Roy T. Shaw
College of Business and
Graduate School of Business
University of Utah

Richard J. Semenik
College of Business and
Graduate School of Business
University of Utah

Robert H. Williams
College of Business Administration
Northern Arizona University

Marketing
an integrated analytical approach

Published by

S73 **SOUTH-WESTERN PUBLISHING CO.**

CINCINNATI   WEST CHICAGO, ILL.   DALLAS   PELHAM MANOR, N.Y.   PALO ALTO, CALIF.

ISBN: 0–538–19730–7

Library of Congress Catalog Card Number: 80–50115

1 2 3 4 5 6 7 8 D 6 5 4 3 2 1 0

Printed in the United States of America

preface

This fourth edition of *Marketing: An Integrated Analytical Approach* retains the traditional depth and rigor of the best early marketing texts while incorporating contemporary marketing approaches. The text integrates each marketing function and institution within the context of the modern marketing program. This approach enables students to learn quickly the relationship between marketing's fundamental elements and recently developed techniques.

This revised edition also maintains a strong analytical orientation which is achieved in two ways. First, the subject area of marketing is divided into its separate components (i.e., concepts, functions, and institutions); then each part is discussed in sufficient detail and depth to allow a student to visualize how a basic element meshes with the whole. Second, the managerial thinking and analysis necessary to perform the marketing task are emphasized. This is accomplished by illustrating how each concept presented has direct application to the marketing program. Furthermore, numerous examples and cases are included to reemphasize these applications.

This book is not intended for students who require simple illustrations and narrative; it is not developed from a single orientation such as managerial, environmental, strategic, quantitative, or any other restricted approach; it is not an encyclopedia, nor is it simply descriptive. Rather, an attempt has been made to incorporate these various approaches in such fashion that a truly integrated treatment of marketing is achieved.

It is the authors' objective to enable students to complete their introductory marketing course with an understanding of what a marketing program is, how it developed and how it is executed, and to recognize how a proper marketing program contributes to the overall effectiveness of the organization.

A review of the topics covered and their organization, as shown in the Contents, will illustrate how these goals are accomplished. For example, "Marketing Plans and Environments" (Chapter 2) sets the pattern with graphic illustrations of strategy development and the marketing planning guide. "The Consumer Goods

Market" (Chapter 4) shows how marketing principles are applied in the consumer sector of the market. "Marketing Research" (Chapter 7) describes the collection and use of information for the effective management of planning and executing marketing, and "Communications" (Chapter 10) illustrates how one function draws from and contributes to other requisite functions and activities.

Never has it been more true than now that marketing is dynamic. *Marketing: An Intergrated Analytical Approach* anticipates the inevitable and rapid changes to which managers will have to respond. Consequently, this text should help students understand the importance of analyzing both the marketing environment and the organization's capability as prerequisties for effective marketing.

To reflect both the changing marketing environment and the new developments in marketing theory and practice, all chapters in this edition are either completely new or significantly revised and rewritten. Most of the cases provided as end-of-chapter materials are also new. Two appendices--one on careers in marketing, the other on case analysis--have been included in this edition. We believe that these additions increase the content quality of the book and make it more teachable.

Ideas and stimulation for this work came from many sources. Weldon J. Taylor, senior author of previous editions, our colleagues and students, and participants in our research projects are due special thanks.

Finally, we especially acknowledge the contributions of Albert A. Pool, a close friend and respected former colleague whose outstanding academic and business career was cut short by a fatal airplane crash.

Roy T. Shaw
Richard J. Semenik
Robert H. Williams

contents

v

1

Marketing and Its Environment

1

the challenge of marketing

We've got more technology kicking around this country than we know what to do with. What we need is the entrepreneur to put it together and in many cases the big guy who can add the capital, marketing, or whatever's necessary to put it into the marketplace.

I've called him the entrepreneur because I'm interested in innovative activities, not just the across-the-board management and production prob'⸳⸳ ⸳ ."

--Richard S. Morse, chairman of the board of Scientific Energy Systems, Inc.; *Marketing News,* July 13, 1979

The ultimate test of an organization's success is whether its customers remain loyal over a long period. This is true whether a company processes a food product, sells clothing or automobiles, builds houses, or produces machine tools for industrial plants. Service industries and nonprofit organizations, such as some performing arts companies, some health clinics, and charitable organizations, are subject to the same ultimate test. Decisions to buy from, or support an organization, result from weighing satisfaction against cost. The role of marketing is to match the offered product or service with the values sought by the buyer, client, or patron.

SATISFACTION ≥ COST

Marketing in its simplest, yet most profound, sense is expressed in the equation

$$\text{Satisfaction} \geq \text{Cost}$$

that is, satisfaction is greater than, or at least equal to, cost, where *satisfaction* means the value received, or perceived, by the purchaser. The positive qualities influencing a market transaction may include performance of the product, its packaging, the outlets through which it is sold, or the perception imputed through promotion.

Cost is any negative or resistive factor, such as money paid, time used, inconvenience, or dissatisfaction. Having to accept a less-than-desirable alternative is a cost, as are unattractive surroundings or poor service. Marketing, therefore, starts with planning a product or service with want-satisfying values (i.e., what to offer) and proceeds through offering the product or service where and how it can best meet customer desires.

Timex watches serve as an illustration of these definitions. The standard Timex, which, for several years, was promoted as a low-quality, almost disposable watch, now has an electronic companion also carrying the Timex name. It was introduced at $39.95.

In marketing the electronic Timex, some of the negative factors (costs) for consumers included its expensive price as compared with nonelectronic Timex watches, the connotation of lower quality than other electronic watches because of earlier Timex promotions, the unproven performance of the watch, and the low-price, low-quality image of some stores that sold Timex watches. The list of negative influences could be extended; those mentioned here may be considered costs by some potential purchasers. It must be noted, though, that a considerable number of consumers think of some cost factors as being positive or satisfaction-giving qualities. For example, to be among the first owners of a new kind of watch and to pay more than is usual are sources of satisfaction to some people. The test of whether a feature is a cost, a satisfaction, or a neutral is the influence it has on the choice of any one customer.

Timex Corporation's efforts to provide consumer satisfaction, aimed at overcoming customers' reluctance to purchase because of the various perceived costs, included making the watch attractive and dignified looking; telling consumers that through "steady electric energy high standards of accurate time-keeping are possible"; selecting wholesale and retail outlets consistent with quality and good taste; and conducting an advertising campaign which complemented the qualities built into the watch.

Balancing Cost and Satisfaction

At that point where a shopper's judgment of satisfaction and cost finds a working equilibrium a decision to buy is triggered.

Each of us, with rare exception, is limited in how much money and time we can spend. If we want a new car we defer or give up the purchase of something else—perhaps furniture or a vacation trip. We ask ourselves: Do we eat out tonight or do we eat at home so that we can save for something else we want? We can't ski, play tennis, listen to the symphony orchestra, go to the library, and work at the same time. Hence we—wisely or unwisely—make choices.

After we decide that we will use money for a car, a coat, or a new tennis racket, we then must select which brand we wish to purchase and from which store we will make our selection. Faced with these decisions, we weigh the satisfaction against costs: of an immediate purchase; of an array of choices.

If we pay $35 for a sport coat rather than $200, we have $165 to apply toward a car, for example. Another person may insist that only a $200 jacket will do.

Thus, we see a wide range of prices charged, services offered, and locations employed by retail stores in response to the variety of choices.

Manipulating the Elements of the Formula

If quality is reduced, can we increase satisfaction? Yes, for part of the market, if the price is decreased more sharply than the quality of the product is decreased.

If the price is raised, can we increase satisfaction? Again, yes, for some customers if quality and services are perceived as being increased more sharply than price.

A plain store in an unpretentious location can provide satisfaction through low prices and reasonable service; an elegant store in a high-rent area can provide satisfaction via carefully selected, high-quality products and extensive services, even though prices are high.

It is the balance between satisfaction and cost that is important. It must also be recognized that not all customers will perceive the same value for each element of cost and satisfaction. Hence, in the chapters that follow much attention is given to how and why customers—either for household goods or for industrial goods—make purchase decisions and what the marketing manager does to assure that proper goods are made available at the right place, at the right time, at the right price, and in the right quantity to enhance satisfaction.

MARKETING DEFINED

Combining the needs and selection process of customers with the marketing organization's desire for a long-lived, profitable venture serves as the foundation for the definition of marketing. The definition offered here is useful for management purposes as well as for the academic study of marketing.

> Marketing is an *integrated* analysis and execution of those activities necessary to *plan, distribute, price, promote,* and *effect exchange* of satisfying products and services to present and potential users.[1]

You can see from this definition that marketing is more than one simple activity. Hence, to carry out the marketing task, we need *concepts*—the ideas and philosophies that underlie company policies; *functions*—the activities that must be performed; and *institutions*—retail, wholesale, advertising, design, and research establishments or facilities.

These components of marketing are introduced in this chapter and are explained further in subsequent parts of the book. One useful concept that contributes to effective marketing originated some years ago with a description of business executives as "deciders" or "mixers of ingredients." Neil H. Borden developed that idea and began using the term *marketing mix.*[2]

---

[1] Adapted from William J. Stanton, *Fundamentals of Marketing,* (4h ed.; New York City: McGraw-Hill Inc., 1975), p. 5.

[2] The first written discussion of this subject is included in the report by Neil H. Borden, "Note on Concept of the Marketing Mix," No. 2M4R, Adv. 720R (Soldiers Field, Mass.: Harvard Business School, Intercollegiate Case Clearing House). The story of the development of the concept is presented

MARKETING MIX

Ingredients that a marketing manager can mix are conviently classified as *product, price, promotion,* and *distribution.* [3]

Buyers purchase a package of value, and that package of value consists of more than the generic product. Hence, the marketing manager identifies the customers and then determines which of the marketing mix ingredients should be emphasized to attract and serve those customers. Those identified customers are the organization's *target market.*

Marketing Mix Ingredients: the Elements of Marketing Strategy

It is important to understand that external environments influence and constrain the marketing manager's actions. (Chapter 2 discusses these factors in depth.) Within the constraints imposed on the manager, his or her task is to use the strengths of the organization—the power and resources which exist in the firm's internal environment. Tools to carry out strategies are those we identified as the marketing mix ingredients—product, price, promotion, and distribution, which means placing the product in the most suitable outlets by utilizing the most appropriate channel.

In manufacturing a technical product, the chosen strategy may be to emphasize product quality. For example, a manufacturer of safes for commercial use may emphasize that its policy is to build the most secure safe regardless of cost. However, a manufacturer of home safes may adopt a different marketing strategy by competing through low price and widespread distribution. Strategies are developed that are appropriate for the selected (i.e., the target) market and the internal capabilities of the firm. One clothing manufacturer produces expensive coats that are sold in only one or two stores in a city. Another produces for the mass market and makes good, but not the best, quality garments which are distributed through medium- and low-price stores.

Emphasizing a Mix Ingredient for Competitive Advantage

A common example of marketing strategies based on the distinctive use of several components of the marketing mix is food retailing. Despite competition from supermarkets, most cities have a few highly profitable small food stores that maintain their strong position based largely on the excellent products they sell. A small store that stocks and sells a wide variety of carefully selected cheeses, specialty bread products, and some imported delicacies provides an excellent example of emphasizing mix ingredients for competitive advantage. A recent survey of the customers of one such store identified shoppers from all parts of the metropolitan

---

in an article by Neil H. Borden, "The Concept of the Marketing Mix," *Journal of Advertising Research,* Vol. IV, No. 2 (June, 1964), pp. 2–7.

[3]McCarthy has popularized these as the four *P*'s of marketing—product, price, promotion and place; *place* meaning *distribution.* E. Jerome McCarthy, *Basic Marketing* (6h ed.; Homewood, Ill.: Richard D. Irwin, Inc., 1978), p. 39.

area. You, no doubt, know of similar stores which do almost no promotion, maintain rather high prices, and are not conveniently located. Yet they prosper by catering to a discriminating clientele and emphasizing an assortment of specialized products—in other words, they gain competitive advantage from a product strategy. Quality and assortment are of more importance to the target market they serve than are location and price.

In food marketing one also finds low-price stores with sales of several million dollars annually. Their basic strategy revolves around price. Other similar size stores may not meet all low prices but advertise heavily to maintain their sales volume. These stores emphasize promotion. Every part of the country has a regional chain that retains its position by being competitive in price, even though it may not have the lowest prices. Such regional chains do some advertising and provide their customers with the cleanest stores, the most attractive displays, and a considerable amount of service. Similar examples of a variety of marketing mix ingredients are emphasized in other kinds of retailing and by various manufacturers.

MARKETING FUNCTIONS

Whenever the consumer or user of something is not the producer, certain economic activities must be performed. These activities are called *marketing functions.* One way to evaluate a marketing program is to examine the costs of performing each function and to determine whether there is a more efficient way to accomplish it. Remember that no function can be eliminated. We can eliminate a position in the organization or cut out a middleman, but the functions they performed still must be done by someone. It is useful to identify these marketing functions.

1. Functions of Exchange
   a. Buying and merchandising
   b. Selling
2. Functions of Physical Supply
   a. Transporting
   b. Storing
3. Facilitating Functions
   a. Financing
   b. Risk-taking
   c. Standardizing and grading
   d. Market information

Functions of Exchange

Buying and merchandising involves the activities required to get the right goods for the needs of the market.

Selling consists of the promotional activities necessary to attract customers. Advertising, personal selling, displays in stores and at, for example, industrial fairs are included in this function.

Functions of Physical Supply

Having the right goods at the right place at the right time and in the right quantities is the contribution of transport and storage. This function has received great attention out of which, in recent years, has grown the major management area of *physical distribution.*

Facilitating Functions

As the name implies, each of these functions facilitates the execution of the exchange and physical supply functions. Likewise, each facilitating function is helpful in the execution of other facilitating functions.

Financing is necessary to provide for the acquisition of goods by both suppliers and customers. Also, in the flow of materials and finished goods there is a need for financing for building inventories, shipping, promoting, and providing credit to consumers. For example, the infant automobile business was able to expand when financing was provided to customers. Before that manufacturers demanded full payment on delivery to dealers and they, in turn, sold on a cash-only basis. Consider the staggering increase in automobile ownership since long-term financing has been available to Joe and Joan Public.

Risk-taking is generally assumed to be a primary part of entrepreneurship. There are two types of risks: controllable and uncontrollable. *Controllable* risks are defined as damage or loss of property through fire, flood, or theft. These risks frequently are diminished by purchasing insurance; that is, the risk is passed on to an outside agency. *Uncontrollable* risks arise from conditions largely external to the firm. Changes in general economic conditions and large price increases, such as the current acceleration in the prices of petroleum products, are examples of uncontrollable risks. These risks cannot be passed on to an insurer. The best protection is guaranteed by unique product features, such as those found in Polaroid cameras or in the new IBM 4300 series of computers; or a strong market position based on outstanding service, or excellent marketing management.

Marketing between physically separated businesses is greatly facilitated by *standardizing and grading* because the need for physical inspection is reduced or even eliminated. Machine parts, fuels, and cereal grains, for example, are purchased according to specifications. The buyer knows that the couplings will fit, that the fuel has a specific Btu capacity, and that the grain will contain only the allowable impurities.

In addition, matching a product to the needs of the market is impossible without a flow of *market information.* To plan and execute a marketing program it is necessary to collect, analyze, evaluate, and use information.

We should observe here that the market does not perform its function of allocating goods and services at the best price in a perfect manner. In large part, imperfect communication of information is responsible for that failure. When you buy clothes and subsequently find others that meet your needs better, or when you suspect that advertising is misleading, you are a victim of imperfect communication. The failure of many products or organizations is frequently the result of the organization's ineptitude in gathering and using proper information.

Who Performs Functions?—A Management Challenge

You can eliminate a middleman, but you cannot eliminate the functions performed by that middleman. As an example, the functions of physical supply may have been performed by a series of specialists: The transportation agency hauls goods from the producer to a regional storage area; after several weeks a trucking company delivers the goods to a wholesaler, who stores them for two more weeks and then hauls small quantities to each of many retailers. That method appears inefficient—and it is. Hence, it could be that a large retailer, instead, makes arrangements to buy full truckloads of goods and has them shipped directly from the producer to the store. The function is performed even though several institutions have been bypassed. These examples do not mean that it is always, or even usually, more efficient to eliminate middlemen. If a store cannot receive, stock, and sell large quantities in a short time, the costs of hauling small quantities directly from the producer are prohibitive. Conversely, if the store takes large quantities in order to achieve transportation economies, but has to stock them for some time, the cost of capital tied up in inventory is probably prohibitive.

The point here is that determining when to perform functions yourself and when to use the services of a specialized agency or middleman is one of the manager's important decision-making duties. How to make such decisions is explained in the chapters on wholesaling, distribution channels, and logistics.

PRODUCTS

The product, as was mentioned, is more than a mere physical object. Each product is a complex bundle of satisfactions which are related to the manner in which the product is perceived by the prospective buyer. Throughout the book considerable emphasis will be given to the problems of supplying the desired product at the most opportune time and place. At this point we will present only the basic classifications of products used in marketing literature.

Industrial Goods

Approximately half of all manufactured goods are consumed by business firms in the course of trade or manufacturing. Called *industrial goods,* these are defined as goods which are destined to be sold primarily to *industrial customers* for use in producing other goods—as contrasted to goods destined to be sold primarily to the ultimate or household consumer. Industrial goods may be divided into five groups: raw materials, fabricated parts, operating supplies, installations, and accessory equipment. Chapter 5 is devoted exclusively to a discussion of the industrial goods market.

Consumer Goods

Consumer goods reach the *ultimate* or *household consumer.* They are destined for use by ultimate consumers or households without further commercial processing. Consumer goods are not classified in the same way as industrial goods but are sometimes divided into three groups which are determined by the attitude of the buyer at the time of purchase. The classification is based on how important the purchase is perceived by the consumer. The product classification has great influence in determining the best type and number of outlets, the amount and type of promotion the product will receive, and the number of variations in product types that will be most effective for each class of goods. A discussion of these decisions is a major part of Chapter 4.

MARKETING INSTITUTIONS

Marketing institutions are of two general types. The first type includes the primary producing industries, such as farming, mining, fishing, forestry, and manufacturing. Firms in this group are distinguished by the fact that their principal interest is in the production of goods. We shall observe, however, that they also perform significant marketing functions.

The second type of marketing institution includes middlemen—those firms that are usually located in the channel through which goods and ownership of goods flow from the producer to the ultimate consumer. These firms are concerned primarily with distribution.

As the name implies, *middlemen* are firms between the producer and the consumer. Since their function is to buy from one source and sell to another, directly or indirectly, these firms may be termed *pure market institutions.* The primary producer and the manufacturer, on the other hand, may be termed *hybrid marketing institutions* because their interests are divided between producing and marketing.

A chain of transactions is necessary to get a bushel of apples from the grower in Washington to the consumer in New York. The aid of a farmers' cooperative, a broker, an auction wholesaler, and a retailer may be necessary for the consumer in New York to enjoy an apple grown in Yakima, Washington, at the price and with the facility which is now possible. Essential though these firms are in bringing the producer and the consumer together, they do not change the form of the product. They perform all the transactions between the producer and the consumer and are therefore properly called middlemen.

Two general classes of institutions perform this interconnecting function, and there are specialists within each of the general classifications. One class is designated merchant middlemen, and another type is called agent middlemen.

Merchant middlemen are distinguished from agents in that the former actually buy or take title to the products in which they deal. There are two types of merchant middlemen—wholesalers and retailers. *Wholesalers* purchase from primary producers, manufacturers, or other wholesalers a supply of goods which they sell to customers who purchase for resale or for furthering production. *Retailers* are those who acquire stocks of goods and sell them to ultimate consumers.

Agent middlemen, though performing many of the functions necessary to distribution, do not take title to the goods. They facilitate buying and selling and may perform other necessary services. Their compensation comes as a commission or a fee for performing the services.

COMPANY-CUSTOMER ORIENTATIONS

A concept that will color, shape, and determine how effective an organization's marketing efforts will be is the basic philosophy the company has regarding company-customer relationships. It is possible to identify three broad company-customer orientations: product orientation, sales orientation, and market orientation.

Product orientation is a concept which assumes that a good product, fairly priced, will find consumer acceptance.

Sales orientation assumes that no matter what the qualities of the product are consumers will not buy enough unless the company provides aggressive and extensive sales and advertising effort.

Market orientation, which is what this book and the best managed firms are devoted to, is a company philosophy that holds that the task of management is to identify the needs and wants of a target market and integrate all functional areas —production, finance, marketing, personnel—toward satisfying the needs and wants of consumers.

Movement to a Market Orientation

One of the clearest explanations of these different orientations has been provided by Robert J. Keith, former president of the Pillsbury Co., a firm which saw its beginnings in flour milling and has since expanded into marketing a diverse number of food-related products.[4] Over the years the firm's orientation, like its product lines, has shifted from production, to sales, and, finally, to marketing.

According to Mr. Keith, the firm's founder, Charles Alfred Pillsbury, decided in 1869 to start a flour mill because of "the availability of high-quality wheat and the proximity of water power, and not from the availability and proximity of growing market areas or the demand for better, less expensive, more convenient flour products." The basic function of the firm at that time was to mill high-quality flour and, almost incidentally, to hire salesmen to sell it. It was the epitome of the product-oriented firm.

In the 1930s, though, a change in philosophy took place which led the company to a sales orientation. Pillsbury became truly aware of the customer and established a research department to obtain facts about the market. According to Mr. Keith, the firm's management also began to realize the importance of wholesale and retail grocers in providing a link between the company and the homes of consumers. At that time Pillsbury's concept was that the firm manufactured products for a consumer market and ". . . must have a first-rate sales organization which can dispose of all the products we can make at a favorable price." The sales force, in what had then evolved into a sales-

---

[4]Robert J. Keith, "The Marketing Revolution," *Journal of Marketing,* (January, 1960), p. 35.

oriented firm, was supported by advertising and consumer information.

A marketing orientation developed in the 1960s, when a marketing department was established to determine *which* products to market. What elements did Pillsbury use in making product selections? Those selection criteria, according to Mr. Keith, "were and are nothing more or less than those of the consumer herself."

The company had indeed evolved to the stage that its purpose was not merely "to manufacture a wide variety of products, but to satisfy needs and desires, both actual and potential, of our customers."

Today the Pillsbury Co., manufacturers of prepared baking mixes, powdered drink mixes, frozen pizza, and refrigerated fresh dough products and owners of Burger King restaurants, identifies itself as a *marketing company* with *all* company functions and activities aimed at satisfying the needs and desires of consumers.

The differences in orientation can be simplified as follows: Product orientation advertises, "Here is a superb posthole digger. The spades are twice-tempered steel, and the handles are of second-growth hickory."

Market orientation, on the other hand, recognizes that no one buys a posthole digger merely to have a posthole digger. The purpose of buying such a tool is to build a fence. If it were possible to send an order to Sears or Montgomery Ward for twelve postholes to enclose a garden, that's what the majority of today's consumers would do. Similarly, most of us are less interested in knowing how a pocket calculator works than we are in the ease with which we get answers to problems.

Product orientation is the oldest of these concepts and quite naturally evolved when many goods, even those that we would consider essential, were in short supply or were not available at all. That concept also is understandable in firms that develop new, complex products because those who conceive the idea are aware of the problems of development and of the technical details. They also see the benefits and do not always realize that most of us may not see why a product is something we can use to our benefit. Two of the early producers of electric refrigerators for home use were General Electric and Frigidaire. GE's sealed unit, which enclosed all functional parts, operated more efficiently than did the open-unit Frigidaire. Yet Frigidaires were easier to sell. GE's sales message to consumers was, in effect, "Here is a rugged piece of machinery that will operate efficiently" —a product-oriented approach. Frigidaire, however, appealed to the senses of consumers: "Here is an attractive addition to your kitchen that adds convenience to your life"—a sales orientation.

General Electric was an engineering, production-oriented company whose principal customers were users of heavy, technical industrial equipment. Frigidaire was a subsidiary of General Motors, which had been selling to household consumers for a long time. GE soon developed a market orientation and became a major factor in the household appliance market.

IBM became dominant in the electronic data processing field because its management identified the problems companies needed to solve and then showed them how IBM could provide the answers. Other computer manufacturers had sales presentations that explained how their equipment worked. IBM's approach was a market orientation; others had a product orientation.

Company Benefits of Market Orientation

The major benefit of market orientation is that it focuses all functional areas on the goal of customer satisfaction. Thus, it is easier to break down the barriers that naturally surround production, sales, research, accounting, finance, and personnel, when there is not a common goal.

THE MARKETING CONCEPT

Many of the ideas regarding market orientation have been expressed and acted upon for quite some time. Those ideas started crystalizing into company policies in the mid-1940s.

One of the earliest formal statements indicating corporate interest in the marketing concept was a paper by J. B. McKitterick, of General Electric, in 1957. He stated the central theme of the marketing management concept:

> . . . the principal task of the marketing function in a management concept is not so much to be skillful in making the customer do what suits the interest of the business as to be skillful in conceiving and then making business do what suits the interests of the customer.[5]

That concept has three basic elements:

1. *Customer Orientation.* This requires knowledge of the customer's needs, wants, and buying-decision criteria. The focus of product development is on those needs and wants.
2. *Integrated Effort in the Organization.* Emphasis is placed on integrating the marketing function with research, product development and management, sales, and advertising to enhance the organization's effectiveness.
3. *Profit Reward.* Attention is focused on profit rather than on sales volume and the concept that if the organization does a good job customer loyalty, repeat business, and favorable attitudes will be developed.

The ultimate may well have been expressed by Peter F. Drucker when he said:

> . . . the aim of marketing is to make selling superfluous . . . to know and understand the customer so well that the product or service fits him and sells itself. Ideally, marketing should result in a customer who is ready to buy.[6]

That goal does not eliminate the communications role of personal selling and advertising. However, it does negate the notion of the "hard sell, get-rich-quick, con game" approach.

---

[5]J. B. McKitterick, "What Is the Marketing Management Concept?" edited by Frank M. Bass, *The Frontiers of Marketing Thought and Science* (Chicago: American Marketing Association, 1957), p. 71.

[6]Peter F. Drucker, *Management: Tasks, Responsibilities, Practices* (New York City: Harper & Row Publishers, Inc., 1973), p. 64.

MARKETING COSTS

Estimates of the costs of marketing all the goods produced in the United States range from 45 to 60 percent of sales. That is higher than marketing costs were 75 and 100 years ago. Why the increase?

The increase is partly an illusion because retailers and wholesalers assumed some of the functions previously performed by customers or producers. Retailers and wholesalers now search out and gather goods into assortments that are attractive to consumers.

As production moved from individual craftsmen, who dealt face-to-face with each ultimate consumer, to large manufacturing units, goods moved farther to market. Overall costs were reduced, even though marketing activities increased.

Additionally, the variety, range, and timeliness of goods demanded by the market have increased. An examination of the labels in a pharmacy or supermarket is impressive proof of the great variety of goods available and of the wide range of places from which they come.

Another reason for the higher marketing costs is that marketing, especially retailing, is highly labor intensive. It is self-evident that "goods are produced by horsepower but distributed by manpower." Hence, productivity per employee in distribution has not increased as much as in manufacturing.

A final explanation for the increase in marketing costs is the fact that built-in services have increased. In the United States we demand that food products, for instance, be hygienically packaged and that much of the preparation for the table be done before the product is purchased by the ultimate consumer. Refrigeration, speedy shipment, and other marketing costs are required to enable consumers to purchase precut, cellophane-wrapped chicken; these are eliminated when consumers buy a live chicken.

The important thing to consider when measuring marketing costs is not so much the portion of the price that is allocable to production and to marketing but rather the total delivered price when all costs are considered. By that measurement, costs of products in the developed economies have actually declined.

WHY STUDY MARKETING?

A large laboratory exists for studying marketing. During the coming weeks observe the various activities in retail stores, on highways, at airports, and on shipping docks of factories. Marketing techniques abound—vibrant, alive, and changing every day. Let yourself be caught up in these fascinating phenomena.

Relate what you see to what you are reading and discussing in class and you should finish the course with a good idea of what marketing is about, where you might fit in (even though you may be majoring in another field), and, above all, how you can contribute to a more effective and efficient means of allocating needed goods and services.

But why should you study marketing? It is advantageous to study marketing because it is a major activity in any economy, because of its importance to you as a member of society, and because it can be a source of gainful employment to you as a manager

Marketing Is Important to the Economy

In the past one hundred years the number of people engaged in wholesaling and retailing has increased roughly twelvefold, while the number engaged in production has approximately tripled. This gives us an indication of the importance of marketing today and also may suggest a cause for concern or an indictment of the way things are allocated in the United States economy.

Responsible Marketing Contributes to Human Welfare

As populations continue to expand and production costs increase it becomes ever more important to match available goods and consumer needs more effectively.

In the 1960s it was found, for example, that about 30 percent of *harvested* produce from the eastern side of the Andes in Peru was never consumed on the west coast of South America, its destination point. That failure is tragic, especially in a country that needs food. Poor packaging, inadequate transportation facilities, as well as some monopolistic practices, contributed to piles of spoiled produce in an area of destitution.

On the other hand, in the United States the farm-to-market roads that were built in the 1930s were part of a marketing program for Midwest food products.

These examples prove that the marketing process is more than demand creation. They illustrate that there are opportunities for challenging careers in the field of marketing that can be socially as well as financially rewarding.

As we shall see in Chapter 2, the marketing program is a planned process to accomplish the following:[7]

1. Produce goods and services needed and wanted in proper quantities and qualities and provide them where and when they are needed.
2. Provide goods and services at fair prices, that is, at prices which cover long-run costs of producing and distributing them.
3. Assure fair dealings in all transactions
4. Provide adequate information from consumers to the marketing entities and from the marketers to consumers to enhance wise producer and buyer decision making

These goals can be accomplished only by the integration of all economic activities of the organization.

---

[7]For an excellent extended discussion of these goals see Theodore N. Beckman, William R. Davidson, and W. Wayne Talarzyk, *Marketing* (9h ed.; New York City: The Ronald Press Company, 1973), p. 608.

You Will Be a Better Manager

No one can be a truly effective manager without understanding something about all the functional areas in the organization. A good marketing decision is based on how that decision will be influenced by financial considerations, accounting and control procedures, personnel, and production capacity. These subjects are discussed in Chapter 2, where we consider the environments of the firm.

QUESTIONS AND ANALYTICAL PROBLEMS

1. Define:
   a. Marketing mix;
   b. Marketing functions;
   c. Industrial goods;
   d. Consumer goods;
   e. Merchant middleman;
   f. Agent middleman;
   g. Wholesaler; and
   h. Retailer

2. State three specific examples of lowering quality but increasing satisfaction. State three examples of increasing costs and increasing satisfaction. State three examples of lowering costs and decreasing satisfaction.

3. Give examples, not from the book, of four retailers, each of whom emphasizes one of the ingredients of the marketing mix.

4. Which marketing functions are eliminated when a farmer sells produce directly to consumers who drive to the farm and pay cash for the produce?

5. Give an example of how market information facilitates the performance of other marketing functions. Do the same for financing and standardizing.

6. You buy a 100-pound bag of fertilizer to use on your home garden. Then you buy 50 similar bags to use on a small produce farm. Is the fertilizer an industrial good, or is it a consumer good?

7. Clearly distinguish between (a) product orientation, (b) sales orientation, and (c) market orientation.

8. Define the marketing concept.

2

marketing plans and environments

Marketers who fail to analyze the divergent values and lifestyles of the American people have an incomplete and inaccurate picture of current buying patterns, according to SRI International, Menlo Park, Calif.

"Although the skepticism has not disappeared, there is a growing awareness that the conventional marketing or planning approaches involving only the classic variables of income, age, place of residence, and so forth, often miss the essential ingredient of what the individual values, and the manner in which he or she lives," noted the firm's president.

--Marketing News, October 5, 1979

"Success is best explained by unremitting attention to purpose." Disraeli

For long-term success the people in marketing must plan their present and future strategies. This must be done in the face of constant changes, as well as in light of present conditions.

An understanding of the environments within which the organization functions is essential in the planning process. This chapter introduces you to marketing planning and then to the environments which exert influence on the planning and execution of marketing activities.

THE PLANNING PROCESS

A complete planning process involves defining the basic interests and objectives of the organization, establishing policies, formulating strategy, developing tactics to implement policies, and creating a control provision for monitoring results and making adjustments to keep plans on track.

At this point our concern is with purpose, objectives, policies, strategy and tactics. (Control is discussed in subsequent chapters.) Definitions of these terms as they relate to planning are:

Purpose: The values the organization seeks to satisfy. The purpose, or the organization's mission, is defined by specifying some need of consumers to be satisfied in a manner that is congruent with the desired values of members of the organization.

Objectives: The goals toward which strategies are directed which, if met, will achieve the purpose. They are stated expectations regarding results to be achieved.

Policies: A set of rules that defines limits of acceptable and unacceptable actions.

Strategy: A plan of action to achieve the objectives.

Tactics: Detailed methods used to carry out the selected strategy.

Purpose and *objectives* establish strategic requirements; *policies* provide the rules for satisfying them; available *power/resources* provide the means.[1]

In developing well-stated purposes and objectives it is useful to answer the following three questions:

1. Where are we now, and why are we here?
2. Where do we want this organization to be in one year? five years from now? Will we achieve our goals if we continue with the present policies and strategies? If not, what changes should be made?
3. Is what we are doing and what we plan to do in line with the kind of organization we want to be?

To answer those questions, to review purpose, and to focus on the basic plans, the following steps should be undertaken:

1. Evaluate the power/resources of the organization (the internal environment in Figure 2-1). Is each of the power/resource elements of the nature and sufficient strength that our goals can be achieved?
2. Analyze present sales. First, analyze by customers and geographic areas. Why do we serve those markets? What are the current trends in volume, profit, and market share? What factors affect these trends? Which are most profitable? Who are our competitors? What are their strengths and weaknesses?

   Second, analyze sales by product. Which products appeal to specific types of customers? Which products are sold in specific geographic areas? What are the current profit volume trends of each product? Which are profitable?

   Third, take a look at sales by distribution channels. What are the profit and volume trends of each channel?

Goals are achieved by serving a target market well. A *target market* consists of selected market segments. A *market segment* is defined as a group of customers who

---

[1]Marketing managers will find it instructive to read literature on national planning and strategy; for example John M. Collins, *Grand Strategy and Principles* (Anapolis: Naval Institute Press, 1973).

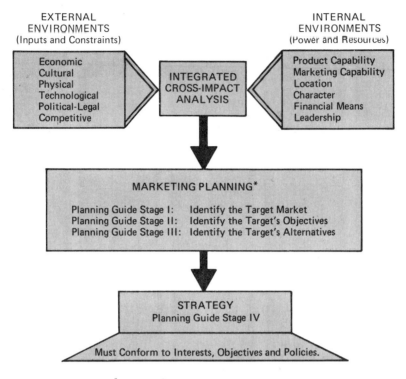

EXTERNAL
ENVIRONMENTS
(Inputs and Constraints)

INTERNAL
ENVIRONMENTS
(Power and Resources)

Economic
Cultural
Physical
Technological
Political-Legal
Competitive

INTEGRATED
CROSS-IMPACT
ANALYSIS

Product Capability
Marketing Capability
Location
Character
Financial Means
Leadership

MARKETING PLANNING*

Planning Guide Stage I: Identify the Target Market
Planning Guide Stage II: Identify the Target's Objectives
Planning Guide Stage III: Identify the Target's Alternatives

STRATEGY
Planning Guide Stage IV

Must Conform to Interests, Objectives and Policies.

*Planning Guide Stages refer to Illus. 2-2.

Illus. 2-1   Integrated Analysis for Stategy Development

have something in common which causes them to respond in a similar fashion to marketing stimuli. Members of that particular group can be distinguished and differentiated from other groups. No one product or marketing approach will be suitable for everyone; hence, one can see the need to define the target that your organization can best serve.

An environmental analysis is required, first, to identify opportunities for satisfying customers through identification of problems the customer needs to solve. Second, it facilitates examination of the firm to see how its resources can cope with external changes. Third, it keeps the firm from staying with a good thing too long. Fourth, it forces the manager to look at conditions and products from the customer's point of view—a consumer-oriented rather than a production-oriented approach. Finally, the manager must, in this review, examine the purpose—values and objectives—and use of resources of the organization, thereby discouraging diffusion of effort.[2]

[2]For guidance in this phase of planning, see Wroe Alderson and Paul E. Green, *Planning and Problem Solving in Marketing* (Homewood, Ill.: Richard D. Irwin, Inc., 1964), especially Chapters 13–16; Douglas W. Foster, *Planning for Products and Markets* (London: Longman Group, Ltd., 1972),

GOAL OF MARKETING PLANNING

As pointed out in Chapter 1, the goal of marketing planning is simply to be in the right market with the right product at the right time. To do that, one must identify the specific segments of the market to be served, offer a product that meets the needs of those market segments, make certain that buyers recognize it as the right product, and get it to the right places.

We know that disposable income alone does not determine what we buy. Each of us decides which activities or products give us the greatest satisfaction. Further, we know that it is frequently difficult to state precisely why we choose one way to spend time and money rather than another. To understand this is to recognize that no person, family, or organization functions in isolation. *Macro-influences*—external environments—affect choices. It is essential to realize this in planning strategies that help customers choose the right product.[3]

Strategies

Marketing strategies for the growth of an organization are focused on three categories: intensification, integration, and diversification.

Intensification means selling more of your present product in present markets by stimulating increased use by present customers, attracting competitors' customers, or getting nonusers to become customers. Coca-Cola advertises *Coke* as a winter drink to stimulate more use; potato chip manufacturers promote the use of chips with party dips, thus broadening the market beyond summer picnic use. Paying attention to advertising over the next week will provide many other examples.

Intensifying also means reaching into other geographic markets, as when Dr. Pepper moved from the Southeast and Southwest into other regions; or into other market segments, as when Levi-Strauss promoted blue jeans as leisure clothing in urban areas rather than only as farm and ranch wear. The modification of commercial food preparation devices for home kitchen use and different quality versions of power tools—one for carpenters and one for home workshops—are examples of product modification strategy to intensify marketing.

Integration means extending ownership vertically, or horizontally. A manufacturer may own and operate some retail outlets—forward, vertical integration—or a retailer may purchase wholesaling or manufacturing facilities—backward, vertical integration. Horizontal integration is the purchase of additional operations on the same level. Chain store and multi-unit wholesale operations are examples of horizontal integration. Criteria regarding the desirability of integration are discussed in subsequent chapters on retailing, wholesaling, and distribution.

Chapters 2 and 9; David Ewing, *The Practice of Planning* (New York City: Harper & Row, Publishers, Inc., 1968), Chapter 3.

[3]For an explanation of how one major company anticipates environmental effects on its marketing plans, see Ian H. Wilson, William R. George, and Paul J. Solomon, "Strategic Planning for Marketers," *Business Horizons,* Vol. 21, No. 6.

Diversification means adding products to the present line. This can be done by adding products that are technologically compatible with present products, such as when a paint manufacturer adds stains and wood sealers, or by adding products that appeal to present customers, even though the products are technologically unrelated. One such example would be a cereal manufacturer broadening the product line to include shoe polish, furniture wax, and cleaning agents.

Finally, some manufacturers add products for entirely new classes of customers. For example, Thiokal Corporation, a supplier of solid propellants for space vehicles, also manufactures tracked snow vehicles. John Deere, a manufacturer of tractors for over 140 years, recently added a line of recreational snow vehicles and winter clothing.

Tactics

The tools of strategy include product design and attributes, pricing, promotion, and placing of the product—that is, the type and number of outlets, as well as the channels to be used in getting products to consumers.

Tactics are the specific activities undertaken to assure success of the strategies. For example, our strategy may be to invest heavily in promotion, especially advertising. Tactics to accomplish that strategy include the *definition* of the advertising message; the medium to use; the type of advertisement—large illustrations with very little printed copy and determining the number and frequency of advertisements to run. Definitions of *strategy* and *tactics* here refer only to marketing plans. A strategy for the entire enterprise, for instance, might be to increase marketing effectiveness. The marketing manager will then have that corporate strategy as a marketing objective and will establish strategies to accomplish it.

A MARKETING PLANNING GUIDE

A marketing planning guide provides an organized approach to planning the strategies and tactics that will be used. Marketing plans must agree with and contribute to the purpose and objectives of the whole organization.

There are five steps in developing a marketing plan. First, identify the *target market.* What market segments, individuals, firms or organizations can gain satisfaction from your product or service? Determine where they are, how many there are, and what environmental factors will affect their response to your offering. Second, determine the objectives—missions or goals—of that target market. What problems do the members of your target want to solve? Answers to those questions will tell you why, or whether, customers need or want your product. If the target market wants clean clothes for the family, an automatic washer offers a solution. If the target wants a rapidly cooked meal at breakfast and dinner time, a microwave oven provides a way to solve the problem of time requirements. Third, identify the *alternative* means available for meeting the target's desired objectives. How are

TOAST

Marketing Planning Guide

I.   Identify the market **Target** -- the individuals, firms, or organizations to whom or which the product is addressed; the specific market segments.

II. Identify the target's **Objectives.** What is the mission or goal of the target? What problems must the target solve? Answers to these questions tell why the target needs or wants the product.

III. What **Alternative** means of meeting goals or solving problems are available to the target? How do they compare with our product and resources? How are goals or mission requirements now met? How is the target now solving problems? With what results? Satisfactory? Unsatisfactory?

IV. What **Strategies** should the marketing enterprise develop to serve the target market and insure long-term success?

V.   What **Tactics** will assure success of the strategies?

Illus. 2-2   **Marketing Planning Guide**

the target market members presently solving problems to achieve their desired objectives? For instance, to get clothes clean one can boil them, beat them on a rock at the river side, or send them to a laundry, among other ways. Does your product or service offer a better, faster, less expensive, or otherwise more desirable alternative?

Analyses of information gathered to answer those questions will assist in determining the strategies to use in making a market offering. Fourth, and only after completing the first three steps, decide what strategies to use. Finally, determine which tactics will most nearly assure success of the selected strategies.

This sequence is emphasized to avoid the common fault of pushing ahead with a strategy that is destined to fail because it is not based on understanding the needs of the market. The plan culminates in developing strategies and tactics.

Using the guide shown in Figure 2–2 to outline and identify what is learned from an analysis of environments reinforces a consumer orientation. It also helps avoid the total-market fallacy. Managers must realize that there is no total market—each market is made up of a number of market segments identified by demographic attributes, geography, income, cultural characteristics, and other bases.

NEED FOR INTEGRATED ENVIRONMENTAL ANALYSIS

How conditions in the world outside the firm always have and will continue to have an impact on business and marketing is illustrated by looking at current trends in housing and personal transportation.

Consider some of the influences that have affected the housing market. High mortgage rates, environmental restrictions on large tract development, a continuing increase in the number of unmarried professionals, and a host of other factors have contributed to a considerably changed housing market from that of previous times.

As a result, in many areas single household dwellings in desirable locations have become priced beyond the purchasing ability of an estimated 75 percent of the nation's population. At the same time rising prices have boosted the portion of personal income that must be allocated for housing. Out of these factors have grown new housing lifestyles including a greater reliance on housing clusters, apartment living, and the purchase of condominiums. That, in turn, results in purchases of different kinds of furniture; yard care, for instance, gives way to other activities, and leisure time is used differently, among other effects of the change in housing patters. The only way to anticipate and react to such changes is to monitor the forces that are external to the firm.

Similarly, there are changes in personal transportation. Smaller automobiles are selling well, fuel costs are increasing, the prices of cars continue to rise, and there is a developing demand for efficient mass transit.

How will these changes affect the allocation of disposable income? What effect will these changes have on the types and locations of retail stores? Will people still go downtown to shop or to see a play or a movie? What kinds of goods and activities will people prefer? What values will change?

The only way to answer these questions is to attempt to analyze how the external environments affect and are affected by all other external environments. Once again it is apparent that the keen marketer, in order to satisfy customer demand, must be aware of the forces that affect the consumer.

THE ENVIRONMENTS

Various environments make up the total climate in which the selected consumers and their suppliers function:

1. *Economic environment*—determines total disposable incomes of individuals and the funds available for business investment.

2. *Cultural environment*—influences and reflects values which determine how individuals and organizations apply resources. It also, through ethical judgments, circumscribes actions.
3. *Technological/Physical environments*—together determine what and how much can be produced
4. *Political-Legal environment*—reflects social goals in the allocation of tax receipts, thereby influencing the allocation of resources; and circumscribes the actions of organizations and individuals.
5. *Competitive environment*—determines opportunities for and restrictions on tactical actions.
6. *Internal environment*—reflects objectives and values of the enterprise; limits money and management resources available to the marketing manager.[4]

Economic Environment

One must keep current on trends in the economy to know the disposable income of individuals for the purchase of consumer goods and of firms for the purchase of industrial goods and services. Absolute current rates and trends of growth, interest charges, availability and costs of basic resources, and employment must be considered.

Cultural Environment[5]

Culture to an individual or society is the sum of traditional ideas and their attached values. Patterns of behavior and distinctive achievements derive from a society's culture.[6] Characteristics of culture are that it is *learned,* "the various facets of culture are *interrelated*—you touch a culture in one place and everything else is affected; it is *shared* and, in effect, (it) defines the boundaries of different groups."[7]

Determining cultural values and monitoring changes in them are vital in long-range planning. Shifts in culture do occur. Attitudes toward society's basic institutions—home, church, and education—can and do change. Married women (with a husband present in the home) comprised 30 percent of the female labor force in 1950 and nearly 60 percent by 1976. One-person households increased from 13 percent to 20.5 percent during that time. For the most part organized religious institutions have experienced upheavals in recent years, and registered church membership fluctuates widely. University and college enrollment is heavier in professional and technical schools than in the liberal arts disciplines, which were the foundation of most universities years ago. Further, many intellectually competent people choose not to complete a university program.

---

[4]See W. Thomas Anderson, Jr., Louis K. Sharpe, and Robert J. Boewadt, "Environmental Role for Marketing," *MSU Business Topics,* Vol. 20, No. 3, Summer, 1972, pp. 66–72.

[5]One of the best recent discussions of the influence of culture on marketing is Vern Terpstra, *The Cultural Environment of International Business* (Cincinnati: South-Western Publishing Co., 1978)

[6]Alfred L. Knoeber and Clyde Kluckhow, "Culture: A Critical Review of Concepts and Definitions," *Papers of the Peabody Museum of American Archeology and Ethnology* (New York City: Alfred A. Knopf, Inc., 1963), p. 357.

[7]Edward T. Hall, *Beyond Culture* (Garden City: Anchor Books, 1977), p. 16.

Societal Value

1. Personal effort—society's attitude toward work; its personal motivation to improve life-style or to be satisfied with it as it is.
2. Personal mobility—extent to which members of society are satisfied with their physical well-being and social position.
3. Financial success and material possessions—their importance to society.
4. Optimism versus pessimism—well adjusted and realistic? Extreme in moods? Low self-image?
5. Individualism—importance of equal opportunity, personal liberty and freedom, status achieved through efforts of members of society.
6. Competitiveness—importance of competition and cooperation. Is competition completely opposed to cooperation? Is competition acceptable in some activities?
7. Honesty—belief in complete integrity, or only if convenient.
8. Education—society's attitude toward, interest in, extent to which it will sacrifice for. Level of education. High school? College? Other?
9. Law—generally law-abiding citizens? Or only when detection likely?
10. Morality—subjective or objective?
11. Home and family—importance to society.
12. Religion—fervent in religious beliefs? Or cool toward?
13. Politics—interested in, or indifferent toward?
14. Social institutions such as civic, charitable, and other volunteer organizations, etc.—active in, not interested in?
15. Prestige—measure of. Acquisition of wealth? Professional accomplishment? Good home and family? Other?

Illus. 2–3   Various Components Comprising a Society's Values

How does a firm evaluate a society? It must analyze the cultural values and monitor changes within the various components that comprise a society's social values. Illus. 2–3 illustrates the social components that firms might examine in evaluating a culture. While it is unlikely that all these values would be considered in a specific marketing strategy, in all likelihood many of them would be of importance in developing an overall plan.[8]

Technological/Physical Environment

Technological developments are important in marketing for two reasons: first, because of new product availability, which affects the way people live and how and what they buy; second, because of their effects on the organizations, institutions, and methods of marketing.

---

[8]For an anthropologist's discussion of values in the United States, see John Gillin, "National and Regional Cultural Values in the United States," *Social Forces,* Vol. 34 (December, 1955) pp. 107–113, reprinted in Montrose S. Sommers and Jerome B. Kernan, *Comparative Marketing Systems* (New York City: Appleton-Century-Crofts, 1968) pp. 171–182.

Every technological change threatens present or traditional products and ways of doing things. Changes in technology, however, present many opportunities for developing new products and innovative methods for serving consumers. The first workable, pocket-sized calculators, for example, were a threat to the makers of slide rules; the development of mechanical refrigerators threatened the entire industry that made and distributed ice. Through hindsight it is easy to see that both developments, rather than merely drawing customers from existing industries, resulted in the creation of new markets and marketing institutions.

Technical Influence on Market Institutions. The influence of technical innovations is usually broader than its impact on a particular product. Consider, for example, why supermarkets developed around 1930 instead of fifty years earlier. Certainly the economic, competitive, political-legal, and cultural conditions were favorable at the time. Even so, without the right technology, supermarket development would not have been possible.

The technological development (and subsequent increased ownership of) automobiles and refrigerators played an important role in the evolution of the supermarket. When automobile ownership increased, retailing patterns shifted, as retailers opened stores in the areas to which people were moving—away from the traditional business district. And, indeed, the population was relocating! Automobiles were providing unlimited flexibility for home ownership away from the city and for new work locales and places to shop.

At the same time that the automobile was revolutionizing the whole concept of where people must live, work, and shop, the refrigerator was providing consumers larger food storage capacity and better food preservation methods than its predecessor, the icebox. This permitted consumers the luxury of not having to make daily trips to the corner market, on foot, to stock up on perishable items.

Improved refrigeration, however, did not affect the consumer alone. On the supply side, refrigeration of railroad cars and storage facilities meant that perishable goods could be shipped from remote areas. Hence, the consumer was able to choose from wide varieites of foodstuffs.

Additional technological advances aided supermarket development. Data processing advances, for instance, along with improved communications equipment, meant that inventory control and information on available goods at a central location were enhanced. Even the promotion of supermarket goods was facilitated by the radio and improved, less expensive printing processes.

Influence on Lifestyle. Look carefully at how meals are prepared and clothes are laundered in your home and compare these techniques with general household practices of the nineteenth century. Gas or electric ranges have replaced the wood-burning stove, greatly lessening the amount of effort expended and time consumed by the homemaker in food preparation. A cookbook by Mrs. M.H. Cornelius, *The Young Housekeeper's Friend,* published in 1858, noted that "because heating an oven takes so much time and wood, the prudent woman uses good planning to accomplish five successive bakings with one heating: the bread first, then the puddings; afterward, pastry; then cake and gingerbread; lastly, custards."[9] She also used considerable muscle.

Push-button clothes washers and dryers have replaced the tub and washboard in the laundry, drastically changing a family's activity patterns. Selling and servicing these complex appliances resulted in distribution patterns and retail institutions quite different from those used to sell a washboard in the old general store.

Influence of Competition. In recent years the pocket-sized calculator has illustrated the ability of technology to effect changes and to impinge on the competitive environment. Not only has a new industry developed to replace the old ways of computing, but within that new industry further technological developments increase competition by reducing costs and adding improvements.

In 1972 Texas Instruments introduced its simplest model with a suggested retail price of $147.95. The TI 100, performing all the functions of the 1972 model (but in a reduced size), was generally available at the end of 1978 for $9.95. When Pittway Corporation introduced residential smoke detectors in 1971, the lowest priced model retailed at about $100. Now one can purchase a slightly improved model for $10 to $15. Improvements in components and in manufacturing processes reduced manufacturing time of the unit from one hour in 1971 to six minutes in 1978.

Currently the U.S. Patent Office receives over 100,000 patent applications for inventions each year and issues over 70,000 new patents. Not many of those inventions are marketed with product success. More about why products succeed or fail is discussed in Chapter 8, but here we reflect on how new ideas succeed only if there is a proper fit with the external environments. A recent Canadian study showed that highly successful managers of new product introductions devoted more than three times as much study and worry to each innovation as managers of less successful firms.[10]

In each decade technological developments accelerate. There is so much change in electronics, for instance, in a period of three years that product leadership in the industry swings from one company to another. Similarly, within a period of six years a small company that developed a fiberboard can for motor oil captured 80 percent of the market from metal can manufacturers. Rechargeable batteries for dictating equipment and electric razors are causing similar changes in product and market leadership.

---

[9]Quoted in a column by Bettina Bier Greaves in *The Wall Street Journal,* December 29, 1978, p. 6.

[10]Blair Little, "New Technology and the Role of Marketing," *The Business Quarterly,* Spring, 1978, pp. 55–59.

Seat-of-the-pants management cannot survive in such a dynamic environment. Firms with *business-as-usual* attitudes will not survive. Managers must consciously monitor and assess developments and plan for change.[11]

Political-Legal Environment

Government policies, laws, and regulations which generally affect marketing can be placed in the following four categories:

1. Those which influence the economy and, hence, the purchasing power of individuals and organizations
2. Those which affect competition
3. Those designed for consumer protection
4. Those which enhance, restrict, or regulate access to and use of society's collective goods, especially the natural environment (*Collective goods* are those for the use of large groups, i.e. society, as opposed to those purchased for use by a family or a firm. Cathedrals, subsidized arts, parks, wilderness areas, and lakes are examples of collective goods.)

The influence of government action can both indirectly and directly affect the scope and activities of a marketing organization.

Indirect Effects on Marketing. Some governmental action indirectly affects the individual marketing organization. The use of power to tax personal and corporate incomes; the incidence and rate of excise taxes imposed on goods such as gasoline, tobacco, and theater tickets; and the rate and methods of allowing credits for corporate investment in capital goods—all affect disposable income and, hence, the amount and type of goods purchased.

Similarly, attitudes on foreign trade, including tariffs and quotas, affect the availability of goods and competition with domestic producers. The tax rates and the method of taxing incomes of persons and firms engaged in domestically owned enterprises established abroad also affect the domestic economy.

Direct Effects on Marketing Marketing is directly affected by laws and regulations which establish the actual boundaries within which business must operate.

Laws and Regulations Affecting Competition. Maintaining competition is deemed important because of the belief that consumers and, hence, society benefit when firms vie for acceptance by providing new and better products at lower prices.

Adam Smith, in *Wealth of Nations* (1776), stressed that *monopoly* (control of an industry or service) in any form is an enemy of society because monopolies impede the working of the market. The market system could not yield its full benefit when no master hatter could employ more than two apprentices and where no master cutler could employ more than one. It was essential to remove all

---

[11]Foster, *op. cit.,* pp. 6–8.

impediments to competition imposed by government, journeymen, or combinations of manufacturers.[12]

A few rules restricting restraint of trade practices such as price fixing, the allocation and control of markets (monopoly), and the combinations of independent firms into trusts existed in the United States early in the 1800s. They were common law (i.e., arising from litigation and not written down as statutes) rulings. Also, a few laws regulating business were enacted in the United States prior to that time—a criminal fraud statute in 1872 and in 1887 a law establishing the Interstate Commerce Commission, with its aim of curbing discriminatory railroad pricing tactics. In the nineteenth century, however, powerful individuals and groups in the United States engaged in such flagrant market abuses in their formation of petroleum, sugar, meat, and coal combines that public resentment required the passage, in 1890, of the Sherman Antitrust Act, which became the major base for regulating business practices. A summary of the major legislation affecting marketing decisions, including the Sherman Antitrust Act, is shown in Illus. 2–4.

Activities Illegal Per Se.   As the result of legislation aimed at preserving competition certain business activities are illegal *per se* (of themselves). Proof of the activity is proof that a violation of the law has occurred. In these cases it is not necessary to show a direct effect of restraint of trade.

The following conditions are regarded as business activities which inhibit competition, and thus, are illegal *per se:*

1. To fix the price of goods or services through an agreement with others. For many years it was contended that persons who performed services were not engaged in commerce and also that the learned professions were exempt from the Sherman Antitrust Act. Both contentions have recently been overturned. Hence, barbers, television and auto repair workers, and other service suppliers may not agree to fix the price of their services. In 1975 *(Goldfarb* v. *Virginia State Bar),* the restriction on price fixing was extended to lawyers.
2. To divide up territories among competitors, such as establishing cartels.
3. To limit the supply of a commodity.
4. To extend the economic power of a patent or copyright to unrelated products. (This is characterized by a refusal to grant access to a desired patent unless the licensee agrees to purchase other specified products.)[13]

Activities Regulated by the Rule of Reason.   Certain other activities may be held to be illegal if the result of the actions excessively restrains trade. In deciding whether trade is restrained, a *rule of reason,* which asks whether there is justifiable reason to anticipate that an action will result in harm to competitors or consumers, applies. The rule itself evolved out of the 1911 case of the *Standard Oil Company of New Jersey* v. *United States.*

---

[12]Robert L. Heilbroner's *The Worldly Philosophers,* 4h ed. (New York City: Simon and Schuster, Inc., 1972), "The Wonderful World of Adam Smith," p. 40–72, is a delightful essay on what Smith said and what other people said he said.

[13]Robert N. Corley, Robert L. Black, and O. Lee Reed, *The Legal Environment of Business* (4h ed.; New York City: McGraw-Hill, Inc., 1977) pp. 260–264.

1890 **Sherman Antitrust Act.** Prohibits contracts, combinations, or conspiracies which restrain trade. Also makes it illegal to monopolize any part of trade or commerce.

1906 **Federal Food and Drug Act.** Forbids the manufacture, sale, or transport of adulterated or fraudulently labeled foods and pharmaceutical products (superceded by the Food, Drug, and Cosmetic Act of 1938, which created more stringent standards, to which amendments were added by the Food Additives Act of 1958).

1906 **Meat Inspection Act.** Requires federal inspection to assure compliance with sanitary regulations for processing of all meat sold in interstate commerce.

1914 **Federal Trade Commission Act.** Prohibits unfair methods of competition and (by the Wheeler-Lea Ammendment of 1938) unfair or deceptive acts or practices.

1914 **Clayton Act.** Supplemented the Sherman Act and defined more precisely certain prohibited practices regarding price discrimination, tying clauses, interlocking directorates and ownership of stocks in directly competing companies, and acquiring stock in another company where the effect "may be to substantially lessen competition."

1936 **Robinson-Patman Act.** Amendment to the Clayton Act which makes it illegal to discriminate in price or terms of sale between purchases of commodities of like quality and quantity; prohibits brokerage fees except to independent brokers; forbids promotional allowances or provisions of services except on "proportionately equal terms," and outlaws the exploitation of independent merchants, customers, and suppliers by unfair competition.

1975 **Magnuson-Moss Act.** Expands Federal Trade commission power over unfair or deceptive practices. Gives the FTC greater power to make trade rules and rules regarding product warranties.

"Consumer Movement" Legislation

Product Safety Act (1967)
Toy Safety Act (1969)
Automobile Information Disclosure Act (1958) and **Automobile Safety Act** (1968), which specifies safety standards for tires as well as automobiles

Illus. 2-4   Major Federal Laws Affecting Marketing Decisions

The Clayton Act of 1914 provided legislation dealing with the right to select customers, exclusive agency agreements, and exclusive product agreements. A seller, according to the Act, has the right to select customers, but some conditions of sale are illegal. A manufacturer may not require wholesalers and retailers to report retailers who are selling the manufacturer's goods at prices lower than those dictated by the manufacturer (*Federal Trade Commission* v. *Beech-Nut Packing Co.,* 1921, and *United States* v. *General Motors,* 1966.)

Exclusive agency agreements in which a manufacturer enters a long-term agreement to supply all or the greater portion of a customer's orders for a product can be beneficial. However, these agreements are illegal if they "substantially lessen competition." In cases where a manufacturer holds the dominant share of the market, any exclusive contract that maintains or increases the share of the market by that manufacturer has been declared illegal.

Other contract provisions that have been determined to lessen competition are those that require a customer to handle *only* the manufacturer's products or prohibit the customer from carrying competing products.

Court decisions on whether certain pricing activities are regarded as discriminatory are vital to marketing. The guiding law prohibiting price discrimination is the Robinson-Patman Act, passed in 1936. An important element of the Act makes buyers who accept discriminatory prices as liable for penalties as sellers. Price discrimination is not illegal *per se;* only those price differences which adversely affect competition are prohibited. Some of those differences include:

1.   Selling in one geographical area at lower prices than in other markets with the intent to eliminate competition
2.   Granting quantity purchasing discounts on such large quantities that the quantity is likely to be purchased by only one or very few customers
3.   Selling a private brand at a price less than the manufacturer's widely advertised and distributed brand.

Controversy surrounds the final prohibition, which came from a price discrimination complaint filed against Borden, Inc. for charging more money for its own brand than for its chemically and physically identical private brands. Borden claimed that customer perception of the Borden brand provided a quality difference. The company also claimed that its extensive distribution precautions with its own brand—precautions it claimed were not always adhered to by its private brand customers—contributed to a difference in quality which merited a higher price.

A majority of the U.S. Supreme Court held that there was illegal price discrimination because the product was the same regardless of the brand.

The court's dissenting minority, however, disagreed. It claimed that an important, nonmeasurable content in the Borden brand was the customer's perception, measured by the brand's past performance, that there was a difference in quality.

Many marketing people tend to agree with the dissenting view, relying on the argument that a product is "a complex bundle of satisfactions" rather than merely a physical object.

The courts' judgments of illegal competitive acts do change, forcing firms to be alert to changes in the legal environment surrounding competition. The decision in the Schwinn Bicycle Company case of 1967, for instance, declared that restrictions placed by a manufacturer on the methods of sale and the selection of territory or customers by a dealer after the title to the goods had passed to that dealer were illegal *per se.* In 1977, however, in a case involving

GTE Sylvania *(Continental TV, Inc.* v. *GTE Sylvania, Inc.),* the power of a manufacturer/supplier to set restrictions on wholesalers and retailers was liberalized. The court stated that in certain cases interbrand competition (that is, horizontal competition, which is the competition between manufacturers of the same generic product—in this case television sets) could possibly benefit through intrabrand competition (vertical competition, which is competition between distributors of the product of a particular manufacturer). Each case is determined on its own merits as it relates to restraint of trade and whether such restraint is excessive.

Unfair competition.   The Federal Trade Commission Act prohibits "unfair methods of competition and (by the Wheeler-Lea Amendment) unfair or deceptive acts or practices . . ." The Magnusson-Moss Act provides that the Federal Trade Commission may ". . . prescribe rules which define with specificity acts or practices which are unfair or deceptive." *Unfair* is difficult to define and its meaning is not static. It appears safe to assume, however, that the following acts will be held to be unfair practices: actions which offend public policy; immoral, unethical or unscrupulous acts such as fraud, misrepresentation of goods as to origin, quality or effectiveness, and misrepresenting one's business; and actions which cause substantial injury to consumers or competitors, such as allowing a trade association to restrict information to consumers (prohibiting price advertising of eyeglasses, for example), commercial bribery, deceptive selling schemes, style piracy, and harassing competitors through spreading false information about them or interfering with their sources of supply. The FTC has, in recent years, been aggressive in monitoring and acting against such practices.[14]

Laws Protecting the Consumer.   Some degree of regulation of goods and services sold to consumers started in 1848 with the Edwards Law, which banned the importation of adulterated drugs. The year 1906 brought passage of the Meat Inspection Act for sanitary regulation of meat packing and federal inspection of all establishments selling meat in interstate commerce. The same year brought passage of the Federal Food and Drug Act, which prohibited the manufacture, sale, or transport of adulterated or fraudulently labeled foods or drugs in interstate commerce.

Those acts paved the way for the rigorous policing of foods and drugs of recent years. You will remember the banning of cyclmates as well as certain cold remedies and sleeping pills, for instance. It was in 1962 that consumer legislation became an important force with a special address by President John F. Kennedy to Congress in which he proclaimed that "the federal government—by nature the highest spokesman for *all* the people—has a special obligation to be alert to the consumers' basic needs and to advance the consumers' interest." The President listed four basic rights of consumers:

---

[14]Theodore N. Beckman, William R. Davidson, and W. Wayne Talarzyk, *Marketing* (9h ed.; New York City: Ronald Press Company, 1973), p. 86.

1. The right to safety—protection against goods or services hazardous to health or life.
2. The right to be informed—protection against fraudulent, deceitful, or grossly misleading information from advertising, labeling, or other means of communication.
3. The right to choose—access to a variety or goods and services at fair, competitive prices.
4. The right to be heard—provision for fair consideration of consumer interest in government policy and legislation affecting commerce, and opportunity for complaints to be heard.

Actions by subsequent administrations have made specific provision for protecting these four consumer rights, as well as for the right to a safe and clean environment. The rationale for government intervention in dealings between buyers and sellers was explained in a special message by President Lyndon B. Johnson in 1963:

> A hundred years ago, consumer protection was largely unnecessary . . . most products were locally produced, and there was a personal relationship between the seller and the buyer. If the buyer had a complaint, he went straight to the miller, the blacksmith, the tailor, the corner grocer. Products were less complicated. It was easy to tell the excellent from the inferior. Today . . . a manufacturer may be thousands of miles from his customers—and even farther removed by distributors, wholesalers, and retailers. His products may be so complicated that only an expert can pass judgment of their quality.
>
> We are able to sustain the vast and impersonal system of commerce because of the ingenuity of our technology and the honesty of our businessmen.
>
> But this same vast network of commerce, this same complexity, also presents opportunities for the unscrupulous and the negligent.
>
> It is the government's role to protect the consumer—and the honest businessman alike—against fraud and indifference. Our goal must be to assure every American consumer a fair and honest exchange for his hard-earned dollar.

That message was the introduction to the establishment of the President's Committee on Consumer Interests. That committee was absorbed into the Office of Consumer Affairs, which was created in 1971.

Appointment of the committee reflected increasing interest by members of Congress and their constituents in further strengthening the federal government's role in consumer protection.

In the brief discussion of consumer legislation that follows, you will notice that much of the legislation designed to protect consumers and honest businessmen from sharp practices of some sellers antedated the establishment of the committee. During the period following President Johnson's 1963 message, however, there was an increased interest in the interpretation and enforcement of those early laws, along with the introduction of new consumer protective legislation.

Important acts included in the *consumer movement* are defined here.

Truth in Lending.   This is the popular term for the Consumer Credit Protection Act of 1968. It was aimed at (1) eliminating the lack of understanding by many

consumers of provisions of credit contracts and (2) the failure of adequate disclosure of all provisions of the credit contract. The Act requires written disclosure of
true costs and all substantive facts in any credit contract, prohibits misleading
advertising of credit arrangements, limits garnishments of wages, and makes it a
federal offense to engage in loansharking.

Truth in Labeling. The Fair Packaging and Labeling Act and the Federal Hazardous Substances Labeling Act require that labels include names and
addresses of producers, descriptions of products, exact quantities of contents
(rather than such descriptions as *King Size* and *Giant Size*), safety warnings on
all potentially hazardous products, and first aid instructions on poisonous
substances.

Kefauver-Harris Drug Amendments Act, 1962. This Act strengthens new drug
clearance procedures to assure more safety, effectiveness, and reliability in prescription drugs.

Truth in Advertising. This is a function of several agencies and laws. The
Wheeler-Lea Amendment to the Trade Commission Act specifically provides for
monitoring ads and prosecuting the sponsors of fraudulent or misleading advertising. The Food and Drug Administration can issue injunctions and seize foods,
drugs, cosmetics, and therapeutic devices if there are misleading or false claims or
misrepresentation.

Considerable policing of advertising claims is accomplished at the state level.
All but six states have adopted the *Printer's Ink* Model Statute or a modification
of that statute.[15] *Printer's Ink,* an advertising trade journal, proposed and sponsored
the bill in 1911 (it was revised in 1945) and urged state legislatures to adopt it
because it was believed that action would be obtained more readily in state courts
than in federal courts. That law makes it a misdemeanor to present to the public
any advertising which contains "any assertion, representation or statement of facts
which is untrue, deceptive, or misleading."[16]

Deceptive or false advertising is legislatively regulated by the Federal Trade
Commission. An advertiser who makes a claim for a product must have evidence
to support it.

Popular titles and principal provisions of other significant laws passed during
the 1960s include the Wholesome Meat Act (1967), which extended inspection
and enforcement of sanitary standards to meat processed and sold in intrastate
commerce; the Product Safety Act (1967), which enabled study and action on
potentially hazardous household appliances and home-care products; the Flamma-
ble Fabrics Act, which established standards of flammability of clothing, carpets,
blankets, and other fabrics in the home and public places; and the Automobile
Safety Act (effective 1968), which specified safety standards for automobiles and

---

[15]Alaska, Arkansas, Delaware, Georgia, Mississippi, and New Mexico.
[16]A copy of the statute may be obtained from the secretary of state or attorney general of any
of the adopting states.

tires. In addition to the federal actions, a majority of the state governments have enacted consumer protection measures.

The thrust has been to make consumers aware of corrective actions available to them and to specify fraudulent or harmful practices. Studies of repairs and guarantees, automobile insurance, land sales, securities, and mutual funds have resulted.

Regulation of Society's Collective Goods.[17]   Society's natural collective goods are regulated by the Environmental Policy Act of 1970, which sets standards limiting the kinds and amounts of waste materials which can be introduced into the nation's land, skies, and waterways. In addition, the Act establishes specific requirements that must be met when a business firm or an individual embarks on new construction that will alter the existing natural setting. Environmental impact studies, preconstruction studies of the impact on the physical environment of any structure, including roads and transmission facilities, are costly and time-consuming governmental regulations.

The impact of collective goods regulation becomes clear when one considers, for instance, the restricted use of phosphates in detergents and the ban on certain insecticides. Both restrictions caused changes in whole product lines and marketing tactics, emphasizing the alertness marketer must maintain with respect to the principal provisions of collective goods regulations.

Competitive Environment

The basic question to answer here is, Can you compete? To answer that you must have information on the intensity of competition, the number and size of competitors, and the methods of competing. Do you, for instance, face price or nonprice competition? Focus on specific market segments in analyzing the competition and examine promotion, product differentiation, and services.

What forms of competition might a business face? There is *direct competition,* which means that another product meets the same general needs as yours. There is also *indirect competition*—competition among sellers of different products. For example, a family may decide to buy new carpets instead of a new car; an industrial customer may decide to contract out an item rather than use your machine to make that product.

It is frequently beneficial to obtain information on each competitor in the following areas: market position, product line, and market areas; the state of competing technology; financial strength; production capacity; and the competitor's marketing strategy and tactics, including price, promotion, logistical services, and the general pattern of the competition's market behavior. Is the competitor an innovator, a follower, or an imitator? Is there no clear pattern? What are the competitor's relationships and reputation with suppliers, financial institutions, and

---

[17]A special section, "Over Regulation," *Saturday Review,* January 20, 1979, pp. 24–41, reviews the effects of the regulatory agencies that carry out provisions of the acts on environmental protection, occupational safety and health, consumer product safety, and others.

workers? What is the character of the management team? From all of this, you can determine the capabilities and likely response to a new market situation, including your entry into the market.[18]

Internal Environment

In order to make use of what we learned from the external environment features, we must understand the firm or nonprofit organization with which we are working. Items to consider are:

1. Problems of integration and difficulties in achieving coordinated action if, or as, operations are expanded
2. Complexity and number of product lines
3. Ability to expand over wide geographic areas
4. Management specialization and specialization of skills within the firm[19]
5. Recognition of the inevitability of change and provisions for managing change
6. Provisions for management of environmental constraints

A marketing manager must know how things get done in the organization. What are past practices and habits? Above all, what are the values of management? In summary, what is the company's subculture?

As will become clear in subsequent discussions of pricing, product development, promotion, and distribution policies and methods, all organizational strengths and weaknesses have an impact on what the marketing manager can achieve.

The main thing to remember from this chapter is that there are some factors, or forces the marketing manager can control. Those are the tools of strategy—price, product, promotion and distribution. But the use of those tools is constrained by the forces that the manager cannot control. Those are the external environmental factors. Consequently, effective marketing strategy can be developed only if one understands the influence those uncontrollable factors will have on customer needs, wants, and reactions.

QUESTIONS AND ANALYTICAL PROBLEMS

1. Define the terms *purpose* of the *organization, objective, policy, strategy, tactic.*
2. How do external environments affect a firm's internal environment?
3. What factors are included in an environmental analysis?

---

[18]See George Downing, *Basic Marketing* (Columbus, Ohio: Charles E. Merrill Publishing Company, 1971) pp. 215–216, for a matrix on competitive retaliations.

[19]The principal functional areas are accounting and control, financing, marketing and production. The principal tasks to be performed should be listed under each functional area. Under marketing, for example, one should list searching for information (including marketing research), the difficulties of controlling a widely dispersed sales organization, the integration of promotion, product knowledge, and knowledge of the target market. The functional areas may have diverse operating objectives. This subject will be further developed in Chapter 13.

4. Examine an advertisement (newspaper or magazine) and list the external environment factors that were considered in preparing the central theme of the advertisement.
5. Examine a shopping center. Observe its location and the types of goods offered for sale. What environments affect the location and the types of stores and merchandise in it?
6. Explain how the information obtained for Stages I, II, and III in the Marketing Planning Guide on page 21 can suggest marketing opportunities.
7. What is the principal effect on marketing strategy of each of the environments discussed in this chapter?
8. Define the term *culture.*
9. Make a list of the items you or your family have used in your home over the past three days. What cultural factors have influenced the purchase and use of those items?
10. What have been the technological advances that have affected your favorite recreational activity? Discuss the question with someone at least 20 years older than you are and compare the answer with yours.
11. Define the terms *tariff, trust* (referring to combination of organizations), and *price discrimination.*

12. List the federal and state laws mentioned in this chapter. State the principal provision of each. Some actions are illegal *per se* and for other the rule of reason applies. What is the difference between *per se* and *rule of reason* as the terms are used here?
13. For each of the laws listed below, write three statements reflecting your reaction to the law if you were (1) an independent merchant, (2) an independent manufacturer, and (3) a spokesman for a consumer group.
   a. Federal Trade Commission Act
   b. Wheeler-Lea Amendment to the Federal Trade Commission Act
   c. Robinson-Patman Act
14. How can an income tax affect markets for consumer goods?
15. What is the basic underlying philosophy of all the laws discussed in this chapter; that is, can you find one characteristic that all the laws have in common?
16. According to President Johnson's statement, what is the rationale for the consumer protection laws and regulations of the federal government?
17. What is the correct name of the Truth-in-Lending Act? What are the principal provisions of the Act?
18. What acts and agencies are included in Truth in Advertising?

Case 2-1 • SNUG-FIT JEAN SHOP

Yvonne Smith inhaled and pulled up the zipper. She had just successfully squeezed into the latest fashion designer jeans purchased at the Snug-Fit Jean Shop. Yvonne observed the fit in the mirror and wondered whether being in style was really worth the discomfort.[1]

---

[1]Much of the information for this case is drawn from Jeffrey Birnbaum, "The Squeeze Is On: Snug Designer Jeans Capture a Market," *The Wall Street Journal,* March 13, 1979, p. 1.

The Snug-Fit Jean Shop was started by Denise Mitchell about six months ago. She had worked in several clothing shops before opening her own shop in a medium-sized shopping center in Fresno, California. Denise had been a part-time college student for several years and, although she had not graduated, she had taken marketing, retailing, and fashion merchandising courses. Because of the classes and her work experience she was confident that she had the necessary ability to open and run her own shop.

After Ms. Smith paid the $36.40 price for the jeans and left the store, Denise wondered whether she would see her again. She hoped Yvonne Smith would become a regular customer.

Later that evening, Denise reviewed the factors that had made her shop a success. She concluded that the shop's location, the designer merchandise she carried, and the advertising she used were the most important things. The designer merchandise was perhaps the most important of the three.

Tight-fitting jeans have been around ever since cowboys began wearing them to prevent saddle sores. However, tight-fitting designer jeans are a rather new phenomenon. Fashion designers such as Calvin Klein, Geoffrey Beene, Gloria Vanderbilt, and Anne Klein design the jeans and put their names on them. Customers like the jeans because some women find the fit and style more flattering and enjoy the status and sex appeal associated with the jeans.

A number of environmental factors, Denise thought, also contribute to the success of designer jeans. First, with a price of $30 to $200, the economic environment must be favorable for demand to be very high for this type of product. Second, certain technological innovations had improved both the fabric and construction of the jeans. Finally, the cultural environment had to be favorable to such a fashion evolution. That cultural environment was particularly relevant for designer jeans.

Denise Mitchell pondered the environmental factors that had led to the success of designer jeans and her own specialty shop. She wondered if these factors were going to change in the near future. If so, she wondered what effect they would have on her business.

What environmental factors could change in the future that might drastically affect the success of the Snug-Fit Jean Shop?

Case 2-2 • KAGGS SUPER DRUG

Kaggs Super Drug is a chain of large drug stores, operating in the Southeast. The chain was started by Bobby Lee Snyder, of Northport, Alabama. Mr. Snyder started with one store in his hometown. From that store, opened in 1954, he has slowly expanded until he now operates 22 stores located in Alabama, Georgia, Mississippi, and Tennessee.

Mr. Snyder is currently contemplating his future plans. In fact, Mr. Snyder is rethinking his basic reason for being in the business. At one time his personal, but unstated, objective was to earn enough money to be comfortable and to allow him enough free time to pursue his favorite pastime, bass fishing. Unfortunately, he recalls, in his efforts to build the business he forgot about why he was doing it. In fact, just this morning he had complained to his wife that he hadn't been fishing in three years!

Now Mr. Snyder is seriously considering a major change in strategy for Kaggs Super Drug. The change, briefly stated, will be to deemphasize expansion and growth and to emphasize profit. Moreover, the emphasis on profit is going to be achieved by vertical integration. Mr. Snyder is thinking specifically about the possibility of buying a small manufacturing plant. The plant will be used to produce private-label products to sell in his chain of 22 stores. Finally, Mr. Snyder is considering taking a less active role in the business.

One good way to slow his involvement in the business would be to turn the retail management end of the business over to a newly hired assistant. Mr. Snyder would then concentrate on getting the production plant going.

Mr. Snyder has three basic concerns about this plan. Will the strategy of concentrating on manufacturing pay off? Will the tactic of no more retail store expansion seriously affect his market position in the next five years? Will his assistant, a recent engineering graduate from Georgia Tech, be able to handle the merchandising end of the business?

What other factors and options should Mr. Snyder consider before going ahead with the project?

2

Buyer Behavior

3

consumer decision making

--"Oil Profits Running Wild?"
a copyrighted article in the
November 5, 1979, edition of
U.S. News & World Report.

For the marketing concept to be fulfilled and put into operation the firm must understand the intricacies of the consumer decision-making process. This chapter will address the many aspects of consumer decision making as well as examine the factors which influence that activity. An overview of the consumer decision-making process will be presented along with a discussion of the psychological inputs to the process.

It is important to realize that the study of consumer buying behavior is merely a matter of studying basic behavior in a specialized context: consumption. As such, concepts from psychology, interpreted within the consumption context, are useful in understanding the decision process. Additionally, since consumers engage in decision making within a social setting, knowledge of the sociological influences on the decision-making process provides insights important to the marketing process.

The Consumer Decision-Making Process

Years of developmental marketing research allow for a generalized portrayal of several stages of the buying decision process. While few consumers are fully aware that they are systematically and methodically working their way through a decision process, consumer behavior and decision practices suggest that such a process is taking place. In order for the marketing decision maker to effectively plan a marketing program, the needs and demands of the consumer must be met in each stage. The consumer decision-making process can be portrayed as consisting of the following six stages:

1. Need recognition
2. Information search
3. Evaluation of product alternatives
4. Evaluation of shopping alternatives
5. The purchase decision
6. Post-purchase behavior[1]

Few consumers will act out each stage with full awareness that they are engaging in a buying-decision process. Furthermore, the elaborateness of each stage and the duration of the process will vary depending on the nature of the decision and the type of product being considered. For frequently purchased, low-cost items consumers spend little time deliberating over which product to purchase. There is little negative consequence to the purchase of an inappropriate product, and a decision error can be quickly and easily corrected. However, if the product has a high price and a long life (such as a durable good), then the decision process is long and involved. The differences in the elaborateness and duration of the process should not lead to the conclusion that the stages in decision making are eliminated in some instances. Even in routine purchases the consumer initiates the decision sequences. It may take only an instant review at each level, but it does occur.

Because of managerial and strategical implications for designing a marketing program that fulfills consumer needs at each stage, it is important to examine in detail the many aspects of the decision-making process.

Need Recognition

Entry into the decision process is initiated by the consumer's recognition of a need. Need recognition is stimulated by one of three conditions: an out-of-stock need, a functional need, or an emotional need.

The *out-of-stock* condition is the most simple of the need states. It is the common situation occuring when a frequently purchased, low-cost item is restocked on a regular basis. Toothpaste, laundry detergent, and food items are typical of products in the out-of-stock condition. The consumer feels very little uneasiness during the decision process and is likely to spend little time fulfilling the subsequent stages. The introduction of new brands may result in further deliberation, but the relative insignificance of the consequences results in a rather routine decision effort.

Entering the decision process by virtue of a *functional need* recognition is considerably more important. A functional need arises when the consumer is seeking a solution to a specified and generally more important need. The need for

---

[1]For a more elaborate treatment of the decision-making process, see Fleming Hansen, *Consumer Choice Behavior,* (New York City: The Free Press, 1972), pp. 297–408.

transportation (an automobile), a more comfortable living environment (furniture and appliances), or clothing are some examples. Functional needs can arise because of the breakdown or obsolesence of currently owned items or a significant change in the consumer's life (for example, buying a home). Situations where a functional need is the catalyst for the decision process result in a more time-consuming and thoughtful progression through the stages. Since decisions in this need area tend to be of greater consequence, by virtue of higher prices paid for the items and their longevity, the decision process is more elaborate and a more concerted effort is made at each stage.

The decision process that is motivated by the recognition of an *emotional need* is a difficult one to handle for both the consumer and the marketing decision maker. The difficulty in understanding the resultant decision process stems from the fact that it cannot neatly be positioned in terms of the cost of the product or life of the product; that is, consumers can seek satisfaction to such emotional needs as status, prestige, belonging, or achievement with almost any product. While an emotional need can be legitimately isolated as a separate recognition category, such needs vary with the consumer who is seeking satisfaction. For example, many consumers will enter the decision process for laundry detergent based on an out-of-stock need recognition. But what about the consumer who purchases laundry detergent and is sincerely concerned that the family is satisfied with the result? There is clearly an element of emotional need in that context.

Perhaps a more conspicuous example is automobiles. If functional needs were the only motivation for seeking satisfaction, few buyers would require the luxury and expense of many of the available alternatives.

The marketing decision maker must understand the various need states that can motivate a product purchase decision. Such an awareness of the need states can be directly translated into a product design, pricing, or promotional strategy that attempts to directly address the desires of the potential customer.

Information Search

Once a need state emerges, a search for information begins. The consumer relies on two basic sources of information: internal and external.

Sources of *internal information* are the consumer's past experiences and stored information. Past experiences with different products and brands provide the consumer with firsthand information regarding a particular product's capabilities in satisfying the aroused need. This type of information results in products being categorized as unacceptable (due to previous dissatisfaction) or as potential solutions to a current need.

Stored information can come from sources other than direct experience. Stored information on various products or product categories is created by media exposure or friends' usage, resulting in a general predisposition (favorable or unfavorable) toward various products.

If reviewing internal information sources does not produce a clear alternative or alternatives for need satisfaction, the consumer will then turn to *external information* sources: the media, friends or relatives, and objective product evaluations (such as buyers' guides or product tests). These sources of information can be distinguished from stored information by virtue of how specific and current they are. If consumers are not satisfied with their knowledge of available alternatives, magazine, newspaper, and television advertising can provide such information. Friends and relatives can provide insights based on their current and past experiences. Conscienteous buyers may turn to specialized publications that test various products and include this information in their decision-making process.

Once the potential buyer is comfortable with the amount of information obtained from both intenal and external sources, the decision process continues.

Evaluation of Product Alternatives

In some cases the search for information will result in a clearly superior alternative for the consumer. In many instances, however, several products seem suitable and an evaluation of product alternatives takes place. Consistent with the need states discussed earlier, the consumer can evaluate product alternatives using three general criteria: functional product features, emotional satisfaction provided by each product, and benefits that accrue from individual product alternatives. It is important to note that the reliance on these three areas will vary from consumer to consumer based on the initial need state and the consumer's own set of values.

An evaluation of *functional product features* includes factors such as price, product performance characteristics, unique features of each product, and any warranties or guarantees offered with the product. Evaluation of the functional features relates most directly to the economic considerations of the purchase.

The *emotional satisfaction* that each alternative provides is, of course, the consumer's perception. This may be stimulated by the manufacturer's portrayal and positioning of the brand (i.e., establishing a distinct market image) and is only useful as an evaluation criterion by those consumers seeking satisfaction of an emotional need. Products may be evaluated on their potential for providing prestige or success with the opposite sex, for example. Evaluating products on an emotional dimension is certainly more a matter of conjuring mental images about the product than examining tangible features.

The evaluation of products based on *benefits* is an area that fills a void between the functional and emotional evaluative criteria. For example, one could evaluate the functions of a riding lawnmower based on the fact that it has three forward gears, a large gas tank, and a grass catcher (all of which are functional features). It is also possible, however, to evaluate the product from a benefit standpoint, taking into consideration that the use of this particular product makes lawn mowing easier and faster so that more time and energy are available for leisure activities. Many products are designed so that their functional features relate directly to further use benefits, such as leisure time depicted in the example above. Consumers often focus on the benefits themselves, thereby highlighting this area of evaluation.

It is the task of the marketing decision maker to accurately identify the type of criteria that are imposed during an evaluation of the firm's market offering.

Again, proper design of the marketing program will require meeting consumers' demands.

Evaluation of Shopping Alternatives

Once a product evaluation is completed, the consumer will begin to evaluate shopping alternatives. The most important aspect of this stage is the consumer's decision regarding which retail outlet to patronize. However, marketers should be careful not to overlook alternatives other than retail shopping. Several firms, most notably Avon, Amway, J.C. Penney, and Sears, have successfully initiated in-house and catalog selling programs, eliminating retail shopping. After evaluating product alternatives, a consumer may discover that the product is available by mail or telephone order. In this case, the trip to the retail store is eliminated. It must be recognized, however, that many consumers opt to avoid the risk of mail-order shopping and also seek additional benefits from the retail store shopping experience.

When the retail store decision is embarked upon, the consumer evaluates the choices at this stage along criteria commonly referred to as *retail store patronage motives.* [2] While the list of motives can become quite extensive, consumers will evaluate a store on the following:

1. *Convenience.* This dimension includes location, parking, ease of movement through the store, and store hours.
2. *Store appearance.* Many consumers consider the store decore, cleanliness, and layout in making their patronage choice.
3. *Products.* Whether a retail outlet handles many different types of products and brands or specializes in its offering can influence the buyer's choice.
4. *Services.* Consumers evaluate the nature of the services, such as repair, delivery, installation, and credit, offered by a store. Some buyers prefer fewer services and lower prices.
5. *Store personnel.* The friendliness, helpfulness, and courteousness of store personnel can frequently affect consumer's patronage of the outlet.
6. *Advertising.* The quality and informativeness of a store's advertising has been determined to be an element of the consumer's store evaluation process.

Beyond the patronage motives, consumers also rely on the retail setting as a final opportunity for product information and evaluation. Especially for higher cost items, the in-store experience can be critical. The purchase of many products requires a judgment and evaluation at the point of purchase, forcing consumers into making a shopping trip. Sales personnel in a store can be an important source of information and advice. (These factors are discussed in greater detail in Chapter 11.)

This stage in the consumer decision process immediately suggests several requirements for the marketing program. The marketing planner must be fully aware of the consumer preferences and desires at this stage of decision making.

---

[2]For a good listing of variables used to measure retail store patronage motives see Robert Kelley and Ronald Stephenson, "The Semantic Differential: An Information Source for Designing Retail Patronage Appeals," *Journal of Marketing,* Vol. 331, No. 4 (October, 1967) p. 43.

The Purchase Decision

Little needs to be discussed about this stage, where the consumer incorporates the knowledge gained through the information search, product evaluation, and shopping evaluation and makes a choice. A final decision is made to satisfy the need structure, and the decision includes selecting a product type, a brand within the product type, a retail outlet (or other source), and a method of payment for the product.

The process is not completed at this stage, however. A critical step for the consumer and marketer follows.

Post-Purchase Behavior

Many firms overlook or are unaware of the fact that the consumer may engage in various types of behavior *after* a decision has been made. In general, the postpurchase behaviors are of two types: additional information search and the acquisition of related products.

Seeking Additional Information. When the consumer seeks additional information after making a purchase, motivation for acquiring this added information is the result of the consumer's attempt to relieve cognitive dissonance. *Cognitive dissonance* is the anxiety that results from having made a decision and a purchase commitment. The amount of post-purchase anxiety is related to several prepurchase conditions: the unit value of the item, the number of close alternatives identified before the purchase, the longevity of the product, and the importance of the decision to the buyer. As each of these factors increases, more cognitive dissonance will result. The uncomfortable mental state generated by the anxiety causes the consumer to seek additional information to reaffirm that the correct purchase decision was made. The recent buyer will scrutinize media advertising in a search of reinforcement. Friends and relatives are also bombarded with requests to view the new item and offer their praise to the consumer for making "such a wise and wonderful purchase."

The astute marketing manager will recognize situations where cognitive dissonance is likely to affect the buyer and will develop strategies that help relieve buyer anxiety. Many firms include a congratulatory note in the product package to immediately provide the buyer with reinforcement. For example,

> Dear Zenith Owner:
>   It is our pleasure to welcome you into the family of satisfied Zenith customers. Over a period of many years, Zenith products have earned a reputation for quality and dependability, and it is our desire to maintain this reputation with you.
>
>   Sincerely,

Other firms will include some comments on their advertising that are directed at recent buyers, thus providing these consumers with an opportunity to support their decision.

It is important for the firm to recognize the potential for postpurchase anxiety and to develop tactics that help the consumer relieve the problem. Consumers will repeat behavior that is rewarding and enjoyable. Postpurchase anxiety threatens the euphoria of product acquisition. Therefore, if the firm hopes to promote brand loyalty and repeat behavior (repurchase of the firm's offering), then tactics that help relieve the anxiety contribute directly to such objectives.

Acquiring Related Products.   The consumer's acquisition of related products generally (though not necessarily) results in a demand for complimentary products from other manufacturers. Procter & Gamble was quick to enlist the support of Mr. Coffee in promoting its Folger's brand coffee. Similarly, consumers who buy a new car frequently stock up on various products (polishes, waxes, vacuum cleaners) to maintain the car properly. Either through necessity or a sense of enthusiasm for the new purchase, consumers purchase several other items related to an initial purchase.

As with other stages in the decision process, post-purchase behavior will vary from consumer to consumer and is based on the importance and value of the item purchased.

The decision process discussed here is meant to point out that consumers are not as capricious or unsystematic as one might intuitively believe. The underpinnings of human behavior are not always obvious, and the stages of consumer decision making are intended to identify that consumption behavior is, in fact, methodical.

At this point it is necessary to go beyond the mere description of the decision process. Numerous influences act on consumers as they work their way toward a buying decision. These influences are psychological and sociological in origin.

PSYCHOLOGICAL INFLUENCES

As a consumer progresses through the decision-making process several individual or psychological influences help shape the nature of the decision and the behaviors in which the consumer is engaged. Marketing has progressed rapidly in its understanding of the relationship between psychological factors and consumption behavior. While all aspects of psychological influences on the consumer are not completely understood, the following areas provide further understanding of consumer decision making and behavior: needs, learning, attitudes, self-image, and perception.

Needs

Basic human needs provide the goal-oriented foundation for the consumer to seek satisfaction in the marketplace. A useful, well-organized description of how needs motivate behavior is provided by Abraham Maslow.[3] Maslow, a pioneer in

[3]A.H. Maslow, *Motivation and Personality* (New York City: Harper & Row, Publishers, Inc., 1954).

the study of human motivation, conceived that human behavior progresses through the following hierarchy of needs:

1. *Physiological needs:* Biological needs that require the satisfaction of hunger, thirst, and basic bodily functions.
2. *Safety needs:* The need to provide shelter and protection for the body and to maintain a comfortable existence.
3. *Love and belonging needs:* The need for affiliation and affection. A person will strive for both the giving and receiving of love.
4. *Esteem needs:* The need for recognition, status, and prestige. In addition to seeking the respect of others, there is a need and desire for self-respect.
5. *Self-actualization:* The highest of all the needs and achieved by only a small percentage of people, according to Maslow. The individual strives for total fulfillment of maximum capabilities.

It should be clearly understood that Maslow was describing basic human needs and motivations. Within the context of a high mass-consumption society, the attempt to satisfy the needs partly manifests itself through acquiring goods and services. Many products directly address the requirements of the need states. Home security systems and smoke detectors help satisfy certain safety needs. Love and belonging needs can be pursued through the use of many products portrayed as representing love, affection, and affiliation within a particular group. Many personal care products such as cosmetics promote greater acceptance by the opposite sex. In their pursuit of esteem, many consumers buy products that are perceived to have status and prestige; expensive jewelry, automobiles, and residences are examples. It is, however, difficult to *buy* self-actualization. There is evidence, however, that product perception is effected by this need state.[4]

An important aspect of Maslow's description of human motivation is that it is strictly hierarchical in nature. Thus, the individual cannot and will not proceed through the need structure until a level of comfort and satisfaction is achieved for the current need state. Beginning with the physiological needs, a routine must be established for the regular and satisfactory fulfillment of the needs. When such a routine is established, the next level of needs, safety needs, emerges as the most urgent. Again, the individual seeks a systematic means of satisfying those needs. The process continues as the individual continually attempts to satisfy the urgings of several levels of the hierarchy. Maslow contends, however, that the vast majority of people in industrialized societies never progress beyond the love and belonging needs and spend their lives trying to achieve satisfaction of the first three levels of the hierarchy.

Learning

In discussing the consumer decision-making process it was noted that consumers rely on past experiences and various sources of information en route to making a purchasing decision. The result of these efforts, over the long run, is learning. Consumers behave differently based on learned information. While there are

---

[4]Curtis Hamm and Edward W. Cundiff, "Self-Actualization and Product Perception," *Journal of Marketing Research* (November, 1969), pp. 470–472.

several comprehensive learning theories, the critical elements of learning, for marketing purposes, are stimuli and reinforcement.[5]

Stimuli are the many sources of information to which the customer may voluntarily or involuntarily be exposed. Several information sources are marketer controlled. Advertising, salespeople, the product package and label, and even the product itself stimulate the consumer. The marketing strategist attempts to design these sources of information in a fashion that has meaning and use to the consumer. In the decision process the consumer is seeking relevant information to aid in the product choice, and these marketer-controlled stimuli will enter the process.

Many other sources of information are beyond the control of the marketing process, though. The consumer's reliance on friends' recommendations or publicity about the product also help the consumer learn. The end result of encountering various stimuli is that the consumer's behavior will be altered based on the newly learned information.

Reinforcement, the second basic element of learning, can have a powerful effect on consumers' subsequent decisions and activities. The direct source of reinforcement in a marketing context is the use of the product. The consumer can be positively or negatively reinforced depending on the level of satisfaction obtained from product use. If the product fails to meet the consumer's expectations, negative reinforcement results. This provides a barrier to the subsequent use of the product. Conversely, a rewarding experience will motivate the buyer to engage in the same behavior again (that is, to repurchase the brand). Several marketing efforts can facilitate a positive reaction on the part of the consumer. The most obvious is that the product be properly designed and meet the consumer's needs as closely as possible. Beyond this requirement, prompt and proper servicing of the product is important. Also, as pointed out in the decision process discussion, post-purchase communications which support the buyer's decision can relieve cognitive dissonance and serve as a positive reinforcement.

Consumption behavior is learned. Marketers must understand that elements of the marketing process can promote consumer learning and enhance a firm's market position. Learning relates directly to the consumer decision process in that stimuli and consumer experience are part of the ongoing product evaluation process.

Attitude

Over the last ten years there has been a flurry of marketing research directed at identifying the relationship between attitudes and consumer behavior.[6] It is currently believed that attitudes are an extremely useful factor in understanding

---

[5]See, for example, Ernest R. Hilgard and George H. Hower, *Theories of Learning,* 3d ed., (New York City: Appleton-Century-Crofts, 1966).

[6]For a look at representative literature in this area see Michael B. Mazis and Olli Ahtola, "A Comparison of Four Multi-Attribute Models in the Prediction of Consumer Attitudes," *Journal of Consumer Research,* Vol. 2, No. 1 (June, 1975), p. 38; and Michael J. Ryan and E.H. Bonfield, "The Extended Fishbein Model and Consumer Behavior," *Journal of Consumer Research,* Vol. 2, No. 2 (September, 1975), p. 118.

consumer decision making and behavior. The usefulness of attitudes in understanding behavior stems from that basic nature of attitudes.

Attitudes represent a mental state of readiness resulting from past experiences and prior information. This state of readiness exerts a directive force on behavior. Therefore, it can be seen that as a consumer reviews experiences with a product and is subject to information about a product, an attitude will result. Depending on whether the resultant attitude toward the product is positive or negative, the consumer's readiness to respond to that product will change. Under conditions of a positive attitude, the response readiness will take the form of approach behavior (that is, purchase and use). When a negative attitude has formed, the consumer will be predisposed to avoid a particular product and seek alternatives.

The marketing role in dealing with attitudes, as part of the consumer's resultant market behavior, is to provide information and product capabilities that will promote a positive attitude. Attitude structure and function are complex elements in basic human behavioral tendencies. In general, however, the marketing practitioner needs to recognize that there is a direct link between attitudes and consumer behavior in the marketplace.

Self-Image

Self-image is the relatively straightforward notion that each of us sees ourselves in a certain way and perceives that others have exactly the same image of us. In the marketing process, consumers choose products they view to be consistent with their self-image;[7] that is, products that they believe represent the type of person they are will seem appropriate and stimulate a favorable reaction. For the person whose self-image is progressive, modern, active, and so on, similarly portrayed products will reaffirm that identity and elicit a favorable response.

There are actually several components involved in self-image. First, the *real self* is the actual, objective view of the person as he or she truly is. The *ideal self* is the type of person the individual is aspiring to be; this may form the content of career plans and aspirations. The *perceived self* is the way people think others see them. There may be a great deal of consistency between the real, ideal, and perceived self. In many cases, however, the three are diverse and affect the decision process as the consumer strives for products that fullfill ideal self-motivations.

To fulfill the expectations of perceived and ideal self, consumers may turn to *conspicuous consumption,* that is, purchasing products they believe represent their desired image. Conspicuous consumption need not be restricted to ostentatious, gaudy products, as is sometimes popularly believed. Rather, products that the consumer believes accurately portray the self-image are used, helping symbolize the image to others.

The notion of self-image provides the marketer with another opportunity to interject meaningful information into the consumer decision-making process. Since self-image manifests itself in an evaluation of the appropriateness of each product

---

[7]E. Laird Landon, "Self-Concept, Ideal Self-Concept, and Consumer Purchase Intentions," *Journal of Consumer Research* (September, 1974), pp. 44–51.

alternative, the marketing strategist can attempt to provide information and product design features which address basic dimensions of the factor.

Perception

Perception is the manner in which an individual relates to the external environment. The orientation to the outside world formed by perception is the product
of past experiences, attitudes, self-image, and various relevant stimuli that serve as
information. It can be seen that perceptions are actually the combined influence
of many of the psychological influences discussed so far.

The implications to the marketing process of perceptions are that consumers
will interpret their marketplace encounters within the context of their perceptions;
that is, consumers' reactions to products, advertising, and the selling environment
are shaped by the factors of perception. Furthermore, consumers' perceptual processes screen out impertinent and irrelevant information. What is important and
meaningful to consumers is defined by their perceptions of the outside world. As
such, information about products, their use, and benefits must be consistent with
the definition of what is relevant.

It is important to realize that perception enters the consumer decision process
by virtue of its effect on the way consumers evaluate products and process information about products. The only goods and services that will enter the realm of
possible consumption by consumers are those that meet this test of perception and
directly address the needs and goals of consumers—the basis for an evaluation for
relevance.

This discussion of psychological influences is intended to highlight their effects
on consumer decision making and subsequent consumption behavior. These internal effects on the decision process must be considered, however, as they apply
within the context of several environmental factors which also affect the consumer.
We now turn our attention to these environmental factors.

SOCIOLOGICAL INFLUENCES

Psychological influences on the decision process do help the marketing manager devise an effective marketing program. The consumer, however, does not
make decisions in isolation. Rather, the individual must cope with and consider the
many influences from the environment in which products are used. Sociological
influences that provide insights into consumer behavior are culture, social class,
reference groups, the diffusion process, and family influences.

Culture

Culture has global influence, the effects of which result in norms for a society.
Culture evolves through the behaviors, artifacts, and symbols that are passed from
one generation to another. It is unavoidable that various cultural influences have
effects on individuals as they fulfill their consumption requirements. The basic
cultural values people learn are transferred, in part, to the evaluation of the

usefulness and appropriateness of products. To understand the effect of culture on the American consumer, several basic and changing cultural influences must be examined.

The American Ethic. United States culture had its beginnings in the Puritan ethic, which dictated that hard work was the essence of a good, clean life. People paid cash for all their purchases and leisure was a sign of laziness and frivolity. The advancement of our society has fostered a new ethic, however, an ethic which values leisure and nonwork activities. Buying by credit is no longer a social stigma and, in fact, is a way of life for many persons. The new ethic places a premium on time itself. People pursue leisure activities and seek ways of increasing the time available for such activities. All this translates into a need and desire for goods and services that help save time.

Convenience is a key variable in the emerging ethic of our country, and its effects are pervasive and conspicuous in marketing. Products that are easy to open, easy to use, and disposable have made inroads in the marketplace as marketers recognized the national desire for convenience. Frozen foods first reacted to the influence. They were followed by products which were pre-prepared or came in plastic bags—ready for preparation and serving. We can now use and dispose of lighters, shavers, and literally every product package we buy. Entire industries have been spawned by the desire for convenience. The fast-food industry and convenience food stores are examples. Similarly, traditional consumer-oriented operations—such as banks and supermarkets—have responded to the convenience movement with 24-hour banking machines and extended store hours.

The United States ethic has simply replaced the live-to-work philosophy of life with a work-to-live philosophy. The desire for a diverse and fast-moving life experience has forced marketers to supply goods and services that fit this evolving norm of behavior.

The Changing Social Institutions. Our society has dramatically altered the nature and effects of our basic social institutions: family, church, school, and government. Both the family and organized religion have declined in their influence on the individual. The once-cohesive family unit has been ruptured by increased mobility, the divorce rate, and economic pressures. Declines in church membership and attendance nationwide are attributed to various causes related chiefly to a desire for personal choice and freedom in worship. The net effect of the decline of these two basic social institutions is that their contribution to transmitting and shaping cultural values has shrunk. No longer are family members or church doctrine a major source of value formation.

Conversely, the influence of educational institutions and government is increasing. Children begin school earlier and spend more years in school than did their parents. Because of the reduced family influence, they receive more of their value standards from the educational system.

Government has also assumed an important role in daily life; however, the influence of government has risen due to an increased awareness of government activities and the availability of services the government can provide.

Changing Roles. Regardless of the constitutional success or failure, such measures as the Equal Right Amendment (ERA), the ERA and similar movements represent a significant restructuring of roles in our society. Changing roles for today's citizens are partly due to the changes taking placing in the family and to the emerging American ethic. Beyond these forces, however, one must recognize that traditional male and female roles are being dramatically restructured. With the restructuring process comes the need and desire for different or altered products and services. Further, as traditional role definitions change, the perception of products will also change. This calls for a different form of communication about products and/or the alteration of product design.

Subcultures

Consistent with the beginnings and philosophy of the United States culture, subcultures continue to exert an influence on behavioral norms. Ethnic affiliations, age groups, geographical residence, and special interest groups—all exert an influence on individual behavior. These groups transmit values and establish norms of behavior. It should be recognized that unique value systems and behavioral tendencies are produced by subcultural influences.

While it may be possible to separate and discuss cultural elements in neat little sections, the identification of their influences should not be misconstrued as being an easy task. The elements of culture discussed here are not singular in their effect. Obviously, there is an interaction and combination of effect from the many changes taking place in our culture. Changing roles are inextricably related to a desire for convenience and the declining influence of the family. Correspondingly the emerging United States ethic is also difficult to separate from the changing institutional structure. The effect of culture on decision making and behavior in the marketplace must be viewed as an overall component of influence rather than several separate forces creating change.

Social Class

An additional influence on the consumer is social class membership. While a fundamental precept of American society is the lack of class structure, social classes tend to evolve as a sociological phenomenon.[8] At the outset, it is useful to describe the factors that define class membership:

1. Education
2. Occupation
3. Area of residence
4. Type of residence

Obvious by its absence is the income variable. Quite simply, income has not proved to clearly delineate the social classes. A plumber and a middle-level execu-

---

[8]The discussion in this section is based on W. Lloyd Warner and Paul Lunt, *The Social Life of a Modern Community* (New Haven, Conn: Yale University Press, 1941).

tive can earn the same income, but their social class membership is different, primarily because their value systems as members of different social classes are also different.

The use of these variables for categorization produces six distinct social classes. These social class designations have provided marketers with insights regarding consumer decision making and behavior:

1. *Upper Upper Class.* This group includes the elite in society. As a very small percentage of the total population (.5 percent) this group represents the old rich, the long-standing families in a community who are thought to (and oftentimes do) live in stately old mansions.

2. *Lower Upper Class.* Often referred to as the *nouveaux riche,* this group is college educated and seeks status. The lower-upper-class person places high value on social interactions and symbols of wealth. This group is alleged to constitute about 1 percent of society. From a marketing standpoint, the small size of this group does not attract the attention of mass-marketed goods and services. However, luxury goods and products that represent prestige and status are pursued by this group.

3. *Upper Middle Class.* Education is the destinguishing feature of this group. The occupational characteristics of the upper middle class can be found in the professions: doctors, lawyers, business professionals. Members of this group place heavy emphasis on career and demand excellence of their children. Products of superior quality are consumed by the group. The high educational level tends to promote product scrutinizing, and items of value complement the household. The upper-middles seek an attractive existence that affects their home, furnishings, clothing, and so on. The upper middle class represents a substantial market segment with 10 percent of society classified here.

4. *Lower Middle Class.* This is the white-collar segment of society. These are conscientious, responsible people who strive for respectability. As such, their value systems emphasize hard work and neatness. They are not a group that demonstrates great confidence in their buying habits and therefore conform to currently accepted norms. Neither are they original in their shopping ideas or behaviors. The female of the household tends to work hard at the decision-making process and tries to stretch the family dollar. Since this group has a large number of members, 30 percent of society, it represents an excellent mass market for standard items of all sorts.

5. *Upper Lower Class.* The "blue collar" class makes up the largest single group of buyers—35 percent. Many members of this class rent rather than own their residence. They lead a structured and unchanging lifestyle, avoiding credit and concentrating their spending on functional items for the home. This class emphasizes investment in durable goods as opposed to the acquisition of conspicuous products. The female of an upper-lower-class household demonstrates the greatest degree of brand loyalty, especially to the national brands, of all the classes. The aspiration level of this group is generally low. Despite the fact that many blue-collar jobs provide considerable income (in many cases higher than their lower-middle-class counterparts), members of this group have little motivation to change their existence.

6. *Lower Lower Class.* These people comprise the uneducated, unskilled, underemployed segment of society. It is estimated that 25 percent of United States citizens are in this social class. The lower lower class lives in substandard housing; many of its members are on welfare. Their plight in life and lack of education results in ill-planned purchase decisions. Impulse buying is highest in this group. Because of its relatively large size and the government assis-

tance this group receives, the individuals cannot be ignored as substantial marketplace participants. The problem in reaching this group stems from the group's unstructured and inconsistent buying patterns.

The value of social class for providing insights to the consumer decision process is related to the values to which these class members adhere. Rather than stress individual classes for describing differences, it is useful to consider the higher classes versus the lower classes.

The higher classes value the impact they can have with their product collection. Products that exude prestige, status, or even class membership are valued. The higher social classes are simply more conspicuous in their consumption. Further, they own their own homes and invest heavily in products to complement the dwelling. On the other hand, the lower social classes place a greater value and emphasis on the family. Products which make life more comfortable and enhance the family's existence are more important. Lower-class group members do not have great aspirations for changing their lifestyles or making them more exciting. In light of this, basic, straightforward communications that highlight fundamental values are more meaningful to this group.

Social class aids in understanding the consumption process in two ways: (1) by identifying the types of products that are likely to be consumed and (2) by identifying the perceptions and life orientation consumers carry with them in making purchasing decisions. Marketers can use the social class variable as another input into the segmentation process, as well as for structuring the precise nature of other factors in the marketing mix.

Reference Group Theory

One of the strongest sources of persuasive pressure and/or influence on the consumer is the reference group or groups to which an individual belongs. Reference groups can be large and diverse, such as college graduates, ethnic groups, or members of a political party. Groups can also be small and intimate, such as the family unit, work peers, or a social club. There is a strong tendency for individuals to conform to the norms of the groups they identify with and engage in behavior the group deems appropriate. There is little mystery to this relationship since the person values group membership and joined the group because of its similar attitudes or interests. The group becomes a reference for judging behavior and determining future courses of behavior.

In the marketing context, reference group theory proves useful in several ways. First, for consumers with little confidence in their buying skills the reference group is used as a substitute for obtaining objective product information. If numerous members of the group are using a a product and gaining satisfaction from it, the consumer can then defer to this information in the decision process. Second, and closely related to the first influence of reference groups, a marketer's portrayal of a product in use by a particular type of person can serve as an added form of relevant purchasing information. Even with potential buyers who do not lack confidence, seeing a person in an advertisement they can relate to and identify with adds another dimension to the image and meaning of the product. Finally, the concept of aspiring group membership is meaningful. Beyond the groups to which individuals actually belong, many people aspire to affiliate with certain groups or to be identified with a particularly revered group. The use of sports heros in children's advertising is an example; witness this in the advertising for Ked's tennis shoes which has adopted the theme: Keds—for those times in your life when you feel like a Pro.

Reference group theory provides the marketer with an opportunity to devise a relevant communication for consumers to use in the decision-making process. Several product types—cars, cigarettes, beer, and instant coffee—have demonstrated strong reliance on reference group influence in consumer choice.[9]

The Diffusion of Innovations

In the specialized context of new products, a mutual relationship between decision making and behavior has been discovered regarding the manner in which innovations are diffused through a society. The key elements of the diffusion process are the *nature of the product and the adopter (consumer) categories.*

Various characteristics of the *nature of the product* will speed or deter the acceptance of a product by consumers.[10] The *complexity* of a product and consumers' corresponding inability to understand its function and operation will slow the process considerably. Also, the compatability of the product with existing norms and behavior affects the rate of acceptance. Microwave ovens (aside from some early safety hazards) were incompatible with the concept of the hard-working mother. Low-suds laundry detergents were viewed as not effective since suds were perceived as related to cleaning power. Similarly, a firm that would attempt to introduce automobile tires in rainbow colors, rather than black, would probably find the color incompatible with consumers' beliefs about what a tire should be.

Three additional characteristics of an innovation relating to its marketability also affect the adoption rate. The *relative advantage* of the product—that is, its superiority over alternative choices—is clearly an influential factor. Relative advantage may be gained through functional superiority, a lower price, or a unique design. The *observability* of the innovation's function can do much to speed or slow the process. It was clear that color television had something different and better to offer than black-and-white models. Finally, if an innovation can be used on a *trial* basis, the adoption rate is bolstered. Many firms, therefore, use free samples or in-home free trials to take advantage of this influence.

The alert marketing strategist recognizes the capabilities or drawbacks of a new product with respect to factors that may facilitate or inhibit its market entry. The other major influence on new product success, *consumer adopter categories,* is equally as informative in designing a marketing program for a new product.

---

[9]*Group Influences in Marketing and Public Relations* (Ann Arbor, Mich.: Foundation for Research on Human Behavior, 1956).

[10]Everett M. Rogers and F. Floyd Shoemaker, *Communication of Innovations* (2d ed.; New York City: The Free Press, 1971), Chapter 4.

DISTRIBUTION OF ADOPTERS

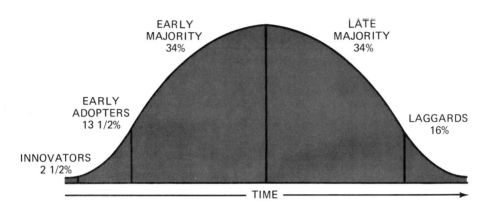

Illus. 3-1   **Adopter Categories**

Some people like to try new products as soon as they are introduced. Others like to wait until the product proves it works. These types of people have been verified to exist en masse and are organized conceptually into what is referred to as adopter categories. The adopter categories are graphically represented in Illus. 3-1 and described as follows:[11]

1. *Innovators.* These people are the first to try a new product. They are high-income, high-social-class consumers who display great confidence in their buying skills. They tend to learn of new products through the mass media. Their higher education and secure financial status make them liberal in their buying behavior. The well-defined demographics of this group and the members' reliance on mass media make them a reachable target for new product introduction despite their small absolute numbers.

2. *Early Adopters.* Still a high-income, high-social-class group, the early adopters differ significantly from the innovators. Most notably, members of this group rely on personal sources of information and also act as opinion leaders once the product is purchased. They tend to have visible positions in the community and therefore greatly speed the diffusion process by their use of the product.

3. *Early Majority.* This group represents the opening of the mass market. It is above average in income, education, and social class and tends to use a broad range of information sources for product awareness, including contact with the early adopters.

4. *Late Majority.* Once a product reaches this adopter category it has firmly established itself in the market. At this stage in the adoption process, buyers are now lower in education, social class, and income. This group has been waiting for price reduction or product improvement before adopting it for use.

5. *Laggards.* This group of consumers is the most skeptical of innovation and the last to adopt the product. The group has a narrow range of exposure and experience and simply delays the adoption decision.

---

[11]This discussion is based on Rogers and Shoemaker, *ibid.,* Chapter 5.

The adoption categorization is a useful conceptualization because it clearly describes the type of person likely to purchase a product at different stages in the product life cycle (see Chapter 8). It should be noted, however, that many products are designed and targeted for consumers who are really somewhere in the middle of the adopter categories. In this situation the diffusion process is minimally useful, and the marketer will proceed with strategies and tactics appropriate for a target group.

Family

The preceding sections have discussed several broadly based sociological influences on the decision and consumption process. The final factor, family, has a more immediate and specific influence on decision making and consumption. Two aspects of family influence are relevant: the family life cycle and the family decision process.

The *family life cycle* is a series of stages in which a family is formed, grows, evolves, and changes consumption patterns. A new family that is establishing a household has a broad range of product needs. The purchase of a home or arrival of a child causes more product needs. As children grow, enter school, learn to ride a bike or drive a car, the need for another set of products evolves. The process continues until the household returns to a two-member unit. The various levels of family development clearly influence the nature and scope of the family's product needs.

The *family decision process* is a complex one that must be clearly understood if marketers are to direct their efforts properly. Although the number of women in the labor force has altered buying patterns, the fact remains that the female member of a family still acts as the major purchasing agent for the household. Because of this, many products are designed for and directed toward women. Within the context of the family decision process, another type of purchasing behavior is that of the female who buys products for other members of the household. As a result, product design and promotion are devised for identification with these family members; whereas the package design or in-store display for the product is frequently directed at the female purchaser. Finally, it must be recognized that many product decisions are made jointly by husband and wife; in such cases the marketing process should allow for this coordinated effort.

QUESTIONS AND ANALYTICAL PROBLEMS

1. What are the main differences and similarities in the way a consumer will engage in a purchase decision for a low-cost, frequently purchased item as opposed to a high-cost durable good item?

2. Describe the three types of needs that can provide the catalyst for consumer decision making. Give an example of a product type that exemplifies each need state.

3. How is the marketer's decision-making power enhanced by knowing the way in which consumers evaluate product alternatives?

4. Define *cognitive dissonance*. Why should a marketing strategy be devised to address this consumer reaction?

5. Give an example of a product that is positioned to satisfy the different levels of Maslow's hierarchy of needs.

6. Why have attitudes emerged as such important factors in consumer decision making? How can an understanding of attitudes aid the marketing effort?

7. What information is relevant to consumers? How does the concept of relevance relate to the process of perception?

8. How does social class affect shopping behavior? What parts of the marketing process must be adapted to comply with the differences in behavior of members of one social class as opposed to the behavior of a different social class?

9. What factors speed or impede the acceptance of a product innovation in society? Cite an example of recent product innovation and how its features aided or hindered its market success.

10. John and Mary (in their early 30s) and Fred and Wilma (in their 60s) are both in the market for a new color television. What are likely to be some significant differences in their decision processes and purchase behavior?

Case 3-1 • CAR SHOPPING WITH THE CAMPBELLS

Jim squirmed uncomfortably in his easy chair as he read that the Organization of Petroleum Exporting Countries (OPEC) just raised the base price of crude oil another 9 percent. Attempting to think through the effects of the increased oil prices on his household, he was especially concerned about his family's driving habits.

Jim and Sue Campbell married in 1972 while Jim was still in school. In the spring of 1975 their first child was born, just three months before the family moved from Bangor, Maine, to Denver, Colorado, where Jim had accepted a job in the public school system. To make the cross-country trip the Campbells sold their sports car and purchased a full-size station wagon. The new car was excellent for cross-country travel, being large enough for carrying the baby, the dog and necessary equipment. Since purchasing the car the Campbells had moved to Georgia, their second child was born, and the price of gasoline had increased by about 25 cents a gallon.

As Jim pondered the last few years he wondered if he had made a mistake by not buying an economy car in 1975. The price of gasoline had risen considerably since they purchased their station wagon, and he was convinced that gasoline prices would continue rising. He decided to discuss the car problem with his wife.

Sue and Jim discussed the car situation and concluded that they were dealing with a very complex issue. To simplify matters they decided to write down all their thoughts about gas prices and the possibility of buying a new car. The following list expressed most of their ideas.

1. Cars are much more expensive now than in 1975.
2. The car loan on the station wagon will be completely paid off in four months.
3. With two kids and a dog they need a full-size car.
4. Gas prices are rising rapidly and will continue to rise during the next five years.
5. As the children grow, they will require more and more transportation.

6. Gas economy and automobile size in general trade off. As the size of the car increases, economy decreases.
7. Cars will continue to be fueled by petroleum-based products for some time.

Suggest a logical approach for the Campbells in attempting to decide whether to purchase a new economy car. What criteria should the Campbells use in making their decision?

Case 3-2 • MANNING CUTLERY, INC.

Manning Cutlery, Inc., is a small manufacturer and marketer of fine cutlery. The 75-year-old firm is well known in the industry for the traditional line of high quality knives and carving accessories the firm manufactures and markets. The cutlery is marketed through selected jewelry and department stores. Independent manufacturers' agents are used to call on the retail outlets. New retail outlets are given distributorships only when a member of Manning's top management team personally inspects a retail store to see if it meets the minimum standards. On the average, twenty new outlets are established every year.

Tom Manning, a grandson of the company's founder, was recently brought into the business. Tom's first assignment was to investigate the possibility of developing an advertising program to increase sales. Tom, being a marketing major, first attempted to identify the primary purchasers of Manning Cutlery. He used the warranty cards sent in by recent purchasers of Manning Cutlery as his source of information. From these warranty cards Tom learned that Manning Cutlery buyers were generally well above average in income, education, and occupational prestige, and that the majority of buyers lived in well above average neighborhoods. From these data Tom reasoned that Manning Cutlery appealed primarily to high social class people.

Help Tom develop an advertising program. Suggest media and creative themes that he might use to effectively advertise to high social class customers.

4

the consumer goods market

LESS MICKEY MOUSE

Disney to Shift Target Of Some Parks, Movies To Teen-Agers, Adults

'Baby Bust' Spurs the Switch

The Wall Street Journal,
January 26, 1979

In working with the Marketing Planning Guide introduced in Chapter 2 the marketer is confronted with two immediate tasks: first, identifying the target at which the marketing effort will be aimed and, second, identifying the objectives of that target in order to know which needs the target wants to satisfy.

Determining the target for specific goods and services is an important task because the needs and perceptions of purchasers are the bases for product type classification. Products are generally placed in two categories: consumer goods and industrial goods. Both consumer and industrial goods must take on specific characteristics which are necessary to meet the objectives of the purchaser.

This chapter is aimed at explaining the consumer goods market. *Consumer goods* are those goods and services purchased by *ultimate* consumers for personal, family, or household use. This discussion of consumer goods shows how consumer goods are classified, the influence of the classification on marketing requirements and the use of market segmentation in effective marketing.

CLASSIFICATION OF CONSUMER GOODS

Three extremely broad categories are used to classify consumer goods. They are convenience goods, shopping goods, and specialty goods.

Convenience Goods

Convenience goods are things such as grocery staples or some kitchen supplies which are purchased frequently, usually at low unit prices. Because demand is defined in the mind of the buyer, the consumer knows when the paper napkins, dish-washing detergent or toothpaste need to be replaced. Also, because of brand similarity, the gain in potential satisfaction from spending a great deal of search time to make comparisons is slight.

Shopping Goods

Shopping goods are those on which consumers spend time shopping to make comparisons among alternatives. Demand is not as clearly defined in the buyer's mind as it is for convenience items. In contrast to buying a package of paper towels, one does not stop at the nearest store and pay cash or use a credit card to buy a radio or dress. Comparisons of price, style, product features, and discernible quality differences among not only alternative items, but also among retailers, are made because the potential gain in satisfaction from making those comparisons is considerable.

Specialty Goods

Specialty goods are those for which no substitute will be accepted. Such items are usually purchased infrequently, and there are unique features that offer sufficient satisfaction to offset the time spent in searching for precisely the right product and price.

Classes of consumer goods are not always precise; neither are they mutually exclusive in every case. It is impossible to fit every product into a consumer goods category. When buying the week's groceries, for example, you may accept buying a loaf of Holsum bread as readily as a loaf of Wonder Bread. Hence, the weekly grocery purchase of bread places bread in the convenience good category. But, when preparing a special dinner, you may drive several miles to a bakery to buy a crusty French bread and special dinner rolls (specialty goods). Thus, it is easy to see that bread, in this case, cannot be placed in a precise product class, since its classification is based on the satisfaction which is desired in the mind of the buyer.

Similarly, a given product class may be perceived by most consumers as belonging in a specific category, while for some other people it may belong in another. For example, many people will shop for a black-and-white TV and select the brand and retail outlet that is lowest in price, thus making the TV a shopping good. Others may read publications such as *Consumer Reports,* question knowledgeable people, make a product determination, and then spend time and effort seeking a specific brand and model. For those people, a TV is a specialty good.

Advertisements courtesy of Faygo Beverages, Inc., Dad's Root Beer Co., and PepsiCo, Inc.

Illus. 4-1   Heavy Promotion of Convenience Goods Is Necessary

MARKETING REQUIREMENTS FOR CLASSES OF CONSUMER GOODS

Convenience goods require widespread distribution because, if the brand is not readily available, a substitute will be purchased. Prices must be competitive because discernible quality differences do not exist. Promotion of convenience goods is relatively more important than it is for the other two classes. Brand A milk and Brand B milk are identical in purity, vitamins, butterfat, and nonfat solids; only the advertising, package design, and display can impute a particular characteristic to cause a buyer to choose one over another.

Because of low unit prices and widespread distribution, almost all convenience goods move through intermediary middlemen (wholesalers, distributors) to retailers. Self-service is well developed for these goods because consumers know the characteristics of several brands through frequent use and purchase.

Shopping goods tend to be sold through relatively few outlets—usually in stores which specialize in goods such as clothing or appliances, or in large department stores in downtown areas or shopping malls. Large retailers dealing with manufacturers that produce a full line make short channels—manufacturer direct to retailer—common in the distribution of shopping goods.

Specialty goods, because of the special qualities which cause buyers to seek them out, are not widely distributed nor extensively advertised. It is important that the retail outlet reflects the special nature of the product and that advice and requisite special services be available.

MARKET SEGMENTATION

Market segmentation is a means used to identify markets and submarkets within a general market. Underlying the concept of market segmentation are the facts that people's wants differ and further, that the wants of one person may be different under various circumstances. As an illustration, there is not only "a market" for automobiles; there are submarkets for different types of cars according to needs, or desires, of various groups of buyers. Identifying those groups, or segments, of the population who want, and will buy, large or small, luxury or economy, sport or conventional models is an important step on marketing planning.

A market segment is a group of people within the general population which can be identified according to the criteria which follow. Marketing managers can give serious consideration to such groups when they:

1. Have something in common which causes members of the group to respond in a similar fashion to marketing stimuli; i.e., homogeneity exists within the group.
2. Can be distinguished and differentiated from other market segments; i.e., heterogeneity exists between groups.
3. Can be reached by available communications media.
4. Are of sufficient size and market potential.

A. What customer classes can I identify?

B. What are the needs (desires) of each class?

C. Which class produces the most profit?

D. Do I have the right mix and resources?

CUSTOMER CLASS	Time of Day	Day of Week	Fast Service	Take-Out	Relaxed-Luxury Atmosphere	Limited Menu	Downtown	Outlying	Epicurean Quality	Superior Service	Wine Service	High Price	Medium Price	Low Price
1. Celebrants of a special occasion					●				●	●	●	●		
2. Family with small children														
3. Teenage after-the-game crowd			●	●		●		●						
4. Downtown worker on lunch break														
5. Tourist passing through														
6. Lunch for executive or professional person														
7. Same as 6 but with guests														

Illus. 4-2   Customer Class/Customer Need Grid for an Eating Place

A simple example serves to illustrate the identification of segments. We know that restaurants which succeed do not attempt to satisfy everyone's needs for every occasion. Illustration 4-2 is an example of a chart in grid form used as a first step in identifying the ideal target market for a hypothetical eating place. The purpose of the chart is to display the service, menu and atmosphere desired by various classes of customers. In the vertical column we list various customer classes that might patronize a restaurant or drive-in at our geographic location. On the horizontal row we list the customer need factors that could influence patronage. Then by observation, experience, or formal research we identify what factors each customer class will want. As displayed in Illustration 4-2 it has been determined that the teenage group usually wants fast service, take-out foods, and a limited menu—at a low price. A group of middle-aged, upper-income couples going to dinner to celebrate a special occasion has other wants. The interior and exterior atmosphere, location, product mix, promotional methods, and price must be designed to appeal to the wants and needs of the segment(s) the restaurant selects as a target market.

VALUE OF SEGMENTATION ANALYSIS

In general the value of segmentation analysis is to identify unfilled consumer needs or wants which may provide marketing opportunities for the firm. Such analysis (1) assists in the establishment of marketing objectives; (2) forces the manager to envision a more precise definition of the needs of consumers; (3) improves management's understanding of why customers make purchases and why noncustomers do not make purchases; (4) helps direct the marketing program, leading to more efficient allocation of marketing resources; and (5) facilitates assessment of the firm's competitive strengths and weaknesses.[1]

Regarding point (4) above, market segmentation guides managers in channeling effort to the most profitable markets; designing products that match consumer needs and desires; and selecting the most effective promotional messages as well as selecting the advertising media most likely to reach the target market.

IDENTIFYING MARKET SEGMENTS

To fully incorporate the marketing concept a firm should construct a *marketing segmentation plan* which consists of (1) selecting a target market from among the identified market segments and (2) generating the proper marketing mix for each selected target market.[2] Identifying target markets for consumer goods is the primary emphasis of this section.

Market segments may be identified by the *consumer characteristics (attributes)* of the population or by *behavioral differences.* The principal bases used for identifying market segments are the following:

Consumer Characteristics or Attributes	Behavioral Differences
Geographic	
Demographic	Volume or consumption rates
Socioeconomic	
Personality and life style	Values or benefits sought

[1]James F. Engle, Henry F. Fiorillo, and Murray A. Cayley, *Market Segmentation Concepts and Applications* (New York City: Holt, Rinehart & Winston, 1972).

[2]*Ibid.*, presents methods of identifying and measuring market segments, in addition to material on strategies for different segments.

A usual procedure in identifying market segments by consumer characteristics is to identify a a number of attributes such as age, income, social class, position in family life-cycle, or life-style. Then marketers attempt to determine how greatly those characteristics relate to, and presumably predict, market behavior such as selection of types of goods, brands, loyalty, media use, and shopping patterns.

A different approach is used in the analysis of consumer behavior. Here, marketers observe and measure variations in response to marketing stimuli. Then they work back to the consumer characteristics which distinguish the segment which behaved in a particular fashion.

Geographic Segmentation.

Commonly used geographic divisions of markets are international, regional, wholesale trading area, metropolitan market area, and local or neighborhood markets within a metropolitan area.

International markets involve trade across national boundaries. Ease of trade between nations varies widely because of the diversity of incomes, goods available, and government policies.

Many corporations in the United States describe themselves as covering the *national market.* Very few actually distribute in every state, and those that do must usually alter their practices between areas to meet varying local conditions. Sears Roebuck and Co., for example, publishes a separate catalog for each of its eleven mail-order houses. Much of the merchandise, such as basic clothing and some household supplies, will be found in every catalog; but a fairly large number of items appear in only one or two because they specifically satisfy local requirements.

Besides the obvious climate-related products, such as home heating and cooling or snow tires, a number of products sell better in specific geographic areas.

In the western states, for instance, there are more power tools purchased for home use than in other regions. Recreational activities also vary by region. The highest per capita participation in skiing, tennis, and backpacking is in the western states; ice skating and outdoor swimming is strongest in northeastern states; boating and fishing are most popular in north central states.[3] Undoubtedly sociocultural factors, as well as physical geographic factors, influence these patterns. An analysis by area enables the marketing manager to focus marketing effort where it is most efficient.

Even though a company may require careful analysis of the numerous markets in a nation to obtain maximum efficiency of distribution, it is still reasonable to speak of large-scale markets. This is possible in the United States due to the ease and freedom with which goods flow from state to state.

Regional markets are those developed within loosely described geographic areas which do not necessarily coincide with political boundaries. For example, firms may sell their products exclusively in New England, the so-called corn belt, or the Pacific Coast states. There are no sharp, sacred boundaries for such trading.

---

[3]*Sunset, The Magazine of Western Living* (October/November, 1978).

Manufacturers that become established in one of these areas may find that contacts are made easily, and channels of communication and transportation may be economical and convenient. It is also possible that the population may cluster in the area, and strong competition may already be established in other areas. For such reasons, a company may choose to sell its product in a regional area.

Wholesale trading areas are sometimes defined two ways. One definition is that such an area includes the territory that covers points commonly reached by wholesale firms in a major city. Since, however, certain kinds of wholesalers can economically operate groceries and pharmaceutical houses in a restricted area, while others serve appliance stores over large numbers of miles, the term is sometimes used to describe the territory covered by one type of wholesaler. Nevertheless, in the broader sense there are several quite well-defined wholesale trading areas. Advertising agencies, chambers of commerce, news media, and wholesale firms collect and furnish market data on such trading centers.

A *metropolitan market,* also called a Standard Metropolitan Statistical Area (SMSA) by the U.S. Census Bureau, is an area in and around a comparatively large city (population of 50,000 or more). The city dominates the retail business in the area, although there may be smaller cities and clusters of shopping centers in the region that are socially and economically integrated with the central city. There are 277 such districts in the United States, plus four in Puerto Rico.

A major factor in geographic segmentation is that most large cities are losing population within their actual corporate boundaries. However, suburbs and satellite cities continue to grow. Hence, data from an area that trades in the city have more significance for market planners than do population data restricted by city limits. Not only do such centers have an effect on sales of the city, but also, as their influence widens, there is a marked effect on small towns that were formerly free of city competition for frequently used items.

Local or neighborhood markets can vary in makeup from those areas served by the old crossroads country store to modern shopping complexes. Data on such markets are often difficult to obtain and interpret from secondary sources because government-generated studies are most often undertaken for political units, i.e., cities, counties, and states. There are, however, two data bases coming into frequent use by market research specialists. They are data from individual census tracts and postal zip code districts. A *census tract* is an area of approximately 4,000 persons with similarity of population and income characteristics. Hence, it is possible to identify areas that have characteristics which indicate possible acceptance of a product or, conversely, to evaluate probable rejection of a product in a specified area. Postal zip code districts often encompass more than one census tract. This factor may be a disadvantage to their use because the demographic characteristics may be spread over a wider spectrum than is true for a census district. However, zip code districts are easy to identify, which is an advantage for the market researcher. The decennial (every ten years since 1790) population census in the United States provides valuable market segmentation information. In years between census taking, data estimates are made. Publications of the Census Bureau, business and economic research bureaus at major universities, and reports such as the annual *Buying Power Index* by *Sales & Marketing Management* are further sources of information geared to geographic areas.

Demographic Segmentation

The story behind the Disney headline at the beginning of this chapter reports that Walt Disney Productions plans to build a theme park to attract adults without children, is making more sophisticated movies, and hopes to build and operate a ski resort.

> "The reason is clear: The number of American children aged five through nine years is expected to decline 5 percent in the next eight years, and the number of 10-to-14-year-olds is projected to drop 14 percent. In the U.S. the prime market for Disney products is the 5-to-8-year-olds . . . Disney can't get much more of that market. So, to grow, it must penetrate the teenage-to-adult market."[4]

Increasing numbers of people in the 18-to-24-year-old bracket, which is the usual time for marriage and family formulation, present marketing opportunities for household furnishings, bridal gowns, and food snacks, among other items. As those persons move into the 25-to-44-year-old group it is expected that their incomes and standard of living will improve, creating marketing opportunities for high-priced carpets, furniture, and recreation equipment, as well as items related to childraising.

Marketers must be aware that age segments of the population are prone to changes. Around the turn of the century, for instance, about 2½ percent of the population was 65 years or older. Now that segment has expanded to 11 percent. Those people in that group who have purchasing power provide a sizable market for travel and recreation goods, mobile homes (although the percentage of mobile homes purchased by young people is increasing as a result of the ballooning costs of conventional houses), and gifts for grandchildren. Even though over 85 percent of married couples over 65 have some retirement benefits or social security, research by zip code areas, when targeting the 65-years-or-older segment, should be undertaken to determine the extent to which disposable income is available in a specific market area for purchases beyond meeting bare living expenses.

According to the birthrate statistics displayed in Table 4-1, a decrease from 23.7 births per 1,000 population in 1960 to 15.3 in 1977 took place. What would you do if you were the manufacturer of Pampers or Gerber baby food and were confronted with these changes? Most likely, you would want to get refined data for regions, and project the number of births to determine where to concentrate efforts on the baby items, as well as to make decisions about diversifying product lines. Gerber Products Company, as a matter of fact, is adapting some baby foods for adult consumers and is adding some adult food items and a line of single-serving canned foods to its product lines.[5]

---

[4] *The Wall Street Journal,* January 26, 1979, p. 1.
[5] "The Lower Birthrate Crimps the Baby Food Market," *Business Week,* July 13, 1974, p. 44.

Table 4-1   Some Demographic Trends in the United States

	1960	1977		1960	1976
Age Groups			Households:		
TOTAL	181 million	217 million	TOTAL	53 million	74 million
Under 17 yrs.	35%	29%	One-person		
18–24 yrs.	9%	13%	household	7 million	16 million
25–44 yrs.	26%	26%			
65 yrs. and older	9%	11%	Families:		
			TOTAL	45 million	57 million
Regions			Female Head	4.5 million	7.7 million
Northeast	25%	23%			
North Central	29%	27%	Birthrate		
South	30%	32%	(Births per		
West	16%	18%	1,000 popula-		
			tion)	23.7	15.3
Metropolitan Areas	71%	73%			

Source: Extracted from United States Department of Commerce, *Statistical Abstract of the United States,* 1978 (Washington: U.S. Printing Office, 1978) p. xiii and p. 29.

Position in the family life cycle is a demographic factor that helps explain differences in a family's demand for some items. The usual stages are (1) unmarried (a single-person household), (2) newly married (no children), (3) full nest I (young married with preschool-age children), (4) full nest II (older couples with dependent children), (5) empty nest (married couples with children grown and gone), and (6) solitary survivor. A neighborhood full of single people living in apartments has different demands from a suburban area made up of young-marrieds with two or three children per household. Census tract analyses can provide information on the family life cycle stage that is dominant in an area.

Some products and activities are closely related to demographic characteristics of a segment of the population. For example, Nordic (cross-country) skiing attracts a wider age range than does Alpine (downhill) skiing, and more people over 60 play golf than play tennis. It is unwise, however, to make armchair analyses to match a product with a demographic characteristic, because primary research will often divulge some surprises. This is especially true in the socioeconomic segments.

Socioeconomic Segmentation

Total income in an area and its distribution are major influences on purchases. Table 4-2 shows that the high-budget family spends nearly $2,000 more for food than the low-budget family and is spending a considerably smaller portion of its total budget for food. The percentage spent for housing increases some as total spending increases; the same percentage for transportation is spent; and for clothing, a slight percentage decrease takes place as budgets increase.

Table 4-2   Annual Budgets for 4-Person Urban Families (1977)

	Low Budget		Intermediate Budget		High Budget	
	In Dollars	Percentage of Total	In Dollars	Percentage of Total	In Dollars	Percentage of Total
Total Budget	10,781		17,106		25,202	
Food	3,190	30	4,098	24	5,159	20
Housing and Household Operation	2,083	20	4,016	23	6,085	24
Transportation	804	8	1,472	9	1,913	8
Clothing	828	8	1,182	7	1,730	7
Income Taxes, Social Security, Disability	1,352	13	3,303	20	5,965	24
Subtotal	8,257	79	14,071	83	20,852	83
Balance for personal care items, misc., consumer spending, medical care	2,224		3,035		4,350	

Note: Based on Autumn prices. Assumes 4-person family of 38-year-old employed husband, wife not employed outside the home, 8-year-old daughter, and 15-year-old son.
Source: Bureau of Labor Statistics, *NEWS,* April 26, 1978, United States Statistical Index entry #6764-4.1.

The rest of the budget goes for personal care items, miscellaneous family consumer items, and medical care. The percentage for those items varies only 4 percent from the low-budget family to the high-level family. However, the high-budget family spends $2,125 more than the lowest for those items.

Discretionary income, which is the amount of money left for a family to spend after food, shelter, transportation, clothing, and taxes are paid for, is an important factor in marketing. The low-budget families in Table 4-2 had incomes approximately equal to their total budgets; intermediate families had incomes about $1,700 over the budget; incomes for the high group were $8,000 more than the budgets shown.[6] Those differences take on considerable importance when estimating the number of new cars, vacation trips, college tuitions paid, and other discretionary expenditures possible at various income levels.

Note that certain patterns can be discerned and that the percentage of total spending allocated to each of the major items changes from one income group to

[6]Derived from U.S. Bureau of the Census, "Distribution of Income," *Current Population Reports,* Series P-60 numbers 114 and 116, and Tables 734 and 735.

When you share that special love, it shows...

...in the sparkle of your eyes, the glow of your smiles, the warmth of your touch. Your joy is complete in the love you share. And your happiness is reflected in your Keepsake diamond engagement ring. A diamond so brilliant in color, so flawless in clarity, so exquisite in cut it's guaranteed perfect, forever, by Keepsake.

Hibiscus

Chelsea

Brisbane

Accent

Keepsake®
Registered Diamond Rings

T-M Reg. A.H. Pond Co.

Lavier

Madera

Bardsley

Keepsake® A perfect way to show your love when it's for keeps.

Courtesy of the makers of KEEPSAKE Diamond Engagement Rings.

Illus. 4-3   **Wedding and Engagement Items Are Marketed to the 18-to-24-Year-Old Segment**

another. Frequently it has been reasoned that, if such changes could be charted and found to be consistent, then a valuable forecasting tool would be developed for planning marketing of consumer goods. In fact, for approximately one hundred years, certain patterns have been observed and used to illustrate the value of income distribution studies. Over 100 years ago the German statistician Ernst

Engel studied the budgets of working men in Saxony. From his data economists deduced that as family income increases:[7]

1. The percentage of the total that is spent for food will decrease.
2. The portion of total spending for clothing will remain approximately the same.
3. The portion of total spending for housing, fuel, and light will remain the same.
4. The portion of total expenditures for sundries, such as education, medical care, religion, recreation, and travel will increase.

For many years such studies of family budgets seemed to confirm "Engel's Laws."

In 1950, 56 percent of families had incomes over $7,000 in constant dollars (1977), whereas by 1977 there were 85 percent. Hence, from the increased income and Engel's Laws we would expect a percentage decrease in spending for food, about the same percentage spent for clothing and housing (including household operation, which includes furniture, equipment, supplies, and utilities), and an increase in the portion spent for sundries. What actually happened illustrates the desirability of *integrating* the analyses of the several factors affecting use of income.

Percentage of Spending on Major Items.   Median income in constant dollars almost doubled from 1950 to 1977. As expected, the percentage of consumer spending for food decreased about 8 percent. The percentage spent for housing and household operations increased by roughly 4½ percent; for clothing there was a drop of over 4 percent, while transportation and recreation increased less than 1 percent.[8]

Income alone does not explain the shifts. Sociocultural factors influence clothing expenditures, for example. The increased portion spent for housing and household expenditures, probably at the expense of recreation and other sundry, nonnecessity items, was partly due to increased utility costs, which rose more than 25 percent from 1950 to 1976, as well as construction cost increases.

---

[7]For detailed analysis refer to two monumental studies on consumption patterns: University of Pennsylvania, Wharton School of Finance and Commerce, *Study of Consumer Expenditures, Incomes, and Savings—Urban U.S.—1950.* This work consists of 18 volumes, largely statistical tables. For more recent, but less detailed, data see Fabian Linden (ed.) *Expenditure Patterns of the American Family* (New York City: National Industrial Conference Board, 1965), p. 18 and periodic studies by the U.S. Bureau of Labor Statistics, of which Table 4-2, p. 72, is an example. Benjamin S. Loeb discusses Engel's Law as a means of predicting sales in "The Use of Engel's Laws as a Basis for Predicting Consumers' Expenditures," *Journal of Marketing,* Vol. 20 (July, 1955), p. 20. Richard D. Millican tests the validity of Engel's Laws in economic affluence in his article, "A Recent Reexamination of Engel's Laws Using BLS Data (1960–1961)," *Journal of Marketing,* Vol. 31, No. 4 (October, 1967), p. 18.

[8]Data derived from the U.S. Bureau of Economic Analysis, *The National Income and Product Accounts of the United States, 1929–1974* and *Survey of Current Business,* July, 1979. A detailed table of personal consumption expenditures by product can be found in each annual edition of the *Statistical Abstract of the United States.*

Even though food expenditures acted according to expectations, a further analysis indicates how opportunities and threats to established products and services can be discovered.

In 1960 people spent 20 percent of their food budgets on meals eaten away from home; in 1976 almost 25 percent was spent eating out. When incomes and food expenditures were tabulated, it was found that in 1960 families in the high-budget group spent 25 percent more *per capita* on food prepared at home than did the low-budget group. However, by 1974 the difference was reduced to only 9 percent. In 1974 the low-income group spent 17 percent of its food budget for food consumed away from the home. Correspondingly the high-income group spent 37 percent. What are the marketing implications of these figures? The figures indicate that as incomes increased, supermarkets lost sales to eating establishments. It is estimated that per capita grocery store sales from 1970 to 1976 declined about one percent and eating place sales per capita rose by approximately 17 percent during the same time.[9]

Other nonincome factors affecting food expenditure patterns include: (1) household size (per capita sales decrease both for eating at home and eating out as the number of people in the household increases) and (2) position in the family life cycle (from young families to those up to 65 years old, the per capita expenditures for consumption at home increases and the expenditures for eating out decreases).

The Working-Wife Family. One of the most important socioeconomic factors affecting consumer goods purchasing patterns is the increasing number of families in which both spouses are employed. Families where both spouses earn incomes have been used to explain the large increase in convenience food sales in grocery stores and take-out dinners from fastfood outlets. Somewhat surprisingly, nonworking wives make more use of take-out dinners, prepared baked goods, and certain convenience items such as instant spray wax. Also, homes of nonworking wives are better equipped with dishwashers, elaborate home laundry equipment, electric carving knives, and frost-free refrigerators.[10] That seemingly anomalous information once more illustrates the wisdom of a cross-impact analysis between the environments discussed in Chapter 2 and carefully defined market segments.

The general category of housewife or working wife can be misleading. It is advisable to study socioeconomic segments, such as age, family size, outside interests and activities, income and education, and personality/life-style within the categories of housewife or working wife. For the working wife a further segmentation should be made according to motivation for work versus the type of employment, i.e., professional or low-status job. Progressive women in professional posi-

[9]David S. Rogers and Howard L. Green, "Changes in Consumer Food Expenditure Patterns," *Journal of Marketing,* April, 1978, p. 14.
[10]Susan P. Douglas, "Working Wife and Nonworking Wife Families as a Basis for Market Segmentation," Marketing Science Institute working paper report No. 75–114, copyright 1975, Marketing Science Institute, Cambridge, Mass.

Courtesy of General Mills, Inc.

Illus. 4-4   A Consumer Product Targeted at a
                            Socioeconomic Segment

tions are involved in a greater amount of housekeeping and cooking than non-working or low-status job-holding women. The progressive woman makes less use of prepared foods and other convenience items, shops at farmers' markets, and spends more time on house decorating.[11]

Promotion by many firms indicates that they view the professional woman as their chief target market for household-help items. Perhaps those firms should make a careful analysis of the socioeconomic and behavioral characteristics of the heavy users of their products to see whether they are targeting most efficiently[12]

Life-Style Segmentation   Life-style segmentation is based on what people do. Suchactivities as church work, movie attendance, dancing, watching sports activities, water skiing, snow skiing, sailing, motor boating, driving, playing cards, reading, and hobbies are identified. One study of car owners found that life-style was a reasonably good predictor or whether a person would own a full-size, intermediate, subcompact, or utility vehicle; demographic attributes were best in predicting only compact car ownership. Authors of the study suggested that life-style works as a discriminator because there is a functional, rather than behavioral appeal, for many people in car ownership. "What people *do* rather than what they *are* may determine the type of car purchased."[13]

Other studies and observations suggest that life-style may be useful in identifying possible markets for sports and hobby products. There is some emperical evidence that sports car owners are more likely to own sail boats than motor boats and that hikers are more likely to engage in cross-country skiing than in snow-mobiling, for example. Marketing students might be interested in carrying out a study to test the validity of those, or similar, observations.

Behavior Segmentation

Segmentation based on behavior, sometimes called consumer response segmentation, is accomplished by studying how people respond to product and marketing variables.[14] The two most used behavioral bases are (1) benefits sought and (2) volume or usage rate.

Benefits Sought.   Toothpaste purchase is an example of benefit segmentation. People may buy toothpaste for decay prevention, fresh breath, bright teeth, good flavor, or low price. A study may show that most purchasers who desire fresh breath are young adults and that decay prevention is most important to families

---

[11]*Ibid.,* p. 20.

[12]See Rena Bartos. "The Moving Target: The impact of Women's Employment on Consumer Behavior," *Journal of Marketing,* July, 1977, p. 31, which presents data to emphasize that the working woman is not a stereotype.

[13]Kent L. Granzin and Clifford E. Young, "How Good Are Value Systems as a Basis for Market Sementation?", paper presented at South Western Marketing Association Conference, March, 1979.

[14]William L. Wilkie and Joel B. Cohen, "An Overview of Market Segmentation: Behavioral Concepts and Research Approaches," Marketing Science Institute, working paper report No. 77–105, copyright 1977, Marketing Science Institute, Cambridge, Mass.

with young children. This provides a clue to the promotional messages and methods best suited to attract those segments.

Benefit segmentation is also useful in developing patronage for particular establishments. It may be as simple as the contrast between a student hangout featuring loud jukebox music versus a barbeque restaurant with live country-

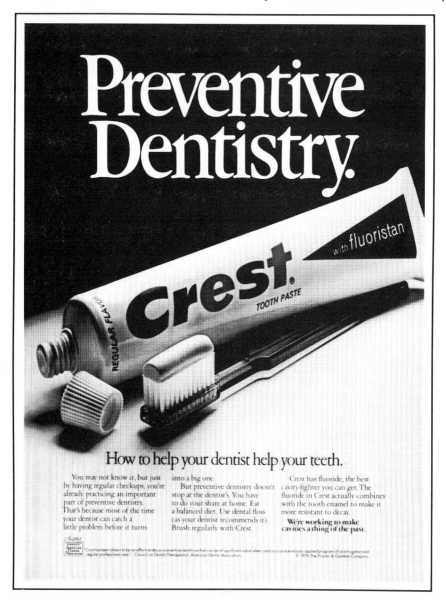

Courtesy of The Procter & Gamble Company

Illus. 4-5   Toothpaste Targeted at a Benefit-Seeking Segment

western music or a continental-menu restaurant with soothing harp music in the
background.

A "benefits sought" study of fastfood outlets, for instance, provided a better
way to measure and predict loyalty of customers than have past attempts using
demographic or other attributes.

How did it work? A consumer panel, drawn at random, furnished information
on the benefits—such as convenience, taste of food, popularity with children,
friendliness of employees, family orientation of the restaurant, and whether the
company was socially responsible—they considered important. Certain benefit
patterns were significantly related to particular outlets. Patrons desiring a pattern
of speedy service, coupon offerings, popularity with children, and a family orientation were most frequently families with young children; patrons for whom speedy
service, convenience, and cleanliness were most important were older, wealthier,
and black customers.[15]

Benefit analysis is particularly useful in explaining why an individual may
respond differently to a marketing stimulus when contemplating the purchase of
items in different product classes. For instance, the importance of price differentials
in furniture may be quite different for a particular person than it is for recreation
equipment.

Demographic and socioeconomic attributes, by themselves, do not relate
nearly as well to camera purchases, for example, as do the particular benefits the
buyer is seeking. Some photographers want precise camera performance that
permits almost complete control to achieve desired effects. There are others who
simply want to take family and vacation snapshots. In both groups there will be
people with widely diverse demographic and socioeconomic characteristics.

Volume or Usage Rate. Sometimes it is useful to classify consumers into
nonuser, light user, and *heavy user* categories. This kind of behavior segmentation
received impetus over a decade ago when it was noted that only 15 to 17 percent
of beer drinkers consumed 88 percent of all beer and that 16 percent of all buyers
of canned hash consumed 86 percent of the product.[16] It was generally noted that
in most consumer product categories half of the consumers purchase around
80 percent of the product.[17] Miller Beer, for instance, has concentrated its promotion on a subsegment of the heavy user group. The company's television advertisements showing men leaving strenuous work at sundown are aimed at beer drinkers who consume more than five cans or bottles of beer between 5 P.M. and
10 P.M.[18]

---

[15]Kenneth E. Miller and Kent L. Granzin, "Simultaneous Loyalty and Benefit Segmentation of
Retail Store Customers," *Journal of Retailing,* Spring, 1979, p. 47.

[16]Norton Garfinkle, "How Marketing Data can Identify Your Target Audience," Address to
Eastern Regional Convention of the American Association of Advertising Agencies, 1966.

[17]Dik Warren Twedt, "Some practical applications of the 'Heavy Half' Theory," presentation at
Advertising Research Foundation 10th Annual Conference, New York, October, 1964.

[18]Jeffrey F. Palmer, vice president, McCann Erikson, Inc., Speech at University of North Dakota
Marketing and Business Conference, April, 1979.

The reasons for concentrating marketing effort on a heavy user segment is that the pay off will be greater per unit of effort than it will be in less concentrated markets. Some caution should be used, however. First, heavy users are often the target of many competitors. Second, not all heavy users are seeking the same benefits; consequently, a heavy use segment may consist of two or more subsegments who respond differently to marketing stimuli. For example, many heavy consumers of ice cream buy mostly inexpensive ice cream at supermarkets because they buy so much it makes sense to save money on each purchase. Others are heavy users because they enjoy premium quality ice cream and to them it is worth the extra money and effort to seek out and purchase the product from a premium quality outlet.

Finally, marketers should not concentrate on only heavy users until they have firm evidence that it is not possible to shift nonusers or light users into a profitable volume category. For example, most opera and symphony companies direct promotion to season ticket subscribers (the heavy use group), even though many of the companies have season ticket sales of less than half their theater capacities. Analyses of audiences of two opera companies revealed that season subscribers, frequent attenders who bought two or more single performance tickets in a season, and infrequent attenders, who were attending a performance for the first time or who had attended once a year, could be identified as distinct segments.[19]

Season subscribers are mature, affluent, highly educated, long-time patrons who have a predisposition toward the performing arts. They are opera fans. The group profile of frequent attenders greatly resembles that of the season subscribers but with enough differences to indicate that separate strategies should be used to attract them. While they are also opera fans, listen to opera music, and watch television opera productions, they are generally younger, less affluent, but moving toward a level of income and maturity likely to make them candidates for the season subscriber segment. Special mailings and advertisements during TV arts presentations should be productive. Infrequent attenders do not consider themselves opera fans but can be reached through the use of featured star performers; they are best reached by newspaper advertisements and the advice of friends.

Segmentation-Use Prudence. Segmentation is not a precise science; it is only a valuable guide. It must be emphasized that buying behavior is almost never explained by reference to only one segmentation factor. Variables from several of the segmentation bases are used to develop productive segmentation. Seldom, if ever, does the market consist of people living in a suburb of a Midwest city, for example. More usually, several combined factors such as "married people between the ages of 30 and 45 with college educations, who live in the suburbs contiguous

[19]Richard J. Semenick and Clifford E. Young, "Market Segmentation in Arts Organizations," *Proceedings AMA Educators Conference, 1979* (Chicago: American Marketing Association, 1979) p. 474.

to a Midwest city, and who have incomes within a certain range" are more likely to identify the segment.

Another caution is that segmentation should not be carried too far. Remember the criterion that a segment must be large enough to be profitable. As prices for goods and services increase many customers are willing to sacrifice an extra feature or extra benefit and get something that does not completely or precisely fit their desires in return for a lower price. Consequently, some product lines can be narrowed without losing profit returns.[20]

Finally, keep in mind that segmentation using the bases described is a first broad cut of the market. Identification of segments will not predict with precision what specific product types and brands people will buy. Segmentation is an important aid to give direction to marketing efforts, but it is not sufficient by itself to guarantee success.

QUESTIONS AND ANALYTICAL PROBLEMS

1. Define the terms *consumer goods, convenience goods, shopping goods,* and *specialty goods.*

2. What criteria are used to identify a market segment?

3. Prepare a matrix to match customer classes and customers needs for a clothing store.

4. What are the principal bases for market segmentation?

5. Examine the Buying Power Index issue of *Sales & Marketing Management* for a recent year. Explain how the index is derived and find the amount of spending on furniture and one other major item in your county.

6. What marketing planning use can be made of the family life cycle?

7. Why is it generally conceded that households data are of more use in marketing planning than are total population data?

8. What effects on spending are evident from income distribution data?

9. What trends in spending on food can you perceive? Consider, at least, family size, income distribution, and working couples.

10. Define *behavior segmentation.* Give examples. Tell how it can be used.

11. Why should marketers attempt to identify market segments?

---

[20]How to identify markets that can be combined and how to estimate the profitability of such clustering is found in Alan J. Resnik, B.B. Turney and J. Barry Mason, "Marketers Turn to Counter Segmentation," *Harvard Business Review,* September-October, 1979, p. 100.

Case 4-1 • BROWN'S FOODKING MARKETS

Generic products in the grocery business refer to brandless items, usually packaged in plain containers which simply state the name of the product.

Generic products were first introduced in the United States by the Jewel Company in 1977. Since then generic products have proved their appeal to customers. A study conducted in the fourth quarter of 1978 revealed that generic products were being offered in more than 8,000 supermarkets across the country.[1] Additional evidence supports the notion that the generic trend is growing.

Dee W. Brown, founder and primary owner of Brown's Foodking Markets, is discussing generic products with his merchandising vice-president, Virginia Martin. The two executives are reviewing a market study on generic grocery products. The study's findings are summarized as follows:

1. The market for generic products is large, especially in certain product categories.
2. Sales of generic products can vary greatly among stores and across markets.
3. The source of sales of generics is hard to identify, but much of the business appears to be drawn from advertised brands.
4. Respected retailers have concluded that, at least in the short run, generics are profitable.
5. It appears that generics will continue to grow, especially in nonfoods and perishables.
6. Generics are not a fad.
7. One component of generics' price differential is a lower gross margin. Nevertheless, retailers believe that generics are more profitable because of increased volume.

Virginia and Dee are in some disagreement about the future of generics and what Brown's Foodking Markets should do about them. Virginia thinks that generics are a hot marketing tool and that the Foodking Markets should introduce them immediately. Dee, on the other hand, believes that generics are a fad and that potential buyers of generics will be the same customers who currently buy Foodking's own store brands. Virginia's counterargument is that a new and different market segment will also purchase generic products because of their novelty. That, she is confident, will boost total sales much higher. Dee, however, still isn't convinced.

Whose view do you support and why?

Case 4-2 • SARAH COSMETICS

The Sarah Cosmetic Company was started by Elbe Norbert and Rita Cascenza in 1973. Elbe and Rita had worked in the cosmetics industry for about ten years before deciding to start their own company.

---

[1]The information for this case was drawn from "Generic Groceries Keep Adding Market Share," *Marketing News,* February 23, 1979, pp. 1, 6–7.

The inspiration for their company was Sarah Ozmun, a 17-year-old country rock singer who had grabbed the national limelight in 1973. Sarah was known as the little gal who could belt out the songs.

Sarah, although a singer by profession, was a favorite endorser of products as well as the subject of numerous posters. Sarah's posters and image were quite different from other poster girls at that time. Always dressed and posed modestly, she was a model for many young girls. Sarah represented traditional American values and believed that women of all ages should have the same educational and employment opportunities as men. However, she stated her opposition to the Equal Rights Amendment, and her desire to settle into a traditional family role was well known. Perhaps Sarah's most unique attribute was that she was sincere and honest about what she said.

Elbe and Rita approached Sarah's agent with a proposal that a cosmetic company be formed using Sarah as the focal point. The cosmetics were to be targeted toward teenage girls, and Sarah was to be used in all promotional advertisements. Sarah agreed with the arrangement, but only on the conditions that the cosmetics be high quality and that she would not be required to say anything in an advertisement that she did not really believe.

The company has been very successful. The products are widely accepted by many teenagers, and Sarah continues to both use and promote the entire cosmetic line.

Now Elbe is working on a ten-year plan for the company. He is somewhat concerned about the company's future because of changing national demographic patterns. He recently learned, while reading *Sales & Marketing Management* magazine, that the youth market increased by 8.7 million during the 1960–75 period; however, it will shrink by 3.5 million between 1975 and 1990. Moreover, the report noted, the number of people in the 14- to 21-year-old range, the primary target for Sarah Cosmetics, will probably shrink from 33.4 million in 1975 to 27.3 million in 1990, an 18 percent drop.[2] As Elbe ponders these statistics, he wonders whether a different marketing strategy is necessary to insure the survival of Sarah Cosmetics in the coming years.

Do you see the changing demographic patterns affecting Sarah Cosmetics' market? If so, what strategy changes do you think should be made?

---

[2]Adapted from, "The Rise and Fall of the Youth Market," *Sales and Marketing Management,* Vol. 121, No. 8 (December, 1978), p. 16.

5

the industrial goods market

Industrial marketing, as a field of study, has often been defined by default. It is not consumer marketing and it is not (necessarily) international marketing. Rather, industrial marketing is said by chroniclers to consist of "other markets" including producer (industrial), reseller (wholesaler and retail), and government markets.

... The dollar volume of sales in industrial markets, however, is about twice that of the consumer market.

--Observations of Thomas V. Bonoma
and Wesley B. Johnson in *Industrial
Marketing Management,* August, 1978.

The same basic functions are performed in both the industrial market and the consumer market. Differences between marketing industrial goods and marketing consumer goods occur mainly because of characteristics and needs of customers. A few distinctive characteristics of industrial goods marketing exist because of the sources of types of goods.

Those differences have sufficient impact on planning and carrying out the marketing task to make industrial marketing almost a separate field of business activity.

In order to emphasize the conditions, problems, and opportunities that are peculiar to the industrial market, this chapter presents, first, a definition of industrial marketing; second, a classification of industrial goods; third, characteristics of demand, including the principal bases for segmenting industrial markets; and, fourth, the characteristics of transactions in this segment of the market.

DEFINITION OF INDUSTRIAL MARKETING

Industrial marketing is the marketing of goods and services destined for use in providing other goods or services. Industrial goods are the products and services purchased by manufacturers, wholesalers, retailers, institutions (such as hospitals or schools) or government agencies for production, resale, capital plant, equipment, maintenance, or for research and development. Products are classified as either consumer or industrial goods, depending on the use for which they are purchased. For example, a small calculator purchased for your own use in school or at home is a consumer good; the same model purchased by a business firm for office or factory floor use is an industrial good.

Since the goal of all production is consumption, it is obvious that the demand for goods used to produce other goods depends ultimately upon individual and family purchases of consumer goods. Hence, the demand for industrial goods is a derived demand and tends to fluctuate. Further, the development of industrial processes and products is marked by increasing complexity. These three features of the industrial market—derived demand, fluctuating demand, and increasing complexity—lie behind the definition of industrial marketing and influence the methods and institutions that move industrial goods. Each is briefly discussed below.

Derived Demand

The demand for machine tools depends upon demand for the items produced by the machine tools which are, let us say, steel brackets. In turn, the demand for the brackets will depend upon the demand for the kitchen shelves and other building items that they support. The same is true for material used in production. The demand for copper depends upon the demand for radios, kitchenware, costume jewelry, and other consumer goods.

Hence, the only reason for extracting or producing a good for the industrial market is that consumers will purchase an item in which the industrial good has played a productive part or an item which is included in the consumer good.

Fluctuating Demand

Heavy commitments of capital are necessary to expand plant capacity or replace obsolescent equipment. During periods of low and falling business activity, it is often convenient, and sometimes wise, for the manufacturer of both capital and consumer goods to delay expansion or replacement until the markets are more promising. On the other hand, regardless of the economic conditions, consumers do not find it convenient to postpone or delay their consuming practices. Consequently, there are greater fluctuations in the industrial market than in the consumer market.

Increasing Complexity

It is said that the Wright brothers purchased all the parts for their first airplane from the shelves of small shops in Dayton, Ohio. It is doubtful that today the simplest craft could be built from parts available at neighborhood stores. Products are increasingly complex. Special metal alloys are being developed and intricate and complicated outputs of screw machines guided by taped programs become parts of objects we handle and enjoy daily, for example

CLASSIFICATION OF INDUSTRIAL GOODS

Industrial goods are usually classified in commerce and in census publications as raw materials, fabricated parts, operating supplies, accessory equipment, and installations.

Raw Materials

The sources of raw materials are the primary industries of agriculture, mining, forestry, and fisheries. Except in some instances of forestry and mining, most of the operations here are comparatively small. The seller has limited choice over where the business is located. Raw materials must be taken at the point where nature provides them. Here we have a problem collecting the materials, a problem aggravated by the number of firms and the distances involved. Usually the problem is solved by a market institution that assumes the responsibility for collecting and distributing; that is, wholesale or cooperative firms collect the products from the numerous small producers, store them for a necessary period, and then sell them to processors. Thus, in the case of both cotton and wool, middlemen collect the crops from the growers. They may process them to the extent of ginning the cotton or combing the wool and then sell them to the manufacturer.

In mining, lumbering, and the production of petroleum, however, direct sale to the first processor is the most common method of sale. Frequently the processor owns the primary source. For instance, U. S. Steel owns its iron mines and Weyerhauser Lumber Company in the Northwest owns its forests. In some industries such integration has been common for several years. Many of the large petroleum companies own their own oil fields or they may achieve control through subsidiary companies. Similarly, steel, copper, and aluminum fabricating companies own their own sources of raw materials.

Fabricated Parts

The buying and selling of fabricated parts exist where industrial consumers, in effect, delegate the manufacture of parts of their products to another manufacturer. These parts are often custom-made according to specification, although, in some instances, a fabricated part may have a general market appeal and be sold to many buyers.

Probably the best example of the purchase and sale of fabricated parts is the automobile (Illus. 5-1). Practically no automobile manufacturer produces its own

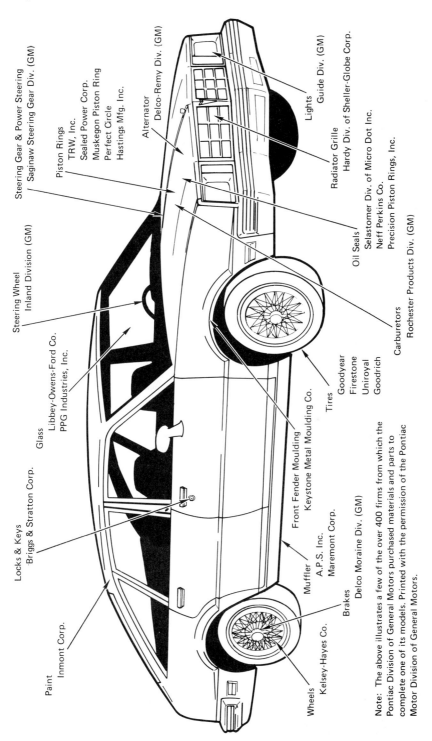

Steering Gear & Power Steering
Saginaw Steering Gear Div. (GM)

Piston Rings
TRW, Inc.
Sealed Power Corp.
Muskegon Piston Ring
Perfect Circle
Hastings Mfg. Inc.

Alternator
Delco-Remy Div. (GM)

Lights

Guide Div. (GM)

Radiator Grille
Hardy Div. of Sheller-Globe Corp.

Oil Seals
Selastomer Div. of Micro Dot Inc.
Neff Perkins Co.
Precision Piston Rings, Inc.

Carburetors
Rochester Products Div. (GM)

Steering Wheel
Inland Division (GM)

Glass
Libbey-Owens-Ford Co.
PPG Industries, Inc.

Locks & Keys
Briggs & Stratton Corp.

Paint
Inmont Corp.

Tires
Goodyear
Firestone
Uniroyal
Goodrich

Front Fender Moulding
Keystone Metal Moulding Co.

Muffler
A.P.S. Inc.
Maremont Corp.

Delco Moraine Div. (GM)

Brakes
Kelsey-Hayes Co.

Wheels

Note: The above illustrates a few of the over 400 firms from which the
Pontiac Division of General Motors purchased materials and parts to
complete one of its models. Printed with the permission of the Pontiac
Motor Division of General Motors.

Illus. 5-1   Partial Listing of Component Parts Suppliers in Automobile Assembly

carburetor. Stromberg and Carter are specialists in this field. Automobile manufacturers generally agree that they cannot duplicate the quality of these products at a comparable cost. The degree of emphasis that the fabricated-part buyer gives to these purchases depends to some extent upon their significance in the economy and the quality appeal of the final product to the consumer. For example, shirt manufacturers make a special point of the fact that their products are made of easily laundered cloth that does not require ironing. In such instances the fabricated part is of significance. In the case of parts with less influence on consumer appeals, the fabricated part may receive less of the buyer's attention.

In most instances manufacturers of fabricated parts cluster in the area of the large assemblers and manufacturers, although there are some exceptions where raw materials and labor resources make other areas more attractive. Usually the sale of fabricated parts is made by the manufacturers' sales representatives making direct contact with the buyer. Naturally the seller wishes to maintain a permanent relationship that assures the buyer's exclusive use of the seller's product.

Operating Supplies

Operating supplies seldom take up a great deal of policymakers' time. Usually much of the responsibility of buying is left to the purchasing agent. However, such supplies as coal and lubricating oil, necessities for the sustained and smooth operation of the plant, must be purchased with care. On occasions, where such items are used in large amounts, contracts run for several years. In some instances flexible provisions are made regarding price. The coal must maintain a certain Btu rating; oil must pass standard tests as to viscosity at changing temperatures and have a minimum flash-point rating. Supplies are necessary for the operation of all industrial and commercial institutions. Although supply costs per unit of output may be small, overall constant use makes their purchase a significant factor in maintaining efficient operations and cutting costs.

For the most part purchases are made directly from the producer. This relationship prevails when the consumer uses a considerable volume of the items. For example, Twenty-Mule Team Borax Company sales representatives contact both industrial and distributing firms that have large volume possibilities. Agreements are made to ship specific amounts at stated intervals, or orders are taken to replenish supplies. In addition to such direct selling, industrial supply houses and wholesalers serve as middlemen between industrial producers and consumers.

Accessory Equipment

The unit of sale in the case of accessory equipment is small when compared with installations. Its sale and purchase does not, therefore, merit as much attention as do installations. The purchasing agent, however, frequently requires the aid of engineers to make a proper selection. For example, the motor of the telescope at

Lick Observatory at Mount Hamilton, California, is $\frac{1}{500}$ of a horsepower. The purpose of this motor is to keep the 14-ton, 36-inch telescope moving slowly enough to hold a star in view. The purchase of this motor required painstaking calculations. Although this may not be a purchase of a typical accessory, fractional horsepower motors fall in this class, and tolerance judgments frequently are very fine. The accuracy with which such motors fit the task and the economy with which they are operated are important factors requiring careful computation.

Tests have proved conclusively that the use of electric typewriters increases production with less fatigue to skilled operators. Thus, a company decision to purchase electric typewriters may be based on both economy and efficiency as well as concern for employees. Similar criteria may be applied in either objective or scientific analysis in many purchases of accessory equipment.

Accessory equipment on the industrial market is sold directly from manufacturer to user and also through regional or area distributors. The relationship between the manufacturer and the user is not so close as that of the installer and the user. Yet large manufacturers of accessory equipment usually have sales representatives who maintain company contacts with large users. Manufacturers' agents, selling agents, and industrial supply houses serve as middlemen for the sale of goods that are not sold directly to users.

Installations

Probably more than any other classification, installations typify the true meaning of industrial goods. No decisions on any type of product merit as painstaking, careful consideration as those relating to major installations. The number of buyers is comparatively small. The cost of installations is great. Negotiations often run over long periods. Usually sales of installations are made directly from manufacturer to ultimate user. Decisions on installations depend on cost reductions, increased production, reliability of machines, financial arrangements, and relationships with the selling company.

SEGMENTATION OF INDUSTRIAL GOODS MARKETS

Industrial goods market segments are identified according to the same criteria as those used for consumer goods. Thus, homogeneity within the group, heterogeneity between groups, availability of communications media to the group, and size of the group to assure profitability are important factors in identifying industrial goods market segments.

Classes of Customers

Three broad classes of customers can be identified in the industrial market:

1. *Industrial users* who purchase finished products for use in the business. The goods are not to be changed or incorporated into other products. Machine tools, typewriters, trucks, and supplies are examples of this portion of the

industrial market. This customer class will include marketing institutions as well as manufacturing establishments.

2. *Assemblers, or manufacturer customers,* who purchase goods such as raw materials, automobile wheels and frames, or other component parts, to incorporate them into products they sell.

3. *Reseller customers* who are distributors who purchase products and resell them in the same form to manufacturers, users, or perhaps to other distributors. This customer class includes manufacturer resellers, design/contractors, wholesalers or retailers.

It is not feasible to make precise distinctions between products that are offered to each customer class. All will be customers for some products but may buy for different uses. Small electric motors, for example, may be sold to some firms to become a part of the equipment they manufacture, but the same type of motors may be used to power small grinders used in the production process in the same plant.

These three broad classes are the primary purchasing mix. The secondary purchasing mix further defines customer classes. In the secondary mix purchases are identified as piece parts, trade components, or subassemblies which are used as is in building up the customer's product; materials, such as sheet steel or plastic that are further processed by the customer; and consumables, such as lubricants and cleaning supplies.

Within those broad classes further segmentation is made on the bases of Standard Industrial Classification (SIC) category, size, location, and end use of the product or service. The SIC, prepared by the Bureau of the Budget, Office of Statistical Standards, classifies types of establishments engaged in extracting, manufacturing, service, and distribution. The SIC provides uniformity in definitions and facilitates the use of data relating to establishments.

SIC category segmentation is one of the most common forms of identifying the target market. Products are made or adapted to meet the requirements of specific industries.

A first identification is made of the type of industry, and requirements are then made according to the detailed classes within the industry.

The upper part of Illus. 5-2 is a reproduction of *Short Title* lists of codes and types of furniture manufacturers; the lower part is an exhibit of detail within the short titles.

Using SIC categories to identify the materials required in the manufacture of items in selected categories, the marketing manager can adapt marketing methods to meet the requirements of the targeted industries.

Size of Customer

Size segmentation may be based on total sales volume of the customer firm, or it may be on the basis of large users or small users of the product. A small or new manufacturer may find a marketing opportunity among low-volume users who are ignored by the large, established suppliers. Conversely, the firm may determine that economies of scale make it preferable to deal only with large users. Such tactics

STANDARD INDUSTRIAL CLASSIFICATION

Code	Short Title	Code	Short Title
25	**FURNITURE AND FIXTURES**		
251	Household furniture	2522	Metal office furniture
2511	Wood household furniture	253	Public building furniture
2512	Upholstered household furniture	2531	Public building furniture
2514	Metal household furniture	254	Partitions and fixtures
2515	Mattresses and bedsprings	2541	Wood partitions and fixtures
2519	Household furniture, nec	2542	Metal partitions and fixtures
252	Office furniture	259	Miscellaneous furniture and fixtures
2521	Wood office furniture	2591	Venetian blinds and shades

STANDARD INDUSTRIAL CLASSIFICATION

Group No. 251
Industry No. 2514

HOUSEHOLD FURNITURE – Continued
Metal Household Furniture

Establishments primarily engaged in manufacturing metal household furniture of a type commonly used in dwellings, whether padded or plain. Establishments primarily engaged in manufacturing dual purpose sleep furniture, such as studio couches, sofa beds, and chair beds, are classified in Industry 2515, regardless of the material used in the frame.

Backs for metal household
  furniture
Beds, including folding and
  cabinet beds: household –
  metal
Bookcases, household: metal
Breakfast sets (furniture), metal
Bridge sets (furniture), metal
Cabinets, kitchen: metal
Cabinets, medicine: metal
Cabinets, radio and television:
  metal
Camp furniture, metal
Club room furniture, metal
Cots, household: metal
Cribs, metal
Dinette sets, metal
Frames for box springs or bed-
  springs, metal
Furniture, household: metal –
  padded or plain
Garden furniture, metal
Gliders (furniture), metal: padded
  or plain
Hammocks, metal and fabric
Household furniture upholstered
  on metal frames
Juvenile furniture, metal
Lawn furniture, metal
Novelty furniture, metal
Nursery furniture, metal
Seats for metal household
  furniture
Smoking stands, metal
Stools, household: metal –
  padded
Swings, porch: metal
Tables, household: metal
Tea wagons, metal

252
2521

OFFICE FURNITURE
Wood Office Furniture

Establishments primarily engaged in manufacturing wood office furniture, whether padded, upholstered or plain.

Benches, office: wood
Bookcases, office: wood
Cabinets, office: wood
Chairs, office: wood – padded,
  upholstered, and plain
Desks, office: wood
Filing boxes, cabinets, and cases:
  wood
Furniture, office: wood – padded,
  upholstered, or plain
Stools, office: wood
Tables, office: wood

Source: *Standard Industrial Classification Manual* (Washington: United States Government Printing Office).

Illus. 5-2   **Examples of SIC Categories**

as allocation of sales territories and frequency of sales calls will usually be determined by present or potential use of the firm's products. For example, suppliers
to automobile manufacturers may have a sales office whose only customer is one
automobile company; and electronic data processing firms may assign only a few
customers to one sales office.

Size also has an effect on marketing channels. Usually, when a large supplier
sells to a large-scale user, the dealing is direct between supplier and customer
rather than through middlemen.

Geographic Location

Geographic location is a frequently used basis of segmentation. Some industries are regional in character, such as those based on mining or other natural
resources. Textiles, automobiles, and furniture are other examples of products with
some degree of geographic concentration. Manufacturers who serve those industries concentrate efforts in those geographic areas in order to provide prompt,
individual service.

End-Use Segmentation

End-use segmentation relates to the final use of the product. If an electronic
component is to be used in an inexpensive radio, the care exercised in the manufacture and the attention paid by the buyer will be considerably different from that
given to a similar component if it is to be used in the control system for a passenger
airplane. Hence, marketing methods are affected by the product characteristics
determined by the quality and precision requirements of the final product.

Purchase Weight Segmentation

Purchase weight segmentation can be used in planning marketing strategies.
Weight here is used in the sense of importance or consequence.

Weight of the purchase decision is determined by the degree of importance
and the complexity of the buying task. That is important to the seller because of
its effect on where authority and responsibility for purchasing will be placed; that
is, by whom and how is buying done.

Importance and complexity of purchasing can be displayed on a scale according to the value placed on the buying decision, as shown in Illus. 5-3.

Weight assigned to a purchase decision can be a function of the complexity
of industrial goods or of the degree of risk and probable impact on company
profitability.[1]

Purchase weight can be assigned as shown in Illus. 5-4.

Purchases with low complexity and low risk weights do not require much
executive time, and purchasing is routine. Those with the highest weights will
require considerable technical and executive effort[2]

---

[1]Lawrence Fisher, *Industrial Marketing* (London: Business Books, 1976), p. 19.
[2]A. Wilson, *Marketing Industrial Goods and Services* (London: Hutchinson of London, 1966) p.
11–23; and R. W. Hill, "The Nature of Industrial Buying Decisions," *Industrial Marketing Management,*
Vol. 2, No. 1, October, 1977, p. 48 and p. 53.

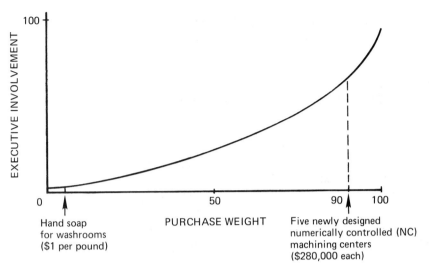

Illus. 5-3   Effect of Purchase Weight on Level of Purchase Decision

As shown in Illus. 5-3, purchase decisions for such items as pencils, cleaning supplies or common stationary will be routinely made at a low administrative level. When the decision involves machinery or equipment that is costly and has an important effect on long-term profitability and effectiveness of the organization, there will be involvement of top executives, technical people, and workers who will use the new purchase.

Complexity of the Product

	Low Weight	High Weight
Standardization	Standardized	Differentiated
Technology	Simple	Complex
Product Features	Established	New
Purchase	Previous and Frequent	First Time
Application to Company	Fits Existing Processes	New Application
Installation Processes	Easy, No New Skills	Specialized
After-Sale Service	None Required	Technical

Degree of Risk and Impact on Future Profitability

	Low Weight	High Weight
Investment	Small	Large
Order Size	Small	Large
Length of Commitment	Short-term	Long-term
Possible Effect on		
Profitability or Loss	Small	Potentially Large

Illus. 5-4   Factors in Purchase Weight Decisions

That explains why General Electric, IBM, and others frequently use sales teams. Such teams include technical experts, market planners, business analysts, and others who learn the problems the customer has to solve and then fit the product and their sales presentations to those problems.

Bases of Buying Decisions

Much of the industrial market consists of firms that have been developed by persons with technical skills for whom careful measurement and calculation are part of their routine. Also, the calculations for profitable operations of manufacturing establishments result in objectification and assignment of numerical measures to expense and income magnitudes. Hence, rational, objective, numerical calculations are to be expected in industrial purchasing decisions. Nevertheless, the industrial seller must consider the emotional responses of the people who are directly and indirectly included in the purchase and use of the product.

CHARACTERISTICS OF DEMAND

Industrial purchases result from a complex mixture of motives. There are, of course, more attempts to support purchases with the aid of objective data than in the case of consumer goods buying. Even in the presence of ample measuring devices and quantitative data, however, an ability to view and properly appraise subjective forces and emotional motives is important. For convenience demand factors may be grouped into the following categories: (1) characteristics of product or service that affect the efficiency of the purchaser, (2) effects of technology and productivity, and (3) effects of innovations.

Demand Characteristics That Affect
Efficiency of the Purchaser

The value of an industrial good to a customer is dependent upon its ability to assure efficiency and profitability in the customer's operations. The highest priced material may be the least costly if it saves time, for example. Even the quantity discount on large purchases may be foregone when small regular shipments reduce storage requirements and provide the materials required in more manageable lot sizes. Demand characteristics usually include those discussed below.

Efficiency of Product Supplied.   This can be based on such qualities as speed of new tools, wearing and lasting qualities of abrasives or bearings, and ease of use or installation. For example, a product might be furnished with features that make possible economies growing out of the use of only semiskilled workers.

Certainty of Supply.   A supplier may entice the buyer with low prices but may not have the competence to meet requirements or guarantee a dependable, long-term supply.

Dependability in Meeting Schedules. Industrial customers must meet schedules in their sales and, hence, must assure themselves of supplies in the quantities, with the specifications, and on the dates promised.

Technical Assistance. This includes information on qualities and use of products or processes as well as advice on maximizing the customer's efficiency in their use. Problems of installing and incorporating equipment into existing productive methods are also important to the customer.

Product Motives and Patronage Motives. In dealing with the industrial consumer, it is advisable to bear in mind that industrial businesses base their decisions on both the product and the institution that sells the product. To clarify some areas of significance in these two classes of motives, the following discussions and listings will be helpful. Some typical product motives are:

Efficiency	Protection from loss
Economy	Dependability or reliability
Quality	Accuracy
Speed	Uniformity and stability
Strength	Low maintenance cost
Durability or endurance	Simplicity

There is some overlapping in these motives. This is especially true in the case of efficiency. Excellence in each of these areas will improve the efficiency of the buying firm. Each item on the list, however, suggests appeal areas, wherein the industrial consumer should respond to a sales approach.

The trigger action that determines choice in the industrial market is often the buyer's image of the selling institution. This is especially important when deciding about goods which are so nearly alike that they provide no basis for a decision. Some of the characteristics that influence market choices are:

Completeness of line	Monopoly position
Completeness of stock	Financial or managerial
Offer of free service	connection
Reputation in trade	Friendship
Reciprocal patronage	Past services
Price and discount policies	Research and pioneering

Quite clearly, the attitude and policy of a firm with respect to increases of new products and the innovation of complex processes have an effect on building a following among its patrons. The discussions on technology and productivity and innovations provide some additional insight into developments in these areas.

Technology and Productivity

The industrial consumer usually chooses to buy a product because it will yield results or profits at a greater rate than its cost. Thus, industrial purchases and sales are closely related to their effect on productivity. The tempo of technological

Anyone can sell you light bulbs.
The Duro-Test specialist also solves your lighting
problems – and saves you money.

The men and women sales representatives from Duro-Test can supply you with a lot more than light bulbs.

They also provide valuable lighting information and expertise you just can't get from a distributor or retailer. They'll tell you which bulbs are right for your particular needs. They'll show you how to save money with energy-saving bulbs that last for years. And they'll show you how to get the *quality* as well as *quantity* of light you

need. Where you need it. In your office, restaurant, hotel, factory, bank, store, hospital, school. You name it.

They'll survey your lighting for comfort, efficiency and safety. And if you've a problem they can't handle, they'll call on Duro-Test's commercial engineers. They're the best in the industry.

Duro-Test – the nation's largest exclusive manufacturer of light sources – markets a full line of energy-saving,

premium-life incandescent, fluorescent and fail-safe vapor lamps. Products include plant-growing lights, the industry's greatest selection of decorative bulbs, and Vita-Lite® – the patented sunlight-simulating fluorescent.

Meet the Duro-Test lighting specialist. Write today to Dept. D, Duro-Test Corporation, North Bergen, New Jersey 07047.

50 YEARS
QUALITY
SERVICE
& LIGHTING
INNOVATION

DURO TEST

Duro-Test Corporation, North Bergen, N.J. • Luxor Lighting Products, Inc., Empire State Bldg., N.Y. • Jewel Electric Products, Inc., Fair Lawn, N.J.
• Duro-Test Electric Ltd., Toronto & Montreal • Duro-Test Int'l., Carolina, P.R. • Duro de Mexico S.A., Mexico City

Advertisement courtesy of Duro-Test Corporation, North Bergen, N. J.

Illus. 5-5   **Industrial Marketing Frequently Includes
Supplying Technical Assistance**

innovations in modern business is such that much of the industrial equipment is less likely to wear out than to become obsolete. Obsolescence results from conditions wherein a new machine or process is more efficient or productive than the one in use. It becomes profitable, therefore, for the producer to discard the old machine and to purchase the new one.

A long-time and a short-time view of productive evolution in industry will be helpful in revealing such trends. For example, in the eighteenth century the average American farmer possessed $15 worth of tools. Today, including the thousands of small part-time farmers, the average farmer owns $2,600 worth of tools or 173 times as much as his great-grandfather. During the early period, 90 percent of the population was required to produce agricultural products. Today, with America consuming an unprecedented amount of food, both in terms of total volume and per capita, less than 6 percent of the population is engaged in agriculture.

In the nineteenth century, chips were cut from metal at the rate of four ounces a minute. Today, with more scientifically hardened metal and improved mechanical arrangements, machine tools trim off 20 pounds a minute. The modern tool is 10 times more accurate and 80 times faster than that of the nineteenth century. Modern machine tools are also multipurpose tools. Some can measure 32 different points simultaneously, and a multiple spindle drill can bore 98 holes at the same time.

Innovations

In the industrial market, change requires the constant purchase and sale of new, different industrial products. This process of industrial evolution includes not only the marketing of installations but also of repairs, fuel, lubrication services, and even the buildings in which production machinery is housed. Constant innovation and the replacing of the less efficient with the more efficient in this market prevent the task of the buyer and the seller of industrial goods from becoming routine to the point where marketing skills are not necessary. While it is true that many industrial goods can be standardized and purchased from specifications, a large part of goods going to the industrial market is being improved constantly. Even a common product such as paint is tested with competitive products for durability before it is purchased by General Motors, and new formulas are announced almost daily.

CHARACTERISTICS OF MARKET TRANSACTIONS

Some features of the industrial market cannot be identified as belonging exclusively to either the demand or the supply side. In this final section some of these features are pointed out: (1) the interdependence of buyer and seller, (2) the decision whether to make or to buy, (3) leasing of installations, and (4) loyalty.

Interdependence of Buyer and Seller[3]

Frequently close relationships develop between suppliers and customers in design and manufacturing of products or techniques. For example, sales representatives of firms that sell data processing equipment must learn enough about a customer's firm to develop and install complete systems for accounting and management control. Business machine companies have specialists in supermarket organization, store layout, and stock control who work with store supervisors of the customer firm. Other examples of this kind of creative selling and engineering that overcome vested industrial inertia will illustrate the value of recognizing the interdependence of buyer and seller.

Creative Engineering and Selling.   Creative is used here (as it is by professional, alert salespeople) in the sense of edifying and conceiving some new or more efficient way to make the customer firm more efficient in its operations. It is just as important to sell a customer on the progressive steps leading to technical efficiency as it is to discover the step or to invent a better process or machine. A study of a large wholesale firm that was losing money is an example of the inertia in existing methods. The study indicated that this company was located in a five-storied building and that merchandise was stacked by hand. The expense ratio of this company was 7 percent of its sales. The two firms with which this house competed had modern one-storied warehouses, and all merchandise was handled by a pallet and trucks. Out-going orders were loaded from the merchandise stacked in the same sequence as it was listed on the order forms. This arrangement made it possible to load an order on a truck that was attached to a power line which was constantly moving through the warehouse. This operation, along with other similar modifications, enabled these two firms to operate on an expense margin of 4 percent of sales.

The policy decisions that would have kept the losing firm up to date in the installation of cost-reducing innovations could have been influenced by reliable data, skillfully organized and effectively presented. This is the domain of the industrial representative. Viewed in a social perspective, an industrial sales representative performs the service of keeping the lag between the technology of the laboratory and that of the industrial plant at a minimum.

Close Relationship of Buyer and Seller.   The product that the industrial consumer chooses to buy must be reliable and productive. The reliability and productivity of major industrial sales in many instances are subject to test and calculations. This situation requires a close relationship between the firms of the buyer and the seller in transactions of major significance. Frequently negotiations

---

[3]There are two excellent articles on requisite knowledge and the important expanded role of industrial salespeople: Gary M. Grikscheit and W. J. E. Crissy, "Personal Selling: A Position Paper," in Ross L. Goble and Roy T. Shaw, *Controversy and Dialogue in Marketing* (Englewood Cliffs, N.J.: Prentice-Hall, Inc., December, 1975), p. 270, and by the same authors, "Communication Correlates of Sales Success," *Industrial Marketing Management,* Vol. 5, No. 2/3, June, 1975, p. 175.

reach a point where the engineering departments of the buyer and the seller confer at length on the needs of the buyer to determine how well the seller's product meets the buyer's needs.

Reliability Plus Confidence.   To be successful in selling the industrial market, firms must first obtain the confidence of their prospect. Buyers must be convinced that the selling company knows its business and will support its claims. Second, industrial selling entails the proper conveyance of the technical information which will convince the buyer that the seller's product will maximize the former's productivity more than other possibilities. It should not be presumed that the latter function is sufficient to the exclusion of the first requirement. Calculations are more applicable in determining acceptability of industrial goods than of consumer goods, even though exact calculation cannot anticipate all the possible problems of operations or measure with perfect accuracy the comparative value of complex technical machines. Realizing this fact, the buying firm is influenced by the confidence it has in the seller's past history and its reputation for standing behind its product. For this reason, on important installations the staff of the seller, from the president to the production engineer, may be brought into contact with the staff of the buyer.

To Make or To Buy

One of the significant decisions all industrial concerns must make with respect to the fabricated parts entering into their products is whether to make the parts themselves or to buy them from other manufacturers. We have noted that automobile manufacturers buy a large percentage of their parts. How far should they go in this practice? Henry Ford became famous for building an industrial empire wherein he purchased virtually nothing. He even made his own glass, rubber, and steel. He built his own railroad and provided much of his own transportation. He found such complete independence from specialized fabricators unprofitable, however, and discontinued this policy. The amount of preprocessed food purchased by restaurants, even many of the most famous, further illustrates the willingness of some managers to hand over problems to specialists.

The alert enterpriser will decide whether to make or to buy a part on the basis of the cost and satisfaction involved. It is possible that the prospective supplier who specializes in a particular type of part can routinize production of the specialty part and achieve economies not possible to the large assembling firm. It is also conceivable that the assembling firm's quality reputation may enhance the overall salability of the assembled product.

Other considerations are the reliability of the supply of the parts and the willingness of the selling firm to meet certain quality specifications important in the final product. It is also apparent that when suppliers with parts of acceptable quality are available, the management problem is not so great as it is in the case of making the part. Manufacturing of parts involves finance, material, labor, and engineering problems that expand the scope of management responsibility.

Leasing of Installations

In some instances agreements are made by the seller of installations to lease the equipment to the user instead of selling it outright. Leasing is common with such products as ships, trucks, railway cars, derricks, machinery, steel machinery, and office machines. Several factors favor this practice. In the first place, the high cost of most installations creates a problem of financing. Since the leasehold method permits payments to be made as the machine is used, the net amount of working capital required is reduced. Second, some machines are complex and require special servicing. If the purchasing firm does not obtain skilled, competent service, the work may be poorly done. Improper repairs will result in inefficient operations, which will reflect on the quality of installations and on the manufacturing firm that made them. The lease arrangements include provision for service by the lessor.

Third, manufacturing firms are hesitant to make large financial commitments for new installations when equipment in current use is operating in a satisfactory manner. With a lease arrangement, however, the manufacturer can introduce the machinery or any of its parts with little extra cost to the user. What might have been a major capital expenditure is changed to a relatively small operating cost. The user is less reluctant to adopt a new method, and sales resistance is overcome. Fourth, property taxes are not charged against installations that are leased. Thus, there is a tax advantage in leasing. To determine net savings one must calculate whether the property tax advantage offsets the depreciation that could be charged against owned equipment.

The seller benefits from the steady income from lease payments. This arrangement enables the manufacturer of installations to escape in part the impact of cyclical declines, which are usually quite severe in the area of capital goods. The manufacturer also enjoys a captive market for supplies and parts that may comprise a substantial portion of profit business. The seller of such equipment can also charge each customer on the basis of the amount of use to which the latter puts the machine. If an outright sale is made, the Robinson-Patman Act prevents the manufacturer from charging different prices to buyers regardless of the amount of use intended.

On the other hand, the seller must arrange for the financing of the equipment that he owns and, in addition, must bear the cost of obsolescence and tax. At present the favorable factors for both the lessee and the lessor seem to indicate the soundness of this method of marketing certain installations.

Loyalty

Many firms build long-term relationships with customers, and it is useful to determine why some potential customers are reluctant to consider new sources of supply.

Loyalty may result from any or some combination of the following:

1. Administrative inertia, limitations on capacity of people in an organization to respond to change. It may also be the result of a considered judgment not to spend time and effort on low purchase weight items.

2. Familiarity with a vendor's policies and performance which have met the customer's needs; hence, risk is reduced.
3. Long-term relationships sometimes persist because the supplier understands the customer's processes and problems. When a supplier seriously keeps up with a customer's needs and adapts service requirements to those needs, loyalty quite naturally develops.

Sometimes short, approved lists of suppliers are developed because of difficulties in evaluating financial strength, policies, and technical capabilities of many possible sources of supply.

Reciprocity is sometimes used. There is no way to measure accurately the amount of business that comes to industrial sellers because they do business with their prospective customers. Many business deals are the result of friendships, and friendships are the result of doing business. This circle of buying and selling can be described as spontaneous, arising from mutual friendship and confidence. In their eagerness to build sales, however, some firms have pressed the accounts from whom they have purchased goods to buy their own goods in return.

This type of business give-and-take is more popular during downturns in the business cycle than during prosperous times. When sales drop to near break-even-point levels, and every dollar of sales counts, many firms consider the companies from which they buy as sales prospects. Sometimes this goes so far that a manager threatens to change suppliers unless reciprocity is practiced. On occasion situations such as the following can develop: Company A buys heavily from Company B which buys heavily from Company C. Company A will put pressure on Company B to get Company C to buy A's product.

During periods of prosperity less use is made of the reciprocity method of acquiring sales. Theoretically such a policy is sound only if the extra costs to the seller are less than the income from extra sales. All other factors being equal, the firm should buy its industrial products from the supplier that gives the most value for the money. Reciprocity influence that tends to deter a buyer from this procedure cannot be justified on the basis of efficient management.

How and by Whom Are Purchase Decisions Made

At the outset of this chapter it was stated that there are sufficient differences between the consumer goods market and the industrial goods market to cause significantly different emphases in marketing methods.

The locus of the purchase decision is a factor that causes many of those different emphases. In the discussion of purchase weight segmentation that was pointed out. It is worth re-emphasizing, because is it unusual for only one person to influence the purchase of industrial goods; buying influence is found at all levels of executive and productive ranks.

In new industries, an electronic component manufacturing specification may go out from the research laboratory, the production developing department, or the production facility. Conversely, it is difficult to determine who is responsible for the sale of new technical products. The research people often claim credit for the sale, as do engineers in development engineering departments and, naturally, the marketing division. The understanding and acceptance of the marketing concept enables these divisions to see this seeming diversity of views as a unified, coopera-tive effort.

In any event the industrial sales representative must learn enough about each customer's processes and problems to identify the level at which purchase decisions are made. In general it is reasonable to assume that for new products or technicques top management will be involved. As a product enters the routine productive phase, either engineering development or production executives make buying decisions. The selection of possible suppliers and negotiations for price and terms, based on specifications, are usually handled by the office of the purchasing agent.

Planning

Planning for growth assumes greater importance each year. Many existing industrial markets are shrinking or, at best, are not growing as rapidly as the economy.

Effort must be balanced between selling existing products and finding new or improved products and techniques. Provision must be made for planning to take advantage of change in social patterns. Increased leisure time, recreational oppor-tunities, and demand for housing influence the dynamics of the industrial market. Progress in technology, resulting both in and from increasing research, military demands, new fuels, and space exploration, require an alertness to opportunity which distinguishes today's industrial market from that of former years.

Pressures arising from population growth around the world, with consequent instabilities in social and economic environments; the conflicting demands for use or conservation of natural resources and the apparent irreversible despoliation of some resources; and increasing dependence on technology—all are essential com-ponents of long-term plans.

This section does not include a catalog of the kinds of market institutions and channels required to distribute industrial goods effectively and efficiently. Chapter 15, on wholesaling and wholesaling institutions (which by definition includes industrial marketing), and Chapter 12, on the selection of marketing channels, explain the types of institutions and proper linkage required to meet the needs of the industrial market.

QUESTIONS AND ANALYTICAL PROBLEMS

1. Define: (a) industrial goods, (b) industrial marketing.
2. Explain each of the following state-ments:
   (a) The demand for industrial goods is a derived demand.
   (b) There tend to be greater fluc-tuations in the industrial market than the consumer goods market.

3. What are the characteristics of each of the three broad classes of customers in the industrial market?
4. Compare the classification of con-sumer goods with the classifica-tion of industrial goods. Do those classifications have anything in common?
5. Clearly   distinguish   fabricated

parts, accessory equipment, and operating supplies.

6. What is the significance of Illus. 5-1, which shows the source of some parts in the automobile?

7. Define each of the three customer classes for industrial goods.

8. List the bases used in defining marketing segments for the industrial goods market. Find an example—an advertisement, display, or operating method—that illustrates each segment.

9. Find five advertisements in trade magazines—preferably those used by production specialists—that make use of emotional appeals. Discuss their probable effectiveness. Do rational appeals or emotional appeals predominate in the advertisements of such journals? Why?

10. Can industrial goods be sold? Is it more nearly correct to say that industrial goods are purchased be-

cause of a recognized need and that they cannot be sold in the sense that a second television set is sold to a householder?

11. Explain SIC segmentation.

12. Explain purchase weight segmentation.

13. Use Illus. 5-3 as a reference. At what management level and what kinds of personnel are likely to be involved in purchases at the 5, 50, and 95 purchase weight categories?

14. Select three kinds of manufacturers and identify five of the demand characteristics of product or service that affect the efficiency of the purchaser that will be of significant importance to each of the three.

15. Which of the characteristics of market transactions in this chapter differ from important transaction characteristics for the consumer goods market?

Case 5-1 • PARKER PUMPS, INC.

Parker Pumps, Inc., was started in the early 1900s in Oklahoma City. The company initially manufactured and marketed water pumps for agricultural use. The pumps were particularly suited for the semiarid climates of Texas, Arizona, and California which were being farmed by pumping out ground water for irrigation.

The company had expanded its product offering into many other industries but always in the pump line. Following the dictum of, "Cobbler, stick to your last," Parker's unstated motto has been, "Pumps Are Our Only Business."[1] This theme was even used in industrial advertising campaigns to emphasize that Parker Pumps, Inc., was a specialist in manufacturing, marketing, installing, and maintaining pumps of various kinds and types. So far this strategy had been very profitable for Parker as profits and sales rose dramatically in the 1970s.

At the end of 1978 Parker Pumps, Inc., was well established in the chemical industry, the pulp-paper industry, the agricultural industry, and the petroleum industry. Additionally, Parker had recently acquired a majority holding in the major manufacturer of pumps for coal slurry applications.

---

[1]Colin Ungaro and Don Korn, "Gould Keeps On Pumping," *Sales and Marketing Management*, Vol. 121, No. 8 (December, 1978), p. 27.

The marketing director, Roy Bowden, a fifteen-year veteran of the firm, was currently in the process of reevaluating the firm's selling strategy. The original product line, agricultural pumps, is sold through a company sales force. The company sales force also sells to the pulp-paper industry. Independent sales representatives currently sell to the chemical and petroleum industry. The company's sales force accounts for 70 percent of the sales revenue even though the chemical and petroleum markets were on the whole much bigger. Mr. Bowden is contemplating a series of reorganizational alternatives. First, he is considering doing away with the independent representatives and having the company's sales force sell all the company's products. Second, he is considering forming a new sales force made up primarily of sales engineers to contact the chemical and oil companies directly. Finally, he is contemplating the utilization of team selling: an experienced sales representative accompanied by a supporting technical engineer calling on all types of customers.

What other alternatives do you recommend to Mr. Bowden? Which alternative do you find most acceptable?

Case 5-2 • GLASS FLEX SIDING

Glass Flex Siding was started in the early 1960s. The company, originally named simply Glass Flex, was started by Henry Jacobs to make fishing rods and sailboats. Mr. Jacobs had developed a new curing process to strengthen fiberglass and hoped that his superior products would sell themselves. Unfortunately, customers did not beat a path to the company's Phoenix, Arizona, location and the firm was soon in financial trouble.

A local contractor in the Phoenix area bought the business, fired Henry Jacobs, and began to manufacture fiberglass siding for residential and commercial use. He hired a marketing director and gave her full authority to set up the marketing program for the product.

The new marketing director took three major steps in the first year. She hired three sales representatives and put them on the road selling the siding to building material outlets and lumber yards. She instituted a direct-mail program advertising the siding to building contractors. And she conducted a study to determine the best channel of distribution for the product. The study revealed that lumber yards, hardware stores, and do-it-yourself centers were the most profitable way to distribute the product. The study, along with feedback from the sales representatives, also revealed that most of these potential outlets did not want to carry the product and would usually only do so when pressured or induced to do so.

The marketing director realized that the prospective outlets must be made to want to carry the product. To achieve this objective she attempted to design a dealer development program to achieve retailer cooperation. Her initial ideas for the program included price incentives to carry the product, display racks and brochures for installation in the retailer's showroom, and a rather favorable quantity discount policy.

What else do you think the dealer development program should include? Are the items mentioned by the marketing director of concern to the retailer?

3

Science in Marketing

6

marketing management

You're looking for a guy who is broad enough to be able to understand the various facets of business. He's got to have depth of intelligence to sort the big ones from the little ones and to do the analytical thinking. He's got to have the ability to make a decision and to live with himself and the decision. He's got to be able to influence people without issuing commands.

--Edward G. Harness, Chairman and Chief Executive Officer, Procter & Gamble, Inc., discussing the qualities of a potential P&G leader in *The Cincinnati Enquirer,* July 8, 1979.

Management is a pervasive and common word in the academic world and in our society. The term means at least two things: the people in an organization who guide and direct the organization, and the actual practice of guiding and directing the organization. The second meaning, the practice of guiding and directing the organization, is the focus of this chapter.

This chapter emphasizes the management of the marketing function within business organizations. However, numerous marketing management practices which are useful to business firms are equally as valuable to nonprofit organizations.[1] The emphasis here on marketing management in the business organization is based on two concepts: first, management evolved and developed as a concept in business organizations; second, the widely held belief that marketing is the most basic and fundamental purpose of a business. This second point was addressed specifically by Peter Drucker, a business consultant and management expert:

---

[1]For example, see Philip Kotler, *Marketing for Nonprofit Organizations* (Englewood Cliffs, N.J.: Prentice-Hall, Inc., 1975).

Marketing is the distinguishing, unique function of the business. A business is set apart from all other human organizations by the fact that it markets a product or service.[2]

Thus, the very roots of marketing and management are found within business organizations.

MARKETING MANAGEMENT: OVERVIEW AND DEFINITION

Although there are numerous definitions of management, the following definition is particularly useful:

Management is a practice, rather than a science. In this, it is comparable to medicine, law, and engineering. It is not knowledge, but performance. Furthermore, it is not the application of common sense, or leadership, let alone financial manipulation. Its practice is based both on knowledge and on responsibility.[3]

This definition tells us a number of things. First, management is a behavioral skill; that is, management is action. Therefore, management can be learned and correspondingly, managers can improve and become better managers. The definition also implies that students of management can learn only so much in the classroom. A great deal of the ability to manage must be learned on the job.

Finally, management is more than common sense and leadership, although both of these factors are important. Numerous skills—communicating, thinking, creating, planning, and the ability to get things done—go into making a successful manager. Additionally, management is based on responsibility. The managers of a firm are responsible to the owners of the firm. Similarly, managers are responsible to the society within which they operate. Businesses are, after all, simply organs of society, and must therefore meet society's requirements.

The following question is frequently asked: What do managers do? One thing that managers do very frequently is make decisions. Management is more than decision making, but decision making permeates the management process. A second task of managers is performing specified functions. A frequently mentioned list of these functions includes planning, implementation, and control. The meaning of these and similar terms will be discussed later in this chapter.

A final point about management is worth noting. All executives in a firm manage. Production people manage, financial people manage, and marketers manage. Management skill is valued regardless of the functional area in which a person works.

---

[2]Peter F. Drucker, *Management: Tasks, Responsibilities, Practices* (New York City: Harper & Row Publishers, Inc., 1974), p. 61.

[3]*Ibid.,* p. 17.

Marketing Management

Marketing management is essentially the practice of management in the marketing area. One definition of marketing management is

> the analysis, planning, implementation, and control of programs designed to bring about desired exchanges with target audiences for the purpose of personal or mutual gain. It relies heavily on the adaptation and coordination of product, price, promotion, and place for achieving effective response.[4]

In other words, when marketers manage, they perform activities to bring about the desired exchanges between the firm and the firm's target markets. Marketing managers assume that desired exchanges, like effective management, don't just happen. Instead, the marketing management philosophy proclaims that these exchanges must be planned and guided.

Planning and guiding marketing exchanges implies far more than simply planning effective sales efforts. Selling essentially tries to get a customer to buy what the firm has to offer. Selling is important and necessary to effective marketing. However, marketing is more encompassing than selling. Marketing management attempts to insure that the firm will have what the customer *wants* to buy. To do this effectively marketing managers must find out what the firm's customers need and desire. Therefore, only through two-way communication between marketing management and the firm's customers can the company develop a market offering that potential customers want to purchase. If a firm is effectively marketing, selling becomes much easier.

The two-way interaction between marketing managers and customers gets marketers involved in product mix decisions. Specifically, marketers are perhaps best qualified to decide which models, styles, or even product lines the firm should offer. Consequently, marketing managers play a central role in the most basic of all managerial decisions: (1) determining what kinds of companies they are managing and (2) deciding in what primary business they are involved.

Supervision of Channel Flows

One way to visualize what people must do when they engage in marketing management is to consider items flowing between the customer and the marketing firm. The management of these flows is the essential function of marketing management.

Perhaps the two most important things that flow between the firm and the consumer are the product and payment for it. Therefore, marketing managers must manage the actual transportation and storage of the product, as well as the payment for the product. Factors such as inventory management and control, traffic management, dealer development, distribution channel design, and the management of accounts receivable fall into this category.

Another important flow between consumers and firms is communication. Communication can take many forms, but one of the primary ways that firms

---

[4]Philip Kotler, *Marketing Management: Analysis, Planning, and Control* (2d ed.; Englewood Cliffs, N.J.: Prentice-Hall, Inc., 1972), p. 13.

communicate to potential target markets is through promotion. Additionally, many firms attempt to receive feedback from their customers. Accordingly, customer service and marketing research are utilized to insure that communication takes place in both directions.

Finally, the title of the product must usually also flow through the channel of distribution. In total, many things must move between the manufacturer and the eventual consumer or purchaser of the product. Insuring that these flows occur efficiently and effectively is one of the primary jobs of marketing management.

MARKETING MANAGEMENT IN THE FIRM

The role that marketing management plays in the firm can vary greatly. Consider what Robert Townsend said about marketing management in his critical book about management experiences at Avis Rent A Car.

> Marketing, in the fullest sense of the word, is the name of the game. So it had better be handled by the boss and his line, not by staff hecklers.[5]

Mr. Townsend may be a little strong in his convictions that top management should be responsible for the marketing in an organization. Perhaps a more balanced view is put forth by one of marketing's strongest proponents, Theodore Levitt, when he stated:[6]

> Vigorous but naive proponents of the marketing concept have gone so far as to suggest that the corporation president's major preoccupation and perhaps even competence should be in the marketing area. To such a formula or job description no knowledgeable man can comfortably subscribe.[7]

> Marketing men have to see that marketing has no automatic claim to superior virtue in the business organization. There are two sides to the marketing matrix, not one. It may be right to say that marketing is a consolidating view of the business process. But that is not the same as saying that marketing must therefore, and in all cases, have the last word. It is a question of balance: What is the proper balance between the demands of the manufacturing department and those of the marketing department? What is the proper balance between the demands of the marketing services department and those of the sales department, between the demands of the marketing vice-president and those of the regional sales manager, between the demands of the treasurer and those of the manager of distributor sales, between the demands of R & D and those of market development?[8]

In summary, marketing management plays a pivotal role in many firms. Through effective marketing management, revenue is earned for the firm and product market selections are made. Moreover, the process of product market selection

[5]Robert Townsend, *Up the Organization* (Greenwich, Conn.: Fawcett Books, 1970), p. 87.
[6]Theodore Levitt, *Marketing for Business Growth* (2d ed.; New York City: McGraw-Hill, Inc., 1974), p. 201.
[7]*Ibid.*, p. 202.
[8]*Ibid.*, p. 204.

determines the firm's business. However, marketing is not the only function that leads a firm to success. The importance of the marketing function will vary according to many factors. Several are discussed below.

The Marketing Concept

The marketing concept has been defined as a business philosophy that places the customer at the center or focus of all business activity. Three principal ideas are associated with the marketing concept. First, the firm should be customer oriented; that is, the firm should attempt to provide meaningful products that provide for long-run satisfaction to the individual and products that match the welfare needs of society. Second, all individuals and departments in the firms, not merely the marketing department, should be concerned about customer satisfaction and welfare. Somehow that idea must be instilled in assembly-line workers, accountants, customer service people and all others whose actions have a direct effect on customer satisfaction. Finally, the marketing concept states that firms should concentrate on profitable sales, not just sales volume. Incorporated in this statement is the idea that through marketing a firm attempts to offer what customers want, rather than to sell what the firm can make.

Some firms have adopted the marketing concepts, others have not. Firms that are still production or sales oriented do manage to perform well in the marketplace. To understand why, one must look at a number of factors, including a deeper understanding of the marketing concept, characteristics of the industry, and the nature of competition.

The Marketing Concept: A Deeper Meaning.   The marketing concept is a normative prescription of how a business should operate. The philosophical foundation of the marketing concept is that in a free enterprise economy individual customer satisfaction is the primary value served by the economic system. Specifically, the creation of customer satisfaction is the rationale for the economic system. This rationale is far different from that in command economies, where values other than the economic well being of consumers are frequently followed. Examples of such command-economy values include the national development of heavy industry or the building up of defense capability.

The marketing concept emphasizes long-run customer satisfaction. The thinking goes that to provide this satisfaction firms must be customer oriented. Furthermore, at times people may not have appropriate alternatives and they, therefore, will accept products and services that provide some satisfaction, but not the entire satisfaction they would like. This is especially true in times of material or resource shortage.

During much of the economic history of the United States (and of the world) production has been the primary problem. However, in the United States during the early 1950s, production problems were largely solved. In fact, many firms found themselves with the capability to produce more than they could sell. Consequently, it was during a time of economic affluence that the idea of the marketing concept was first discussed.

Industry Characteristics.   Particular industry characteristics, usually relating to supply considerations, may allow a firm not to adopt the marketing concept and still be successful—but only to a limited extent, since all firms face either direct or indirect competition. Consider the oil industry today. The dependence on petroleum products is enormous in our lives. We use petroleum-related products for heating, transportation, and deriving chemicals used in wide ranges of products. Without oil, our life-styles would be drastically affected.

Firms in an industry with supply problems, such as the oil industry, can frequently be nonmarketing oriented and still be successful. However, any firm not practicing the marketing concept may be somewhat vulnerable because competition can exist on more than one level. Exxon not only competes with Texaco, for instance, but also with other energy-producing companies such as those marketing natural gas or devices that transform solar energy into useful forms for man's immediate needs.

The U.S. Postal Service is a prime example of an organization losing out to other forms of competition. As the level of service provided by the Postal Service declined, long-distance telephone and private carriers such as United Parcel Service (UPS) have challenged the Postal Service, once the dominant carrier of personal and business messages.

Nature of Competition.   Firms in industries characterized by monopolies or weak forms of competition may also not practice the marketing concept and still be successful. Monopolies made possible by unique processes or product characteristics may give a firm a true advantage over competitors. To rely on this protection to guarantee demand and profits may be short-sighted. Failure to be concerned about customer satisfaction may lead to the firm's failure in the long run.

Perhaps the best example of an entire industry that refused to provide true customer satisfaction is the railroads. In the 1920s and 30s, the railroads in the United States were unchallenged and highly profitable. Today many railroads are either going broke, have gone broke, or are pleading for government relief. Competition from the trucking and airline industries and other factors have led to the decline of the railroads. Yet this decline did not have to occur. Refusal by the management of many large railroads to be concerned about the customer led in part to the decline of the railroad industry.[9]

Implementing the Marketing Concept

At the most fundamental level, implementing the marketing concept means introducing a customer orientation throughout the entire firm. Inculcating concern for customer satisfaction in every individual in the organization can be accomplished in at least three ways: first, top management must set the example; second,

---

[9]For a discussion on the railroads and marketing, see Theodore Levitt, "Marketing Myopia," *Harvard Business Review,* Vol. 38, No. 4 (July-August, 1960), p. 45. Also see Levitt's retrospective commentary on "Marketing Myopia" in the *Harvard Business Review,* Vol. 53, No. 5 (September-October, 1975), p. 11.

organizational changes may be required; and third, a procedure to collect and process information from the marketplace must be established.

The leadership role in effectively implementing the marketing concept is critical. If top management merely espouses the philosophy of the marketing concept, but by plan or example does not attempt to practice it, little will change in the firm. Top management, including the president, must understand and practice the marketing concept. Additionally, top management must communicate the importance of the marketing concept to the firm's employees.

Some organizational changes may be necessary to implement the marketing concept. Perhaps the most fundamental change that many firms must make is to centralize all marketing activities under one person. This allows coordination of the entire marketing effort. Secondly, other organizational changes may be required to insure that the marketing aspect of various decisions are considered before decisions are finalized. Such an example would be the inclusion of the top marketing executive, and perhaps the sales manager, in the firm's executive committee.

To be customer oriented, a firm must know and understand present and potential customers. To achieve this understanding and knowledge, an organized system or method of communicating with customers is frequently required. Marketing research and the marketing information system are usual methods used to establish the necessary communication. These topics are discussed in Chapter 7.

The Role for Marketing Management

Marketing is one important aspect of a business. Firms may prosper without good marketing but usually only in the short run. Because marketing management is fundamental to a business, marketing management should play a large role in developing and formulating company strategy. Also, because marketing is the revenue-earning function in a firm, marketing factors must be considered in most business decisions. The marketing function is not always dominant, but how marketing factors relate to other business decisions must always be considered.

Marketing is not the entire business. Chief executive officers must be concerned about more than marketing. However, marketing is fundamental and important to most businesses—or it should be. Therefore, marketing management should play an important role in guiding and directing the entire organization.

MARKETING MANAGEMENT FUNCTIONS

The traditional functions that managers at all levels engage in are analysis, planning, implementation, and control. These functions have been mentioned previously, and the planning function will be discussed in more detail later in this chapter. However, a more specific statement of what managers do has been presented by Peter Drucker. A discussion of Drucker's points relating to marketing management follows.[10]

---

[10]Drucker, *op. cit.,* p. 400.

Managers Set Objectives

Marketing managers deal with objectives in at least two ways. First, marketing managers may assist in the objective-setting process for the whole firm. Many factors are considered when the firm's objectives are stated. Nevertheless, marketing must offer input and assistance in the development of the firm's objectives.

The firm's objectives are not based entirely on opportunities, resources available, or marketing factors. Instead, these objectives are related to the values of the owners and managers. To a degree, the firm or corporate objectives are value related. For example, consider the folklore about how objectives differ between small and large businesses. Big business objectives are frequently enshrined in terms of growth, market share, and return on investment. Small business owners, on the other hand, may have objectives relating to things other than simply business success. Examples include providing a place of employment for family members, providing a steady income, or providing the necessary financial freedom to do other things that are more interesting.

In addition to being value related, objectives are only meaningful within a specified time frame. For example, the meaning of the commonly stated objective of profit maximization depends on the time period specified. Different marketing strategies are required for long-term profit maximization than for short-term profit maximization. Well-managed organizations have both short- and long-range objectives. Short-range objectives are usually stated for periods of one year or less; long-range objectives are for periods greater than one year.

The second way marketing managers deal with objectives is by setting specific objectives for the marketing area. The objectives set for the marketing area must be consistent with and supportive of the firm's overall objectives. Marketing area objectives frequently cover such aspects as market share, sales accounts or customers, and products. Both the level and growth of these factors can be important. For example, a firm's objectives may be stated as follows:

1. Maintain 20 percent share of the market.
2. Increase sales by 10 percent.
3. Develop 20 new retail accounts.
4. Introduce one new product into national distribution.

Once the marketing objectives are stated, they must be communicated to the members of the organization. The members of the organization will have to assist the marketing manager in achieving the objectives. If the objectives are not communicated effectively, they cannot serve as a focus for organizational effort.

The actual process of setting objectives can assist a manger in at least two ways. First, setting objectives and formulating plans to achieve the objectives are not totally unrelated activities. Therefore the one contributes to the other. Second, many firms employ a Management by Objectives (MBO) system. These systems frequently stress setting objectives from the bottom up. When this occurs, the objective-setting process can also serve as a method of motivation. When managers are allowed some freedom to set objectives within certain overall guidelines, these same managers are frequently more committed to the objectives and therefore try harder to accomplish them.[11]

Managers Organize

Organizing refers to building the type of organization necessary to achieve the previously stated objectives. Two typical marketing organizations are shown in Illus. 6-1 and 6-2. The first organization revolves around functions to be performed. Sales, advertising, marketing research, and physical distribution are com-

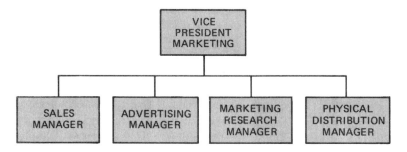

Illus. 6-1   Functional Marketing Organization

mon functional areas in marketing. Purely functional organizations are best suited to firms with a relatively small product mix of similar or related products.

The second organizational chart, shown in Illus. 6-2, depicts a typical marketing organization where product managers are used. The product manager may be

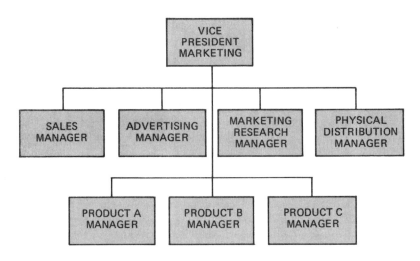

Illus. 6-2   Product Manager Marketing Organization

---

[11]For a complete discussion of MBO, see George S. Odiorne, *Management by Objectives* (New York City: Pitman Publishing Corporation, 1965).

given all or some of the responsibility for the product or products he or she is managing. Because of this, product managers must spend a lot of time in coordinating efforts among the various functional areas of their products.

Organizing includes tasks other than designing the organization. First, individuals must be selected to perform the various functions. Second, authority must be delegated to the chosen individuals. The authority delegated should be commensurate to the responsibility placed on the individual. In summary, organizing implies setting up the structure and selecting the people who will accomplish the objectives.

Managers Motivate

After objectives are set and the organization built, the manager must direct the organization toward the objectives. Direction is accomplished through effective leadership, motivation, and communication.

One of the prime areas for motivation is sales. Mental attitude frequently is *the* factor that is the difference between a successful and an unsuccessful sales representative. Personal employee motivation, important in all phases of management, is especially important in the marketing and sales area.[12]

The manager has many tools available for use in motivation. First, clear objectives and a healthy organizational climate can be of great value. Second, a manager can use pay, promotion, and job positions as tools to achieve motivation.

Leadership is also important for marketing managers. Implementing a true customer orientation in an organization requires that top management be committed to the goal and that top managers support and encourage the goal in others.

Managers Measure

Perhaps one of the most important tasks a manager can undertake is to measure and evaluate performance. The marketing organization in total, and each person in it, must be evaluated and controlled. This process requires that standards of measurement be set and actual performance compared with these standards.

The setting of standards and their comparison with actual performance allows management by exception to take place. *Management by exception* implies that managerial time and attention will be devoted to an employee or process only when the employee or process is failing to perform adequately. Consider a sales manager who has established minimum target goals for each of the firm's regional areas. Only when the target goals (sales quotas) are not being met is the sales manager forced to devote special time and attention to that particular area. The process of measuring facilitates management by exception.

Additionally, measuring is valuable to a marketing manager in a number of other ways. The value of sales quotas has already been mentioned. The effectiveness of advertising and sales promotion devices can also be evaluated. Finally, measuring allows a marketing manager to better perform the last and final function: developing people.

---

[12]For insight into the role of motivation Og Mandino, *The Greatest Salesman in the World* (New York City: Frederick Fell Publishers, Inc., 1968) is highly recommended.

Managers Develop People

Marketing managers must develop people, including themselves. Indeed, one of the basic functions of management is to train and coach people to improve and to learn from their experiences, successes, and mistakes. Developing people is valuable to the individuals involved as well as to the organization. Good sales managers were once fledgling sales representatives. Product managers probably performed many functions, including that of sales representative, before moving to more responsible positions. The growth individuals go through is a function of both their own interest and their determination to improve, plus the coaching and training provided by their superiors.

All five of the basic managerial functions are somewhat interrelated. Setting objectives assists in organizing as well as in motivating, measuring, and improving performance. Through good organization, communication is improved; and good communication assists managers in measuring and developing personnel.

These five functions are not fundamentally different from the more common list of analysis, planning, implementations, and control. A comparison of the two ways of looking at the manager's job is shown in Illus. 6-3.

SETTING OBJECTIVES REQUIRES
1. Analysis
2. Planning

ORGANIZING REQUIRES
1. Analysis
2. Planning
3. Implementation

MOTIVATING AND COMMUNICATING REQUIRES
1. Analysis
2. Planning
3. Implementation

MEASURING REQUIRES
1. Analysis
2. Planning
3. Implementation
4. Control

DEVELOPING PEOPLE REQUIRES
1. Analysis
2. Planning
3. Implementation
4. Control

Illus. 6-3   **Comparison of Managerial Functions**

MARKETING MANAGEMENT'S PRIMARY TASK

Of all the tasks that marketing managers must perform, perhaps the most important is that of developing an effective marketing strategy. Strategic planning was discussed in general terms in Chapter 2. Marketing management strategic planning includes three different, but necessarily interrelated steps: (1) identifying opportunities, (2) selecting a target market, (3) formulating a marketing mix.[13]

Identifying Opportunities

The old adage about opportunity staring us in the face (if we could just see it) is probably true. Frequently the ability to see an opportunity is the key difference between a truly effective and an ineffective marketer. Opportunities usually are all around us, if we could only see them.

As a firm's management seeks opportunities, two factors usually narrow the search. First, the firm's resources may severely limit the types of opportunities a firm is able to take advantage of. Resources, here, mean more than financial resources alone. Perhaps equally important as financial resources are human resources, such as management capability. Sometimes physical assets such as production capacity may be important. A resource of growing importance is information, which is discussed in the next chapter.

The role of resources in limiting a firm's search for opportunities is complemented by the firm's objectives. The objectives of a firm may define the type of business a firm should be in, and may also include statements relating to growth, use of outside capital, and even the type of organization the business will have. These objectives narrow the types of opportunities that managers seek. However, a firm may find that the constraints of resources and objectives leave the organization with no promising opportunities. In this situation either the firm's resources must be expanded or its objectives changed.

Selecting a Target Market

The second step in marketing management strategic planning involves selecting a target market. Naturally target market selection is related to the favorable opportunities identified in the search for opportunities.

To select a target market means to consciously choose a total or portion of a market that the firm hopes to satisfy with an offering. The target market, defined as people with purchasing power and the willingness and authority to buy, is chosen on a number of bases. First, the market must be of sufficient size to merit the time and resources expended on cultivating the market. Second, the target market must have either an unmet, or poorly met, need for certain benefits or satisfactions. Third, the target market must offer the possibility that members of

---

[13]The basis for this discussion is drawn from E. Jerome McCarthy, *Basic Marketing: A Managerial Approach* (Homewood, Ill.: Richard D. Irwin, Inc., 1978), p. 52.

the market will respond in a like or similar manner (homogeneously) to the firm's marketing mix.

Target market selection is somewhat similar to market segmentation. However, the two concepts differ. For example, a market segmentation study may indicate that the market for wall-cleaning soap includes four market segments. However, two of the segments may be quite similar, but not identical, with respect to their needs, attitudes, and wants. In this situation the firm may decide that a marketing mix to appeal to the two similar segments will be appropriate. The previously identified market segments are now grouped together and treated as one target market. This strategy has been called a *combining strategy* by McCarthy.[14]

Target market selection is helpful to a marketing manager in many ways. First, the process of consciously selecting a target market partially insures that the marketing manager knows something about the people in the market. Second, when the target market is identified and defined, the marketing manager is given a standard by which to evaluate how well the firm is meeting the needs of the target market. Finally, knowing the characteristics of a target market is tremendously useful in the design of the marketing mix.

Two additional points on target market selection are worth noting. First, the selection of a target market does not mean that sales will be lower than if the entire market were chosen. Frequently a target market will include fewer people than the whole market, but purchases made by members of the target market may be at a higher level. Second, target marketing is one way to truly implement the marketing concept. The marketing concept incorporates the idea of customer orientation. By selecting a target market, and by providing an o fering to satisfy the needs of the target market, firms display a true customer orientation.

Formulating a Marketing Mix

The final stage in the marketing management strategic planning process is that of formulating a marketing mix. Formulating the marketing mix means mixing the right amount of promotion and proper distribution with the optimal price and product design. Of course, the marketing mix is designed to promote a satisfactory offering to the potential customers within the target market.

Ideally the marketing mix is also designed to provide for a differential advantage to the offering firm over competing firms. *Differential advantage* means that from a competitive viewpoint the firm has at least one unique aspect that gives it a strong position in the market with respect to achieving customer loyalty or patronage.

The differential advantage can come in many forms. In some cases a unique product design, perhaps covered by a patent, may provide a differential advantage. In other cases the differential advantage may be achieved through lower prices or superior distribution or promotion. Regardless of the factor from which the differ-

---

[14]*Ibid.*, p. 68.

ential advantage is derived, the marketing mix is ideally designed to incorporate the advantage.

The marketing mix is formulated by the marketing manager with knowledge about the target market and with the concept of differential advantage in mind. However, the actual process of designing a marketing mix is still considered more of an art than a science. No specific rules guide a marketing manager in that decision. Nevertheless, a few generalizations can be stated.

Consistency. One generalization that should be followed is that all elements of the marketing mix must be consistent and supportive. To most people, mink coats and diamond jewelry would be totally out of place in a discount store. The products and the outlets are not consistent and would probably confuse the buyer. It is extremely important that promotional programs be consistent with the other elements of the marketing mix. Promotional messages that promise more than the product can deliver or which present a message or theme that is inappropriate for a particular medium face a high possibility of failure. For example, consider the negative reactions of most consumers to a billboard advertisement for a *very* intimate personal care item.

Marketing managers must also keep in mind that what is appropriate or consistent must be evaluated from the consumer's viewpoint. Also, they must remember that what is appropriate or consistent changes, and may be in a continuing state of flux. Scrambled or mixed merchandising, discussed in Chapter 14, is ample evidence of this type of change.

Consideration of Competition. The marketing mix must also be designed with competition in mind. Generally direct, head-on competition with an established brand leader is rarely successful. On the other hand, some direct competition may be necessary. The marketer of a new food product really has little choice but to attempt to get widespread distribution in the same outlets, and perhaps even on the same shelves as its major competitors.

Feasibility. This generalization simply means that the marketing mix must be possible for the firm. For a small marketer to use a national television campaign is probably not feasible. Using low prices as a differentiating factor for a small convenience store is also probably not feasible.

Frequently beginning small business owners make unreasonable assumptions, because of their lack of experience, about the feasibility of their marketing mix. Common misconceptions of advertising and personal selling often lead to impracticable approaches. Expecting personal selling and advertising to make up for an inferior product is not reasonable, and therefore not feasible.

Matching Target Market Expectations. One of the key elements in designing a marketing mix is that the mix must match what the target market expects. Knowledge of what the target market expects can come only from a thorough understanding of the potential purchasers in the target market. This knowledge can come through intuition about the target market based on familiarity and experience or on formal market research conducted for that purpose.

The marketing management decision about the marketing mix is similar to most business decisions. A combination of information and managerial judgment is required, and the decision is made in spite of some uncertainty and, in fact, risk. The design of the marketing mix is an art. However, logical thinking and scientifically collected marketing information can be of value to the marketer as the marketing mix is created.

QUESTIONS AND ANALYTICAL PROBLEMS

1. Why do you think that Peter Drucker made the statement, "Marketing is the distinguishing, unique function of the business"?
2. Do you agree or disagree with the statement that only so much can be learned about management in the classroom?
3. Why is marketing management so critical to the success of many firms?
4. How are selling and marketing related? Will selling always be a necessary function in most businesses?
5. Can firms in a free enterprise economy survive and prosper if they fail to practice the marketing concept?
6. What are some of the most difficult obstacles to overcome when implementing the marketing concept in a firm?
7. Differentiate between firms providing short-run and long-run customer satisfaction. Illus-

trate your point using an industry example.
8. To insure that companies are marketing oriented, should company presidents always be chosen from the marketing end of the organization?
9. Do you believe that the managerial function of developing people is profit oriented?
10. Why are the three steps of the marketing management strategic planning process necessarily interrelated?
11. Of what value is it to a marketing manager to consciously select a target market?
12. How have convenience type stores established a differential advantage?
13. List a number of methods by which a marketer can achieve a differential advantage over competitors?
14. Marketing managers have been compared to good cooks. Why is this comparison made?

Case 6-1. DUNN GUN COMPANY

The Dunn Gun Company has a long and interesting history. The firm was founded by Michael J. Dunn in 1852. Mr. Dunn had emigrated from England in 1849. Along with his family, he eventually settled in a small town in Pennsylvania, where he opened a gun shop to sell and repair all types of guns. His son, Dennis, began working in the shop at age 14.

Dennis developed into an expert gunsmith and a gifted inventor. He developed and sold many designs for the major gun manufacturing companies in the United States and Europe. Eventually, Dennis and his brothers started their own company to market Dennis's inventions in the United States.

The guns were not manufactured by the Dunn Gun Company. Manufacturing was contracted out to various firms, mostly in Europe. After they were manufactured, the guns were shipped to the United States and distributed to authorized retail dealers. Prior to 1957 no company sales representatives were used. Orders and merchandise were received and shipped by mail or other delivery firms such as United Parcel Service. After 1957 company sales representatives were hired to call directly on retailers.

In the early 1960s the firm began to expand its product mix from guns to other types of sports equipment such as camping gear; fishing rods, reels, and accessories; hunting and outdoor clothing; and golf and tennis equipment. In 1960 the marketing organization was organized on a functional basis. The general sales manager was in charge of all marketing operations. He supervised the sales force, the advertising department, and a products department. The principal responsibility of the products manager was to arrange with suppliers to manufacture Dunn-designed equipment. Product development, distribution, and pricing were not part of the responsibility of the general sales manager.

In 1979 the organization chart of the marketing area still looked about the same, except that the general sales manager was now called the vice-president of marketing. Also, the Dunn Gun Company was no longer a family-owned business, having sold out to a major supplier. William Greenwell, a nonfamily member, was now the firm's president. Greenwell had been with the company since 1952, and therefore was knowledgeable about all aspects of the Dunn Gun Company. One other change had also occurred. Dunn Gun Company was manufacturing some of its own sports equipment.

Greenwell is considering reorganizing the entire firm, as well as the marketing area. He is currently contemplating which functions to make the marketing area responsible for, and also whether to use a functional or product manager type of organizational structure.

What do you recommend to Mr. Greenwell? In addition to thinking about functions the marketing area should be responsible for, you might draw an organization chart that you believe will be effective for the marketing area.

Some assumptions about the firm and product line may be necessary to create a detailed marketing area organization chart.

Case 6-2. FIRST NATIONAL BANK OF HUNTSVILLE

Mrs. Katherine H. Richards, president of the First National Bank of Huntsville, Indiana, recently read a *Wall Street Journal* article entitled "Consumers Find Credit Is Easy as Banks Compete for Business."[1] The article impressed Mrs. Richards in a number of ways, including her amazement at how liberal many big city banks were in granting relatively large amounts of consumer credit. An example was given in the article of one individual who received a $10,000 line of credit by simply completing a mail application. This line of credit was granted, even though the individual in question earned only $28,000 a year.

---

[1]Edward P. Foldessy, "Consumers Find Credit Is Easy to Get as Banks Compete for Business," *The Wall Street Journal,* March 19, 1979, pp. 1, 37.

Mrs. Richards also was astonished to learn that at the end of 1978 approximately 23 percent of the average American's paycheck was going to pay off interest and principal on consumer loans. This percentage figure was up significantly from the 1975 figure. The high inflation rate and the buy-now-pay-later philosophy were two reasons given for the increase in the use of consumer credit.

Mrs. Richards called in her three chief assistants, Gerald Gray, the marketing director, Matthew Wilson, the head commercial loan officer, and Karen Pearson, the head consumer loan officer, to discuss the article. Specifically, Mrs. Richards wondered whether the First National Bank of Huntsville should ease its consumer credit policies.

Karen spoke first: "We should establish two new programs," she began. "We need to start offering lines of credit by mail, and we must adopt a policy of automatically raising a customer's credit limit on Visa and Mastercharge cards when the limit is approached."

Matt Wilson, always profit-oriented, agreed. "Consumer loans in today's economic environment are our most profitable business. Let's increase them. Karen's ideas are good," he stated.

Gerald Gray, however, was less sure. He generally favored various methods to make banking easier and more enjoyable for customers, but in this particular situation he had different feelings.

"Maybe we should consider other factors beside just profit in this case," Gray argued.

Gray proposed two questions: First, is it best in the long run to offer consumers unlimited amounts of credit? He reasoned that the debts must eventually be paid. Second, when this occurs, and life-styles have to be adjusted to make the payments, will customers still be satisfied with First National for granting them so much credit?

At that point both Karen and Matt became irritated with Gerald's apparently inconsistent remarks. "What's the matter, Gerry; have you forgotten about the marketing concept you have been preaching to us for the last five years?" chided Matt.

Whose views do you support? Why?

7

JC marketing research

As American industry has grown more complex, business people have found themselves increasingly removed from the actual marketplace. At one time business owners met directly with their customers on a daily basis. Today, however, management often finds itself isolated from the buying public. As a result of this change, business people have found that keeping in touch with the needs and wants of the marketplace forces greater reliance on formalized information collection systems and less direct contact with the public. However, to effectively implement the marketing concept—that is, to find a need and to satisfy it—requires that marketing managers constantly monitor the ever-changing marketplace.

The J. C. Penney Company exemplified this change when it underwent a major strategy adjustment in 1977–78. Through market research Penney's management discovered that the only way to build market share and profitability was by capturing more of their customers' dollars. Research indicated that one way to do this was to offer more fashionable and contemporary clothing. Therefore, more than ever before, Penney's began to emphasize brand name fashion clothing.[1]

---

[1]"J. C. Penney's Fashion Gamble," *Business Week,* No. 2517 (January 16, 1978), p. 66.

ROLE OF MARKET RESEARCH
IN MARKETING MANAGEMENT

The actual work that management performs includes such basic functions as analysis, planning, implementation, and control. The one skill that predominates in all phases of management, however, is that of decision making. In fact, this term is often used interchangeably with the term management.

Illus. 7-1 presents a visual image of the decision-making process. The inputs into the system are managerial judgment and information. These inputs are then processed and a decision is made. The final outcome is a commitment to a certain course of action, one that leads to the accomplishment of one or more previously selected objectives. Whatever the result, feedback—which contributes to the judgment of the decision maker—occurs.

The figure demonstrates that information is one resource the manager utilizes in making decisions. Naturally current, relevant, and accurate information yields the best decisions.

Unfortunately marketing managers seldom have time to conduct lengthy, expensive data collections before making decisions. The business world often demands quick decisions. These kinds of decisions require marketers to rely heavily on judgment, and good judgment derives from having experience at basing decisions on limited information.

In some situations the cost to obtain the type of information necessary to make a completely informed decision is simply too high. For example, suppose that a sales manager expects next year's sales to vary between $50 and $60 million. Also, suppose it is known that if sales are $55 million or less, five sales representatives will be adequate; but if sales are over $55 million the sales manager needs to hire another salesperson. Along with this information it is known that the minimum cost to conduct a study to pinpoint sales is $25,000. In short, based on this information, the sales manager is simply better off to make the best sales estimate and

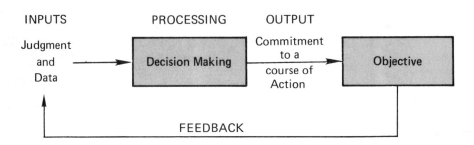

Illus. 7-1   The Decision-Making Process

Source: Ben M. Enis, *Marketing Principles—The Management Process* (2d ed.; Santa Monica: Goodyear Publishing Co., 1977), p. 272. Reprinted by permission.

then decide whether to hire an additional salesperson. The necessary research required to provide a better forecast of sales will cost more than a mistaken estimate.

One common element of business decision making is that of risk. Information collected through research may provide the potential for an accurate decision, but the information can never completely eliminate the risk involved. Risk can be reduced and, perhaps, better understood, but it can never be eliminated. Consequently, the role of marketing information collected for decision-making purposes is simply to create better and more informed decisions by marketing managers. Market research can help managers make better decisions, but it can never make the decisions for the managers.

THE MARKETING INFORMATION SYSTEM

More than ever before managers are recognizing that good marketing information leads to better marketing decisions, and, consequently, to more efficient, effective operation of a firm. Information is looked upon as a new resource, an addition to human resources (labor and management), physical resources (land and buildings), and financial resources (cash).

This new view means that information, like other resources, must be managed. The marketing information system concept has developed from this need to organize and manage marketing information. A *marketing information system* (abbreviated MIS) has been defined as:

> . . . a structured, interacting complex of persons, machines, and procedures designed to generate an orderly flow of pertinent information, collected from both intra- and extra-firm sources, for use as the basis for decision making in specified responsibility areas of marketing management.[2]

The definition stresses the need to collect data both from inside the firm and from outside in the marketing environment. A careful analysis of monthly sales to determine if actual and projected sales were in line exemplifies data collection within the firm. However, an analysis of internal sales is often insufficient. The firm's management is also interested in sales volume relative to competitive firms, since management must be concerned about its share of the market relative to its competitors. Thus, information from both inside and outside the firm must be gathered and analyzed.

The MIS concept also emphasizes the need to collect data on a continuing, regular basis. This differs from the traditional role of marketing research which directs resources into particular problem areas that are of concern at any one time. For example, if a firm is considering whether it should market a new product, marketing research is directed at measuring and describing potential market segments. However, as the product is launched, the research staff is asked to monitor

---

[2]Samuel V. Smith, Richard H. Brien, and James E. Stafford (eds.) *Readings in Marketing Information Systems* (Boston: Houghton Mifflin Company, 1968), p. 7.

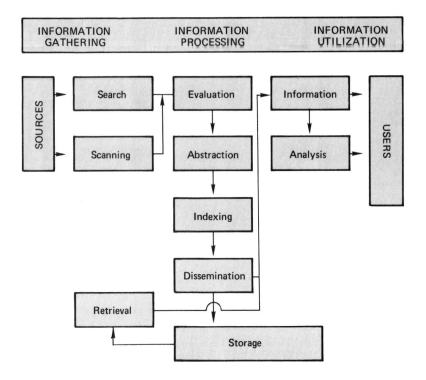

Source: Adapted from Philip Kotler, "A Design for the Firm's Marketing Nerve Center," *Business Horizons,* Vol. 9, No. 3 (Fall, 1966), p. 63.

Illus. 7-2   **The Marketing Information System**

and evaluate the advertising for the new product. This monitoring is a function of the ongoing marketing information system.

The MIS system within the firm is made up to accomplish information gathering, to process information, and to facilitate information utilization. Illus. 7-2 clarifies these functions.

First, data are gathered from primary and secondary sources. Next, the data are processed. This stage includes subjective evaluation of how accurate, credible, and relevant the data are. Also included is an abstraction of the data into a more concise, usable form, and indexing and disseminating the same data. After processing, the body of data is called information and is ready for direct use by marketing managers. The key element in the design and implementation of any MIS system is that it must meet the needs and capabilities of the users.

Marketing research serves as one of the data collection elements of the MIS system, and it is perhaps the most important element. Performance of marketing research is best illustrated by discussing the steps taken to conduct a market research project.

THE MARKET RESEARCH PROJECT

Marketing research, defined as "the systematic, objective, and exhaustive search for and study of the facts relevant to any problem in the field of marketing," is accomplished by completing marketing research projects.[3] Usually a research project is initiated when a problem is encountered. But the case can be made that market research should be used *before* problems arise. For example, one of the most important management functions is that of setting objectives. A market research project to assist management in the objective-setting process may be far more valuable than conducting a study a year later to determine why the objectives were not met. Regardless of when the study is conducted, however, six steps which lead to completion of the project are followed. The initial step is problem formulation.

Problem Formulation

Problem formulation is the recognition that for some reason a goal or objective of the firm is not being met. The problem formulation stage concentrates on choosing various alternatives related to why the goal or objective is not being achieved. As an example, suppose for the last three months that sales have been 10 percent below expected levels. In the problem formulation stage two or three potential causes of falling sales will be identified. For example, further investigation may reveal that sales are normal in all sections of the country except one. Given that situation, one would expect the problem to relate to the personal sales function or to the fact that a competitor is taking extremely aggressive action in that one geographical area. Research may then be used to investigate those two alternatives.

One aspect of problem formulation is identifying the problem situation model. A *problem situation model* is a formal or informal model that a manager believes in and that relates desired outcomes to specific variables affecting the outcomes.[4] Problem situation models are important because they provide researchers with ideas and clues about which variables may be important to investigate.

The output of the problem formulation stages is a sentence that asks a question which relates two or more potentially measurable variables. For example, is the decline of sales in Territory *A* related to the poor performance of the sales manager? Or, is the decline of sales in Territory *A* due to the introduction of a new product by our major competitor?

Research Design

Research design is the second step of the marketing research project. The output of this step is a set of procedures to follow to answer the question stated

---

[3]Richard D. Crisp, *Marketing Research* (New York City: McGraw-Hill, Inc., 1957), p. 3.
[4]Donald S. Tull and Del I. Hawkins, *Marketing Research Meaning, Measurement, and Method* (New York City: Macmillan, Inc. 1977), p. 38.

in the research problem. The research design specifies the exact data to be collected, the data collection methods, and the types of data collection forms to be utilized. In general, the research design is the blueprint the researcher follows for guidance in conducting the study.

The research design includes the plan, the structure, and the strategy necessary to conduct the research.[5] The research plan is an outline of every step the researcher will follow. The research structure states the actual variables of interest and explains how the variables are related. For example, Illus. 7-3 pictures what the owners of a convenience store chain perceived as the variables leading to high gross operating margins. In this example, the managers believe that heavy auto traffic, neighborhood loyalty, convenience of location, operating hours, and items carried, along with radio and newspaper advertising, yield a high level of gross operating margin.

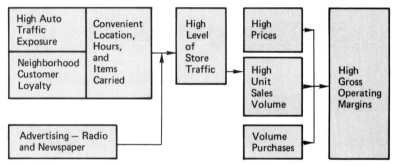

Source: Adapted from Donald S. Tull and Del I. Hawkins, *Marketing Research* (New York City: Macmillan, Inc., 1977), p. 40.

Illus. 7-3   **Structure of Variables Leading to
                            High Gross Operating Margins**

The research strategy is more specific than the research plan and includes the exact methods to collect, organize, and analyze the data to solve the research problem. Various methods of data collection are discussed later in this chapter.

Selecting the Sample

The next important step in the research project is choosing the sample. Certain types of market research use large samples. For instance, W.R. Simmons and Research Associates, a collector of data on magazine readership, usually gathers samples in the range of 15,000 readers. The researchers believe that such a large sample is necessary to obtain accurate statistics on magazines with limited

---

[5]Fred N. Kerlinger, *Foundations of Behavioral Research* (New York City: Holt, Rinehart & Winston, 1964), p. 275.

readership. On the other hand, a small business owner, concerned about potential customers' perception of the value of a new, personally developed product, may give the product to ten persons believed to be average customers. These persons may be asked to use the product to see how well it satisfies their needs; thus, an individual business owner's decision will be based on this more limited selection.

The key to sample selection is that the sample must be representative of the overall population. Ideally the most representative samples are random; that is, each member in the population has an equal chance of being selected for the sample. However, random samples are often difficult to select and expensive. These problems force market researchers to rely on convenience samples, on quota samples, or on some other form of nonrandom sample. The question the researcher must attempt to answer is: Will a nonrandom sample affect the results enough to make them invalid?

The key to answering the question often rests on the researcher's judgment. The important point is that the sample is representative of the population concerning those factors of interst to the researcher. A sample of women from one church group and from one local PTA, for instance, may be representative of various types of women's hair care problems; thus, a firm interested in studying the problems women have with hair care products could derive an adequate sample from such a relatively small group.

Data Collection

The next stage in the research project is data collection. If data collection is not carried out conscientiously, the project may fail to assist management decision making no matter how well the project is planned.

A common form of data collection is interviewing. Interviewers are given a list of names of people and their addresses. The interviewers contact each person on the list and conduct a personal interview.

What type of person makes the best interviewer? The answer varies and is in many cases dependent entirely on the specific situation. The subject matter of the interview, the sex and social class of the respondent, and numerous other factors can affect interviewer effectiveness. One field director in a market research firm listed the following qualifications for an interviewer. Notice that the field director felt that the interviewer should be a woman.

> She should be healthy, active, energetic, intelligent, have a sense of humor, be tactful, persistent, adaptable, tolerant, interested in people, with a sense of responsibility, careful attention to details, etc. She should be 25 to 55 years, have 20 hours available including A.M., P.M., and weekends, have high school or better, a car, legible handwriting, stenographic skills, membership in organizations. She should be willing to work on demand for a relatively low hourly rate.[6]

---

[6]Gerald Zaltman and Philip C. Burger, *Marketing Research: Fundamentals and Dynamics* (Hinsdale, Ill.: Dryden Press, 1975), p. 298.

It should be understood, however, that this description is probably most suitable for a door-to-door interviewer whose subject matter is common household products and problems.

Data Analysis

After the data have been collected they must be analyzed. Often data analysis is accomplished by computing some basic calculations in the data. Example calculations include averages, percentages, or cross tabulations. Cross tabulation is the process of classifying people on the basis of two variables. Using the example of women's hair care problems, assume the researcher wondered whether the use of hair spray differed by age. To determine this, Table 7-1 was computed. From the table the researcher was able to see that the tendency to use hair spray decreases as age increases. Whereas 86 percent of the 15-to-25 year age group use hair spray, only 40 percent of the 45-and-over group use hair spray.

Table 7-1   **Cross Tabulation Table**

		Age Categories		
	15–25	26–35	36–45	45 and over
Use Hair Spray	43(86%)	35(70%)	26(52%)	20(40%)
Don't Use Hair Spray	7(14%)	15(30%)	24(48%)	30(60%)

Data analysis can be simple or complex. Regardless of the level of complexity, however, the general purpose of the analysis remains the same: to summarize and present the data in such a way that drawing implications from the data is facilitated.

Preparing the Research Report

The final stage in the research project is preparing the reserach report. Uppermost in preparing the final report is considering the reader (or audience, if the report is to be presented orally). The purpose of the report is to convey to the reader in a clear, explicit manner the findings and implications of the research project.

The report must present both the strong and weak points of the research. The researcher has an obligation to recognize—but not necessarily to emphasize—unanswered questions or weaknesses in the research project. However, as with almost any aspect of human interaction, the research report should be marketed to the readers in such a way that the strengths of the study are evident to the decision maker. Marketing research can reduce uncertainty and help managers and proprietors make better decisions. However, the element of judgment will always be required in both evaluating the research and making the decision for which the research was conducted.

METHODS OF DATA COLLECTION

Data collection usually means the collecting of information from and about people. Although other types of information can occasionally be considered market research (i.e., product performance data), the focus of most market research efforts is concerned with what people think, what people do, and what people have done.[7]

Marketing information can be collected in either primary or secondary form. Secondary information, usually published material, originates for some reason other than the immediate problem facing the researcher. Nevertheless, the information may still be very useful in solving a number of market research problems. Sources of secondary data include various local state and federal government agencies and industry trade associations. Census material is perhaps the most frequently used secondary data in market research.

Secondary data should always be consulted before any data collection is undertaken, because obtaining it is less costly in time and money than primary data. However, there are times when secondary data will not answer the research question. In these situations primary data must be collected. The three principal ways to collect primary data are surveys, experiments, and observation.[8]

Surveys

Information from surveys is collected by asking respondents questions about current states (i.e., what is your age?), past behavior (i.e., what brand of catsup did you purchase last?) and future intentions (i.e., do you plan to purchase an automobile in the next month?). Surveys can generally be conducted personally, where an interviewee is asked the questions by a live interviewer, or impersonally, where the respondent answers questions on a printed questionnaire. The type of questions on the survey can also vary. What attributes are most important to you about your favorite grocery store? exemplifies a total free response question. Please indicate whether each of the following attributes which describe grocery stores are not important, somewhat important, or very important to you in your selection of a favorite grocery store. Attributes such as prices, quality of products, and cleanliness of the store exemplify a closed-end question. Generally closed-end questions are fairly easy to analyze; unfortunately they frequently provide only superficial responses. Open-end questions, on the other hand, are difficult to analyze and interpret but do provide the researcher insight into what thoughts and concerns the person has.

Surveys have both advantages and disadvantages. Their major advantage is the ease and speed by which large amounts of data can be collected. Also, in some situations, surveys represent the only method to collect data. For example, if management is interested in the attitudes nonpurchasers have about the firm's product, asking questions is usually the only method available to get the information.

[7]Philip Kotler, *Marketing Management: Analysis, Planning and Control* (3d ed.; Englewood Cliffs, N.J.: Prentice-Hall Inc., 1976), p. 129.
[8]*Ibid.*, p. 429.

Survey methods also have some disadvantages. One of the greatest of these is that respondents may not provide accurate information for a number of reasons. Frequently questions are asked which require respondents to call upon their memory (i.e., when did you last buy flowers for someone?). Some questions delve into private or personal topics that some people do not like to answer (i.e., what was your household income last year before taxes?). Finally, some questions are more likely to elicit socially acceptable responses rather than true ones (i.e., what were your dollar expenditures on alcoholic beverages last month?). Either because of memory lapse, a desire not to reveal personal information, or a desire to appear socially acceptable, information may be provided by respondents which is simply not correct. Consequently, a market researcher must be careful not to accept survey information totally at face value.

Experiments

Surveys, the most frequently conducted type of market research, are not necessarily the only type. Experiments are one type of data collection being used more and more frequently. Experiments are different from surveys in that the researcher plays a more active role in the study. The researcher actually changes a variable of interest, which causes a reaction by the people involved in the study.

One very successful example of the experiment is the study done when instant coffee was first introduced in the United States. Instant coffee was a disappointing seller. Survey research conducted on the topic revealed that coffee drinkers, in general, didn't like the taste of instant coffee. However, when taste tests were given, few respondents were able to tell the difference between instant and regular coffee. Something was obviously wrong.

To solve the problem, the following experiment was conducted.[9] The researchers devised two shopping lists. The lists included one-half pound of hamburger, two loaves of Wonder Bread, one bunch of carrots, one can of Rumford's baking powder, two cans of Del Monte peaches, five pounds of potatoes, and a can of either drip-grind Maxwell House coffee or Nescafe instant coffee. Next, one hundred women were asked to visualize a word picture of the type of woman who would purchase the shopping list. Fifty women evaluated the list with the instant coffee; another 50 women evaluated the list with the regular coffee. On the list that included instant coffee as the final item, 48 percent described the woman who would make those purchases as being lazy, a person who did not plan her purchases well. On the list that included the Maxwell House regular coffee, less than 10 percent made the same criticism. Obviously instant coffee at that time carried the connotation of an easy way out. Any homemaker buying instant coffee was thought to provide inadequate care for her family. The results of the study were used by the Nescafe product manager to alter the advertising theme and thereby overcome the bias against instant coffee.

---

[9]Much of this discussion was obtained from Mason Haire's article, "Projective Techniques in Marketing Research," *Readings in Marketing*, edited by Phillip R. Cateora and Lee Richardson (New York City: Appleton-Century-Crofts, 1967), p. 149.

The Nescafe study was an experiment, because the researchers controlled the subjects' response to the regular coffee list or to the Nescafe list. The researchers were interested in whether a difference would occur in how women evaluated the potential purchaser of the shopping list. Experiments are often conducted when test marketing new products and when attempting to determine which of two advertisements is more effective.

Observation

Observation is often used when survey questioning fails to produce the desired information. As shown in Illus. 7-4, a researcher may face four different situations when attempting to gather information from respondents.[10]

The first situation occurs when the respondent has both the ability and the willingness to verbalize the type of information desired. In this situation, the researcher asks direct questions. Two other situations require indirect questioning; that is, questioning techniques which make it easier for subjects to respond because potential embarrassment is reduced, potential hurt feelings are eliminated, or because the respondents may simply not have the ability to put their feelings into words if asked a direct question. The fourth situation, when respondents have neither the ability nor the willingness to answer, is the situation when observation is most appropriate.

		HAS ABILITY TO VERBALIZE	
		YES	NO
WILLING TO VERBALIZE	YES	DIRECT QUESTIONING	INDIRECT QUESTIONING
	NO	INDIRECT QUESTIONING	OBSERVATION

Illus. 7-4   **When to Ask and When to Observe**

Merely observing behavior and attempting to infer underlying beliefs and attitudes is a difficult process because different people can engage in the same behavior for different reasons. The following example is illustrative.

> In a supermarket a man with his arms full of cans throws the armful into a cart at the beginning of the aisle. He pulls the cart by the front along with him through the aisle. He examines a Rinso Blue box and reads the front for a moment. Then he walks back to the beginning of the aisle and looks at Oxydol, regular size. He hesitates, then picks up a large package of All with the rosebush offer. He then reads an All box (in a display with other All boxes) and puts it back. He backs down the aisle halfway and reads the Dreft box, then further up he reads the Ivory Snow box. He then takes a box of Instant Fels and puts it in the cart.

[10]Adapted from Paul E. Green and Donald S. Tulls, *Research for Marketing Decision* (3d ed.; Englewood Cliffs, N.J.: Prentice-Hall, Inc., 1975), p. 158.

What was the man looking for? Was he comparing prices? That's hard to tell. When asked various questions the respondent answered as follows:

> *I am allergic and was looking for one with* **soap** *marked on it. I have a terrible reaction to detergents.* He pointed to Salvo and said, "That kills me." He went on to discuss septic tanks, saying that people with septic tanks are told not to use detergents, that it is against the law in some places, and related an army experience. The observer commented that the shopper had a hard time choosing and asked, "Haven't you found one that you like?" The shopper said, "Every once in a while I get allergic to the one I am using so I have to switch." The observer asked, "Do you think this Instant Fels will do it?" He answered, "I haven't tried it. I hope so."[11]

Frequently only observation will provide the information necessary to make a better decision. Conducting a correctly designed observation study, however, is not easy. And, just as importantly, interpreting the data collected from observation studies is difficult. In fact, different researchers may draw different conclusions from the same data. Nevertheless, observation is one method the researcher has available to provide information on a topic area that is difficult to research.

In summary, data can be collected from respondents through surveys, experiments, or observation. Each data collection method has its advantages in terms of both expense and the validity of the data collected. The researcher must weigh the costs relative to the advantages of each method and choose the most appropriate method for each research project.

TYPES OF MARKET RESEARCH

Market research can be conducted on many topics. Typical problems include measuring the size and location of potential markets, identifying and selecting market segments, product testing, and measuring communication effectiveness and consumer attitudes. Each of these areas must be discussed in some detail.

Market Potential Studies

One of the most important tasks of marketing research is measuring and predicting the future sales levels in a particular market for a specific product or product type. Marketers would ideally like to know if adequate demand exists for a product before deciding whether to develop and market that product. Product failures are so expensive that research is often a requirement. Retailers, likewise, attempt to determine whether a town, city, or area of a city will support a new store before the decision is made to open the store.

Sales Forecasting.   Frequently the most important piece of information necessary for management planning is the sales forecast. The sales forecast is used as a planning base in both the marketing and financial areas. Consequently, the accuracy of the sales forecast is important.

---

[11]William D. Wells and Leonard A. Lo Sciuto, "Direct Observation of Purchasing Behavior," *Journal of Marketing Research,* Vol. III, No. 3 (August, 1966), p. 227.

Top-Down Method. One method to compute the sales forecast is the top-down method. The top-down sales forecast procedure requires an initial estimate of what industry sales would be under various levels of marketing effort in a given time period. This figure, called the market potential, is actually a function or series of points. The graph in Illus. 7-5 demonstrates that for a given time period sales could fall along any point on the chart depending on how much industry marketing effort was expended. Marketing effort is the entire industry's expenditures for items such as advertising, sales representatives' salaries, and sales promotion. If industry marketing effort is projected at Point *A,* industry sales will be forecast at Point *S.*

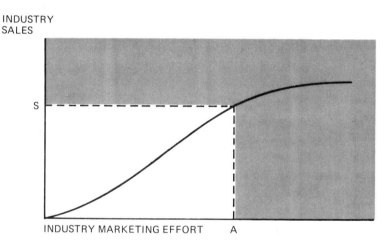

INDUSTRY SALES

S

INDUSTRY MARKETING EFFORT   A

Illus. 7-5   **Industry Market Potential**

The next step involved in the top-down method is forecasting the company's market share. Company market share is the percentage of total industry sales that the firm expects to capture. For example, if industry sales of fast-food hamburgers are 10,000,000, and McDonald's sells 1,200,000, McDonald's market share is 1,200,000 ÷ 10,000,000, or 12 percent. Market share is an indicator of the amount and effectiveness (how good are McDonld's advertisements compared to Burger King's?) of the firm's marketing effort.

The development of a company's sales potential function (as shown in Illus. 7-6) occurs after the market share has been determined.

To determine the sales forecast, managers select the level of marketing effort they either desire or can afford. The computation of the sales forecast in this manner emphasizes the idea that sales result from a marketing effort; that is, sales result from the firm's expenditures for activities such as product development, advertising, and distributor development.

Build-Up Method. A second method to forecast sales is the build-up method. One aspect of this technique involves thorough questioning of the firm's sales

COMPANY
SALES

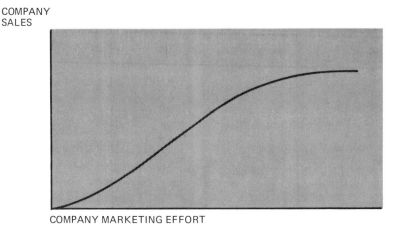

COMPANY MARKETING EFFORT

Illus. 7-6   Company Sales Potential Function

representatives. This method, called the sales force composite, requires sales representatives to estimate the volume of sales they will most likely make for each of the products in the product line. The total forecast is computed by adding the various estimates of each of the sales representative and by adjusting the figure on the basis of management's judgment.

Each of the two sales forecasting methods are effective in given situations. Many firms utilize two or three different sales forecasting methods and look for consistency in the results.

The Measure of Market Areas. The tie between geographical areas and marketing is very strong. Sales representatives are frequently assigned geographical territories within which to travel; and promotional expenditures —advertising, for example—are often allocated to geographic market areas. Finally, store, warehouse, and plant location are of vital concern to many marketers.

Establishment of Sales Territories. The direction and management of the sales force is often critical to the success of a firm. The often repeated statement that "you don't have marketing without a sale" is undoubtedly true. Effective sales force management depends, to a degree, on the definition of the sales territories. Ideally sales representatives are assigned to sales territories that have the same sales potential and work load. Work load is usually determined by the number and size of customers and by the travel time required to serve the customer. If the work load and sales potential of all sales territories are approximately equal, quota setting and sales force evaluation and compensation becomes a much easier job. Marketing research is often used to assist sales managers in properly determining the firm's sales territories.

Location of Retail Stores. Location is one of the most important determinants of the success of a retail store. Regardless of product mix, price level, or sales promotion, a poorly located store will have a difficult time making a profit. This is especially true when competition in the marketplace is fairly strong.[12]

In the past the usual emphasis was on the location of a single store. Today, however, the location of shopping centers is of equal or more importance. Again, market research can be tremendously valuable in selecting optimum sites. Data most frequently utilized in store and shopping center location include income and other descriptive characteristics of households in the vicinity of the proposed site and information on stores and shopping centers already serving the same marketplace.

Warehouse and Plant Location. Marketing research can also be extremely useful in determining the best sites for warehouse and plant location. Factors considered when making these decisions include the accessibility of highway, train, and air routes; the location of the firm's primary markets; and the relative costs of land, labor, utilities, and construction. Aspects of growing importance include the tax treatment of business firms by local and state governments and environmental constraints on construction. Warehouse and plant locations are complex decisions that tend to commit the firm's resources for a fairly long period of time. Consequently, managers and researchers attempt to collect and process as much relevant information as possible before making a decision.

Market Segmentation Research

Market research is often applied to determine market segments. Market segmentation research is a three-step process. First, groups of people who share certain similar traits are identified. Common bases for identifying these groups of customers are geographic location, demographic characteristics, socioeconomic characteristics, psychological characteristics, and product-related characteristics.[13] Next, the responsiveness of the identified group to various marketing tools is evaluated.[14] With this information at hand, management selects which market segments represent the best match between the firm's competencies and resources and the segment's sales potential. Target market is the name given to a chosen segment.

Market segments based on geographic location are identified by logic as well as by research. For example, the geographic market segment for warm clothing will obviously be found in cold climates. Geographic market segments can also be identified through a detailed analysis of sales records. Sales records, when maintained on a geographic basis, will quickly allow the researcher to determine where the product is performing best. However, before the cause of the sales differences can be attributed to geography alone, other potential causes must be eliminated. Examples of these other causes include more effective sales representatives, wider distribution, or more intense competition in one area than in another.

---

[12]A large amount of marketing research literature is available on retail location—for example, William Applebaum, "Methods for Determining Store Trade Areas, Market Penetration, and Potential Sales," *Journal of Marketing Research,* Vol. III, No. 2 (May, 1966), p. 127.

[13]Donald S. Tull and Del I. Hawkins, *Marketing Research* (New York City: Macmillan Inc. 1977), p. 554.

[14]Adapted from Ben M. Enis, *Marketing Principles, The Management Process* (2d ed.; Santa Monica: Goodyear Publishing Co., Inc., 1977), p. 241.

Market segments based on demographic or social economic variables are also determined by identifying differential purchase rates and patterns among different types of customers. Surveys are frequently conducted which ascertain both product usage patterns and demographic and socioeconomic variables. Cross classification procedures can then be used to identify if a particular age group, income level, etc., is associated with a particular brand or usage pattern (i.e., a heavy user).

Some firms utilize market information cards (referred to as warranty registration cards in the past) to determine whether the product appeals to a particular market segment. The product purchasers are asked to complete the card and mail it back to the manufacturer. The cards usually include demographic and socioeconomic data on the purchaser plus questions which attempt to determine where the purchaser found out about the product.

Psychological variables have been used with some success in market segmentation. Life-style is one type of psychological variable frequently employed to identify potential market segments. The most frequent applications of life-style market segmentation research requires that people state their agreement with a series of statements. An example statement is:

A person can save a lot of money by shopping around for bargains.

Agree Completely   _____
Agree Somewhat _____
Neither Agree or Disagree   _____
Disagree Somewhat   _____
Disagree Completely   _____

From a series of statements of this type, a researcher can determine whether a person has a convenience orientation, a price orientation, or some other shopping-orientation. Marketing managers then utilize those conclusions in designing creative promotional strategies, developing distribution policies, and evaluating how to price the firm's products.

Often market segments can be identified in terms of a product-related characteristic. Brand loyalty and product benefits are two examples. Researchers frequently identify heavy users of a product. The assumption behind this identification is that heavy users of a product are more inclined to respond favorably to a firm's marketing program than are light users. Also, segments are often identified in terms of the exact benefits derived from using the product. Consider toothpaste. Do people use it because it whitens teeth, because it freshens breath, or because it stops tooth decay? Customers desiring the same benefit from a product will often respond in a similar manner to a firm's marketing program.

When market segments have been identified, research must then be conducted to determine how the segments will respond to the firm's marketing effort. Test marketing is often employed to evaluate this segment responsiveness. For example, a firm may direct three different advertising appeals to three different market segments in a number of test market cities. The most responsive segment is then selected as the firm's target market for its overall product marketing program.

Product Research

Market research is frequently employed to test and evaluate the sales potential of new products. Frequently management wants an evaluation of whether a new product will be a marketing success before distribution to the entire marketplace is undertaken.

Concept Test. A *concept test* determines whether an idea for a product receives a favorable reaction from potential purchasers. People may be asked to view a film, a picture, or a sketch, or to listen to a description of the product. Then they are questioned about the product and their feelings toward it. How the product will fit into the consumers' life-style, what products currently used by the consumers will be replaced by the new product, and how much the new product will be worth to the consumers are questions that the concept test helps answer.

At each step in the new product testing process, management must decide to either stop the development process or to continue it. If the concept test has a disadvantage it is that negative evaluations of a new product sometimes result simply because the concept is new and different. In other words, when consumers cannot visualize how a product will enhance their life-style, they often respond negatively to it.

Bench Test. A second market research test in the development of a new product is the bench test. A *bench test* is conducted when a prototype of the product is developed. The prototypes, though often handmade, represent what would result from the production process if the product were given the final go-ahead by management. The example product is then exposed to potential customers and middlemen. The reaction of these two groups is then evaluated. Because the product is in a much more concrete form than during the concept test, consumers are often able to be more definite in their statements about preferences and their intentions to purchase.

Frequently a business analysis is conducted along with the bench test. A *business analysis* is the managerial process of projecting future levels of costs, revenues, and profits related to that product. If the business analysis indicates negative profits through all phases of product testing, the product development process is usually halted.

Test Marketing. The final step in the product development stage is the test market. The test market accomplishes two purposes. First, management will make a decision whether to put the product into full-scale distribution or to shelve the product—either temporarily or permanently—after test marketing. The projection of costs, revenues, and profits based on test market results is usually the most accurate available. Consequently, if test market results are poor, management may be fairly confident that the product will not be a success.

The second purpose of the test market is to develop the optimal marketing program. This program is developed by trying various combinations of price, distribution, promotion, and product alternatives in different test market cities. Because the number of combinations of price, product, promotion, and distribution are so great, management frequently devises four or five alternative marketing mixes. These alternative marketing programs are then tried in selected test market cities. Hopefully the best of the four or five marketing alternatives will be identified.

As discussed earlier in this chapter, the test market truly is an experiment. Here, the variable manipulated in the experiment is the type of marketing mix used in the test market city or cities. The variable of greatest interest is the level of sales under each of the test market conditions.

Test markets are not, however, without problems. One study found that of all the products receiving positive results in test markets run by well-managed companies, 60 percent of the products failed. Results of this type indicate that test markets are probably an unnatural situation in which everyone either consciously or unconsciously hopes the product will succeed. Consequently, sales personnel work harder, middlemen cooperate more fully, and the process of getting the product to the ultimate consumers is handled more effectively than in nontest market situations.

Competitors can (and do) disrupt test markets. Through such activities as price cutting, increasing or decreasing advertising budgets, and flooding the test market area with sales promotion devices such as cents-off coupons, two-for-one sales, and even free samples, competitors can confuse test marketing results. As a result of these activities, managers have difficulty interpreting test market results.

Test marketing also allows competitors to copy the new product. Consequently, the advantage of being the first in the marketplace may be sacrificed. In more than one case a competitor has actually beaten the test marketing firm into national distribution.

As with any marketing research techniques, test marketing has its advantages and disadvantages. The judgment and experience of marketing managers and researchers needs to be applied to the problem of whether to test market certain products.

MEASURES OF COMMUNICATION EFFECTIVENESS

Communication effectiveness refers to research conducted by marketers to evaluate advertising and other promotional efforts. The scope of these evaluations varies from measuring exposure to outdoor advertising on billboards to determining the cost per thousand of reaching various customers by different types of media.

Many difficulties in measuring communication effectiveness exist. Probably the most serious is that communication measurement techniques often measure only potential exposure to an advertising message, not how effective the message is in building sales. The usual assumption is that without proper exposure any message, regardless of its quality, will be only partially effective.

Television advertising illustrates the weakness of relying on communication measures of exposure. Television is considered a low involvement media because it requires little effort on the part of the viewer to absorb a commercial message. Consequently, little of what is supposedly observed on television is ever consciously remembered. Research conducted by asking respondents if they remember observing advertisements and the content of those advertisements usually results in a low percentage of positive answers. Yet sales figures indicate that commercials are very effective. Behavioral scientists hypothesize that television advertisements are stored in the unconscious part of viewers' minds. Then, when they see the product in a store, they are cued or reminded of the commercial and as a result purchase the product.[15]

There are three primary ways of evaluating television viewership. The A. C. Nielsen Company, for one, places audiometers on the television sets of a selected sample households. The audiometers tell the Nielson researchers when the television sets are on and to which channel the set is tuned. From these viewership figures, Nielson can compute rankings for the networks and the television shows being watched. The audiometers do not tell the researchers which members of the household are watching. The assumption is made that if the television is on, some household members are watching. Furthermore, the company assumes that the more sets are tuned to a particular channel, the more people in total are viewing a particular program. Firms utilize the Nielsen viewership ratings to decide the channels, programs, and time to advertise their products. Like the Nielsen Company, the advertisers assume that if people are watching a show, they will be exposed to the advertising aired during the show.

Exposure to various programs and advertisements is also measured by telephone surveys and by people keeping diaries about their television viewing habits. Telephone surveys are often conducted on a one-time basis to evaluate the popularity of a given TV show. A sample of respondents is selected and then called while a show is on the air. The interviewer usually asks people which program they are watching and how many members of the household are watching it.

Diaries are detailed records of what television or radio stations certain family members watch or listen to. Diaries are often kept for long periods of time, enabling experts to evaluate the changing popularity of TV shows and radio programs. Diaries are especially useful in determining the audience composition of various television and radio programs. Market researchers are able to look at the demographic or socioeconomic profile of people viewing particular shows on TV and of people listening to various radio stations. The programs or stations with audience profiles most closely matching the demographic and socioeconomic profiles of the firm's target markets are then used for placement of advertisements.

The growth of cable TV will undoubtedly have an influence on advertising evaluation. Cable television will present an opportunity for experiments to be conducted by allowing market areas to be split into equal halves. This action will give management another perspective about the message that is most effective in obtaining sales.

As with television and radio, newspaper and magazine readership is also measured and evaluated. Demographic and socioeconomic profiles of magazines are frequently developed. Advertisers again attempt to match the firm's target market profile with those of various magazines and newspapers.

In the market for consumer products, advertising and promotion receive frequent emphasis in the marketing mix. Consequently, an evaluation of the effectiveness of promotional messages is important. Ideally researchers would like to relate advertising effectiveness directly to sales, but because other elements in the marketing mix also affect sales the establishment of a direct tie is sometimes difficult. To

---

[15]Herbert E. Krugman, "The Impact of Television Advertising: Learning Without Involvement," *Public Opinion Quarterly.* Vol. XXIX, No. 3 (Fall, 1965), p. 349.

skirt that problem, researchers use such measures of communication as exposure and remembering, along with sales figures, to evaluate the firm's promotional program.

MEASUREMENT OF CONSUMER ATTITUDES

The attitude consumers hold toward a product is often pivotal in determining whether the product will be a marketing success. Because attitude is so important, increased work in the area of attitude research is being conducted. Several attitude models exist, but the expectancy value type model is perhaps the most frequently utilized in marketing situations.[16] Attitude models of the expectancy value type attempt to identify the primary attributes or characteristics of a product and to determine which attributes consumers think are most important. Information of this type can provide insight for the formulation and adjustment of marketing strategy.

Attitude research can be exemplified through the previously mentioned toothpaste example. Toothpaste attributes can, in general, be identified through research or, simply, through experience with the product. Among these attributes are price, whitening ability, decay prevention, and breath freshening. Obviously some customers are more concerned about one attribute than another. Therefore, market segments can be identified in terms of the importance given to any one attribute. This procedure was discussed earlier in the benefit market segmentation section.

Once management understands the attitudes of various groups of customers toward the firm's brand, various attitude change strategies can be followed. First, using primarily promotional tools, the firm can attempt to increase the rating of its own brand on a particularly important attribute. For instance, even though a toothpaste is not *known* for decay prevention, this fact can be emphasized if the product effectively prevents cavities. A second strategy is to attempt to increase the importance of an attribute to potential customers where the firm's brand does well. For example, advertising for a toothpaste which makes teeth very white may provide reasons why white teeth are to be valued. Finally, the firm may point out to the market the presence of a new attribute which should be considered by customers but which is currently not being considered—that is, if the firm's toothpaste has a good taste, management may want to stress the fact that if a toothpaste tastes good, the kids will want to brush their teeth more frequently and for longer periods of time.[17]

Attitude research is another available tool of the market researcher to assist marketing managers in making better decisions. The attitudes customers hold toward products are factors that must be analyzed when designing and implementing a marketing strategy.

---

[16]William L. Wilkie and Edgar A. Pessemier, "Issues in Marketing's Use of Multi-Attribute Attitude Models," *Journal of Marketing Research,* Vol. X, No. 4 (November, 1973), p. 428.

[17]Harper W. Boyd, Jr., Michael L. Ray, and Edward C. Strong, "An Attitudinal Framework for Advertising Strategy," *Journal of Marketing,* Vol. XXXIV, No. 2 (April, 1972), p. 27.

QUESTIONS AND ANALYTICAL PROBLEMS

1. In your own words, what function does the MIS perform?

2. What is the relationship between the MIS and marketing research?

3. Describe the role of managerial judgment in the market research process.

4. What rule should the marketing manager follow in deciding whether to fund a research project?

5. Which step in the market research project do you consider the most important? Why?

6. Why should secondary data always be investigated before collecting primary marketing data?

7. What are the advantages and disadvantages of test marketing?

8. Why are marketers so interested in the attitudes of consumers toward various products?

9. How can market research be helpful to a marketing manager in designing and implementing a market segmentation strategy?

10. Why is market research conducted at various stages in the new product development process?

Case 7-1 • MORRISON'S MEDICAL MART

James Morrison, the manager-owner of a small medical supply store, is in a dilemma. He is considering opening a new store, but is unsure of this decision.

Mr. Morrison opened his first store shortly after his discharge from the United States Army in 1958. Returning to his hometown of Syracuse, New York, he borrowed some money from a close relative and was soon in business. His store, which stocked a full range of medical equipment for in-home use, was very successful. In addition to his complete product line, he emphasized personal selling service in his marketing strategy. Full-time employees, trained personally by Mr. Morrison, made up the sales force. They were all well compensated for their efforts. Because some medical equipment was personal in nature, the customer needed to rely on the advice provided by the sales personnel; therefore, Mr. Morrison believed that competent, helpful, friendly employees were critical to the success of his store.

The Morrison Medical Mart was located downtown near a fairly busy intersection. Parking was not a problem, since there was a free parking lot adjacent to the building.

Mr. Morrison once before opened a second store in a neighboring community. The store did fairly well, but Mr. Morrison was never able to find a trustworthy manager. Consequently, the store was not profitable and was eventually closed. Mr. Morrison attributed the store's failure totally to employee theft, not to a lack of demand.

For two reasons Mr. Morrison is contemplating a second store in Syracuse. First, his oldest daughter is about to graduate from the local city college. Both father and daughter want to work together in the family business. Mr. Morrison is confident that in time his daughter can take over management of the new store. Secondly, a new hospital is being constructed in the new, fast-growing area of Syracuse. Mr. Morrison believes that a store in this area, near the hospital, will have a very high chance of success.

Mr. Morrison, a careful and thoughtful businessman, has some questions about what effect a new store might have on his current downtown location. As a matter of fact, he is not totally sure why his first store has been so successful. Additionally, he is unsure whether this success can be transferred to another store. Mr. Morrison, although not the least bit egotistical, thinks that a large degree of the success of the first store is due to his personality and concern for his customers. He is unsure whether he can spread his attention between two stores and still maintain the friendly, helpful atmosphere which he deems so critical. Mr. Morrison knows that one method to get some information about this problem would be to ask his current customers some questions about the store: why they shopped there, where they heard about the store, and where they lived. Mr. Morrison has also decided that a short questionnaire, handed out and completed by his customers in the store, will be a good way to collect this information.

What information should Mr. Morrison ask of his customers? Design a short question-naire to incorporate this information

Case 7-2 • THE COLLEGE SURVIVAL KIT

Hope Ryan, a divorced mother of two college-aged children, is a sales representative for the advertising department of a large daily newspaper. She has an idea for a unique product and is now in the process of changing the idea to a reality.

Briefly, Hope had observed her two children struggle through their first two years in college. She soon recognized that part of the difficulty was that her children were not prepared emotionally, academically, or even physically for the different, and sometimes demanding, requirements of college. At first she simply discussed the issue with her friends and acquaintances. She found that many of their children experienced the same sort of difficulties. Next, Hope began doing library research on the issue. Her investigation revealed that others had observed the phenomenon.

Hope first thought what was needed was a college survival guide for students. Then she realized that what was necessary for students to be better prepared for college were various behavioral skills. An incomplete list of such skills included good study habits, good eating and health habits, good social skills, domestic ability, and personal care and dress habits. To develop these skills, she reasoned, would take some time. Therefore these skills would have to be developed while the student was still in high school.

It was at this point that Hope conceived her idea. What was needed was a college survival guide for parents. Parents of potential college students could use the guide to help prepare their children for the first one or two difficult years in college.

Hope initially thought some type of book or manual would be appropriate. But she gave that idea up because so few people actually take the time to read a book. Instead, she slowly developed a kit which included various kinds of practice exercises, short readings, and case studies. Additionally, the kit included a master calendar around which a parent could schedule the training program. It was at this point that Hope became concerned. She felt confident that a demand for her product existed. However, she was unsure how to reach potential customers to make them aware of the product. She planned to use direct-mail to distribute the product. That still didn't solve the problem of how to promote the product.

Because of budget constraints Hope knew that radio, TV, and direct-mail advertising were not possible. Consequently she felt that magazines and perhaps newspapers were her only real alternatives. Hope discussed her problem with a marketing professor at a local college. He recommended that she first attempt to describe her target market in terms of demographic, socioeconomic, and attitudinal variables. Next, he recommended some type of research effort to identify print media readership of the target market. The professor felt that, at least initially, a sample of target market members of as little as 200 might be adequate to identify commonly read print media.

Using your own experience and intuition, describe the nature of the target market in broad demographic, socioeconomic, and attitudinal variables. Next, identify several ways target market members could be identified. Finally, what method of market research would you judge most effective in obtaining the desired information?

4

Marketing Functions

8

χ product

Of the four marketing mix variables, the product often is considered the critical element of the marketing decision process. It is from product decisions that the related pricing, distribution, and promotion strategies flow. Because the ultimate success of a product or service depends on consumers' voluntary choice, management's task is to design and market products or services that satisfy these choices.

This chapter focuses on the fundamental elements of the product as a decision area within a marketing-oriented firm and the strategies of product management. Besides defining what a product is, product-related topics such as new product development and the product life cycle, product line and mix strategies, branding, packaging and labeling, the role of merchandising, and the primary producer's and manufacturer's merchandising problems will be discussed.

THE DEFINITION OF THE PRODUCT

Before decision making in the product area can begin, it is important that a clear understanding of what constitutes a product must exist. A product is more than a physical, tangible object that performs a specific function. To be sure, a product is designed to serve its user and provide conspicuous, identifiable results. Beyond this obvious purpose for a product, however, the enlightened marketing decision maker realizes that consumers seek more than a functional benefit from many products. The classic article in the area points out that the products people consume include a wide range of related expectations and benefits beyond functional benefits.[1]

For example, when a person purchases an automobile, the purchase certainly includes an engine, tires, seats, windows, etc. The automobile buyer may also be seeking comfort, style, prestige, service, and economy. For a product to be developed and marketed in a fashion that truly satisfies consumer desires, all the potential attributes—tangible or intangible, functional or emotional—must be considered by the marketing manager in the design.

With the marketing concept as a framework, it is useful to define the *product* as a set of tangible or intangible attributes that provide real or perceived benefits to the consumer. It is also useful to include in the definition of the product the warranty and service elements at both the manufacturer and retail level as part of the benefits consumers seek. By including many elements of the consumer choice criteria in the definition of the product, the marketing decision maker increases the probability that buyers will gain satisfaction from the purchase and use of the product.

NEW PRODUCT DEVELOPMENT AND THE PRODUCT LIFE CYCLE

A prime management task in the product area is continually pursuing the development of new products and monitoring the health and viability of existing products. For a firm to perpetuate its existence it must be organized for the development of new products and must generate a flow of new product ideas. Further, it is necessary to plot the performance of existing products so that decisions about changing the product or pursuing new segments can be made at appropriate times. The procedures in new product development and the concept of the product life cycle relate to these important decision areas.

New Product Development

It is important to realize that new products take many forms. The firm does not need to discover and introduce a world phenomenon to legitimately call a product new. Certainly revolutionary inventions such as television and the telephone were new products; so are products that are significant improvements over existing products, such as automatic coffee makers. From a standpoint of strategy, it is also useful to consider improved products—products that have been

---

[1]Theodore Levitt, "Marketing Myopia," *Harvard Business Review,* Vol. 38 (July-August, 1960), p. 45.

redesigned or have new features—as new products. Approaching a product with any changes as a new product forces decision makers to be aware of tactics and practices that can enhance the performance of an altered product in the marketplace.

One of the first requirements of building a successful new product development program is to accept as reality the need for new product development. The emphasis given this subject by industry during the last decade is consistent with the progressive changes that have characterized every significant field where new knowledge and administrative skills have been factors. Further, the improved capability to identify consumer desires and competitive pressures for market share have made new product development a must for survival of the individual firm.

Organizing for New Products.   There is no place where the marketing concept, with its implied unity and interaction of all divisions of the business, has more impact on a business organization and its planning than in the area of new products. Programs for established products often can be routinized. Their continued sale and delivery may require minimal interaction between the specialized divisions of a firm. However, in the instance of new products, there must be constant interaction and free communication between specialized divisions. The most important divisions in developing a successful new product are marketing, technical research, and production. It is inconceivable, however, that technical research could turn out a product that meets the highest standards in market desirability and production feasibility without active collaboration and feedback from marketing and production. It is also quite likely that marketing and production could supply information which would reduce significantly the amount of research necessary by making strategic information available. Similarly, marketing must be completely aware of the needs and limitations of technical research and production. In other words, the amount of interaction and interdepartmental communication necessary to bring all relevant data into focus at the time and place of significant action taking requires these specialized areas to operate almost as a single division.

Organizations may take many forms to achieve such unity of action. In some organizations there may be no formal new product organization at all. Interaction may take place entirely on an informal basis. When a positive and communicating attitude prevails among staff members, interaction in the process may be quite satisfactory. In other organizations, there may be a new product team composed of personnel from each of the strategic areas. Members meet to discuss and execute new product ideas and strategy. Other organizations may have new product committees which synthesize data and serve as helpful informational and motivational catalysts to the operating divisions. Finally, there may be a new product development department whose staff specializes in each of the vital areas, serving as a liaison with each area of specialization. Although the incidence of failure in new product ventures is great, it can be decreased significantly by having an organization for new product development with the ability to bring the many skills required for new product development and marketing into a completely unified action.

Corporate Policy for New Product Development.   Choosing an organizational approach for new product development is one thing; having a corporate policy regarding new products is quite another. The reason policy is so important is that while corporate growth thrives on new product development, the risks are great. Booz, Allen and Hamilton report that of 60 ideas that appear to have promise as new products, only one succeeds (see Illus. 8-1).

Corporate policy on how the company will grow and stay abreast of market activities is important. Some companies have grown by acquiring other companies with successful products. Others wait until new products cross the threshold of development and then enter their brand and profit by growth sales in the industry. Home freezers provide an example of this practice. Deepfreeze, Inc., promoted the idea, but other brands entered the scene and profited even more than the originator of the product. If a company chooses this course of action, it should be aware of the necessity to organize quickly and to achieve selling and producing impact equal or superior to the company that marketed the product first. This may be a management challenge as difficult as developing the product from the beginning. However, some companies have the management skill and promotional resources required to profitably imitate other companies' products.

Maintaining a growth position in an industry presupposes a carefully planned and vigorously administered new product program. Specific corporate policies for

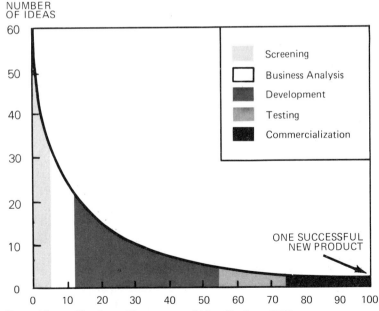

Source: Booz, Allen & Hamilton, *Management of New Products*, 1968.

Illus. 8-1   **Decay Curve of New Product Ideas**
by Stage of Evolution (51 Companies)

the development of new products involve the design and introduction of new products, copying others, or acquiring companies with successful products.

Criteria for Judging New Product Ideas.   Beyond organizational efforts to generate new product development and the use of corporate policies in determining new product procedures, there are general criteria that can be used to judge new product ideas and possibilities. The criteria listed below identify basic considerations relating to the potential for new products and the consistency of a new product proposal with existing corporate operations.

1. Does the new product have a well-defined and obtainable market segment? Competitive activities should be carefully considered here. Also, the possibility of securing protective patents should be fully investigated.
2. Can the firm use existing production facilities to make the product? The financial burden of new capital investment may reduce the feasibility of some new products.
3. Can existing distribution channels be used for the new product? Venturing into new relationships with wholesalers and retailers is expensive and sometimes difficult to accomplish.
4. Is the firm's sales staff qualified and large enough to handle a new product? Retraining or adding to the staff may need to be considered.
5. Are current managerial skills suitable for marketing the new product? Products that reach beyond the expertise and experience of current management have a high probability of failure.
6. Does the new product fit the company image? Products that differ from the company image may need to be marketed under a different brand name to insure a consistent public image.
7. What will the effects of the new product be on other products in the firm's product line? The danger of "cannibalism" is ever present with new product introduction.

By asking the above questions management can evaluate new product proposals in a method which emphasizes the efficiency of adding a product to the firm's marketing offerings. Further, several of the criteria attempt to judge the potential for success of the new product.

The Product Life Cycle

Even before the recent trend to develop new products, marketing experts observed a tendency of new products to mature, grow old, and die. This tendency is more apparent today and has become a center for management concern.

Illus. 8-2 shows how the product life cycle is typically divided into four stages. First is the *development stage.* Here management carefully makes its way into the market with test marketing or other techniques devised to obtain consumer reaction to the new product. During part of this process, the product may actually undergo certain changes in response to research findings. The final period of this stage takes place when the product, then being produced in its maximum quantity, is offered to the market with a complete commitment of funds for selling and advertising. Many firms which introduce truly new and different market offerings (such as microwave ovens), absolutely *must* supply consumers with information regarding the unique benefits of the *type* of product. This strategy is known as

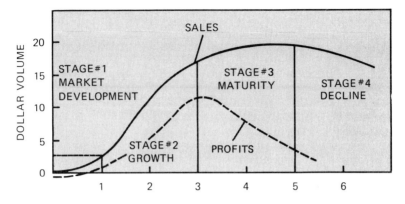

Illus. 8-2   **Stages in the Product Life Cycle
and Profit Curve**

primary demand stimulation. The great majority of products fail in the development stage.

Those which do not fail, however, enter the second stage of the product life cycle, *market growth.* The beginning of the growth stage is marked by a rapid increase in the sales curve over the development stage. This is often described as the "takeoff" period. Success in the introduction of a product frequently results in attempts by other producers to copy features of the product and win part of the market. Since inventories have to build up with the distributors and dealers, the factory sales are greater than consumer sales. This phenomenon inflates the hopes for projected sales. Price competition enters the picture and, if the company itself fails to innovate, its competition will. This is also the stage in which the firm will begin to engage in *selective demand stimulation.* As opposed to primary demand stimulation, this type of promotion emphasizes the superiority of one *brand* of the product type over competitors' offerings.

At the point when most of the prospective users have adopted the product, the *maturity stage* begins. Sales level off since inventories are well stocked and the number of new users or adopters decreases. In spite of these developments, firms attempt to achieve and hold brand preferences. These attempts frequently involve creating product differentiations, many of which are quite minor. In most instances these differentiations are sufficient to justify an entirely new promotional campaign. In contrast to the development stage, when the manufacturer depends on the distributor and dealers to push the product, the manufacturer, in the maturity stage, may be forced to use advertising to gain the acceptance of the consumer. The distributor and dealer may, in the maturity stage, handle similar products of several manufacturers since they can no longer profit by giving undivided attention to the brand that entered the market first. Each manufacturer must continue to court the distributors and dealers with discounts, price concessions, and special deals. But even these special efforts are often insufficient to hold a firm's market share when its competitors are doing the same thing.

The *decline stage* begins when, for one or more obscure reasons, the sales of the product level off or decline. Such an eventuality often means that the sales of some of the competing companies fall off, forcing the weaker ones out of the market at great costs. The remaining companies are those that have been the most successful in anticipating the changes in the marketplace. By revitalizing its marketing program with a realistic plan relating to the product, its price, the channels through which it is sold, and its promotion, a company may preserve the market share of the product.

Profits in the Product Life Cycle.   A common profit curve is shown by the broken line in Illus. 8-2. During the development stage profits are less than zero because of the large expenses that accompany market entry. Profits tend to peak near the end of the growth stage and then fall off during the maturity stage since, by definition, the maturity stage is characterized by stiffened competition. Companies increase promotional efforts, and price competition becomes strong—resulting in lower profits.

Anticipating the Decline with a Plan.   Knowing the nature of the life cycle and the forces that influence it is important to the marketing decision maker. Such knowledge prompts advanced planning with programs aimed at preventing the losses accompanying the decline stage. Decline can be anticipated as a result of one or a combination of the following developments:

1. The product's novelty wears off.
2. New developments render the product obsolete.
3. After the development stage, competition is so great that excess profits and growth potential are nonexistant.

Corporate management should be aware of all these dangers and plan to offset them. The program to accomplish this objective should be explicitly set forth and given as much support as the new product program itself. Some of the possibilities for offsetting declines include:

1. Discovering (via product and market research) new uses for the product among its present users. Such usage might become the new copy theme to preserve the rest of the advertising programs. DuPont accomplished this goal when it tinted nylon hose so that rather than wearing a few neutral shades, women began wearing a different shade of hose with each outfit.
2. Stimulating, with new advertising programs, more frequent use of the product by present users. Coca-Cola's "Have a Coke and a Smile" campaign is a good example of the use of this tactic.
3. Expanding the market to include new users. Different age groups, social classes, or reference groups might be brought within the circle of the company's target even though they were once outside the company's original market. Johnson & Johnson successfully used this technique by stimulating demand for its *Baby Shampoo* in many different age groups.
4. Developing new uses for the product if the company sees no prospect for the implementation of any of the above alternatives and is committed to a source

of new motivations for the product. Perhaps the best example of use of this strategy is Arm & Hammer's revival of baking soda with several new uses for the product.

Timing in all these techniques is important. The firm should always be aware of what is likely to happen in the marketplace within six months so that the plan can be ready to execute before a market decline becomes a deflating and costly experience.

PRODUCT LINE AND MIX STRATEGIES

Every new product must be considered on its own merits. As discussed earlier, the development of new products provides growth opportunities for the firm. New products and changes in existing products, however, must also be evaluated as they relate to the firm's other market offerings. This leads the decision maker to consider a new realm for strategy planning: the product line and the product mix.

A *product line* is a group of similar products that serves a similar purpose. A line of soap products and a line of cosmetic products are examples. A firm's *product mix* is the sum total of all the different product lines that the firm manufactures or markets. Procter & Gamble Co. has a soap products line, a personal care products line, and a grocery products line. Together, these different types of products constitute the product mix for P & G.

Product Line Strategies

Three basic types of strategies are employed in managing a firm's product line(s). Decisions must be made concerning (1) product positioning, (2) the breadth and depth of the line, and (3) expansion or contraction of the product line.

Product Positioning.   Very early in the life of each product in the line the firm should determine the market position targeted for the product. Positioning depends on the range of competing products in the market. Individual products can be designed, priced, and distributed in such ways that they are positioned at the very top of the product category (for example, a Cadillac Seville or Pierre Cardin clothes). Conversely, the decision can be made to position the product at the low end of all market offerings (as Chevrolet did with the Chevette). The positioning decision will be influenced by the firm's ability to design, produce, and gain distribution of a particular type of product. Further, market opportunities and competitors' products and practices will influence product positioning strategy.

Breadth and Depth of the Line.   The firm must also determine the appropriate breadth and depth of the product line. As an example, consider tennis products. A firm could achieve great product line breadth by marketing tennis rackets, tennis balls, tennis shoes, men's and women's tennis apparel, ball machines, etc. As the firm attempts to supply many types of related products, the line has greater breadth.

This concept can also be applied in a larger context. Continuing with the sporting goods example, consider the products marketed by Spalding. Spalding could organize its product lines according to general categories such as equipment (balls, rackets, skis, helmets, etc.), apparel (uniforms, shoes, socks, etc.), and so forth. The product lines retain the similarity in nature and purpose but are somewhat broader.

The concept of depth in a product is evident when a single firm offers a wide variety of choices of the same type of product. Procter & Gamble Co. offers the consumer a choice of ten laundry detergents: Tide, Salvo, Dash, Bold, Dreft, Gain, Cheer, Era, Duz, and Oxydol. Each comes in different sizes, and some are available in different forms (tablets, powders, and liquids). Similar depth in the product line is achieved by Adidas and Nike in the tennis example used previously. Each of these firms markets several types of running and tennis shoes in different styles, sizes, and colors for men, women, and children.

Breadth and depth in a product line allow the firm to penetrate different market segments. Products in the line are designed with slight differences to satisfy varying consumer needs and desires. Further, the strategies can enhance the firm's retail shelf position and establish a strong relationship with distributors and retailers.

Expansion and Contraction of the Line.   Expansion and contraction of the product line involves the addition or deletion of a product from the company's line of offerings. The decision to cease the production and marketing of an item in the line is influenced by profitability, cost of production, consumer behavior, competitive pressures, or changes in corporate objectives. A good example of a recent contraction of the product line is United States automakers' decision to stop producing convertibles. Consumer demand had reached such a low level that the model was an economic infeasibility.

Product lines are expanded to provide firms with greater market coverage in the product group or to take advantage of excess production capacity or existing distribution opportunities. Two related concepts in this regard are trading up and trading down. If a firm introduces a new product that is priced high in the range of products available on the market, then *trading up* has occurred. *Trading down* results when a product is targeted at the low end of the competitive structure. Trading down was successfully accomplished by Marantz in the stereo industry in the early 1970s.

Expansion of the product line allows the firm to take advantage of newly emerging market segments. Also, the addition of a new member of a product line may attract new consumers to existing products in the line.

Product Mix Strategies

Changing a firm's product mix is a major corporate maneuver. Expansion or contraction of the mix means adding or dropping an entire product line. In some instances the expansion of the mix is a relatively smooth operation. When a firm is in a business related to the area in which it wishes to expand, existing management skills and marketing mix efforts can be employed. For example, if a major sporting goods firm were to add skiing apparel to its mix of sporting goods lines, the expansion would be facilitated by the firm's presence in the industry and its past experience.[2]

Frequently product mix expansions are achieved through corporate acquisitions.[3] Some expansions, however, lead a firm far afield from its base of expertise. A hotel chain contemplating the addition of a fast-food chain to its product mix may find fast-food marketing practices vastly different and unwieldy to manage.

The contraction of a product mix is typically a difficult decision. Such a move could involve deleting an entire group of products from a firm's business operations. The impact on capital equipment, employees, and other product lines must be weighed. The decision usually rests with the elimination of low-profit items facing a declining market, rigorous competition, or shortages of raw materials.

BRANDING, PACKAGING, LABELING

Branding, packaging, and labeling are factors in the product area that must be carefully considered. While tactics in these three areas will not be the foundation of the product strategy, they function as supplemental efforts that can have a crucial effect in overall product performance in the market plan.

Branding

A brand permits a company to crystallize positive goodwill associations around a name. The brand name becomes a symbol of quality that influences the person to choose the company's product. The more favorable and the more powerful such associations are, the greater the selling power of the product.

Positive brand associations may be the result of many factors. The product itself may yield a high degree of satisfaction that recalls favorable association when the name is spoken. The package may be attractive. The company that sells the product may have achieved a good name because of its public relations policy or its reputation for selling a prominent line of products.

If there were no name with which to associate the experience of, for instance, drinking Coca-Cola, the consumer would find it difficult to repeat the experience. The information and motivation that were a part of this experience would not be preserved. Information and motivation about a product cannot be recalled or transferred unless that product has a name.

Brands are classed as manufacturer brands and as middlemen brands. As the name implies, a *manufacturer's brand* carries the name the manufacturer gives it. It is not necessarily the name of the company; Lincoln and Mercury, for example, are products of the Ford Motor Company. In some cases, however, the product does carry the name of the company, as in the case of the Ford Pinto, Fairmont,

---

[2]"Dean Foods: Diversifying to Supplement a Low Growth Business," *Business Week,* December 18, 1978, p. 74.

[3]"Beatrice Foods: Adding Tropicana for a Broader Nationwide Network," *Business Week,* May 15, 1978, p. 114.

and so on. Usually, although not always, the manufacturer's brand is marketed on a national scale and is therefore called a national brand. Middlemen may also adopt brand names to identify their products. In most instances the middlemen operate in a restricted region of the nation. For this reason middlemen brands are sometimes called local brands.

Manufacturer's Brand.   The manufacturer's brand usually carries a stronger selling impact than the distributor's or middlemen's brand. Frequently the national brand has the advantage of advertising through national magazines and television networks. Since the national brand is sold in greater volume and can support a much larger advertising budget, it may carry the selling impact of Coca-Cola in soft drinks or Del Monte in canned foods.

For this reason, nationally branded items can command a higher price for comparable quality. Since the nationally branded product usually has won a consumer preference, it maintains a stable price more easily during periods of price declines than does a local brand, making it a desirable product for the distributor to stock. Such preference gives the manufacturer easy access to the market.

As in the case of the good name of an individual, the branding of a product carries with it some responsibility. If the product quality fails to meet expected standards, ill will can result and discourage the use of the product as easily as goodwill can support it positively.

Some distributors may intentionally avoid the use of national brands because of their higher price and narrower profit margins. Some retailers and distributors stage large campaigns to place their own private brands ahead of national brands. Such policies can boomerang, however, when the national advertiser has established a strong preference with the ultimate consumer.[4]

Middlemen Brands.   The materials shortages of World War II had a negative impact on middlemen brands. These brands have not made a strong comeback since then.

Middlemen brands are found mostly in food items. An example is A&P's Eight-O-Clock brand coffee. Also, outside the food line, Macy's department store has 20,000 items, with its own private brand label, manufactured especially for its own business.

There are advantages that distributors enjoy if they are successful in establishing and maintaining brand prestige in their own products. Placing a better quality product on the market at a low price is possible since distributor brands do not have to bear the brunt of nationwide advertising costs and can win goodwill and prestige. Also, a certain amount of independence results when distributors have brands of their own, since they are not at the mercy of disadvantageous price, margin, or promotional changes of the national brands.

It appears that there may be an increase in the number of middlemen brands in the future. The goodwill that is attached to a brand name is a property right.

---

[4]Recently many grocery chains have initiated "no-name" products. This low-cost appeal to consumers is expected to be proved as a reliable alternative to strongly supported branding.

Attached to it is a certain amount of strength and security. As distributors become larger and stronger, they tend to want to strengthen their positions by acquiring the brand goodwill for themselves.

Packaging

Packaging adds several additional dimensions to the product and can serve as an important promotional or differentiation factor in overall product positioning.

As a promotional device the package serves two important purposes. First, in the myriad of products displayed at the retail level, a well-designed package can aid in attracting the buyer's attention. The package that is capable of catching the shopper's eye and inducing the potential buyer to examine the product more closely adds considerably to the product's potential for market success. The market entry of L'eggs pantyhose was successfully aided by a unique package that gained shoppers' attention.

The attractive, distinctive package can facilitate recognition. Both in the retail setting and in the user's home, a package that clearly and immediately stimulates brand recognition provides the firm with an added opportunity to communicate.

As a differentiating feature, the package can achieve this effect for the firm in several ways. For the household consumer, the product with a package design that makes the product easy to use gives the buyer an added convenience. Products that are easy to open, come in "boilable bags," or have pump spray applicators are examples. Also, those products that are made more safe by the package provide a basis for differentiation. A child-proof cap or unbreakable package distinguishes one brand from its competition.

Differentiating package features are not only important to the household buyer but also to the trade (wholesalers and retailers) purchasers. Products that have protective packages or packages that facilitate storage and display of the brand provide members of the trade with another reason to sell and promote the product.

Packaging efforts can provide the firm with supplemental product tactics. Both for the ultimate consumer and the trade, package features are meaningful elements in the overall consideration between brands.

Labeling

There are several requirements that the product label must fulfill. These relate to conveying various sorts of information to the consumer. First, the label should provide the buyer an indication of price. Though this responsibility frequently falls on the retailer, the manufacturer can aid in this process either by prepricing the item or providing a clear space on the label for the price. The label must also indicate proper use of the product and/or instructions for using it. Many firms have discovered that consumer dissatisfaction with a product is the result of its improper use. If a product is designed to function through particular application, the firm must insure that the consumer is informed of the nature of the application. The label also provides the manufacturer with a method of communicating warranties and warnings. If the manufacturer backs the product with a warranty, the label provides an opportunity to indicate the nature of the warranty. Additionally, any dangers that may result from the use of the product should be indicated, accompanied by preventive and corrective measures that can be initiated. Finally, by

virtue of several legislative mandates, package contents and nutritional information
(if applicable) must be provided on the label.

THE ROLE OF MERCHANDISING

The coordinating function designed to assure the availability of the right
product at the right time and in the right place is known as *merchandising.* Success
in meeting the product availability challenge is at the heart of market strategy
decisions and applies at all levels of the product flow. The product flow consists
of a channel of distribution with a series of systematized inventory storage points
to supply projected needs. At each of these points, decisions regarding which
products, the quantity of each item, and the time to make or buy specific products
are vital issues affecting a company's growth and profitability. Examples of the
success or failure of tactics at different levels of the market are helpful in visualizing
the importance of the merchandising effort.

Applicability of Merchandising at All Market Levels

At the primary market level farm surplus problems, over several decades, have
exemplified a failure to coordinate product availability with market needs. The
tremendous costs of these surpluses to the nation's taxpayers have provided evidence of the undesirable results of the failure to coordinate product availability
with market demands in agriculture.

At the manufacturer's level 80 percent of the new food products that are
offered on the market fail. In these instances the problem is not only how much
to make or buy but also what to make.

A study by Theodore L. Angelus of 75 new products that failed determined
that the major reason for new product failure was a lack of significant difference
from existing products serving the the same purpose.[5] Other reasons for failure
were: poor product positioning, bad timing, poor product performance, and the
wrong product for the company. For example:

Insignificant product differences
1. Hunt's flavored catsups (pizza, hickory) were not sufficiently different
   from regular catsup.
2. Easy-Off Household Cleaner. The aerosol foam cleaner was not, to consumers, significantly easier or better than liquids such as Formula 409.

Poor product positioning
Revlon Super Natural Hairspray. To consumers *super* means extraordinary
holding power; *natural* means ordinary holding power. Consumers did not
know what the product represented.

Bad timing
In 1968 seventeen new brands of household cleaners entered the market;
Easy-Off, Whistle, Power-On, and several others failed.

---

[5]Theodore L. Angelus, "Why Do Most New Products Fail?", *Advertising Age* (March 24, 1969),
p. 85.

Poor product performance
> General Foods cereals with freeze-dried fruit failed because the cereal became soggy before the fruit became soft enough to eat.

Wrong product for the company
1. Even giant Procter & Gamble failed twice trying to get a large share of the hairspray market (Hidden Magic and Winterset/Summerset).
2. Colgate, after several tries, has not made a success of food products.

At the retail level the basic problem is the same, although the administrative challenge is somewhat different. In the case of the farmer and the manufacturer the problem is what to produce or what to make; but the retailer must determine what, when, and how much to buy. Failures in retailing are as common as manufacturer flops and just as costly. A study conducted by IBM indicates that, for every dollar's worth of merchandise which the average retail store sells, sales of 98 cents are lost because the stores do not have available the merchandise that customers want. A continuing study indicates that for medium-sized and small distributors and for small retailers, almost 35 percent of the merchandise accounts for over 90 percent of the profits; approximately 20 percent of the stock in most stores should not be on the shelves because it is not wanted by customers.[6]

The extent to which a condition of unbalance exists was made evident in a survey of eight typical retail stores that compete in general merchandise lines (see Illus. 8-3). Three of them are nationally known chain stores. Surveyors shopped these stores for items that should have been a regular part of their stock. For 43 percent of the requests, the specific item was not in stock. Even the store with the

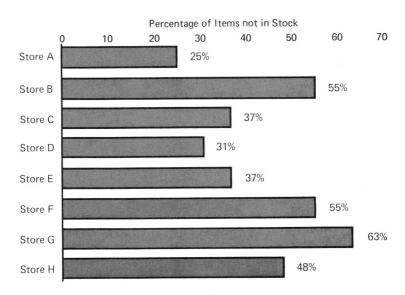

Percentage of Items not in Stock

Store A — 25%
Store B — 55%
Store C — 37%
Store D — 31%
Store E — 37%
Store F — 55%
Store G — 63%
Store H — 48%

Illus. 8-3   **Out-of-Stock Conditions in Eight Retail Stores**

[6]Continuing and unpublished study by Lloyd C. Pierce, co-director, University of Utah Small Business Management Development Program.

best score was out of stock on 25 percent of the items. One store in the group was out of stock on 63 percent of the requests. The results of the survey were presented to the store managers, and each agreed that the items requested should have been a part of the stock.

Marketing activities should impel people to buy. Certainly the merchandising process possesses such quality. To have available the exact goods that the customer wants, when and where he or she wants them, decreases sales resistance and encourages the movement of goods. On the other hand, failure to have the right goods encourages sales resistance. Merchants, however, should not expect this coordination process alone to move the goods. They should be aware of the fact that price, for example, is an equally important factor which influences the consumer's decision on whether to buy. Even when the product is attractive and the price fair, some selling or promotion may be a necessary ingredient in triggering the sale. Thus, all the elements of the marketing mix operate together as one. Price, promotion, and place must be integrated into the program with the product offering to achieve maximum sales.

Definitions of Merchandising

The Committee on Definitions of the American Marketing Association defines *merchandising* as "the planning and supervision involved in marketing the particular merchandise or service at the places, times, and prices, and in the quantities which will best serve to realize the marketing objectives of the business."[7] The word *merchandising* has had so many and varied meanings that this definition has not been readily accepted. However, the concept of coordination of demand and supply is one of the most vital in successful market management. The term *merchandising* is used to describe the planning and administration necessary to achieve an optimum coordination of product availability with current demand.

Relationship of Buying to Merchandising

Is buying synonymous with or a subordinate part of merchandising? These two terms are often used together. Occasionally they are used as synonyms. Certainly, as merchandising is described, buying is an essential ingredient. In retailing or wholesaling the decisions of what and how much to buy are usually made by buyers who frequently decide sources from which merchandise will be purchased. Such execution of the immediate purchases, however, is not all there is to the coordinating process. The buyer in a retail establishment usually operates within the range of maximum and minimum stock allowances. Buyers are also advised of a price range. On the other hand, the merchandising function includes the formulation of policies to guide the buyer. Policymakers set the maximum and minimum stock figures and the price ranges.

Department stores separate the functions of buyer and merchandise manager. The latter coordinates the activities of the buyers, but does no buying. Frequently

[7]Committee on Definitions, *Marketing Definitions* (Chicago: American Marketing Association, 1960), p. 17.

the merchandise manager is aided by divisional merchandise managers. Thus, we see the buying function as one activity in the execution of the merchandising plan. Behind the act of buying, however, research into product demand, formulation of policies, and coordinating and altering policies are all parts of merchandising and serve as guides to the buyer.

Buying and merchandising can be mroe clearly differentiated in the field of manufacturing. The merchandising responsibility here is in making a product line that will stimulate and satisfy a demand. This is in contrast to retailing and wholesaling, where the task is to buy the products. In both cases the coordination of demand and supply is essential. It is true that there are buyers in the manufacturing business. Yet the purchases here are composed of raw materials, fabricated parts, or other goods that are not products for resale. Thus, we see buying as a supporting and subordinate function included in the merchandising program. The term is not synonymous with merchandising. Merchandising is broader and includes the buying operation.

Ingredients to Be Coordinated

It may help us to see why merchandising should have a meaning distinct from promotion if each of the fundamental elements of its components is viewed in relief. First, the product itself must be considered. To what degree is it desired by the buying public? How does it compare with new products that competition is offering? What degree of preferences do past responses indicate? Is it holding its own in the race with existing products on the market? Thus, the whole question of product desirability must be considered.

Then, in view of product desirability, what amount should be purchased or made? This decision must be made by manufacturers, such as Remington Rand and International Business Machines, when they contemplate a year's production schedule. It applies to typewriters as well as to electronic data processing machines. The same problem confronts the retailers who sell these products to the public. The intensity of desire for the product and the number or volume required to satisfy the desire are strategic factors. They must be appraised and coordinated to obtain an accurate projection of the number to make or buy.

The third ingredient is time and place. IBM must have an adequate number of typewriters in Los Angeles, or within a few days of Los Angeles, if it is to realize the sales potential which exists in that area. The market for these typewriters in the Los Angeles area cannot be projected perfectly. Time is required if they are to be shipped into the area. Yet a decision must be made as to how many should be available at specific times in that area; sales may be lost if the wrong decision is made. Thus, the problem of product adjustment involves the following: first, the desirability of the product itself; second, the amount of the product required for the market; third, the time period over which the demand will be expressed; and, fourth, the administrative planning and activity to meet the demand at the appointed place. There is ample evidence supporting a need for emphasis of this function in view of the present failures to achieve satisfactory performance.

Coordination of product offerings with current demand, or merchandising, provides a quality of availability which is essential in the movement of the products toward their ultimate market. This function of coordination is nothing more or less than management's market forecasts successfully administered into sales. In accomplishing this administrative task, the buyer's intuition, unaided judgment, or memory are not enough. A method or a system and a carefully formulated policy used as aids to judgment are essential. By examining merchandising problems at each of the institutional levels—primary producer, manufacturer, wholesaler, and retailer—the nature of management's challenge in merchandising will be more clearly understood.

THE PRIMARY PRODUCER'S MERCHANDISING PROBLEMS

Product coordination can be a difficult problem for primary producers. Lack of proper balance of output with demand for products of mines, forests, fisheries, and the problem of surpluses from farms are evidences of failures to coordinate supply with demand.

Extractive Industries

Within limits, the rate of production in mines can be controlled by management decisions. Supply of and the demand for the product are such that predictability of both factors with a minimum factor of error is possible. Although producing and consuming firms are comparatively few, they are competitive. They supply as much as the market demands at prevailing prices, and the supply of these products has a tendency to be highly elastic. As demand pushes the price to higher levels, the volume produced increases greatly.

Mine operators do not have the powers of adjustment by innovation possessed by the manufacturer. Kennecott Copper Company, in its smelting processes, may change the form or shape of its product to make it more convenient to industrial uses; but it cannot invent a new item that will give the company a definite advantage over competition and make other products obsolete. Its customers, General Electric and Westinghouse, introduce changes in the models of their appliances almost annually to increase the demand for their product, but such a course is not open to Kennecott. The area of management activity available to this company is confined to determining how much can be sold, finding a buyer, and reducing unit costs.

The adjustment of the supply of timber to demand is a long-run problem. Reforestation and the development of new timberland are activities performed now to meet a demand that will exist years hence. The nature of this business is such that the coordination of supply with demand extends over a period of years. Furthermore, decisions and policies often transcend the interest and the initiative of the firm and become a matter of public policy.

Coordination of Supply and Demand in Agriculture

In agriculture the problem is different. Farms in the United States number approximately 2.6 million. Farms are increasing in size as the number of farms shrinks. Although they are operating more as businesses, there are still problems of coordinating the immediate supply with the immediate demand. Each farmer is geographically limited to a few crops. The uses to which these crops are applied are also limited. For example, southern farmers cannot drastically change their basic pattern of production from cotton and tobacco. Those in the Midwest have little that can be planted except wheat, corn, and soybeans. General Motors can develop a new automobile model that will make old models obsolete, thus creating a market. Farmers are not in a position to influence either the supply or the demand in this manner. Furthermore, there are so many farmers that the decision of one farmer has little influence on either the supply or the demand.

The area in which farmers can adjust their product to meet a current demand is very narrow. If we take an overall and practical view of the farm, it is very closely related to a merchandising failure. Simply stated, the current status of farming in the United States is evidence of a failure to coordinate the immediate supply with the immediate demand.

THE MANUFACTURER'S MERCHANDISING PROBLEMS

Two principal areas confront manufacturers in their merchandising problems. The first is adjusting the flow of currently used products to meet the demand. The second is in developing new products.

Established Products

Two difficulties are present in merchandising established products. First, there is the danger of losing sales because of not having a sufficient supply in stock or of becoming overstocked in terms of a falling demand and being forced to take markdowns. The second problem, which is closely related to the first, is the danger of a product losing its market position.

Before corrective action can be taken, however, management must know how serious the trouble is and the specific reason for the maladjustment. We recall the example of the large pipe company that was overstocked with obsolete pipe valued at $100,000. Until an inventory was taken of the stock, the management was not even aware of this waste. When the inventory was computed, corrective action was taken by cutting down on the production of slow-moving items with which the firm was overstocked and by cutting out those products for which there was no demand.

Inventory Control.   Stock-control programs can avoid such costly experiences and frequently reduce capital requirements for a desirable inventory level.

The following is an illustration of a simple inventory control method employed by a medium-size distributor. Note that this simple system incorporates all the elements required to assure the proper item at the right place, time, price, and quantity.

Step 1: Prepare a card for each item (there are approximately 700 items).

$$\text{Item \#UC} \times \text{Usage} = \text{UV}$$

Item #UC	× Usage	= UV
(unit cost)	(number of sales of the item in the past year)	(unit value)
	UC × Usage	=UV
Item #1234	2.00 × 50	=$100
Item #4321	5.00 × 0	=0

Step 2: Fill all cards in a box in order according to UV. Place the highest unit value card first moving down to 0-value cards.

Step 3: Total the unit value shown on all cards.

Step 4: Start with the highest unit value card and add unit values shown on cards until 90 percent of total unit value is determined. In this example that was 35 percent of the items carried.

Step 5: Count all 0-unit value items. That was, in this company, 20 percent of all items carried. These items were disposed of.

The distributor now carefully watches the inventory to discern any shifts in demand, examines new items for possible inclusion in inventory, and establishes a program to dispose of 0-value items.

A firm with several thousand items must have a more elaborate system, very likely computerized, but the basic ideas are the same. A commonly used method is that installed by a large shoe machinery company that had to keep thousands of parts available for both repair and manufacture. In this method an established figure for stock minimums and maximums on each item serves the purpose of control. Each time a withdrawal is made, the number of parts withdrawn is entered on the record, and the balance is recorded. When the minimum is reached, enough stock remains to provide for a production period and a safety factor in case of trouble. A notice of this stock condition is returned to the control office whenever minimum stock conditions are recorded. The return of the record is the signal to replenish the stock to the maximum again. At the end of a period, the total sales figures yield the rate of sale and become the basis for a production schedule. The maximum and the minimum stock figures can be revised if tolerances have been narrow or if stock has been greater or less than needed.

Another example in a different area—food manufacturing—also reveals the nature of the merchandising problem and how to meet it. The problem here is different because the product has an element of perishability as do the products from which it is made.

Therefore, the company has to watch its stock carefully. The unknown factor with which the company has to contend is the amount purchased by the ultimate consumer. The inventory reserve has to be kept at a minimum and never is allowed to become greater than a two-week supply. Company sales are approximately $40 million a month, or $500 million annually.

The company goes directly to the consumer level to get its coordinating information. The following steps are used: District sales managers are required to submit projected budgets of sales three months in advance. One month later each manager reviews the report, notes changed conditions, and then reviews it with the division manager. Necessary revisions are made as a result of this final discussion. One month before shipment is due the division manager compiles his or her reports with last-minute revisions and sends them to the central office. The central office then makes a master budget and assigns the production to plants throughout the nation. Raw material orders are placed, and production is effected to meet the demand as estimated. Differences can be absorbed by the inventory, which is controlled on a first-in, first-out (FIFO) basis. Naturally a district manager who is constantly off on estimates will be given help. However, seldom does such action become necessary.

In other instances the manufacturer's product is not perishable, and a significant portion is sold to retail stores through wholesalers. Since the product is not perishable, it can remain on the shelves and in the warehouses of retail and wholesale firms. Such an arrangement makes it very difficult, however, for the manufacturer to control production so that it coordinates with consumer demand. After subscribing to a store audit service, one manufacturer of drug and cosmetic items discovered that there was a six-month lag between the time that consumer sales at the retail stores began declining and the time warehouse sales reflected this decrease.[8] For example, warehouse sales increased through the period January to December, but consumer sales fell off sharply in June. Wholesalers and retailers continued to order and fill their shelves throughout the year since the product had experienced a rapid growth during the previous months. After a period, wholesalers and retailers found their shelves full of a product that was not selling. Had the manufacturer been informed of the slowdown in sales six months earlier, the difficulty could have been corrected by changing the product, by a price adjustment, or by a selling appeal, whichever the situation required.

Influence of the Computer.[9]   The essence of merchandising as related to established products is time. If the manufacturer could know exactly what product the consumer wanted at a given moment in time and had the capacity to supply it immediately, merchandising problems would not exist. The less time that exists between the decision to produce and buy and the expression of customer choice,

---

[8]The best known store audit service is that provided by A. C. Nielsen. In providing this service Nielsen selects a sample of stores and during specific periods makes a record of the stock on hand of the item being studied at the beginning of the period in each of these stores. The merchandise purchased and placed in stock during the period and the amount in stock at the end of the period are then used to compute a specific sales figure.

[9]An excellent description of the impact of the computer on marketing is presented in "Computers Begin to Solve the Marketing Puzzle," Business Week (April 17, 1965), p. 114. Even though fifteen years old, the article presents the topic well.

the smaller the risk. Such a shortening in time decreases the amount of merchandise that needs to be impounded at storage and reservoir points and reduces the incidence of loss on merchandising failures.

Introducing computers into the scene has brought a veritable revolution in reducing the time required to get feedback on sales at different market levels. Rapid transmission of sales data, broken down by unit sales, margin, location, and time, is made by possible by the systems being installed in certain retail outlets. The standard cash register has been replaced by small computer terminals which, in addition to totalling sales and storing money, translate and relay the information to a data processing center as the sales are rung up by the checkout cashier.

Owens-Illinois is one company among hundreds that have automated the merchandise system into a computer program at the manufacturer and distributor levels. The Owens-Illinois headquarters in Toledo, the processing headquarters, is connected by wire to 100 different sales and manufacturing headquarters. When an order comes in, the computer system determines if the product ordered is in stock (and its location) and sends a release and a shipping order for the plant to ship it. A most significant part of this transaction is being able to supply the merchandise to the customer in 35 hours instead of taking a period of several weeks; in addition, the information is made available at every point in the reservoir or storage system.[10] Printouts from the computer can inform every person responsible for storage or production of stock conditions at a moment's notice. If management wished to do so and had the production-marketing flow sufficiently routinized, the computerized system could order the production department to order the new materials for a production cycle that would replenish stock by the amount of the sale. A part of this same computer printout can compile the rate of sale. Computers make it possible to improve the quality of the merchandise forecast by enabling management to include many more market influences in the sales forecast.

Corrective Action. The merchandise control system, whether automated or traditional, exists for one purpose alone: to inform management of what is happening to the merchandise flow so that proper action may be taken to keep it flowing at an optimum rate. When sales of a well-established product increase or decrease, a corresponding increase or decrease in production may be all that is required. When the decrease is chronic and the product is a significant part of the company line, however, more analysis may be required. The product may need revising or replacing. It may be that a new advertising slant, a new package, or an entirely revised sales program may be required. Possibly, the product should be eliminated from the product line. The additional analysis may require market reserach that will reveal why the product is slipping or which competitors have the market and why. Corrective action is usually possible once the facts are known. Any system of control adopted should enable management to avoid delays and point to the problem areas.

---

[10]*Ibid.*, p. 115.

New Products

The merchandising problems associated with new products is unique in several regards. First, there is no history associated with the product, so routine inventory control procedures cannot be applied. Second, the merchandising tasks associated with a new product differ from established products in that efforts to cultivate the market must be executed. This requires coordinated activities at all levels of the marketing effort. Finally, as discussed earlier in this chapter, the process of introducing a new product has special considerations, and these must be carefully implemented.

QUESTIONS AND ANALYTICAL PROBLEMS

1. Why is the product considered by many the critical decision area in the marketing mix?
2. What advantages does the decision maker gain from using a broad definition of the product?
3. What is a *new* product? Give two examples of recent new products.
4. Why do so many new products fail? How can careful analysis of new product ideas increase the probability of success and improve the efficiency of new product introduction?
5. What is the relationship between the product life cycle and promotional strategy? Give an example of a new product that is entering the growth stage of the life cycle and cite the distinctive promotional effort being used.
6. When a product begins to decline, which types of efforts on the part of the firm can be used to extend the life cycle?
7. Explain the difference between a *product mix* and a *product line.* Choose a company you are familiar with and describe the firm's product mix and product line.
8. What advantages accrue to the firm by branding a product? What responsibilities does the firm accept by establishing a brand name?
9. How is merchandising distinguished from other product area tasks? Explain how merchandising strategies relate to a firm's profitability.
10. Using a riding lawnmower an an example, explain how one buyer might judge this product by its *tangible* attributes while another might evaluate it by its *intangible* attributes. How do these two buyers establish different market segments for the same product?

Case 8-1 • MORRISON ENVIRONMENTAL PRODUCTS

Morrison Environmental Products is a $5 million firm located in Houston, Texas. Andrea Morrison, the firm's founder, is a marketer by trade and training, having spent a number of years working for a large advertising agency on the East Coast. While in the agency she was exposed to a procedure used to detect consumer problems. When the problems were detected, the agency personnel would develop a promotional message to show potential customers how a particular product could solve the problem.

Ms. Morrison believed that the problem detection system could be used in new product development as well as in developing advertising appeals. Because of this conviction she started her own firm with the specific intention of developing and marketing new product ideas to other firms.

The problem detection system was developed by Batten, Barton, Durstine and Osborn Advertising Agency (BBDO).[1] The problem detection system is based on the assumption that consumers cannot tell someone what types of products they want, but they can describe their problems. The system consists of two steps. First, a long, thorough list of problems that could be solved by a particular product or service is developed. This is a creative step and one that is extremely important. Usually a hundred or more potential problems are developed around a particular topic or subject. Ms. Morrison and her associates develop the problem list from in-depth interviews of consumers and experts in the field, by reading about the subject, by direct observation, and by just thinking about the topic. Second, the major problems are identified by interviewing 150 prime prospective customers. These potential customers are asked to evaluate each problem with respect to whether it is important, whether the problem occurs frequently, and whether a current product or service already solves the problem. The three rankings are weighted and coded and then added together in such a way that the higher the total score, the greater the problem to the consumer.

This procedure is generally fairly easy on respondents. Respondents are not questioned beyond their ability to respond accurately. Moreover, many respondents find the experience somewhat enjoyable.

Ms. Morrison has just been approached by a national builder of homes, apartments, and condominiums. The builder wants Ms. Morrison's firm to identify key problems that potential customers have with nonsingle unit dwellings (i.e., apartments, condominiums, townhouses, etc.) and to suggest product design features to solve these problems.

Evaluate the problem detection system developed by BBDO. Do you think it is appropriate for new product development? Is new product development appropriate for a house, apartment, and condominium builder?

Case 8-2: GODDARD BUILDING MATERIALS

Goddard Building Materials is a manufacturer of roof trusses and a wholesaler of other building materials in St. Cloud, Minnesota. Boyd J. Goddard is the owner and manager of the business. Mr. Goddard started out as a building contractor. He prospered as a contractor but soon identified a new opportunity.

Goddard spotted his opportunity when he noticed that roof trusses for houses and industrial buildings were not being manufactured in the St. Cloud area. In fact, the closest factory was about 45 miles away. Goddard borrowed some money, started a small factory, and was soon providing trusses for the entire St. Cloud area and much of northern Minnesota.

---

[1]Adapted from E. E. Norris, "Your Surefire Clue to Ad Success: Seek Out the Consumer's Problem," *Advertising Age*, March 17, 1979, p. 43.

Although Mr. Goddard got his start in manufacturing roof trusses, he soon began to act as a wholesaler of other lines of building materials he did not manufacture. As time passed, the wholesaling business first equaled and then exceeded the truss manufacturing business. The primary purchasers of both the trusses and the building materials were contractors operating in the retail trade area of St. Cloud. Mr. Goddard relied mainly on walk-in business, but he tried to visit all the contractors in the area at least once every six months. He knew many of the contractors personally and was confident that the personal attention he gave them was responsible for most of his sales volume.

Mr. Goddard is currently wrestling with a product line decision. Specifically, he is concerned about the different lines of insulation to stock. Currently his product line consists of fiberglass bats for insulating walls and under floors and one brand of cellulose insulation which is commonly blown into attics. Although the insulation product line offered by Goddard Building Materials is fairly narrow, he thinks it is adequate for most types of construction in the St. Cloud area.

The decision he faces is whether to expand his product line to include both additional brands and new types of insulation. He is considering the expansion for several reasons. First, many custom-home buyers are now specifying not only the amount but also the type and frequently the brand of insulation they desire in the home. Second, the emphasis on fuel conservation has stimulated interest in many new types of insulation. One type of insulation that is of particular interest is foam. This insulation is squirted into the walls after the exterior siding and interior wall board are in place.

What factors should Mr. Goddard consider as he makes his decision about the insulation product line? Should he be concerned about brands or just generic types of insulation?

9

price

Regional Slump

*Prices of Homes in Chicago Suburbs Begin to Fall
Amid Glut Due to Bad Winter and Gasoline Pinch*

--*The Wall Street Journal,*
July 20, 1979

The price of a product or service plays an important role in most economies. Price is particularly important in free enterprise economies such as those in the United States, Canada, and Western Europe. Consequently, marketing managers need a basic understanding of how overall economic factors are affected by the pricing practices of businesses. Also, marketing managers should know how economic forces affect the pricing strategies that management implement. These economic forces not only limit the pricing practices of management, but they also present many opportunities. Consider the Volkswagen Rabbit with the diesel engine. In 1978 the Rabbit was rated as the automobile with the highest miles per gallon rating of any automobile marketed in the United States. This miles per gallon rating, along with fuel shortages and rising fuel prices, caused consumers to greatly desire high mileage cars. Because of this, dealers began asking and receiving from $500 to $2,500 above the suggested retail price.[1]

Many people think that business people who mark up prices exorbitantly are unethical. Actually the raising or lowering of prices based on the willingness of

---

[1]Amanda Bennett, "Rabbits Multiplying, But a Bit Too Slowly to Suit Most People," *The Wall Street Journal,* March 23, 1979, p. 1.

customers to pay serves two vital functions: the balancing of supply and demand and the allocation of more resources to produce the desired product—high mileage automobiles, for example.

This chapter will discuss the balancing function and the supply and demand function of price setting. Additionally, both the theoretical and practical aspects of setting a price are presented. Finally, the strategic implications relating price setting to the marketing mix are discussed. Included in the strategic pricing area are pricing strategy, pricing objectives, pricing methods, and pricing policies.

PRICE IN THE FREE ENTERPRISE ECONOMY

The role of price in the free enterprise economy is important and, in fact, fundamental to the operation of the economy. Because of the importance of price and the fact that this importance is frequently misunderstood, we should consider the following:

Economies: Two Types

To better visualize the role that price plays in the United States economy it is useful to contrast the two general types of economies found in the world—free enterprise and command. These two economies are shown in Illus. 9-1 as end points of a continuum. Positioned along the continuum are the approximate locations of various national economies.

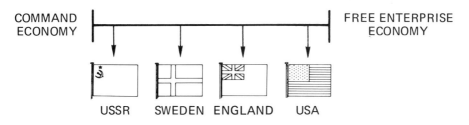

Illus. 9-1   Continuum of World Economies

Two factors differentiate predominantly command economies from predominantly free enterprise economies. First is the rationale or chief value the economy serves. Second is the role of price in balancing supply and demand. Directly related to supply and demand is how economic resources are allocated to meet the ultimate consumer and business requirements.

What Values Should the Economic System Satisfy?   A fundamental question to be asked of any economic system is what primary value the economy serves. An even more basic question is whether the economic value is inherent in the system or imposed from the outside. All economic systems, to one degree or another, have to provide a standard of living for the people working and living in the system. In free enterprise economies this goal, to provide a standard of living, is the fundamental reason the economic system is organized as it is Theoretically the economy exists for no other reason. If resources are drawn from the economic output of the country to satisfy a need other than consumer well-being, these resources are collected through taxes levied on the members of the economy. Basically the very reason for the economy's organization and operation is the consumer's material well-being.

Command economies also must provide a standard of living for the members of the economic system. However, the percentage of the country's output that is funneled to the individual consumer's well-being is often dependent on or subservient to other goals. These goals can be determined by a political process representative of the people, or more frequently imposed by the desires of the country's leaders.

In actual practice the economies vary in operation because of their differences. In free enterprise economies demand for goods and services by ultimate consumers serves as the organizational motivation for collecting resources and manufacturing and marketing of products. Individuals perceive that a demand for a particular product exists. Resources are collected and used to acquire the means necessary to manufacture and market the product. The individuals who collect the resources and bear the risk of success or failure do so because of the possibility of earning a profit.

The organizational motivation in command economies is somewhat different from consumer demand. Economic planners take into consideration previously decided goals and then assign each economic unit certain goals or objectives. The motivation in the economy does not come through the desires of consumers, but through the goals, objectives, and quotas set by the economic planners.

In the two types of economies, the function a product's price carries out is entirely different. In a free enterprise economy product prices reflect relative value, that is, the ability of the product to command other goods in exchange.[2] Prices are simply reflections of value in monetary terms. In command economies prices are used more as a rationing tool. By economic plan, only a certain number of products will be produced in a given time period. To attempt to balance the supply of the product with the demand, the price of the product is arbitrarily set hopefully to insure that supply will not outstrip demand, or vice versa.

One other interesting difference in the two economies is the location of the planning function. Critics of free enterprise economies have frequently questioned the free enterprise system's viability because economic planning does not take place. This criticism is not correct, however. Economic planning does occur, but at a much lower level than in a command economy. Among other things, business firms plan, on a very frequent basis, the product lines they will offer, the manufacturing equipment in which they will invest, advertising budgets which they will

[2]Theodore N. Beckman, William R. Davidson, and W. Wayne Talarzyk, *Marketing* (9h ed.; New York City: The Ronald Press Company, 1973), p. 358.

expend, building expansion, and so on. Similarly, consumers frequently plan the purchases they will make. A more appropriate question is whether economic planning at the national level is more effective than at the individual firm and consumer level.

How Are Resources Allocated?   The two types of economies also differ with respect to how scarce economic resources are allocated. In free enterprise economies, price plays an important role. The price a product sells for is a direct reflection of how much or how little consumers value the product. If consumers are willing to pay a high price for the product, the company offering the product stands a good chance of earning a high profit. High profits encourage both the original company and other firms to offer more of the product. In this way prices, serving as a direct reflection of how people value products, determine how resources are allocated to various end uses.

In command economies, resources are allocated by decision making at a much higher level than individual consumer or company levels. Consumer demand or willingness to purchase certain products may or may not be taken into consideration by the decision makers. Shortages of many consumer goods may exist, but other goals may simply have higher priorities. A competing goal with the production of consumer goods could be, for example, the construction of a new steel mill.

The price consumers are willing to pay is fundamental to the operation of a free enterprise economy. Because of this importance, price has always been considered a major factor in both marketing and economics. The result of this price emphasis over time has been the development of a rather elegant model of how businesses should price their products to maximize profits. This model, although unrealistic in many ways, can be useful in gaining perspective on the price-setting process.

Economic Foundations for Price Determination

For two given products having similar characteristics, costs of the products tend to approach a uniform figure. Also, preferences people have for such products have common characteristics. Based on these realities, economists have developed a conceptual scheme which describes the means by which prices of such products are influenced by costs and consumer preferences. Product costs and desire for products operate in a dynamic market to establish limits on the amount that is produced and sold and on the prices that are charged. In order to understand how this price-making process operates, basic economic concepts will be introduced and illustrated in a model: and this model will be examined in relation to realistic market place situations.

Costs and Revenues   This discussion is based on money costs and revenues and on the assumption that the firm wishes to maximize its profits. To illustrate the economic process involved, the model used will be a hypothetical shoe manufacturing company seeking an optimum point at which to price its shoes. The product is sold in competition with other similar shoes in a specific market. The shoes are a popular brand, and some prestige accrues to them because of the brand name. It is assumed that the shoes should sell at different prices than competitive shoes and that more units will sell at lower than at higher prices.

Basic to the whole concept of discovering the price that will maximize profit is the determination of the point where total revenue exceeds total costs by the greatest amount. This computation is complicated somewhat by the fact that unit costs tend to vary according to the amount produced, and unit revenues vary according to the amount placed on the market at a given time. To discover the point of optimum balance between total costs and total revenues, marginal costs and marginal revenues must be determined. Knowing how these magnitudes are determined and how they are interrelated is essential to an understanding of the price-determination process.

Marginal Cost.   It has already been stated that costs vary according to the volume of units produced. Economic studies show that in most instances where fixed and variable costs are involved a point is reached as volume is increased where the cost per unit increases with each added unit of production. As volume of production and sales increases, the per unit fixed cost diminishes. On the other hand, as the output increases and the production and management coordination processes grow more complex, the variable unit cost decreases at a slower rate or increases. Frequently such costs increase faster than unit fixed costs decrease; therefore, the total costs increase—a phenomenon described by economists as the law of diminishing returns. Strategic to this discussion, though, is the cost element called *marginal cost*— the amount of cost that is added as a result of producing and selling one additional increment of the product. This phenomenon will be understood more clearly when it is introduced in the model illustrating the production and sale of shoes.

Marginal Revenue.   The price or the average per unit revenue that is received is influenced by the amount of a product that is offered on the market. When a useful and desired product is offered, there are usually a few buyers who are willing to pay a comparatively high price for it; but there are more people who are willing to buy the product only at a lesser price. Therefore, when only a few products are offered, a high price can be obtained. Theoretically, however, each additional unit that is offered must be sold to a person who is willing to pay less than the previous buyers. As a progression of this process continues, the price continues to decrease. All purchasers of the product will then buy the product at the lesser price since theoretically it is impossible to sell to each buyer at the highest price that the buyer is willing to pay. Regardless of the intensity of the buyer's desire to buy the product, he or she will insist on paying the same price as the lowest buyer. The strategic question then is what change will the sale of each succeeding increment of the product make in the total revenue of the firm. This amount is the *marginal revenue*—the amount by which the total revenue is changed by the addition of one more unit of product to sales. It should be noted that this amount will not be the same as the price received for the additional unit. When the additional unit is offered at a reduced price, the price of all other sales will decrease to the amount of the lowest price at which there was a sale.

Therefore, the marginal revenue will usually be less than the price or the average revenue.

Optimum Price for Maximum Profits. This brings us to the hypothetical shoe company which is presented as operating at different production levels of from 1,000 to 9,000 pairs of shoes (see Table 9-1). The company judges that any change in production levels, to be economic, should be at least in increments of 1,000 pairs. For example, note at the production level of 3,000 pairs that the average variable cost (determined by dividing the number of pairs produced into total variable costs) is $7.66 per unit. The average fixed cost (total fixed cost divided by the number of shoes produced) is $4, making the average total cost $11.66 per unit. At this production level the total cost would be $35,000, which is $4,000 more than the total cost of producing 2,000 pairs of shoes. The $4,000, then, is the marginal cost at this level of operation.

**Table 9-1   An Illustration of the Laws of Increasing
and Diminishing Returns**

Quantity (1000's)	Average Variable Cost	Average Fixed Cost	Average Total Cost	Total Cost (1000's)	Marginal Cost (1000's)	Average Revenue (Price)	Total Revenue (1000's)	Marginal Revenue (1000's)	Profit (1000's)
1	$12.00	$12.00	$24.00	$24	—	$17	$17	—	$- 7
2	9.50	6.00	15.50	31	$ 7	15	30	$13	- 1
3	7.66	4.00	11.66	35	4	13	39	9	4
4	6.25	3.00	9.25	37	2	11	44	5	7
5	5.60	2.40	8.00	40	3	9	45	1	5
6	5.50	2.00	7.50	45	5	7	42	- 3	- 3
7	5.86	1.71	7.57	53	8	5	35	- 7	-18
8	6.63	1.50	8.13	65	12	3	24	-11	-41
9	7.78	1.33	9.11	82	17	1	9	-15	-73

The average revenue is equal to the prevailing price for the shoes. We note that, as the amount that is offered on the market is increased, the average revenue (price) decreases from $17 at the 1,000 unit production level to $1 at the 9,000 level. At the 3,000 unit production level, average revenue is $13 per pair of shoes. At this point in production the total revenue of $39,000 is $4,000 greater than the total costs, and this figure represents the company's profits. If the company increases its operation to 4,000 units, the marginal costs are $2,000; marginal revenue, $5,000; and total profits, $7,000. This $3,000 increase in profits is the result of marginal revenue exceeding marginal costs by this amount. The next step in the progressively increasing production point is strategic in this illustration. At the 5,000 unit production level, the marginal cost increases from $2,000 to $3,000, while the marginal revenue decreases from $5,000 to $1,000. Thus, if the company were to increase its production from 4,000 to 5,000 pairs, its profits would be smaller by $2,000.

By presenting these relationships graphically, it is theoretically possible to determine the strategic points with even greater precision. In Illus. 9-2 notice

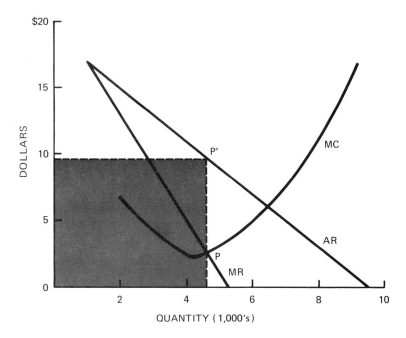

Illus. 9-2   **Graphic Illustration of the Laws of
                                  Increasing and Diminishing Returns**

that the marginal revenue curve and the marginal cost curve intersect at Point
P, or at approximately $2.5. The average revenue is slightly under $10, and
the number of shoes offered on the market is between 4,000 and 5,000 pairs.

The intersection of the marginal revenue curve with the marginal cost curve
is strategic. These magnitudes represent the amount of change in the total revenue
and total cost. Therefore, when marginal revenue is greater than the marginal cost,
the profit spread between total costs and total revenue is greater. When additional
units are added after the point of intersection, the amount added to costs is greater
than the amount added to revenue, and the total profits are smaller. Therefore, the
optimum price is that point where the marginal revenue and the marginal cost
approach equality.

Practical Value of Marginal Concepts This pricing explanation has its
roots in neoclassical, or Marshallian, economics. It represents a sound view of
establishing a price to maximize profits. When this concept was first described by
Alfred Marshall, land, labor, and capital were the basic cost factors; and the
demand for products was much less complicated. The soundness of the basic theory
remains intact, but in its application costs have become much more complex than
the simple measure of the classical factors of production. Also, the competition for
thousands of new and innovative products has added an infinite number of influences to the revenue curve.

Marshall's theory presumes that costs should be computed on the basis of the
entire production cost. On most products sold today, fixed costs should include

costs of developing a product and the cost of product failures before a successful product is developed. Unit product cost should also include a distribution of selling and administrative costs. Frequently many of these costs are incurred at points remote from the time and place where the specific cost they add to each product can be determined. To include them in unit cost figures requires considerable effort and many estimates. Furthermore, a price policy may dictate that a price be established for a period, such as a year, as is the case with automobiles and some packaged goods. In the course of such a period, under a dynamic system of management, a company may change its operations to reduce its costs, thus influencing the point where marginal cost curves increase. It is also likely that in the course of a year the firm's advertising and selling program may influence volume and have an effect on the marginal revenue curve. It is, therefore, impossible for a company to follow the marginal cost and marginal revenue rule in the absolute sense. Such a course would require a change in price with each change in the position of the cost or the revenue curve.

Impact of New Concepts on Cost   Because of accounting difficulties and frequent changes in demand, the rule of maximizing profit by pricing at the intersection of marginal cost and revenue curves has not been given great attention. However, the computers provide instant accounting data. These data will include comprehensive amounts of information formerly beyond the scope of conventional accounting. Another very important feature of modern computer accounting is that when a change takes place in costs, the change can immediately be recorded and become part of the current computation. The same can be said of the revenue side of the equation. Indeed, with these changes it is possible that in modern firms the marginal cost and the marginal revenue intersection may be kept in constant focus.

PRICING STRATEGY AND OBJECTIVES

One of the key factors that marketing management must consider in the design of the marketing mix is the importance of price in marketing the product. The role of price should be consistent with the other aspects of the marketing mix. Additionally, the price of a product or service is frequently the most easily adjusted of all marketing mix factors. Because of this, the marketing mix can frequently be brought into line with changing market conditions or consumers' expectations by simply adjusting the price.

The price of a product is viewed by consumers as much more than what has to be given up to attain the product. Price is frequently used by consumers as a direct indication of quality.[3] Also, the price of many products carries a certain status with it. In *some* situations, and for *some* products, raising the product's price may actually increase demand. Pricing strategy refers to how management uses the

---

[3]Donald S. Tull, R. A. Boring, and M. H. Gonsior, "A Note on the Relationship of Price and Imputed Quality," *Journal of Business,* Vol. 37, No. 1 (April, 1964), p. 186.

price variable of the marketing mix to influence target markets or earn a profit for the firm. A number of pricing strategies and strategy classifications exist. The strategies discussed here are based on product cost and whether the product is a new offering.[4]

Full Cost Pricing

Full cost pricing means that for each product sold, the selling price must cover the product's portion of the fixed costs, as well as the variable costs associated with the product. A full cost pricing strategy emphasizes the importance of covering all production and marketing costs in view of the long run. If these costs cannot be covered, the capability of the firm to survive will be threatened.

Full cost pricing is usually associated with markup pricing methods. *Markup pricing,* frequently employed by retailers and wholesalers, means that the selling price of a product is determined by adding a fixed percentage to the cost of the product. For example, the standard markup in many retail stores is 100 percent. This markup figure may be based on tradition, competitive factors, or it may exist for simplicity. Regardless of the underlying logic, retailers may simply mark the price as double the cost and put the product on the shelf. More formally:

$$\text{Cost} \times (\text{Markup percentage} + 1) = \text{Selling Price}$$
$$\$3.00 \times (100\% + 1) = \text{Selling Price}$$
$$\$3.00 \times 2 = \$6.00$$

If the item was marked up 50 percent, the formula would read:

$$\$3.00 \times (50\% + 1) = \text{Selling Price}$$
$$\$3.00 \times 1.5 = \$4.50$$

The markup percentage used by the merchant will typically vary by product class. It will be selected to insure that all overhead costs are covered and that some profit is earned.

Variable Cost Pricing

A *variable cost pricing strategy* means that at times products are priced simply to cover the variable unit costs of production and marketing and not total unit costs, which include fixed costs. The reasoning for this strategy is that fixed costs will continue whether or not the firm manufactures and markets a product. Therefore, in the short run it may be better to continue to manufacture and market a product even though only variable unit costs are being covered. Employees are kept in jobs, the product is kept in front of consumers, and conditions may change in the near future which will again allow the firm to charge the full cost price.

In addition to the desire to stay in business, variable cost pricing can serve two other functions. Because the cost of the product is lower than full cost, demand may increase (remember the downward sloping demand curve). Demand may

---

[4]The strategy classification and discussion was derived in part from Roger A. Kerin and Robert A Peterson, *Strategic Marketing Problems* (Boston: Allyn & Bacon, Inc., 1978), p. 338.

increase to the point where per unit production and marketing costs drop, total revenues increase, and the product eventually becomes profitable. This argument is especially relevant in industries characterized by high fixed costs, and where the incremental costs of producing one more unit is rather small. Consider the airline industry: the plane must fly the route whether partially full or completely full. By providing standby tickets at reduced prices, less than full-price customers can still contribute to the profit and overhead of the firm.

A second reason for variable cost pricing is to shift demand from one location or time period to another. The net result can be a net overall increase in revenue with more satisfied customers because fewer customers are turned away. Movie theatres frequently feature matinees at lower prices than for the evening shows. Lower afternoon ticket prices help shift attendance from peak times to slow times.

Variable cost pricing methods are also used as a promotion device. Retail stores feature *loss leader* items. These items are priced well below full cost. Hopefully, the low cost items attract customers to the store to purchase other items as well as the loss leaders.

New Product Pricing

The pricing of a new product is particularly challenging. The difficulty lies in forecasting how the market will respond to the product. Simply relying on cost-oriented methods may severely underprice the product relative to what customers are willing to pay. Also, it may initially overvalue the product and therefore prevent the product from being a long-run success.

In new product pricing, a continuum of pricing practices is followed. Perhaps the most conservative practice is to *skim* the market. This strategy implies setting the price high initially and therefore restricting sales to some extent. Through time, the price of the product is slowly lowered. This brings more potential buyers into the marketplace. Skimming strategies are safer in that it is much easier to correct a pricing error. Consumers accept a price reduction on a product with less resistance than a price increase.

Skimming methods are particularly useful when a firm wants to recover the initial costs of product development rather quickly. A danger of skimming is that the high price will encourage a competitor to enter the market and undersell the original product. Therefore, a skimming strategy is easier to implement when the product is technically advanced, covered by a patent, or is in some other way protected from competition.

The opposite strategy of price skimming is *market penetration,* a strategy that implies setting an initial low price. Because of the low price the potential market for the product is very large. The advantages of this strategy include discouraging competition from entering the market and establishing a large and loyal following of customers. This strategy is particularly useful when a product's unit cost of marketing and production decreases rapidly as volume increases.

Skimming and penetration are end points of a continuum of new product pricing strategies. Many firms simply elect an intermediate price and then adjust the price as market conditions and the initial experience with the product dictate.

Pricing Objectives

Ideally all elements of the marketing mix achieve certain objectives which contribute to marketing objectives and overall company objectives. Pricing objectives must be consistent with the general pricing strategy followed by firms. Additionally, the pricing objectives guide the establishment of price policies and the selection of price determination methods. Three general classes of pricing objectives have been identified.[5]

Profit-Oriented Objectives. Profit-oriented pricing objectives imply that the primary concern in setting prices will be the effect the prices have on profits. The effect on profits of overall price levels or price changes are assessed more with respect to profits than to competition, sales, or even public relations.

Three primary profit-oriented objectives have been identified: profit maximization, target return, and satisfactory profit. Profit maximization has already been discussed. This simply means that a firm will price in such a way as to achieve maximum profits, regardless of the effect on competition, society, or even the ultimate consumer. This goal does not lend itself to evaluation and may be socially unacceptable to many members of society. Additionally, a manager following this goal must determine whether profit maximization in the short or long run is desired. In spite of the many weaknesses of this objective, it fits with the economic theory of optional price determination. Following a profit maximization goal will theoretically lead to an optimal allocation of resources in a free enterprise economy.

A more common objective is simply a target return. This return can be in dollar figures or percentage terms. A small business may have a dollar value as an objective to insure that the owner and the owner's family will have the standard of living they desire. Large businesses frequently use a percentage figure. Common percentages used are net profit to sales or net profit to investment. General Motors has popularized the return on investment method. In large, decentralized firms such as General Motors, maintaining control over the various divisions and departments becomes a challenge. Financial controls, such as minimum return on investment figures, facilitate this process.

A final profit-oriented objective is satisfactory profits. The argument goes that managers of some firms determine what stockholders, boards of directors, and others think are acceptable profit levels. The managers then insure that satisfactory profit levels are reached. After the satisfactory profits are achieved, the managers may focus on other objectives besides profits.

Sales-Oriented Objectives. Some businesses may stress sales and sales growth over profits. Although this idea is in conflict with the marketing concept, it is still held by many managers that sales growth must occur first and that profits

[5]The classification of pricing objectives was taken from E. Jerome McCarthy, *Basic Marketing: A Managerial Approach* (6h ed.; Homewood, Ill.: Richard D. Irwin, Inc., 1978), p. 479.

will eventually follow. Many firms are finding out, however, that this is not always the case.[6] Profits do not necessarily follow sales growth in many firms for two reasons. First, the industry may be highly competitive. Consequently, prices lower than what are acceptable for an adequate profit are set to simply compete with the other firms in the industry. Second, lower prices are initially set to encourage brand trial and hopefully brand loyalty. The plan is to raise the price when the brand develops a loyal following of customers. However, because of similarities among competitive products and other reasons, brand loyalty may not develop. Under this condition consumers quickly shift from one brand to another depending on which brand has the lowest price. This practice keeps prices and, therefore, profits at low levels.

In addition to growth in sales, two other sales-oriented objectives have been identified: growth in market share and maintaining market share. Growth in market share and maintaining market share are both pricing objectives that relate to competition. In highly competitive markets and also in slow growth markets, maintaining market share may determine all pricing practices. The usual justification for this type of pricing is the demonstrated difficulty in regaining market share once it has been lost. Therefore, prices are frequently adjusted to prevent losing market share. Moreover, the easiest time to achieve a strong market position (high market share) is when the market is rapidly growing. Frequently price adjustments are made during these growth periods to insure that when the market stabilizes the firm will have an established or strong position.

Status Quo Objectives.   Status quo objectives also relate to competition and refer to pricing in such a way as to meet or avoid competition. At least two reasons may explain the use of this type of objective. First, all firms in the industry may recognize that a cut in price will be followed by all other firms in the industry. Therefore, the net result of the price cut will likely be similar market shares for all firms as before the price cut, but with lower profits for all. A second justification is also based on the recognition that price competition leads to lower profits. Firms, rather than compete on the basis of price, choose to compete on another basis, such as promotional effectiveness, product development, or distribution.

Regardless of the pricing objectives utilized, the pricing system must be managed to reach the objectives. Management implements and manages the pricing system through the establishment of pricing policies and the determination of actual price-setting methods.

PRICING METHODS AND POLICIES

Once a firm's management has decided upon the appropriate pricing strategy and pricing objectives, specific pricing methods and policies must be formulated.

---

[6]"Pricing Strategy in an Inflation Economy," *Business Week* (April 6, 1974), p. 43.

These methods and policies serve as day-to-day guidelines for the actual setting and adjusting of prices.

A number of specific pricing methods are available to a manager. These methods must, however, be used within the context of the situation, the firm, and the marketplace to be truly effective. To help managers price products within the correct frame of reference, three factors should be considered.

Target Market, Image, Marketing Mix

The target market, the brand image, and the marketing mix should all be considered before a final price is decided upon. Firms following the marketing concept should be knowledgeable about the behavior, attitudes, demographics, and perhaps even price expectations of target market members. These factors can give the marketer insight on how the firm's product should be priced; and, more importantly, how the price will be accepted by the target market customers.

The image carried by the product or service is also an important factor to consider in price setting. The product image is, to some degree, already set by the company image. However, product images can be separated from the firm's image. For example, Tide detergent is widely known as a Proctor & Gamble product, yet it still has a distinctive image of its own. The image decision is basically a positioning decision. Specifically, the product is positioned relative to both competitive products and target market members' expectations. Such questions as *What expectations about quality do our target market members hold about the product?* or *Relative to our product's major competition, should our product be positioned as more or less exclusive?* must be asked.

Finally, the pricing decision can be made only within the greater context of the marketing mix. The price chosen must be consistent with the product quality and image, the distribution channel (i.e., type of outlet, level of selectivity, etc.), and the promotional media and creative strategy utilized. Price levels inconsistent with other marketing mix factors are confusing to customers and frequently disruptive of marketing channels. Marketing effectiveness is improved when the marketing mix is both consistent and designed for the selected target market.

Pricing Methods

Specific price-setting methods are usually determined on the basis of cost, competition, and demand. Each of these methods is useful in given situations, and frequently more than one method may be utilized in attempting to identify the best or most appropriate price.

The names of the three pricing methods indicate that either cost, demand, or competitors' prices are considered when the price is set. A more realistic view is that either cost, demand, or competition is emphasized in the decision. All three factors will usually be considered to one degree or another as pricing decisions are made. Like all managerial decisions, pricing decisions require a mixture of managerial judgment and information about the pricing situation.

Cost-Oriented Methods. Cost-Oriented pricing methods were discussed previously in this chapter. Briefly, these methods rely on the cost of the product to determine the selling price. For example, architects and building contractors frequently price their services at a rate of 10 percent of the cost of the project.

Cost-oriented pricing methods are used for a number of reasons. First, in competitive situations cost-oriented methods insure that prices among competitors will not differ drastically. For example, retailers using standard markup percentages can be confident that prices will differ little among them. Second, cost-oriented pricing is relatively simple. Decisions about consumers' expectations and demand curves are not required. Finally, cost-oriented pricing methods are considered more fair by many people. Therefore, firms that are particularly concerned about public relations may utilize some form of cost-oriented pricing to insure that the pricing method chosen will be acceptable to the firm's publics.

The two primary methods of cost pricing, markup and cost plus, have been discussed previously. *Markup pricing,* frequently used in retail and wholesale businesses, simply means pricing the product by using the cost of the product as a base. This base cost is then increased by a commonly used percentage. Commonsense rules have been developed to assist marketers in determining the markup percentage. Although the rules are not always followed by retailers, they are useful to keep in mind.

1. An inverse relationship should exist between markup percentage and unit cost.
2. An inverse relationship should exist between markup percentage and product turnover.
3. Markups should be higher, but prices lower, on middlemen's brands than on manufacturers' brands.[7]

Cost plus pricing, in addition to being used by building contractors and architects, is also used in situations where making cost estimates is extremely difficult or impossible. A firm or a governmental unit may desire a new type of equipment with capabilities exceeding what is currently available. In order to get interested parties to submit bids, a cost plus proposal may have to be offered. Otherwise the uncertainty of the project would be so great that no firm would bid for the job.

Competition-Oriented Methods. Competition-oriented pricing implies that the primary emphasis on selecting a price is the level at which a firm's competitors are pricing. Costs and demand are not totally ignored, but competitor's prices are extremely important to strategic or tactical pricing decisions. Moreover, pricing on the basis of competition does not imply that prices are set identical to a competitor's prices. Frequently a firm may have a policy of pricing a certain percentage above or below a primary competitor's price.

Competition-oriented pricing has been referred to as ball-park pricing.[8] The idea of ball-park pricing is to price products at about the level of the average price

---

[7]Lee E. Preston, *Profits, Competition, and Rules of Thumb in Retail Food Pricing* (Berkeley, Calif.: University of California Institute of Business and Economic Research, 1963), p. 29.

[8]Mark I. Alpert, *Pricing Decisions* (Glenview, Ill.: Scott, Foresman & Company, 1971), p. 43.

in the industry. In many situations products are actually designed and developed to sell for a certain price. First, a decision is made about the retail price of the product. Next, the discounts from list price are calculated to insure high enough margins that retailers, and if necessary other middlemen, will handle the product. Finally, the amount necessary to earn an acceptable profit at forecast volume levels is computed. The remaining or residual figure will be what is available for production and marketing costs. This figure, rather than engineering considerations, may have a dominant influence on the production methods and materials utilized in producing the products.

Competition-oriented pricing is also used where sealed bids are submitted. This procedure is used in numerous and varied situations such as in the purchase of surplus equipment or in the awarding of television contracts. The objective of the bidding firm is to price just beneath the closest competitor. A bid above the competition won't win the contract, and a bid far below the nearest competitor is underbidding the proposal. Competition's price is the point of emphasis.

Competition-oriented pricing has two main advantages. First, the prices competitors are charging can usually be ascertained and are relatively certain. In cost- and demand-oriented pricing, figures of such certainty are usually not easily obtainable. Second, competition-oriented pricing can reduce or eliminate price competition among competitors. As discussed before, using price as a competitive tool is considered disasterous by many business people.

Demand-Oriented Pricing. Demand-oriented pricing means that a high price will be charged when desire for the product is high and a low price when desire for the product is low. The theory of demand pricing was discussed early in this chapter under the heading of "Economic Foundations for Price Determination." In actual practice, much demand-oriented pricing takes the form of price discrimination. Numerous forms of this discrimination can exist. Discrimination can take place on the basis of customers, product version, place, and time.[9]

Consider the following examples: On any Saturday afternoon in the fall, fans pour into football stadiums in Tuscaloosa, Alabama; Norman, Oklahoma; and South Bend, Indiana. Whether the fan backs the Crimson Tide, the Sooners, or the Fighting Irish, those on the 50-yard line paid more for their tickets than those on the 20-yard line. On the basis of geographic location or location in the stadium, differential ticket prices are charged. A second example is the differential pricing practices of some ski lift operators. Frequently, lift passes sold on weekdays are cheaper than those sold on Saturdays and Sundays. The lower ticket prices during the week encourage more people to use the ski lifts during relatively slack periods. On the basis of time, differential ticket prices are charged.

---

[9]Philip Kotler, *Marketing Management: Analysis, Planning and Control* (2d ed.; Englewood Cliffs, N.J.: Prentice Hall, Inc., 1972), p. 527.

Pricing Policies

"Price policies are general guides to action that determine how prices will be used to attain the goals pursued by the firm."[10] Price policies include such topics as price flexibility, price level, pricing over the product life cycle, price discounts, and product pricing related to transportation costs.[11]

Price Flexibility Policies. Price flexibility policies generally relate to whether a one-price or a varying-price policy will be followed. Retail stores in general practice a one-price policy. Regardless of the quantity of purchase or who the purchaser is, all buyers pay the same price. Automobile dealerships, on the other hand, practice a varying-price policy. The price a customer pays for a car may relate directly to the knowledge and negotiating ability of the buyer. This is a form of price discrimination based on the customer.

Price-Level Policies. Price-level policies relate to competition-oriented pricing methods. Specifically, price-level policies describe how a firm's products will be priced relative to competitors' prices. These policies may also describe how the firm will react to a competitor's change in price.

Pricing over the Product Life Cycle. Pricing-over-the-product-life-cycle policies describe practices to be followed as the product moves through its life cycle. Price skimming and market penetration relate to pricing the product in the introductory and growth stage. Policies should also be developed to guide product pricing during the maturity and decline stage.

Price Discount Policies. Price discount policies refer to such things as quantity discounts, trade discounts, and cash discounts. Quantity discounts are given to encourage customers to cluster their purchases with just one supplier. These discounts, which generally must be cost justified, are of two types. Non-cumulative quantity discounts are given on single purchases. The idea of these discounts is to encourage buying in large lots. Cumulative quantity discounts are given for the purchase of products over a period of time. Usually, if some minimum quantity is purchased, a discount will apply retroactively to all previously purchased products during the time period.

Trade and cash discounts are also given for specific purposes. Trade discounts are given off list or suggested retail price. These are awarded to gain cooperation and the performance of marketing functions by middlemen. Wholesalers are frequently given larger discounts than retailers. The reason for the different discounts is that wholesalers are supposed to perform more marketing functions for the manufacturer or supplier than are retailers. Cash discounts are given simply to hasten the payment for merchandise that has been delivered.

---

[10]Rom J. Markin, *Marketing* (New York City: John Wiley & Sons, Inc., 1979), p. 589.
[11]McCarthy, *op. cit.* p. 483.

Usually terms, such as 2/10 net 30, are specified on the sales invoice. This means that a 2 percent discount off the invoice price will be given if the bill is paid within 10 days. Otherwise the bill must be paid in full within 30 days.

Pricing and Transportation Costs.   Pricing policies relating to transportation costs are also important. When a sale is made the buyer should know who pays the transportation costs. The buyer should be particularly aware of whether the price quoted is a delivered price or a seller's origin price.

An additional factor of some importance to the buyer is when the title or ownership for the product changes. The designation *FOB* is used to facilitate title change. *FOB* means free on board. For example, if a manufacturer sells goods on *FOB factory* terms, the buyer pays all transportation costs from the factory and owns the goods from the moment they are shipped. If the manufacturer sells on *FOB destination* terms, the manufacturer pays transportation charges and holds title to the goods until they reach the customer.

Retail Pricing Policies.

Retailers at all levels have pricing problems particular to the retailing function. Two pricing policies particularly suited to retailers, but used to one degree or another by other marketing institutions, are odd-price policies and price lining.

Odd prices were originally adopted as a means of preventing clerks from pocketing money from a sale. If a book sold for $10 and was paid for with a ten dollar bill, it was easy for a dishonest clerk to pocket the money and not report the sale. If the book cost $9.95, however, the clerk had to ring up the sale on the cash register or record the sale with a cashier. In addition, the view has long been held that pricing goods at $4.95 or $4.98 rather than at $5 increases sales greatly. This view presumes that the slight difference in the prices escapes the consumer's consciousness. That the psychological sound of 98 cents creates less resistance than $1 sounds plausible, and the fact that such techniques are universally practiced is an indication that this view is widely held. However, empirical evidence is lacking to prove that this concept is true, and there has been no agreement on which odd prices are most effective. In a study which attempted to gather empirical evidence, a large mail-order firm made a catalog, split-run test on an item. The item was priced in one million copies of the catalog at one-cent intervals from $1.99 to $1.98—that is, one million catalogs priced the item at $1.99; a second million copies, at $1.98; and so on. There was no conclusive evidence that any one of the prices in the series was more effective than another. It would be most helpful if there were more evidence to support the theories that influence the setting of prices.

In the field of shopping goods, retailers must decide whether to use price lines or to price at a variety of levels. A *price-line* policy is followed when a store selects a specific price within a certain price range. For example, instead of pricing suits that cost $40 and $50 at prices yielding a goal of 40 percent markup, or $63 and $83, a specialty store prices all the suits at $75. Extreme examples of this policy were the menswear stores that carried only suits and topcoats at a single price. Although most of these stores have changed their policy today, they still adhere to a rigid price-line policy of offering suits at only two or three prices. There are virtues in such a policy. It is simple. The stock control problem is made easy. It resolves itself into keeping an adequate variety of styles, sizes, and colors in each line. The task of making a choice is also simplified for the consumer. Making the price-quality evaluation is often a frustrating experience for him. Setting a price line tends to avoid much of this confusion and makes a decision easier. Smaller stock may be required to satisfy customers. The purchases may be concentrated into popular price lines. Bookkeeping and marketing are routine, and it is easy to compute the retail price on items of stock.

On the other hand, difficulties may be encountered in using price lines. Some customers may prefer a price between price lines. A store may have price lines including $1, $1.40, and $1.80. Such customers may wish to pay $1.25, but not $1.40, or $1.75, or $1.80 for goods priced in this zone. On the other hand, the store may gain by actually selling merchandise for $1.80 to those who would normally have paid only $1.75.

QUESTIONS AND ANALYTICAL PROBLEMS

1. Price is an adjusting mechanism. Explain.
2. Define (a) marginal costs, (b) marginal revenue, (c) average revenue.
3. What factors are involved in determining the optimum price for a product or a service?
4. Prices can be the basis for an allocation process. Explain.
5. Not always do firms place maximization of profits first in a list of company objectives. Why not?
6. How much control does a manufacturing company have over the price at which it will sell its product?
7. Prices ultimately have their roots in the subjective feelings and choices of people. True or false? Why?
8. Examine the prices of one type of product in your vicinity. Compare the prices, for example of kitchen appliances, television sets, and automobiles. How much price competition exists? Also, look for any relationships between price, location, type of retail store, and advertising policy.
9. Costs should not dominate price setting. Explain and evaluate this statement.
10. Give an illustration of how pricing should conform to other policies in a retail establishment.
11. Evaluate the use of an odd-price policy.
12. Define and illustrate price lines.
13. Evaluate price cutting as a competitive device. Consider probable effects on sales volume and net operating profit.

Case 9-1 • TROUT RODS, INC.

Trout Rods, Inc., is a fairly small company with a large reputation for manufacturing some of the finest trout-fishing fly rods in the world. The company was founded in 1910 and is still located in Burlington, Vermont, in the same building that it started.

For the first fifty years of the company's life, the primary products manufactured and marketed by Trout Rods, Inc., were split bamboo handmade fly rods. Starting in 1960, outside management was brought into the company and changes in the marketing program were instituted. First, the product line was expanded to include other types of fishing rods and equipment. Second, a mail-order program was initiated. A mailing list was developed from previous customers and from the subscribers of *Fly Fishing Magazine.* Catalogs were mailed to mailing list members on a quarterly basis. Additionally, *Trout News,* a six-times-a-year fishing interest paper was also mailed out on a regular basis. The paper was used as an advertising medium to announce sale merchandise.

In spite of the changes in the product line and marketing program, Trout Rods, Inc., was still known for the fine line of fly rods offered by the company. Split bamboo as well as fiberglass, graphite, and boron fly rods were now available. Generally split bamboo was still considered the finest of all material, and some fly rods sold for as much as $600. The other three rod materials were all cheaper than split bamboo; the production costs for the three new rod materials were about the same. Because of this, the marketing manager of Trout Rods, Inc. was uncertain about how to price the entire fly-rod product line. Generally he believed that customers perceived boron to be superior to graphite, and graphite superior to fiberglass. However, each type of rod had its own particular following of customers.

Suggest a pricing approach and pricing method that you think would be most appropriate for the fly-rod product line. Would it make sense to price boron, graphite, and fiberglass differently, even though the costs for the three materials are about the same?

Case 9-2 • WINSLOW UNIFORM SHOP

In 1977, Roberta Briggs and her husband moved from Los Angeles, California, to Winslow, Arizona, where the couple had purchased the Winslow Uniform Shop. Roberta, a former computer programmer, and her husband Bill ran the business. Bill supervised the retail store, while Roberta traveled throughout northern Arizona making direct sales calls on motels, restaurants, hospitals, schools, junior colleges, and the one university in the area. Most of the sales were made in Flagstaff, Williams, and Page, Arizona. She also made some sales to the motels and restaurants serving tourists visiting the Grand Canyon.

Being a programmer by trade, Roberta knew little about marketing. By being a hard worker, friendly, and a logical thinker, she soon developed good selling skills. She actually received a lot of satisfaction from making a sale, which was both profitable to the business and helpful to her customers. Bill handled the book work and the buying end of the business. He had a good sense of style and the ability to spot a good buy when one came along.

Roberta and Bill had difficulty dealing with the many new and unfamiliar situations they faced. After a couple of bad experiences, they worked out an acceptable lay-away policy. With the help of their suppliers, they had also developed a fairly good inventory policy. Pricing, however, was the big problem. Both Roberta and Bill felt totally inadequate in this area, and their experience so far in the business had not helped their confidence.

The pricing policy followed by the Uniform Shop's previous owner was simply to mark up everything 100 percent from cost. The policy was followed by Roberta and Bill when they purchased they store. However, both Roberta and Bill thought this procedure had definite weaknesses. These weaknesses were especially evident when some uniforms had to be marked down to cost or below to sell them, while other merchandise sold out in a week, even though the markup was always 100 percent of cost.

A number of pricing problems perplexed them. First, they didn't know whether a 100 percent markup should apply to all product lines. Second, they were unsure whether the prices charged to Roberta's direct sales customers should be higher, lower, or the same as the retail store prices. Third, they wanted to establish some price lines in the store, but they were not sure at what levels. Finally, they were undecided whether to continue to use a 100 percent markup policy. They didn't like the policy, but they didn't know what to replace it with.

Offer suggestions to help the Briggses with their pricing problems.

10

X communications

The large brass tray that means "Barbershop Here" in Denmark; a red rag or red flower tied on a pole extending over the doorway of an Andean hut to indicate that the chicha, a potent local brew, is on sale; and the man beating a drum crying out his wares in an open market are all means of communicating to potential customers the availability of a product or service. All three actions are aimed at fulfilling the same objectives as the newest, slickest, full-color, completely orchestrated television commercial.

Promoting goods and services is a necessary component of a free economy. Promotion, very likely, lowers consumer costs because of its effect on reducing the expense and effort of searching out desired goods. Additionally, the stimulation of demand from promotional efforts can result in production cost savings, because producers can take advantage of full operating output through full use of existing plants and equipment.

As a marketing function, promotion can be defined as any personal or nonpersonal communication that creates a favorable disposition toward a good, service, or idea in the mind of the recipient of the communication. It should be noted that the definition of promotion used here only implicitly suggests that promotion is a selling tool. Promotion, first and foremost, is the communications tool of marketing.

A sale is the result of a carefully designed and fully integrated marketing mix. Only when a product is properly designed, priced, distributed, *and* promoted will a sale result. The ability of promotion to inform and persuade consumers makes it capable of having a powerful impact on consumer decision making. Promotion, however, cannot be burdened with the entire responsibility for a sale.

Identifying promotion as fundamentally a communications task permits the establishment of a proper perspective regarding promotion's role in stimulating a sale. The broad definition of promotion as communications results in additional insights with respect to this phase of the marketing mix. First, looking at promotion within the communications perspective allows for the consideration of a greater range of strategies by the marketing decision maker. Certainly few of us have considered purchasing duplicating equipment or large-capacity computers. Despite this fact, both Xerox Corporation and IBM direct promotional messages to general consumer audiences. Neither of these highly sophisticated firms intends to sell its products to average consumers. A *sale* is not the objective of these promotional strategies. Rather, establishing a favorable predisposition toward the firm, or an enhanced image of the firm in the minds of consumers, is the intent. Many creative, legitimate promotional objectives do not focus on sales per se.

A second major benefit of using the communications perspective is that greater appreciation for the complexity of the promotional process is gained. Attempting to design a promotional program while relying solely on a sales objective neglects various aspects of message design and media choice which can increase the effectiveness and efficiency of the promotional process.

This chapter and Chapter 11 will discuss the many considerations inherent in the area of promotion. Discussed in this chapter are the nature and purpose of promotion in the marketing program, communications as a process, and the elements that make up the promotional mix.

THE NATURE AND PURPOSE OF PROMOTION

The nature and purpose of promotion is embodied in four essential areas. First, there is a distinctly economic purpose to the promotional process that affects the ultimate cost of goods and services to consumers. Second, promotion is essentially a communications effort which entails a complex of basic communications considerations. Third, how promotion operates within the framework of the marketing mix and its integration with the other marketing variables must be considered. Finally, promotion consists of a number of related efforts; the tasks that make up the promotional mix require identification.

THE ECONOMICS OF PROMOTION

The economic effects of promotion relate to four basic concepts: economies of scale, the shifting of a firm's demand curve, elasticity of demand, and effective competition.

Economies of Scale

It can be argued that a product actually costs consumers less because of promotion. The amounts spent by firms for promotion varies from product category to product category. In general, consumers are paying from 1 percent (automobiles) to 12 percent (cosmetics) for information (promotion) about products. There is no way to estimate, however, how much more products might cost in the absence of promotion.

Promotion stimulates demand. As demand is stimulated, firms are able to take advantage of the economies of scale that accrue from large demand. As production reaches higher and higher levels, fixed costs such as rent, taxes, and equipment costs are spread over a greater number of units of the product being produced. This, in turn, actually lowers the cost of producing an individual item and the cost savings can be reflected in a lower price to consumers.[1] Economies of scale result in savings in areas other than production. If a firm is able to ship products in large quantities resulting from stimulated demand, the cost of shipping is greatly reduced. Further, paperwork and inventory costs can be reduced when large quantities of goods move quickly through the distribution system.

Shifting the Demand Curve

The benefits of economies of scale tend to accrue to both the firm and the consumer. Shifting the demand curve for a product results in direct benefits to the firm alone. The phenomenon of shifting the demand curve for a product simply means that consumers will demand more of a product at all price levels. Illus. 10-1 shows that as demand for a product is stimulated, the demand curve for that product can be shifted upward and to the right. This results in an increase in demand from Q_1 to Q_2. Price level P_2 illustrates a second consideration regarding shifting the demand curve—that is, regardless of the original price (P_1 or P_2), more of the product (Q_2^1 rather than Q_1^1) is demanded when the curve shifts. This effect of promotion on demand allows the firm greater flexibility in its decision making. Under conditions of increasing costs or rigid demands for return on investment, promotion can aid in developing greater sales volume even if price increases are necessary.

Elasticity of Demand

The concept of increasing the inelasticity of demand for a product is shown in Illus. 10-2. When a firm is able to develop a very strong desire for its product (commonly known as *brand loyalty* when such an effect occurs over a long period of time), consumers are less likely to react strongly to a change in the price of the

---

[1]There is debate as to whether the cost savings resulting from economies of scale are ever actually passed on to consumers. See for example, R. Steiner, "Does Advertising Lower Consumer Prices?" *Journal of Marketing,* Vol. 37, No. 4 (October, 1973), p. 19; and Jules Backman, *Advertising and Competition* (New York City: New York University Press, 1967), p. 144.

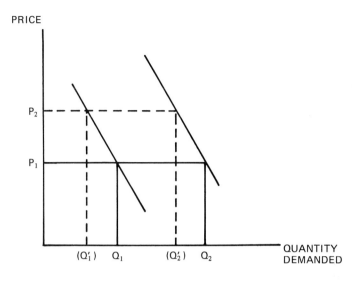

Illus. 10-1   **Effect of Promotion on Demand**

product.[2] Notice that under conditions of a price increase with a firm's original demand curve (D_1), quantity demanded by consumers decreases dramatically (from Q_1 to Q_2). When, however, a firm is able to develop an inelastic demand curve—one which is less sensitive to price changes—(D_2), the same change in price results in only a minor decrease in quantity demanded (Q_1 to Q_3).

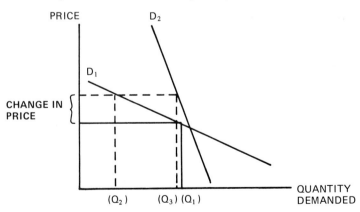

Illus. 10-2   **Effect of Price Increases on**
Quantity Demanded

[2]For a detailed discussion of this effect of promotion see Lee E. Preston, *Markets and Marketing: An Orientation* (Glenview, Ill.: Scott, Foresman & Company, 1970), p. 198.

Promotion plays a large role in developing the inelasticity of demand (insensitivity to price changes). Through the process of identifying for consumers the unique attributes of a product or service, price becomes less of a consideration in purchasing decisions. As a product emerges as superior in the minds of some consumers, their reliance on price as a decision criterion is minimized. The result is a decrease in the elasticity of demand and fewer negative consequences of a price increase to the firm.

Effective Competition

The final economic consideration relates to a firm's ability to compete effectively in the marketplace. With the rapid technological advancement of today's products and increased knowledge by consumers, firms are under great pressure to provide satisfying goods and services. Even if the research and development activities keep abreast of competitors, it becomes the task of promotion to inform consumers of the firm's improved offerings. If promotion fails in this effort, the economic impact on the firm is great. A related consideration is that today's companies face increased competition from different industries. Inter-industry competition provides both competitive opportunities and threats. Promotion, again, is instrumental in the exploitation of new market potential and warding off competitive thrusts. When new industry opportunities for a product are identified, the development of the new market can be aided by promotion. Conversely, reaffirmation of the product's value to its current users helps deter competitive efforts of substitute products.

However, promotion is not universally hailed as a stimulant for industrial competition. Promotion has been charged with actually decreasing the overall amount of competition in an industry. Especially in the case of advertising, critics claim that the amount of money required for the promotional process alone is so great that in some industries many potential competitors are blocked from entering the market.[3]

In summary, promotion has fundamental economic benefits for the firm and the consumer. By contributing to the stimulation of demand, promotion can help reduce the cost of producing a product and potentially reduce the price of the product to the consumer. Promotion can also have beneficial effects on a firm's demand curve, giving the firm more flexibility in its decision making. Finally, as the firm faces increasing competition from its primary industry and between industries, promotion can help maintain the economic stance of the firm.

THE ENVIRONMENT FOR PROMOTION

In Chapter 2 it was pointed out that the overall marketing process of the firm must be designed keeping in mind the particular aspects of the social, competitive,

---

[3]Colston E. Warn, "Advertising: A Critic's View," *Journal of Marketing.* Vol. 26 (October, 1962), p. 12.

and economic environment, along with insight into the firm itself. Similarly, the promotional program must be designed with the same careful consideration of the external and internal environments if the firm hopes to communicate successfully.

The environment for promotion is, therefore, a combination of the internal environment of the firm as it is manifest in marketing decisions other than promotion and the external environment within which the marketing program will be conducted. Examination of how the factors in each of these environments affects promotion will help establish a foundation for understanding the promotional task.

The Internal Environment

Decision making regarding product design, pricing, and distribution affects the promotional program. The internal environment of the firm and decisions made regarding the other elements of the marketing mix must be considered when promotional decisions are made.

Product. It is on this element of the marketing mix that promotional decision making relies most heavily. The firm's offering to the consumer must be scrutinized to determine how successful communication can be achieved. The nature of the product largely provides the informational content of any promotional effort. It should be recalled that consumers do not perceive a product as simply a tangible entity. Many people do not buy dish washing liquid; rather they are buying soft hands, clean dishes, or a pleasant fragrance.

For promotional purposes it is critical to determine all the potential benefits the consumer may perceive in the product. These relate to both the functional and nonfunctional attributes that the product possesses. Functional attributes are the measurable, tangible elements of the product. Product characteristics such as special ingredients, unique features, distinctive design, and guarantees are examples of functional attributes. Nonfunctional product attributes largely relate to the emotional buying motives that consumers may employ in the product purchase. Consumers perceive many products on the basis of providing status, security, affiliation, or respect. If a particular product category is characterized by these nonfunctional criteria, then these elements become relevant information to the consumer. As such, it is necessary that promotion contain this information.

The general nature of the product itself will also affect the promotional program. If a product is infrequently purchased, highly technical, and judged at the point of purchase (such as a stereo system), the requirements for promotion will differ greatly from a product that is frequently purchased, low priced, and self-service in nature (such as toothpaste). The precise nature of the difference and various tactics employed in each situation are presented in Chapter 11. For now, it is important to recognize that the product, as an element of the marketing mix, affects the promotion program.

In viewing the product as an element of the environment that affects promotion, the following questions are useful in determining the nature of such effects:

1. Was the product designed for a particular segment of the population?
2. Were features built into the product design to differentiate it from competition?
3. What are the characteristics of the product regarding frequency of purchase, complexity, and point-of-purchase judgment?

Answers to the above questions will aid in determining the nature of the effect the product itself has on promotional decision making.

Price.   Determination of the price for the product can present distinct opportunities in the promotional program. If the firm establishes a price for the product that is low in the range of prices in the product category, price can then become a differentiating feature in the brand's promotion. If the price is high relative to competitive prices, this can also be implemented strategically to the product's advantage through promotion. For the most part, however, promotion is instrumental in implementing the concept of *nonprice competition,* that is, reliance on the product's attributes and want-satisfying characteristics as the basis for the promotional appeal. If a product has been developed to satisfy particular consumer desires, then the price is a less important criterion in consumer choice.

The influence of pricing decisions on the promotional program should not be misinterpreted or underemphasized. Granted, other product features tend to be emphasized in promotion from a strategic standpoint rather than from a price standpoint. However, one of the major elements of the promotional mix, sales promotion, relies on price as the essence of the persuasive appeal. Sales promotion is that combination of pricing and promotion that consumers encounter daily. Cents-off offers, coupons, rebates, and percentage reductions in price are all promotional tactics that emphasize the pricing element of the marketing mix. Depending on the elasticity of demand (sensitivity of demand for a product to a change in price), price can have an effect on the nature of a firm's promotional program.

In assessing the effects the price of a product may have on the promotional program, the following questions can provide insight:

1. Is the price of the product high or low relative to the price of competitors?
2. Is the product characterized by an elastic or inelastic demand curve?
3. Does the product have unique features that reduce the importance of price as a decision factor in the minds of consumers?

Distribution.   Just as product characteristics and pricing policies provide opportunities and constraints for the promotional program, the firm's distribution network can influence the nature of promotion.

First, the *intensity of the distribution system* must be considered. Intensive, selective, and exclusive distribution calls for different emphasis among the elements of the promotional program. Intensive distribution (placement of the product in as many outlets as possible) requires a large amount of advertising to support retailers' acceptance of the product. Conversely, selective and exclusive distribution generally dictates a heavy emphasis on personal selling and cooperative arrangements for advertising between manufacturer and retailer.

Second, the *type of retail outlet* that characterizes the distribution program affects promotion. Full-line department stores (such as Sears, J.C. Penney, and Dayton-

Hudson) assume a great deal of responsibility for promoting the products in the store. Further, outlets of this type have strong appeal to consumers. The discount store as a mode of distribution is essentially self-service, emphasizing low prices which dictate different tactics in the firm's promotional program. Single-line outlets (appliance stores, sporting goods stores) tend to have more varieties within product categories and more expert in-store sales assistance. Finally, the specialty store method of operation places a premium on personal selling with minor emphasis on advertising. All these factors must be weighed in the promotional program.

A third influence that the distribution network has on promotion is the *geographic scope of the firm's distribution.* National, regional, and local distribution programs call for differences in advertising media choice, size of the promotional expenditure, and potentially different campaigns for different regions of the country.

Finally, the nature of the retail outlet itself can have an important influence on consumers' willingness to stop at the outlet. Known as *consumer patronage motives,* factors such as speed of checkout, return policy, courteousness of salespeople, and location operate as influences on where consumers choose to shop.[4] These characteristics of the retail outlets that make up the firm's distribution system can enter into the appeals in the promotional message.

When considering the influence the distribution element of the marketing mix has on promotion, therefore, the following four questions about the firm's distribution program must be answered:

1. What is the intensity of the distribution system?
2. What type of retail outlet characterizes the distribution system?
3. What is the geographic scope of the distribution system?
4. What consumer patronage motives may influence store choice?

The External Environment

Promotion, as one of the four elements of the marketing mix, logically draws on the assessment of the environment undertaken for the firm's overall marketing program. Knowledge of competitors' efforts, social and cultural trends, technological developments, the political and legal environment, and the economic environment are all important inputs to the promotional program. Determining the nature of these environments has a direct bearing on promotional activities.

Competition. Within a product category firms attempt to gain a differential advantage over their competition. This striving for a competitive edge manifests itself, in part, through promotion. The firm attempts to emphasize that its offering is superior to competitive offerings and points out distinctions that legitimately can be made between the rival product and the firm's product.

---

[4]George Fisk, "A Conceptual Model for Studying Customer Image," *Journal of Retailing,* Vol. 37 (Winter, 1969–1970), p. 1; Robert Kelley and Ronald Stephenson, "The Semantic Differential: An Information Source for Designing Retail Patronage Appeals," *Journal of Marketing,* Vol. 31 (October, 1967), p. 43; Jay Lindquist, "Meaning of Image: A Survey of Empirical and Hypothetical Evidence," *Journal of Retailing,* Vol. 50, No. 4 (Winter, 1974–75), p. 29.

Technology. Technological developments in a product category may provide the firm with an opportunity for effective promotion. Conversely, if the firm has not yet adopted a technical advance, the technological deficiency of the product must be overcome if the improvements are conspicuous (digital watches as opposed to conventional timepieces, for example). If the advancement relates to a less obvious or more-difficult-to-understand product feature, its use in promotion may be obstructed.

Market demand. The overall level of demand in a product category can work for or against the individual firm. In the late 1960s and early 1970s the demand for gas-guzzling recreational vehicles grew rapidly, and manufacturers' promotional requirements were less rigorous. When gasoline prices increased, the recreational vehicle market contracted rapidly, forcing many marginal competitors from the market. The remaining firms found promotion under these market conditions considerably more challenging.

Economic and behavioral aspects of the market are also elements of market demand that can influence promotion. Certain economic conditions are conducive to consumer spending on durable goods and large ticket items. Conversely, under conditions of high inflation and an unfavorable income tax environment, consumer discretionary income is restricted. Behavior population trends (such as the birth rate and mobility patterns of the population) dictate the need for different promotional strategies.

These market forces manifest themselves in the nature of the promotional program. Both long-range planning and the tactics employed in a specific campaign will be developed partly on the basis of varying market demand factors.

Cultural and Social Trends. The evolution of cultural patterns and the currently popular values of a society can translate into promotional tactics.[5] The growing emphasis on convenience and the importance of time have caused these factors to be emphasized in the communications effort. The time-saving nature of a product, its convenient use, and increased store hours are currently important information content for promotion.

As a society focuses on different elements of personal satisfaction and interaction, the promotional program will need to adapt to the changing emphasis. What is deemed important, relevant, and satisfying in a product will be due partly to the value consumers place on different elements of their daily existence.

Legal and Political Constraints. The constraints on marketing communications resulting from various regulations must be recognized. The Robinson-

---

[5]A good discussion of the manifestation of values in promotion can be found in James F. Engle, Hugh G. Wales, and Martin R. Warshaw, *Promotional Strategy.* (3d ed.; Homewood, Ill.: Richard D. Irwin, Inc., 1975), p. 78.

Patman Act of 1936 mandates that any advertising compensation a firm chooses to allocate to one retailer must be available to all retailers on a proportionally equal basis. The Federal Trade Commission Act of 1914 and the Wheeler-Lea Amendment (1938) provide the Federal Trade Commission (FTC) with the power to regulate advertising which is judged unfair or misleading in nature. The FTC has historically dealt with deceptive or misleading advertising by issuing cease-and-desist orders. These orders require the firm found in violation to delete allegedly deceptive claims from subsequent advertising. In 1970, however, the concept of corrective advertising was proposed.[6] Corrective advertising requires a firm to not only delete deceptive claims from future advertising, but also fully disclose to consumers the deception of its previous advertisements.[7]

The legal environment for marketing and, subsequently, promotion constitutes a serious faction of which to be aware. Real constraints exist regarding the tactics that can and cannot be used in promotion.

THE COMMUNICATION PROCESS

Once the overall nature of the environment for promotion has been assessed, the task of communicating within that environment must be undertaken. As mentioned previously, communications is the essence of the promotional process in marketing.

Communications for marketing purposes is undertaken either as mass communications or as personal communications. To fully understand the appropriate application of each of these basic forms of communication, a separate discussion of the fundamental elements of each is necessary.

MASS COMMUNICATIONS

Mass communications is the attempt to communicate an identical message to a large number of people at a particular point in time. Mass communications is truly an impersonal form of communications because the mass media (newspapers, radio, television) are employed as the vehicle for transmission instead of transmitting a message from one person to another. Illus. 10-3 is a basic model of mass communications that provides a basis for understanding how this impersonal method of communication takes place.[8]

---

[6]*Campbell Soup Company et al.* FTC Docket C 1741 (1970).

[7]The Federal Trade Commission's use of corrective advertising as a remedy was confirmed in August, 1977. *Warner-Lambert* v. *FTC.* 562 F. 2d 749 (1977). Research evidence regarding corrective advertising can be found in Robert F. Dyer and Philip G. Kuehl, "The Corrective Advertising Remedy of the FTC: An Experimental Evaluation," *Journal of Marketing,* Vol. 38, No. 1 (January, 1974), p. 48.

[8]This model of mass communication is an adaptation of an excellent model appearing in *Promotional Strategy.* p. 21. See Footnote 5.

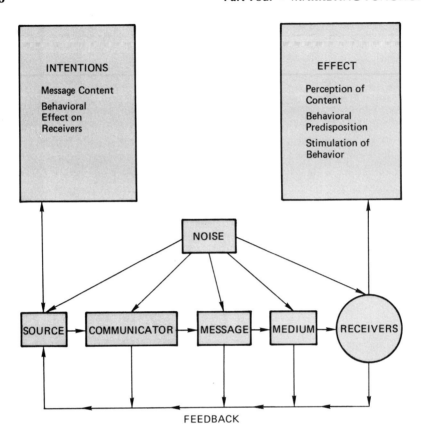

Intentions

A mass communications effort in marketing (typically advertising) begins with the careful specification of intentions for the attempt. *Intentions* refer to the *message content* of the promotional piece and the *behavioral effect* the promotion is expected to have on message recipients. The intended message content is the collection of informational and persuasive elements of the message. It is developed from the information gained from an analysis of the environment discussed in the previous section. Such an analysis determines which criteria consumers are using to judge the want-satisfying nature of a product. Information in promotion that relates to these characteristics is deemed *relevant* information by consumers and thereby has an improved probability of being received and understood by consumers. Recall that relevant information to consumers may be either functional or nonfunctional product attributes.

The intended *behavioral effect on receivers* is rarely realized immediately. In general, it is hoped that the informational content of a message will create a favorable behavioral predisposition toward the product: that is, at some future time, a receiver will judge the product acceptable and make a purchase. (Recall the discussion of the responsibility of promotion for a sale.) In some instances promotion asks for immediate action on the part of the consumer. Advertisements urging the receiver to mail in the coupon before the end of the month or to send $7.95 before midnight tonight ask for immediate response. The characteristic behavioral intention, however, is to create a favorable predisposition toward the product so that purchase behavior may result some time in the future.

Source

The source of a mass communications message in marketing is the organization that is responsible for developing the advertisement. In many instances the source of a message will be a firm's advertising department or an advertising agency. It is important that the intent of a mass communications effort be clearly and precisely identified for the source. People who specialize in the development of creative, attention-getting messages must be guided by the knowledge of which information consumers deem relevant for a product. Without such guidance the firm will find that its advertising is creative, attention-getting, usually enjoyable, and only effective by accident. Unless the source of the message constructs the message on the basis of information gathered from the environment, the intentions for the advertisement have little chance of being achieved.

Communicator

In the model of mass communication on page 198, the *communicator* is separated from the source. The model is designed this way to emphasize the importance of the person speaking for the firm. Research on the effects of the person who actually relays the message indicates that this element of the mass communications system can be tremendously influential.[9] For example, in some product categories receivers of a message react more favorably to a communicator who is perceived as similar to themselves.[10] On the other hand, some messages are better received when the communicator is viewed as a specialist, or expert, and therefore unlike the receivers.[11] Further, reference group theory can also be implemented through a specific portrayal of the communicator(s).

The communicator in a message is perceived as the person speaking for the product. This element of the mass communication effort should be carefully considered and viewed as an opportunity to increase the effectiveness of the message.

---

[9]Carl I. Hovland, Irving L. Janis, and Harold H. Kelly, *Communication and Persuasion: Psychological Studies of Opinion Change,* (New Haven, Conn.: Yale University Press, 1959) or Carl I. Hovland, Arthur A. Lunsdaine, and Fred Scheffield, *Experiments in Mass Communications,* (Princeton, N.J.: Princeton University Press, 1949).

[10]Timothy C. Brock, "Communicator-Recipient Similarity and Decision Change," *Journal of Personality and Social Psychology,* Vol. 1 (June, 1965), p. 650; Franklin B. Evans, "Selling as a Dyadic Relationship—A New Approach," *American Behavioral Scientist,* Vol. 6 (May, 1963), p. 76; and M.S. Gadel, "Concentration by Salesmen on Congenial Prospects," *Journal of Marketing,* Vol. 28 (April, 1968), p. 64

[11]Robert B. Settle, "Attribution Theory on Acceptance of Information," *Journal of Marketing Research,* Vol. 9 (February, 1972), p. 85.

Message

As mentioned previously, the *message* is the firm's opportunity to relay information to consumers and attempt to persuade consumers that the firm's product meets the judgment criteria. In mass communications one difficulty in constructing a message is making it suitable for numerous receivers. As such, the message will ultimately be a generalized representation of many consumer criteria. If done well the analysis of the environment will have produced a profile of which information is relevant to consumers, so that the message can be reasonably specific.

Again, the overriding consideration for message content is that the message contain information which receivers find relevant. If consumers deem the message content of an advertisement irrelevant or contradictory to their existing beliefs, the advertisement will be subject to the perceptual mechanisms of *selective exposure, selective perception,* or *selective retention.* [12] These are defense mechanisms which allow recipients of a message to screen out impertinent or irrelevant information.

If a message is not relaying information that relates to the various criteria a consumer is using to judge a product, the message will be avoided altogether (selective exposure). Should an advertisement achieve the exposure but not provide information in an acceptable form or fall short of emphasizing proper aspects of a product's characteristics, it will again fail to communicate (selective perception). Finally, even if a message gains exposure and is perceived completely, it may not achieve strong enough impact to be stored in memory (selective retention).

The process of developing a successful message is a difficult one. Aside from needing comprehensive and accurate information about the environment, the message must be presented in a format that is capable of breaking through the perceptual defense mechanisms of the receiver.

Medium

The medium employed in mass communications is the vehicle through which the message is carried to the receivers. In marketing, newspapers, radio, television, magazines, and billboards constitute the most frequently used media for the transmission of messages. Each of these media has the capability of reaching a large number of receivers—at low cost per contact and at frequent intervals.

The technical nature of each medium can aid or impede the communications effort. The broadcast media have the advantage of allowing audio or audiovisual presentation of the message. The impression the receiver gets through broadcast media, however, is fleeting. The print media can provide more information but are unable to demonstrate a product in action. The nature of each medium's effect on the promotional effort is detailed in Chapter 11.

---

[12]There is a large body of literature on the perceptual defenses. A good discussion of the literature can be found in James F. Engle, David T. Kollat, and Roger D. Blackwell, *Consumer Behavior.* (2d ed.; Hinsdale, Ill.: Dryden Press, 1973) p. 211.

Receivers

The receivers of a message delivered through mass communications can be determined beforehand by carefully choosing the medium. Most members of the mass media have relatively accurate, up-to-date information on readers and viewers. In this phase of the mass communications process, the most useful information from the environment is the firm's decisions and efforts regarding market segmentation. Based on the firm's attempts to design, price, and distribute a product for a predetermined segment of the population, this is the audience for whom the communications effort should be designed. Media information regarding who is reached through the medium should be employed to match message placement with the group using the medium.

Effect.   The effect of the communication effort will be determined through identification of receivers' perception of the content, behavioral predisposition toward the product, and the amount and type of behavior stimulated.

Identifying what was actually perceived by consumers and their resulting behavioral predisposition toward the product can be a lengthy and costly process. Only through a consumer survey (such as Starch readership scores for print media or on-the-air tests for broadcast media) can such information be obtained. The critical issue about content perception is whether consumers' perception of the message content is what the firm intended to be communicated as the message content. The behavioral predisposition of the consumer relates to the overall image of the product produced by the communication and consumers' resultant intentions to buy after exposure.

The amount and type of behavior stimulated are important measures of the systems effect. Unfortunately, they are also the most difficult to measure. Since a consumer may not draw on the information obtained from a message for long periods of time, being able to attribute behavior to a particular message is nearly impossible. For messages that implore immediate action on the part of the consumer, the task is a bit easier. Monitoring calls received or orders obtained provides some idea of the message impact in this instance. In assessing the behavioral effect a message has, perhaps the least informative measure is sales themselves. Again, promotion will be only partly responsible for sales, and the consumer may have been stimulated to respond from a different source of information or information that had been mentally stored.

Noise.   Noise is any disturbance in the communications system which inhibits transmission to the receiver. Noise affecting intentions comes in the form of inaccurate or incomplete information about the environment. Noise emanating from the source of the message can be experienced when a product's attributes are not portrayed properly or inaccuracies regarding the nature of the product are transmitted. Similarly, the communicator can be a disturbance if he or she functions as a distraction during the transmission of the message. The message itself is an element of noise if the language used or visualization is confusing to the receivers. Clutter in the chosen medium produces noise, as competing messages interfere with one another. Noise is present within receivers, given their attitudinal predisposition toward the product or distractions that may occur during receipt of the message. Overall, noise results in reducing the impact of communications or a complete lack of reception of the message.

Feedback.   Feedback in mass communication is slow and difficult to obtain. The receivers are the main source of feedback and provide information regarding the success of the established system. The information desired in the feedback process relates to discovering:

1. Who are the actual receivers of the message?
2. What was the perceived content of the message?
3. What behavioral predisposition toward the product results by virtue of receipt of the message?
4. What type and amount of behavior was stimulated by exposure to the message?

Since the source of the message and receivers are physically separated, the feedback process in mass communications is greatly delayed. Once this valuable information is obtained, however, changes throughout the system can be instituted. The communication can be changed or portrayed differently, message appeals can be altered, media placement can be adjusted, or new groups of receivers can be singled out and pursued. The feedback process provides the firm the opportunity to enhance its mass communications effort.

PERSONAL COMMUNICATIONS

Personal communications is the transmission of a message in a face-to-face setting. In marketing, personal selling is the system for personal communications. Illus. 10-4 demonstrates the elements of a personal communications system in marketing.

The personal communications system is essentially the same as mass communications. The communicator in personal communication is the vehicle for transmission of the message, that is, the salesperson functions as the medium. The development of intentions and the message and an analysis of effects require the same planning and consideration that were discussed in mass communications. However, the communicator, noise, and feedback elements of the personal communications system entail different considerations.

Communicator

Since the person speaking for the firm encounters the receiver face-to-face, several characteristics of the communicator's task change. Rather than simply relaying a message prepared in advance (or being depicted in a printed adver-

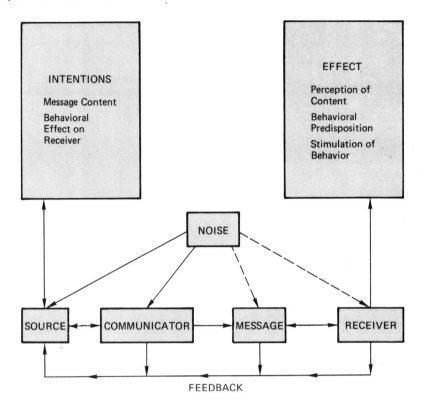

Illus. 10-4 **A Personal Communications System**

tisement as a user of the product) the communicator must physically approach the receiver. This necessitates training relative to product features, use of the product, and preparation to answer any questions the receiver may have. Further, in some personal selling situations, the salesperson (communicator) is also instrumental in the delivery, servicing, or installation of a product. Other non-communications activities, such as order taking and inventory monitoring, can also be part of the salesperson's responsibility. Further, by virtue of the face-to-face nature of the communications situation, the salesperson must realize that his or her manner of speaking, dress, and other nonverbal cues may convey different meanings to receivers. The well-designed personal communications system prepares the communicator for several peripheral tasks and contingency occurences.

Effect

The effect in a personal communications system is somewhat easier to determine than in mass communications. Since the salesperson can alter the message and amount of information between receivers and reply to questions from receivers immediately, there is increased probability that the perceived content of the message will be the same as the intended content. Further, since part of the salesperson's job is to bring about a sale, the behavioral effect of the message is more closely linked to the communications system from the outset. If a sale does not result from a personal communications effort, there still may be a change in the behavioral predisposition of the receiver, but the effect will remain difficult to measure.

Noise

The nature of the interference in a personal communications attempt differs in some respects from the noise in mass communications. The threats of inaccuracies in information and adverse receiver predisposition are essentially the same. The danger of relaying an inappropriate message is lessened due to the communicator's ability to alter the message according to an individual receiver's needs and capabilities for processing information. Noise directly related to the characteristics of the communicator may be amplified, however. Receivers may react to personal characteristics of the salesperson more vigorously due to the close proximity of communicator and the receiver. Again, personality traits, language, dress, and mannerisms may have an effect on the salesperson's attempts to communicate.

Feedback

Feedback in the personal communications system is immediate. The salesperson has the opportunity to alter the message according to the receiver's unique need for information and ability to process it. One of the firm's most valuable monitoring systems for determining the appropriateness of its product design, pricing, and distribution tactics comes from personal contact with the market. Since reporting the results of sales contacts to the firm is part of the salesperson's responsibility, feedback from personal communications is less costly and difficult to obtain than feedback from mass communications.

DIFFERENCES BETWEEN MASS
AND PERSONAL COMMUNICATIONS

The differences between the two basic communication systems used in marketing relate to a few key areas, including cost, the communication setting, and overall efficiency and effectiveness.

Cost

Mass communications provides a great cost advantage over personal communications. Through the media, large numbers of receivers can be reached for (in many instances) less than a penny each. Personal communications is often more expensive per number of persons reached by a message. For instance, with personal selling it is estimated that an industrial sales call may soon cost as much as $200 per contact.[13]

Communications Setting

An obvious difference between the systems is the setting in which communication takes place. In mass communications the receiver may be comfortably situated at home or in an automobile. The communicator is a remote entity who is relatively anonymous. Distractions abound, since the receiver's attention is diverted by competing stimuli, other tasks (driving a car, for example), or general interruptions in viewing, reading, or listening. The probability in the latter situation that the message will fail to communicate is higher.

Personal communications takes place in a vastly different setting. The receiver is face to face with the communicator, many times in an unfamiliar setting (such as a retail store), and with the opportunity to ask questions. In these circumstances distractions are minimized and the chance that a message will be communicated is greatly enhanced.

Efficiency and Effectiveness

A communications system is *efficient* when the largest number of *specific* receivers is reached at the lowest possible cost. A communications effort is *effective* when the intended content of the message is the same as the perceived content of the message in receivers' minds. In the case of mass communications versus personal communications there is a clear case of efficiency versus effectiveness. Mass communications are far more efficient in reaching large numbers of receivers through various media at extremely low cost. However, due to the generalized nature of the message, great numbers of distractions, and the long delay in feedback, the mass communications system is relatively ineffective.

Personal communications, on the other hand, provide a high degree of specialization in the message, a reduced amount of distraction (thereby reducing the probability of defense mechanisms being activated), and immediate feedback to the firm. Promotional decision making is, therefore, faced with the decision between relying on more efficient mass information transmission or the more effective personal relay of the message. Deciding between the two systems or a combination of both will be discussed in promotional strategy (Chapter 11).

---

[13]Edward M. Mazze, *Personal Selling: Choice against Chance* (St. Paul, Minn.: West Publishing Co., 1976), p. 212.

THE PROMOTIONAL MIX

Through careful development of the fundamental nature of promotion and establishment of basic principles relating to communications it is possible to direct attention to more specific elements in marketing communications. Within the framework of the overall effects of promotion and the essential characteristics of communications as a process, it is time to consider the mix of communications techniques the firm can employ in the promotional program. This mix of techniques is called the *promotional mix.*

Just as the firm develops an overall marketing program based on a blend of product, pricing, promotion and distribution decisions, the promotional program is also a blend of four elements: advertising, personal selling, sales promotion, and publicity. Together these components form the promotional mix.

Advertising

As identified in the discussion of mass communications, advertising is the nonpersonal presentation of information to a large number of potential customers. Advertising employs the mass media of television, radio, newspapers, magazines, billboards, and direct mail. The major tasks involved in developing advertising for the firm are:

1. Determining the proper customer audience
2. Placing advertisements in media that reach the desired customer audience
3. Developing a message based on the judgment criteria employed by the customer audience to evaluate the product
4. Measuring the effectiveness of the advertising effort

The principles of demand stimulation and mass communications apply directly to the advertising component of the promotional mix. Firms realize the tremendous worth of reaching large audiences with great frequency, accounting for billions of dollars of advertising expenditures.

Personal Selling

Personal selling can be defined as the face-to-face presentation of information regarding the firm's product or service. The elements discussed in personal communications make up the basic functions of the personal selling component. The major tasks in the personal selling process differ greatly between industrial sales and retail sales. In general, regardless of the selling context, the essentials of the process involve:

1. Identifying high potential prospects
2. Pre-presentation preparation
3. Approach
4. Information transmission
5. Demonstration
6. Order taking
7. Follow-up

Personal selling dominates the promotional mix of many major corporations. Because of the advantages of a specialized message and immediate feedback, personal selling in many instances represents the ideal form of communications. Personal selling constitutes a large percentage of the promotional budget of United States corporations; according to the 1979 United States Census, over seven million people are employed in personal selling.

Sales Promotion

Sales promotion is another form of nonpersonal communication. Historically sales promotion has involved the combining of advertising and pricing as a communication device; free samples, coupons, and cents-off approaches in advertising are typically cited as sales promotion tactics. A somewhat broader definition is useful since point-of-purchase display materials, trade shows, and contests can also be classified as sales promotion. *Sales promotion* can therefore be defined as those marketing expenditures other than personal selling, advertising, and publicity that stimulate consumer purchasing and dealer effectiveness. Sales promotion is most evident in the form of displays, shows and expositions, demonstrations, and various nonrecurring selling efforts not in the ordinary routine.[14]

Sales promotion rarely dominates the promotional mix of a firm, but it does provide a timely alternative for dealing with unique situations. Introducing a new product, attracting attention to new features in an existing product, or attracting new users for a product are all instances of using sales promotion effectively.

Publicity

Publicity is the unpaid for information about a firm or its product that is disseminated to the public. Typically firms prepare news releases regarding new product developments, profit and growth, new capital investments, and the like. These publicity items are sent to major news organizations (such as Associated Press, United Press International, or regional and local counterparts) for inclusion in newspapers, magazines, and trade publications. Firms rarely invest a great amount of time or effort in publicity campaigns. A well-prepared, timely, and informative publicity item, however, can gain widespread distribution and generate great consumer interest.

[14]Committee on Definitions, *Marketing Definitions: A Glossary of Marketing Terms* (Chicago: AMA, 1970), p. 20.

QUESTIONS AND ANALYTICAL PROBLEMS

1. Why is it useful to consider promotion as, first and foremost, a communications effort rather than a selling effort?

2. Cite the economic effects attributable to promotion. Which of these results from brand loyalty on the part of consumers?

3. What is nonprice competition? Where does this strategy enter the promotional effort?

4. How does the nature of a firm's distribution strategy affect the promotional effort? What role do consumer patronage motives play in this effort?

5. Which mechanisms do consumers use to screen out mass communications? How can an advertisement overcome these defenses?

6. What are the fundamental differences between mass communications and personal communications? How do these relate to the concepts of efficiency and effectiveness in the communications process?

7. Define the elements that make up the promotional mix.

8. How does the systems approach discussed in Chapter 1 apply to the promotional mix?

9. What basic tasks will a salesperson be required to perform in a selling effort? Cite the applicability of these tasks to the model of personal communications presented in this chapter.

10. If you were responsible for devising a promotional strategy for Levi Strauss jeans, what is the first decision you would try to make regarding the firm's advertising campaign? What would be the initial decision?

Case 10-1 • DAISY GLUE

Daisy Glue was a new type of glue developed by Jean Estes of Glen Park, Illinois. Jean was a chemist by training, having earned her Ph.D. in 1966 from Indiana University. After earning her doctorate, Jean went to work as a research chemist for a major oil company. She spent ten years with the company, and during that time she developed what she considered a superior glue for construction and industrial uses. Finally, in 1977, Jean quit her job with the oil company and set up her own business to manufacture and market her new glue.

The new glue, called Daisy Glue, is particularly well suited for building and home construction. The glue is waterproof, fairly inexpensive, and extremely strong. More importantly, the glue is a semicontact cement. The glue hardens to full strength in about five minutes. If necessary, simply holding the glued item in place for five minutes allows for a perfect bond. Because of the semicontact feature, the glue is particularly suited to finish carpentry work. Moreover, because the glue is inexpensive and extremely strong it is equally good for rough construction work, such as gluing down floors, adhering siding on walls, or even gluing together pieces of wood to make laminated beams.

Jean Estes is comfortable with production, but is unfamiliar with marketing. Therefore, she has taken a small business marketing seminar at a local university. The seminar has helped her see the importance of identifying a target market and developing a marketing strategy. Jean has selected building contractors in the state of Illinois as her initial target market. She has decided to price the product competitively and distribute the glue through building supply stores, lumber yards, and do-it-yourself centers. The big problem she faces is how best to promote the product.

Jean believes that primary target members will require a technical explanation and demonstration to really see the value of the glue. However, she can't afford TV advertising, and she thinks that sales people calling on various jobs to make demonstrations will be inefficient and will probably cause some resentment among builders and owners. Also, she believes that direct-mail promotion will not be effective since it fails to display the benefits of the new glue.

What suggestions would you make to Jean about choosing the communication medium to promote Daisy Glue?

Case 10-2 • KAUFMAN COLLEGE

Kaufman College is a small private college located in a small town in central Oregon. The college was once affiliated with a major Protestant religion. However, the college is now entirely nondenominational and does not receive any church support.

Kaufman College prospered during the 1960s. However, beginning in the early 1970s student enrollment dropped off and the school began to face serious financial problems. Because of these and other difficulties a new college president was appointed in 1974. The president, Jack B. Davidson, was an alumnus of Kaufman College and a successful business-man. He was offered the job because the board of regents believed that the college needed to be run more like a business.

Mr. Davidson's first major action was to initiate work on a ten-year master plan for the college. He appointed a committee to develop the plan, and he requested that the committee answer certain specific questions. First, he wanted the committee to develop a mission statement for the college. The mission statement was to specify the fundamental purpose of the institution. This mission statement was also to identify the unique aspects of Kaufman College relative to state and other private schools.

Second, one-, five-, and ten-year objectives were to be developed for the college. These objectives were to be both qualitative and quantitative. Number of students, quality of faculty and programs, and types of academic degrees were to be covered by the objectives.

Finally, the committee was to suggest a formal strategy to achieve the objectives. Mr. Davidson had personally instructed the committee on the use of marketing variables such as price, product, distribution, and promotion to help achieve the objectives. Additionally, the committee was instructed to give a lot of thought to the question of the appropriate target market or markets for the college. Marketing variables could be more effectively planned after the appropriate target markets were identified.

The following target markets were identified:

1. High school seniors living in and around the community where Kaufman College is located and who desire a liberal arts education in a small private school
2. High school seniors living in the Northwest who desire excellent preparation for a professional graduate school in business or law

3. High school seniors living in the United States who desire a high-level education in social work
4. Parents of the three groups mentioned above
5. Social work professionals living in the Northwest who desire advanced degrees in social work

These target markets were chosen simultaneously with the development of product and pricing strategies. However, the committee is still developing a complete promotion strategy. Specific questions remain in the committee's mind about how to employ personal sales people, whether to use advertising, and the potential effectiveness of sales promotion devices and public relations.

What recommendations would you make to the committee about the promotional mix for Kaufman College?

11

promotional strategy

The complex task of stimulating demand for a firm's market offering requires the careful coordination of the promotional tools. The specification by a firm of the combined use of advertising, personal selling, sales promotion, and publicity results in the firm's *promotional strategy.* Only after all the elements of the promotional mix have been examined and integrated can a firm hope to effectively communicate with its market segment.

The preceding chapter identified the fundamental elements of the promotional process. This chapter will aim at identifying and investigating the procedures that result in the strategic application of promotional tools. The focal point of the promotional strategy process is the promotional mix. After identifying factors that influence a firm's use of the elements of the promotional mix, the objectives for the promotional program and the budget appropriation can be considered. At this point, each element of the promotional mix must be examined in detail so that the strategies and tactics for advertising, personal selling, sales promotion, and publicity can be specified.

The systematic approach to promotional strategy development presented in this chapter allows for a comprehensive effort in this phase of the marketing mix.

Further, the probability of effectively and efficiently communicating to consumers is increased as the integration of promotional tools is carried out.

INFLUENCES ON THE PROMOTIONAL MIX

The reliance on each area of the promotional mix was discussed in general terms in Chapter 10. When the specification of the amounts of advertising, personal selling, sales promotion and publicity must be made, a more detailed analysis of the influences dictating the choice of each is necessary. Specifically, the first stage of promotional strategy development involves an analysis of (1) the characteristics of the market, (2) the characteristics of the product, (3) the nature of the firm's distribution system, (4) and characteristics of the firm.

Characteristics of the Market

The accurate assessment of market characteristics greatly enhances the strategic use of promotional tools. There are three basic influences of the market that manifest themselves in the final promotional mix.

The Consumer.   A firm will find that it must stimulate demand within one or more of three basic consumer groups: household consumers, industrial users, or middlemen. Each of these types of consumers dictates various degrees of reliance on the promotional mix variables. Typically the industrial user and the middleman are more effectively reached with personal selling. These customers tend to be more knowledgeable and price and service oriented. Under these circumstances the individualized communication provided by personal selling tends to dominate the promotional mix. Additionally, the limited, absolute number of customers in the industrial and middleman markets makes personal selling more economically feasible.

The household consumer, on the other hand, may be reached through a combination of advertising, personal selling, or sales promotion. Certainly the large number of customers in the household market lends itself to the use of advertising; depending upon other considerations, however, some combination of advertising, personal selling, and sales promotion may be appropriate.

Geographic Considerations.   Two basic geographic considerations can influence the promotional mix: the geographic breadth of the market and the geographic concentration of the market. The more geographically concentrated a firm's market is, the more personal selling tends to enter the promotional strategy. Conversely, a widely dispersed market, geographically, lends itself more to advertising.

With regard to geographic breadth of the market the promotional mix can vary dramatically depending on the local, regional, or national scope of the firm's market. As the scope of the market broadens, more emphasis will be placed on advertising. Of course, it is relatively easy to visualize a situation where a local retailer will rely heavily on advertising. Be aware of the fact that the choice in such a situation may be dictated by other influences.

Competition.   The practices of competitors in a market cannot be ignored as an effect on a firm's determination of the promotional mix. In any given industry firms tend to come to the same conclusions regarding the use of promotional mix elements due to the similarity of influences to which the firms adapt. However, strategic maneuvers regarding the use of advertising, personal selling, or sales promotion often dictate that a firm "follow suit" to maintain its market position. For example, a competitor may suddenly increase its use of advertising in an industrial market with heavy geographic concentration (a context typically dominated by personal selling). To meet such a competitive thrust, other firms in the industry may alter their promotional mixes accordingly.

Characteristics of the Product

The general characteristics of the product or service a firm is marketing can have a powerful effect on the use of promotional mix elements. The effect stems from fundamental characteristics of a product rather than from specific differences among brands.

Product Category.   One of the most informative considerations for determination of the promotional mix is to examine the basic product category of the item to be promoted. The use of advertising, personal selling, and sales promotion varies greatly depending on whether the firm is attempting to stimulate demand for a convenience good, shopping good, or a specialty good. Convenience goods, which are purchased with great frequency and are generally simple items, typically have broad market segments. Promotion of convenience goods typically relies on advertising and sales promotion. Shopping goods need a greater emphasis on personal selling because of their high price, complex nature, and the fact that consumers judge the product at the point of purchase. The emphasis on brand names in the specialty goods category reduces the usefulness of sales promotion for this group. However, because of the exclusive nature of the distribution for the products, advertising is typically necessary to identify for consumers the outlet where the product can be obtained (see Chapter 8).

Stages in Life Cycle.   The discussion of the product life cycle in Chapter 8 identified that every product passes through several stages of market development. During the various stages, promotional requirements change. In the introductory stage the need for personal selling is acute, as a firm attempts to gain acceptance for the product at the wholesale or retail level. Also at this stage, advertising may be used to stimulate *primary demand,* that is, demand for the product category in general. The attempt here is to inform consumers of the usefulness and benefits of using this type of product. Two recent examples of products that have required heavy amounts of primary demand stimulation are microwave ovens and television video playback machines. As the product progresses through its life cycle, *selective* *demand* stimulation is undertaken through advertising. This strategy emphasizes differences between the firm's brand and competitors' brands.

The middle stages of the product life cycle require a promotional mix that considers all the influences in its determination. Should a product reach the decline stage, a firm might rely more heavily on sales promotion to liquidate inventory and eliminate advertising to reduce costs.

Product Features.   Individual product features may dictate that heavy emphasis be placed on different elements of the promotional mix. If demonstration of the product in use is necessary to effectively communicate its benefits, then personal selling is indicated as a significant part of the promotional mix. Further emphasis on personal selling is warranted if the product is one where trade-ins, customization, or installation is typical. If the product has a highly elastic demand curve, the firm can use sales promotion to great advantage. Features of the product or consumer behavior relating to the product can cause different emphasis on elements within the promotional mix.

The Nature of the Distribution System

Decisions regarding the distribution system for the product have a direct bearing on the promotional mix. Three types of distribution decisions tend to influence the promotional mix configuration.

Intensity of Distribution.   The total number of retail outlets that sell the product affects promotional strategy. The more intensely a product is distributed (i.e., a large number of retailers sell the brand), the more advertising is used to presell the product. When selective distribution is used (i.e., a relatively small number of retail outlets carry the brand), retailers have a vested interest in generating more store traffic through self-funded advertising or cooperative efforts with manufacturers. Selectively distributed goods require that consumers be informed where the product can be obtained. Advertising is a key element in this effort.

Length of the Distribution Channel.   The channel of distribution is the configuration of wholesale and retail selling operations a manufacturer uses to reach the desired market segment. As more resellers are involved in the strategy to reach the market, channel length increases. One obvious effect of channel length on the promotional mix is the increased need for personal selling as more middlemen are involved. As channel length increases, firms must attempt to gain tighter control over distributor, wholesaler, and retailer activities. Personal selling can be instrumental in this regard.

The shortest channel strategy, manufacturer to user (either household or industrial), will use the direct personal selling technique. In this instance, advertising is often employed as a supportive effort to create a favorable predisposition in the prospective customer. Avon, Century 21 Real Estate, and IBM are good examples of corporations using a short channel and supporting personal selling with mass communications.

Type of Middlemen.   Related influences on the length of the channel are the types of middlemen that constitute the links at various levels of distribution. At the wholesale level, the influence on the promotional mix stems from wholesalers' capabilities regarding promotion and service to the retail market. Wholesalers with large sales staffs and complete service and promotional processes relieve the firm of the responsibilities of stimulating demand at the retail level. If the firm has chosen wholesalers with only minimal promotional capabilities, then these tasks must be undertaken internally. The firm's activities in personal selling and sales promotion to retailers will greatly increase.

At the retail level, the type of retail outlet employed for the firm's distribution to consumers can greatly influence the promotional mix. In some instances, the retailer will be the dominant force in the promotional program. This is especially true in cases where the retailer is better known than the manufacturer of an item or in markets where the retailer's name is more influential than the manufacturer's brand name (such as the furniture market). Another important consideration at the retail level is the amount of in-store personal selling that retailers provide. It is possible to discover many similar items that are sold both in essentially self-service outlets (such as K Mart or Woolco) and in service-oriented outlets. Products such as small appliances and hardware items are examples. The more an outlet is self-service oriented, the more the manufacturing firm must presell the item through advertising. As the retail outlet assumes more of the demand stimulation at the point of purchase (personal selling), the manufacturer can rely on this communication to consumers and alter the promotional mix accordingly.

It should also be realized that manufacturers and retailers have a mutual interest in stimulating demand for the manufacturer's brand. In light of this fact, many items are promoted nationally emphasizing the manufacturer's name and locally employing the influence of consumer awareness of the retailer's name and location.

Characteristics of the Firm

The nature and extent of the promotional mix is also influenced by various internal considerations. Paramount are several characteristics of the firm marketing a product.

Previous Business Practice.   Many firms, either by virtue of inertia or the existence of an unchangeable bureaucratic structure, rely heavily on a particular configuration of the promotional mix. These previous business practices may result in a greater emphasis on personal selling, advertising, or sales promotion than would logically be called for. Reliance on previous practices is especially prevalent among firms that do not systematically develop a promotional strategy. Such programs are easy to administer and employ established resources whether or not they are appropriate.

Funds.   Amounts of funds available for promotion tend to dictate the use of personal selling. A firm with limited funds may well be able to finance a small sales staff but be incapable of launching an effective advertising campaign (even though other considerations may dictate the use of advertising). Under these circumstances, the firm may try to deploy its sales staff in an effort to gain retailer support for the brand. Also, the staff can be used to set up and service dealer displays, thus making effective use of the sales promotion element of the promotional mix.

Size of the Sales Staff.   When the firm has a relatively small sales staff it may defer to other areas of the promotional mix or to the members of the channel for promotional support. A small sales staff can severely constrain the firm's ability to carry out an effective promotional program. The firm must seek alternative sources of effort (such as wholesaler and retailer support) in an attempt to overcome an inadequate sales staff with other strategies.

Extent of the Firm's Product Line.   When a firm has an extensive product line several changes occur in the nature of the promotional mix. Extensive product lines lighten the selling task at the wholesale and retail level. Dealers can be convinced with incentives to carry and promote the full line. Further, the efficiency of the firm's sales staff is greatly increased when several items are involved. Also, depending on the branding strategy the firm employs, advertising efficiency can be greatly increased since communications for each member of the line may have peripheral influences on other members. An additional dimension is also added to the sales promotion effort as joint efforts in couponing and in-store displays become possible.

Each of the elements identified as influencing the promotional mix are not meant to be analyzed or interpreted in isolation. Quite the contrary, it is only through a comprehensive consideration of all the influencing factors that the appropriate mixture of promotional elements can be achieved. While one factor may dictate the use of advertising, another may indicate the use of personal selling, and a third the use of both advertising and personal selling. The final decision regarding the nature of the promotional mix will be the astute intrepretation of the effect of the various influences and the level of each promotional element that results in a forceful use of advertising, personal selling, and sales promotion.

SETTING PROMOTIONAL OBJECTIVES

One of the most difficult tasks in the promotional strategy process is the establishment of objectives. At the outset of attempting to set objectives, it is useful to draw upon the communications models established in Chapter 10. These models provide a basis for the development of appropriate and useful objectives for promotional efforts.

Basic Elements in Setting Promotional Objectives

The basic elements of the promotional strategy process that provide the starting point in setting objectives are the: (1) definition of the target market, (2) intended message effects, (3) intended behavioral effects, and (4) geographic allocation of promotional effort.

Definition of the Target Market. The specification of which group or groups of prospective buyers will be the target for promotional effort is an outgrowth of the consumer analysis conducted for the firm's market offering. Given that the product or service was designed or intended for use by a particular group of consumers, the first stage of setting objectives will be to design the promotional mix to reach this group efficiently and effectively. It should be recalled that the firm may have several target markets it wishes to reach.

First, all levels of the distribution system must be considered so that demand stimulation at the wholesale and retail level is specified.

Second, at the household consumer level, demographic, life-style, and behavioral characteristics of the potential market are used to provide greater direction to advertising and personal selling efforts. An additional consideration at the household consumer level is type of prospective customers the firm chooses to pursue. Even after demographic, life-style, and behavioral descriptors are identified for the potential buyer, there are still likely to be at least three different types of consumers in the group: users of the firm's brand, users of the product category but not users of the firm's brand, and nonusers of the product category. It must be decided which subgroup(s) the promotional effort will be directed to. Such specification can change message content and strategy.

Third, if the firm is marketing an industrial product, again the identification of the buyers with the best potential for using the product in the greatest quantities must be made so that deployment of the sales force and development of message content are efficient and effective.

Intended Message Effects. The next basic element in setting objectives is to specify the intended purpose of the message. Generally messages will be devised to achieve one or more basic effects. First, the message may be intended to *persuade* the target market to try the product or to convince the target market that the product is superior to other market offerings. Second, a message can be devised to *inform* consumers of product attributes: unique features, special benefits, improvements, location, etc. Third, the message may intend to *establish, retain,* or *change attitudes* toward the brand. You will recall from the discussion in Chapter 3 that an *attitude* is that complex cognitive element that has direct bearing on behavior toward a product. Finally, a message may be devised with the intention of *establishing, retaining,* or *changing the image* of the brand. Some messages are only implicitly persuasive, carry little or no objective product information, but rather are devised to change the image of the product.

The type of message that is capable of achieving the preceding intended effects is developed through careful planning and the creative process. Researching the target market and pretesting messages contribute to identification of a message's potential for achieving intended effects.

Intended Behavioral Effects.   Since promotional activities are charged with the responsibility for stimulating demand, objectives regarding the intended behavioral effects are necessary. As discussed in Chapter 10, the promotional strategist has too little control over the many influences on sales to judge promotion on this basis. Appropriate objectives for behavioral effects are (1) stimulating trial use, (2) increasing store traffic, (3) increasing the size of order or quantity purchased, and (4) increasing the frequency of purchase (through the communication of more varied or frequent product uses). Granted, several of these objectives may manifest themselves in an increased sales figure, but then only when the other marketing mix variables are performing their functions.

Geographic Allocation.   Objectives regarding the geographic allocation of promotional efforts are the final basic element in setting promotional objectives. Depending upon the external environment, the nature of the market, and the nature of the distribution system, objectives regarding the concentration of advertising efforts or deployment of the sales staff may change considerably. The firm that faces stiff competition from a regional competitor may find it necessary to invest more heavily in promotional activities in that region in comparison with a similar market area that does not have significant regional competition.

When the market for the firm's product is concentrated in several key areas, the same type of deployment of resources is called for. Similarly, the distribution system needs to be considered with regard to its capabilities geographically. If all regions are equally serviced by the system, then similar objectives will be called for. Should distribution capabilities vary on a geographic basis, then objectives which take account of the differences are called for.

Communications and Sales as Promotional Objectives

It has been stated quite forcefully that communications be retained as the essence of promotional objectives. The question must be asked whether sales are ever a proper objective for promotional tools. On occasion, the answer to this question is yes.

Situations wherein sales can be established as a legitimate objective occur when the promotional stimulus either calls for direct purchase action on the part of the receiver or the promotional input is close in proximity to the culmination of a sale. In the first case, advertising that calls for immediate purchase action constitutes a sales object. With regard to proximity to the culmination of the sale, personal selling strategies that hold the salesperson responsible for closing the sale and writing the order come close to complying with a sales objective. Also, several sales promotion devices such as cents-off coupons and aisle displays can be thought of as direct links to sale volume. In all these cases, however, it is relatively easy to conceive of one or the other marketing mix variables having a confounding effect (price is the most obvious interference).

In general, the promotional strategist should strive for objectives that relate directly to the effect he or she is directly in control of: communication. Marketing students should be aware that this is a controversial issue, with advocates and arguments on both sides.[1]

Measuring the Achievement of Objectives

The most important element in measuring the achievement of promotional objectives is that the objectives be stated in measurable terms at the outset. Whether the objective is persuasion, information regarding product attributes, or any of the other basic goals for promotion, some way to judge the relative effect of promotion is necessary. To determine the impact of promotional efforts, two basic measurement approaches can be used.

Market Survey.   A market survey taken before, during, and after the execution of promotional tactics can provide insights about the achievement of objectives. For example, within the target segment, a survey should be made regarding the percentage of potential customers who are aware of a brand's major attribute. Several times during the promotional campaign, the same segment should be surveyed to see if an increased percentage of consumers are now informed. This will provide a direct measure of achievement of an objective to inform consumers.[2]

Laboratory Pretest.   Due to the high cost and time consumed in conducting a market survey, many firms are opting for rigorous laboratory pretests of promotional devices as an alternative measure. Both advertising and personal selling tactics can be presented to a small group of subjects representing the target segment. In a laboratory setting, the subjects' reaction to alternative promotional materials can be measured against established objectives. The promotional devices which appear to achieve the desired effects in the laboratory are then employed in the marketplace.

The process of setting promotional objectives is an important stage of the promotional strategy. It provides guidelines and a structure to the application of promotional tools. Further, it allows for planning future promotional efforts as the achievement of objectives is monitored.

---

[1]See, for example, E. Jerome McCarthy, *Basic Marketing* (5h ed.; Homewood, Ill.: Richard D. Irwin, Inc., 1975), p. 387 and James F. Engle, Hugh G. Wales, and Martin Warshaw, *Promotional Strategy.* (3d ed.; Homewood, Ill.: Richard D. Irwin, Inc., 1975), p. 173.

[2]Test marketing can be considered an additional measuring device, but the great expense involved in employing such a tactic makes it economically infeasible.

BUDGETING FOR PROMOTION

After carefully considering the objectives to be pursued with promotional efforts, it is necessary to determine the allocation of funds for promotion. This section will discuss the most often relied upon techniques in determining the amount to spend on promotion. The items to be included as charges against the promotional budget will vary from firm to firm depending on accounting and management practices. Two significant items that historically have not been included in the determination of the promotional budget are sales staff salaries and commissions or marketing research. Items that characteristically are always included in the promotional budget are media costs of all types, advertising agency fees, advertising pretest costs, market surveys of promotional effectiveness, cooperative programs with retailers, catalogs and selling aids for middlemen or corporate sales staff, and the firm's advertising department salaries. Beyond these types of items, corporate practice dictates what is and is not charged against the promotional budget.

The traditional techniques used in determining the promotional appropriation are (1) previous business practice, (2) percentage of sales, (3) return on investment, (4) how much the competition spends, (5) funds available, and (6) objective and task.

Previous Business Practice

Many firms consider the prior years' expenditures for promotion and determine the increase or decrease of funds to be allocated for the current campaign. Little sophisticated or quantified decision making usually enters the process. Items such as a projected increase in media costs or an impression of competitive pressure manifest themselves as increases in the budget. Conversely, a general dissatisfaction with results in prior campaigns may stimulate reduced spending in certain categories of the promotional effort. This technique draws heavily on the decision maker's experience and practical know-how. In general, it can be evaluated as a wholly unacceptable approach to the budgeting decision. It does not draw on market information or meeting objectives.

Percentage of Sales

Basing the promotional budget on a percentage of previous years' sales is a standard decision tool. It is the favored approach of many firms because it is easy to calculate, usually provides for more total dollars from year to year, and the decision maker can easily explain how the figure was arrived at. Several problems result from the use of this technique, however. First, when a firm's sales are decreasing, the promotional budget will automatically contract on a total dollar basis. A possible aid to the sales dilemma of the firm is increased stimulation of demand which, of course, will be increasingly difficult as the promotional budget shrinks. Second, this technique for appropriating funds can easily result in overspending on promotion. Once the funds have been earmarked, the tendency is to find ways of spending the total budget amount. Third, and most seriously, the percentage of sales approach does not relate promotional dollars to promotional objectives. It is merely a convenient method of establishing a dollar figure.

Return on Investment

To judge the amount spent on promotion as an investment in the firm's market performance has intuitive appeal. It identifies promotion as making a contribution to the enterprise much the same as a capital investment. While the approach is satisfying conceptually, it is unworkable from an operational standpoint. As discussed previously, it is very difficult to determine the point at which promotional efforts actually affect the message recipient. This results in a failure to specify the time frame over which a return on promotional investment can be expected. Further, a return on investment necessarily must rely on sales revenues as a basis for judging and calculating return. This implicitly holds advertising solely responsible for sales and, in light of earlier discussions, this perspective is unacceptable given the true capabilities of promotion.

Competitive Spending

The promotional budget can be determined by monitoring the amount spent by competitors on promotion and allocating an equal amount or an amount proportionate to the firm's market share relative to competition. There is a question as to whether this technique can ever be actually put into practice. First, even if the total dollar figure expended by competitors on promotion were obtainable, this would still not indicate the amounts expended on *particular* promotional activities. Second, as mentioned in the discussion on "Previous Business Practice," competitors may employ very different allocation procedures, thereby deceiving a firm attempting to copy a competitor's promotional budget. Third, the approach is totally reactive, thereby violating the basic premise that promotion is a tool at the disposal of the firm to strategically market its product or service.

Funds Available

In some situations the corporate environment is so concerned with accountability for funds that the promotional budget is the result of "leftovers." Only after all direct costs for manufacturing and marketing a product have been accounted for, plus a profit allocation, does the decision maker identify promotional funds. The typical result of employing this procedure is that insufficient funds are left over for promotion. Granted, some firms are in a crisis situation regarding cash flow and financial liquidity. Notwithstanding these pressures, budgeting on a funds-available basis is simply inappropriate. As a budgetary technique, it again fails to draw on information relevant to the promotional effort.

Objective and Task

By now it is obvious that the approaches to budgeting for promotion discussed thus far fail to draw directly upon the objectives established for promotional efforts. Therefore, the technique that is most appropriate and defensible is the objective and task approach.[3]

This technique merely begins with the stated objectives for each area of the promotional mix. Given promotional goals for target market reach, message effects, behavioral effects, and geographic allocation of promotional efforts, the decision maker identifies those tasks that will achieve the desired impact. Tasks such as media placement and frequency of advertising, frequency of sales calls, cooperative retail programs, couponing, and the like are specified, and costs are determined. In this fashion, the purpose for promotion is the basis for determining the dollars allocated.

The objective and task approach results in a budget figure that is an *ideal* in many ways. The figure arrived at must then be reconciled with what the firm is capable of investing in promotion. Even if a reconciliation and subsequent reduction in dollars allocated is necessary, at least the firm has identified what should have been expended to pursue its promotional objectives.

At this point we can turn our attention to the individual elements of the promotional mix: advertising, personal selling, sales promotion, and publicity. Through a discussion of the specifics of each area, the intricacies inherent to the application of these promotional tools can be identified.

ADVERTISING

The fundamental elements of the advertising effort were discussed in Chapter 10 within the context of mass communications. It is necessary to expand our dicussion of this area of the promotional mix and examine specific aspects of advertising: (1) types of advertising, (2) the creative effort, and (3) media selection.

Types of Advertising

The first consideration in the use of advertising is to determine the type or types of advertising that will be used. While this may seem simple, a lack of consideration at this stage may result in missed opportunities and/or lack of fulfillment of corporate promotional objectives.

Target Audience. The type of advertising and its execution will differ depending upon whether it will be directed at household consumers, industrial users,

---

[3]For a comprehensive discussion of the objective and task approach and its implementation see *Promotional Strategy,* 3d ed., by Engle, Wales, and Warshaw.

retailers and wholesalers, or professionals (such as doctors, engineers, etc.). The message theme and informational content will vary in these advertisements because of the differences in application of the product and the informational needs of the message recipient. Further, the use of media to reach these audience groups will be vastly different.

Product or Institutional.   All advertising is either product or institutional advertising. Product type advertising emphasizes attributes and benefits of a specific product. The majority of advertisements we are exposed to in the mass media are of this type. A manufacturer or seller of a product attempts to stimulate demand for the product per se with this type of advertising.

Institutional advertising is broader in scope and may have one of several purposes. Corporations often employ this type of advertising to build goodwill and to create a favorable predisposition toward the firm. Associations (such as the Dairy Association or the Board of Realtors) will employ an institutional approach in an attempt to stimulate demand for the product or service of an entire industry. Charitable or service organizations will also advertise to solicit funds or inform the public of available services. Finally, when retailers do not single out a product in their advertising, they are using an institutional approach to pursuade consumers to shop at their store for various product needs rather than at competitors' outlets.

National, Regional, or Local.   Finally, the geographic scope of the advertisers' market also defines the type of advertising to be used. National advertising can be accomplished through the use of network television advertisements or national editions of major magazines. This, of course, is appropriate when the advertiser has nationwide distribution for the product or service. Regional advertising is used by firms with regional markets (such as airlines and some department stores) or by firms with national distribution who face stiff competition in particular regions. Finally, local advertising is employed by the many thousands of retailers having one or a few outlets and competing within a very small area.

The Creative Effort

In discussing the creative effort expended in the development of an advertisement, one should realize that an original and successful advertisement is *not* the result of a jolting inspiration or a bolt from the sky. Rather, the process of carefully examining a number of elements of the advertising context in a systematic fashion is the essence of the creative effort. While the intangible aspect of what is *creative* cannot be taught or even discussed very well, there are many elements that *can* be discussed that form the foundation for the creative effort.

Attracting and Holding Attention.   The first step in the creative process is determining a way to attract and hold the attention of the receiver. The use of

Courtesy of Gulf Oil Corporation

Illus. 11-1   Institutional Advertising Helps Build Goodwill

action, color, and sound can be creatively employed to break through the barriers that screen out a message. Celebrities are also used as a means of attracting the viewer's or listener's attention. The use of a recurring story line that entices the receiver to "catch the next installment" has also proved effective in this regard.

The Old Home Bread campaign and the Miller Lite Beer approach are examples of the recurring story line.

Type of Appeal.   In determining the type of appeal to employ while considering the creative aspects of advertising, the two most basic types are emotional appeals and appeals based on functional product attributes. Appealing to a receiver on the basis of security, prestige, affiliation, or another emotion can be effective if the consumer perceives the product as capable of providing such benefits. Emphasizing functional product attributes can have a powerful effect if the product has unique features that clearly distinguish it from other products.

Beyond the basic types of appeals, several other specific appeals can be employed. The use of humor is a well-favored approach in advertising, but the effects of its use are mixed at best.[4] The same is true regarding fear appeals. Marketing researchers have advocated the use of fear appeals while researchers in other behavioral sciences cite adverse effects on communication through its use.[5]

One of the more recent approaches in advertising is comparison advertising. This type of appeal compares the advertiser's brand with several competitive brands, either explicitly or by inference (i.e., the leading brand). While this technique has never had legal roadblocks, for years advertisers have feared that its use would produce benefits for the competitors' brands. Evidence regarding the specific effects of this technique is still being obtained. However, it appears that comparative advertising is more effective than harmful as a communications approach.[6]

The appeal that will prove most effective relays *relevant* information to the message recipient. Regardless of the specific technique for trying to relay this information, it must be related to the recipient's criteria for judging the product before it will communicate. It is at this point that the promotional strategist relies most heavily on the marketing research information about the product.

The Presentation.   Various aspects of the technical presentation relate to creatively executing the advertisement. Specifically, decisions relating to copy, visualization, and repetition must be made as part of the creative effort.

---

[4]Brian Sternthal and C. Samuel Craig, "Humor in Advertising," *Journal of Marketing,* Vol. 37 (October 1973), p. 12.

[5]For a discussion favoring the use of fear, see Michael Ray and William Wilkie, "Fear, The Potential of an Appeal Neglected by Marketing," *Journal of Marketing,* Vol. 34 (1970), p. 59. For a discussion of the adverse effects of fear appeals see Irving L. Javis and Seymour Feshback, "Effects of Fear-Arousing Communication," *Journal of Abnormal and Social Psychology,* Vol. 48 (1952), p. 78. A general discussion of the use of fear in advertising can be found in Brian Sternthal and C. Samuel Craig, "Fear Appeals: Revisited and Revised," *Journal of Consumer Research,* Vol. 1 (December 1974), p. 22.

[6]A general discussion of the technique can be found in William L. Wilkie and Paul W. Farris "Comparision Advertising: Problems and Potential," *Journal of Marketing,* Vol. 39 (October 1975), p. 7. Empirical evidence of the effects of comparative advertising is found in V. Kanti Prasad, "Communications Effectiveness of Comparative Advertising: A Laboratory Analysis," *Journal of Marketing Research,* Vol. 13, No. 2, (May, 1976), p. 128. Also see Debra Scammon "Comparison Advertising: A Reexamination of the Issue," *Journal of Consumer Affairs,* Vol. 12, No. 2 (Winter, 1978), p. 381.

Too often advertisers believe that a good journalist will make a good copywriter. For copy to be effective, it needs to be far more than grammatically correct. The copywriter, regardless of the medium used for the presentation, must insure that the message theme is unambiguous and highlights relevant decision information. Copy (including the headline in printed advertising) should emphasize the brand name. It should not be a rambling, undirected discourse on the product. Benefits from product use and specific claims should be enthusiastically and forcefully relayed. Unique product features should be emphasized to take maximum advantage of product differentiation. Finally, consistency is a key element. The risk of confusing the message recipient cannot be afforded.

For those media that furnish visual presentation, some basic guidelines can be offered. The picture should tell the complete story. If the viewer sees only the visualization, this is the only opportunity to communicate. The visual should be consistent with the illustration and complement its message.

Although repetition of advertisements in the media (especially television) is a much maligned practice, the truth of the matter (based on learning theory) is that the use of repetition in promotion is an essential factor in achieving message reception, retention, and behavioral effects.[7] Certainly, repetition can be overdone and can introduce annoyance as an effect. The amount of repetition that will be needed for any particular message should be empirically determined. Depending on the characteristics of the audience, the nature of the product, and the type and amount of information being communicated, the requirements for repeating the message to an audience will change.

Media Selection

An advertising effort can be undermined if blunders are made in the selection of media to transmit the message. It is necessary to understand two fundamental elements of the media available for advertising: inherent characteristics and strategic application. The inherent characteristics of the media relate to opportunities or constraints that result from the technical capabilities and consumer reactions to the media. Strategic application of the media can be achieved through *reach and frequency* tactics and *flighting and audience duplication* techniques.

Inherent Characteristics. The inherent characteristics of the media are rated in Table 11-1 as high (H), medium (M), or low (L)—that is, each medium is evaluated according to its capability or application on the basis of the way in which it functions.

The descriptors used in Table 11-1 may need clarification. *Coverage* is merely an indication of a medium's ability to reach potential message recipients within a specific scope. Coverage at both the national and local level are relevant. *Selectivity* is an indication of a medium's ability to reach a specified type of receiver or reach a group of receivers based on geographic location or demographic characteristics.

---

[7] An excellent overview of the effects of repetition is provided by James F. Engle, Roger D. Blackwell, and David T. Kollat, *Consumer Behavior* (3d ed.; Hinsdale, Ill.: Dryden Press, 1978) p. 427.

Table 11-1   Evaluation of Major Media

Characteristics	TV	Radio	Newspaper	Magazine	Direct Mail	Billboards
Coverage						
Local	H	H	H	L	H	H
National	H	L	L	H	M	L
Selectivity						
Demographic	M	M	L	H	H	L
Geographic	M	M	H	H	H	H
Consumer Acceptance	M	M	H	H	L	M
Consumer Attentiveness	L	L	M	H	L	L
Reproduction Quality	M	N/A	L	H	H	M
Flexibility	L	H	H	L	H	M
Use by retailers	M-H	M	H	M	M	M
Cost						
Per contact	L	L	L	M	H	L
For national coverage	H	H	H	M	H	H

Consumer acceptance of a medium relates to how credible consumers view a medium or whether they use the medium as a source of product information. The way in which consumers listen to or view a medium is an indication of *consumer attentiveness.* Some media are carefully examined (such as magazines) while others are glanced at or skimmed (such as television, radio, and billboards) because of the brevity of the presentation. *Reproduction quality* relates to the ability of a medium to produce an accurate visualization. The color capabilities of the media are also evaluated on this dimension. *Flexibility* pertains to two characteristics of a medium: closing times (the length of time an advertisement must be submitted before it appears in the medium) and the ability of the advertiser to actually acquire space. In some media, long closing times and chaotic buying of space can disrupt strategy plans. The *use by retailers* is an indication of the medium's appropriateness for use by retailers or of use by manufacturers in cooperation with retailers. Finally, *cost* must be considered in at least two ways. On a per contact basis, cost is figured on the dollar (or cents) amount it costs to expose each receiver. The cost evaluation can differ when the use of a medium is considered for national coverage, however.

The evaluations in Table 11-1 demonstrate that each medium has its strengths and weaknesses. The creative use of media results from a careful judgment of the needs regarding proper product presentation, adequate transmission of message content, and the nature of the audience. In many instances, the inherently low capabilities of a medium may be less of a liability than the general case where these factors are considered.

Strategic Application. As mentioned previously, strategic applications of the media can be achieved through reach and frequency tactics and flighting and audience duplication techniques.

Reach means the number of different homes exposed to an advertisement during a given time period (typically four weeks). *Frequency* is the number of times a home within the area reached is exposed to the advertisement. A related concept is *GRP* or *Gross Rating Points.* This is a summary measure of Reach X Frequency. An important aspect of GRP is that it can now be calculated for time periods with the elimination of duplicated audience (i.e., reaching the same homes or viewers more than once). If reach (rather than repetition) is a critical creative objective, then GRP ratings that reflect the unduplicated audience should be relied on heavily.

Flighting is a media scheduling technique that has both financial and effectiveness advantages. This tactic is implemented by scheduling a heavy advertising campaign for a period of time, then stopping advertising altogether for a period of time, only to come back at a subsequent date with another heavy schedule. Flighting is used to support special merchandising efforts or for new product introduction. Financial advantages are gained through flighting because better prices for space or discounts may be gained by concentrating media buys in a short time period. Communications effectiveness may be enhanced since a heavy schedule may gain the repeat exposures necessary to achieve consumer awareness. The next *flight* of the promotion can then reinforce the previous communication.

Audience duplication is a technique that can have powerful communications effectiveness. The objective of audience duplication is to reach the same group of receivers through different media. One preferred tactic in this regard is to run the sound track from a television ad as a radio spot. The recall and visualization stimulated in the receiver results in high levels of recognition for the brand. There are difficulties in the precise application of the technique since various media services cannot provide the extent of duplication provided. Advertisers have had to rely on mathematical formulas to estimate the duplication effect.

The advertising element of the promotional mix can provide great benefit to a firm's efforts in stimulating demand. It is, however, dependent upon the precise specification of the factors discussed here. A well-conceived and carefully executed advertising campaign can reach the potential market and communicate the corporate message according to established objectives.

PERSONAL SELLING

The next step in the promotional strategy process is determining the application of personal selling. As discussed previously in this chapter, several influences indicate the need for a personal selling effort. Further, the level at which personal selling will be implemented (industrial, trade, or consumer) should also have been determined. At this point, the specifics of developing the personal selling phase of the promotional mix will be discussed. The fundamental considerations in personal selling are: (1) types of personal selling tasks, (2) operation of the sales force, and (3) evaluating the personal selling effort.

Types of Personal Selling Tasks

The task of personal selling can be described as having one of three basic purposes: order taking, creative selling, or supportive communication. Also, regardless of the type of selling to be engaged in, the general task of preparing for and executing the selling effort is required.

Order taking. The least complex of the selling tasks is order taking. Its importance, however, should not be downplayed, since the number of selling efforts categorized as order taking dominate the selling process in the United States. The retail clerk who takes payment for products is considered an *inside order taker.* In this case, the buyer has already chosen the product and merely uses the salesperson to make payment. The other type of order-taking sales task involves the *outside order taker* who typically calls on industrial buyers or the trade (wholesalers and retailers). This type of salesperson and the task he or she performs is very routine. The accounts have been established, and the order taker merely services them on a reorder basis.

Creative Selling. The creative selling task requires much more effort and expertise in its execution. Situations where creative selling is implemented range from retail stores, through the selling of services, to industrial selling. In creative selling the potential buyer relies heavily on the sales representative for information, advice, and service. At the retail level, those outlets that have a fully trained and experience sales staff and emphasize the in-store selling effort are using creative selling. Products such as clothing or major appliances typify the use of creative selling. The services of an insurance salesperson or a stockbroker represent another type of creative selling. With products or services of this sort the salesperson aids the buyer in determining how his or her unique needs can be best served. Perhaps the most complex of all selling tasks is creative selling at the industrial level. Those salespeople who deal with high cost and complex corporate decisions for purchases of capital equipment or raw materials have tremendous demands placed on them. Many times the salesperson has specific training in a related area (engineering, computer science, etc.) in order to handle this type of selling effort. The salesperson may be required to identify the product that best serves the buyers' needs or carefully calculate the number and type of products necessary for the organization (such as in hospital supply sales). This creative selling task calls for high levels of preparation, expertise, and close contact with the buyer.

Supportive Communication. Some personal selling tasks are very indirectly related to selling per se. Rather, it is the objective of the effort to generate goodwill and insure that the buyer is satisfied with the firm's product and service. The missionary salesperson is typically employed in this capacity. He or she will call accounts with the expressed purpose of monitoring the satisfaction of the buyer. There may be some provision of product information in the process, but only as a service to the customer.

Preparing for and Executing the Selling Effort.   In order to perform
properly the selling tasks just described, preliminary preparation is required.
The preparation for creative selling is more demanding and extensive but the
order taking and supportive efforts should be detailed as well. The first step in
this process is *preparation* for the selling effort. This involves gathering relevant
information about prospective customers, corporate supportive activities (such
as advertising), and information about competitors' activities. The well-prepared salesperson will be confident and efficient in his or her selling efforts.
Further, effectiveness will be enhanced when the salesperson can identify customer needs and point out advantages over competitive products or services.
Next the salesperson must perform the *sales presentation.* Here it is critical that
the salesperson identify relevant information for each prospective buyer and include this information in the sales presentation. All aspects of the product and
related services that form the judgment criteria must be included and effectively communicated. At this point, the *negotiation* stage begins. The salesperson must answer questions, resolve objections to product features or service
elements, and implement corporate pricing procedures.[8] *Closing the sale* is the
next part of the effort. Here the salesperson attempts to persuade the buyer to sign
the order form. This is a delicate stage in the process, and techniques for closing
the sale must be well prepared and judiciously executed. Finally, *follow-up* must be
provided to the buyer. In many selling efforts, it is the responsibility of the
salesperson to make sure that the product is delivered, that the order is correct,
and that the buyer is satisfied.

Operation of a Sales Force

Employing a sales force requires the same kind of structured, detailed planning
as is required in advertising. The effective use of a sales force in promotional
strategy stems from complete attention to several operational elements: job description, recruiting, training, deployment, compensation, and management.

Job Description.   Before a firm can hope to make effective use of personal
selling it is necessary to know the size of the sales force and type of person that
will be needed. A comprehensive, detailed job description that clearly identifies
both the selling task as it will be performed and the number and type of salesper-
sons desired is necessary. Only after the firm is capable of producing such a
description can the development of the sales staff begin.[9]

---

[8]The inside order taker rarely has any authority over pricing but may still have to answer inquiries
regarding price. This stage of the selling effort pertains primarily to the creative salesperson.

[9]The *type* of person needed is left to the discretion of the firm and is based on the type of product
and nature of the selling task. Some evidence does exist regarding personality and personal characteris-
tics that appear to be related to selling success. See, for example, Laurence M. Lamont and William
J. Lundstrum "Identifying Successful Industrial Salesmen by Personality and Personal Characteristics,"
Journal of Marketing Research, Vol. 14 (November, 1977), p. 517; and Richard P. Bagozzi, "Sales Force
Performance and Satisfaction as a Function of Individual Difference, Interpersonal and Situational
Factors," *Journal of Marketing Research,* Vol. 15, No. 4 (November, 1978), p. 517.

Recruitment. Once the number and type of people have been determined, the firm can begin to recruit a staff. Sources for finding qualified people vary from classified advertising to professional recruiting organizations to college campuses. The critical thing to remember in recruiting is that it is a continuous process. The firm should solicit qualified people on a regular schedule so that a file of appropriate applicants is available. The firm that begins to recruit only when the need arises will find itself tempted to accept unqualified or inappropriate people.

Training. Training the sales staff relates directly to the nature of the selling task and the objectives to be achieved. For some order-taking sales efforts, very little training is required. Conversely, some creative selling efforts may require lengthy and costly training programs. One important decision in training a sales staff is the nature of the training experience. The firm must decide the content of the program, when it will be presented, who will do the training, and what training techniques will be used. It is wise at this point for the marketing decision maker to draw heavily on the management expertise in the firm (or elsewhere) to implement an effective training program. What should be taught is, of course, the domain of the promotional strategist and should provide the foundation for the training program.

Deployment. Once the sales staff is assembled and trained the process of making assignments begins. Whether the context for performance is the retail store or a sales territory, the staff must be assigned specific duties. At the retail level, the scope of the salesperson's duties and the range of selling tasks can vary greatly as discussed earlier. Deployment of retail staff can range from merely staffing a cash register to creative selling, restocking, reordering, and soliciting new customers. In field sales, there are greater numbers of deployment decisions. Not only does the scope of responsibility need to be specified, but the number of accounts, number of sales calls (daily, weekly, or monthly), and peripheral activities (service and promotion) must be determined for each member of the staff. Further, the geographic allocation of sales force activity must be specified.[10]

Compensation. There are three compensation alternatives available: straight salary, straight commission, and a combination salary-commission alternative. Illus. 11-2 indicates the factors that influence the emphasis on the use of the salary and commission alternatives.

The more highly skilled the sales staff and the more rigorous the selling effort, the most appropriate compensation method tends to be oriented toward a salary arrangement. As the selling task becomes less complex and embodies few service activities by the sales force, the commission approach to compensation becomes

---

[10]For a specific plan for sales force deployment see A. Parasuraman and Ralph L. Day, "A Management Oriented Model for Allocating Sales Effort," *Journal of Marketing Research,* Vol. 14 (February, 1977), p. 22; and Michael S. Herschel, "Effective Sales Territory Development," *Journal of Marketing,* Vol. 41 (April, 1977), p. 39.

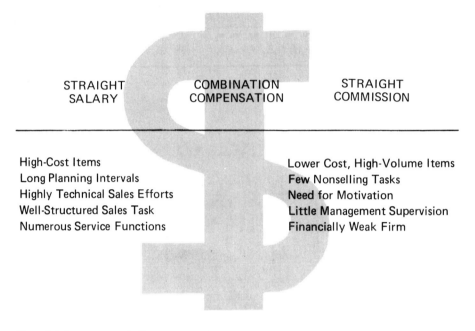

| STRAIGHT SALARY | COMBINATION COMPENSATION | STRAIGHT COMMISSION |

High-Cost Items   Lower Cost, High-Volume Items
Long Planning Intervals   Few Nonselling Tasks
Highly Technical Sales Efforts   Need for Motivation
Well-Structured Sales Task   Little Management Supervision
Numerous Service Functions   Financially Weak Firm

Illus. 11-2   Influences on Compensation Alternatives

more feasible. Many firms are currently using a combination plan since few selling assignments clearly indicate the exclusive use of salary or commission.

Management.   The management of the sales force is the ongoing responsibility of corporate personnel. To ensure that the goals of the promotional mix are being achieved and that company policy and procedure are being followed, the sales staff will need supervision. Further, as a method of interjecting control into the process, management of the sales staff can be most effective.

Techniques for managing the personal selling effort are varied. One consistent conclusion is that personal and individual supervision of the members of the sales force is superior. In this regard, field (or department) supervisors and regional or local sales managers can be usefully employed. It has also been offered that a cooperative rather than a competitive management strategy are more effective as a management style;[11] that is, techniques that motivate cooperation between salespeople rather than competition (for awards or bonuses) are a more effective management approach.

Evaluation.   Evaluating the performance of salespeople is a task that draws directly upon the objectives established for the selling task. Beyond linking evaluation to goal attainment, there are several objective and subjective criteria

[11]See Rensis Likert, "New Patterns in Sales Management," *Changing Perspectives in Marketing Management,* edited by Martin R. Warshaw (Ann Arbor: Bureau of Business Research, University of Michigan, 1962), p. 1.

upon which individual staff members can be judged. Illus. 11-3 outlines the criteria that can be used.

The objective criteria should be carefully implemented. For example, total dollar volume of sales must be judged against order size and expenses generated. A salesperson might be rated highly on total dollar volume at the expense of many small orders obtained at great cost to the firm. Also, depending on the objectives of the sales effort and the selling task involved, it may be that peripheral activities are critical to long-range plans to the detriment of current sales figures. Astute use of objective criteria is the key factor.

The subjective criteria are very difficult to put into operation. Being judgmental by nature, management must be careful to allow flexibility and individual styles to exist. The strength of an individual salesperson may be in his or her unique style. Suppression of individual differences may be inefficient and demoralizing.

The implementation of the personal selling plan of the promotional mix must be performed with great care. In many instances, the consumer decision process and consumer attitude toward the firm is focused directly on personal selling. In many marketing efforts, the consumer or buyer relies heavily on personal selling assistance as a critical variable in the choice of a brand. In these instances, the personal selling effort must be properly designed and put into operation. Further, the sales representative is frequently viewed as the tangible manifestation of a

---

Objective	Subjective
1. Sales • total dollar volume • percentages of quota • by product line • by territory (department) • per sales call	1. Appearance 2. Preparedness 3. Customer Relations 4. Attitude 5. Product Knowledge
2. Profit (margin) generated • by territory (department) • by product line	
3. Orders • number • size	
4. Sales calls executed	
5. Expenses generated	
6. Peripheral activities • service calls • promotion • follow-up	

Illus. 11-3   **Criteria for Evaluating Sales Staff**

corporation. Sales force performance can have an overriding effect on consumer attitude and behavioral predisposition toward the firm's market offering.

SALES PROMOTION

Sales promotion is a very conspicuous factor in the promotional mix. Properly used, it is capable of having important effects on demand stimulation. A major portion of the sales promotion process is the joint use of advertising and pricing. The scope of sales promotion can be broadened, at this point, to identify related activities that are classified as sales promotion. Further, the objectives of sales promotion will be identified.

Types of Sales Promotion

There are various types of sales promotion—all designed to stimulate demand. This phase of the promotional mix is by no means minor since it is estimated that nearly $4 billion was spent on sales promotion in 1977.[12] The basic types of sales promotion are coupons, premiums, contests, point-of-purchase materials, trial offers and sampling, and trade shows.

Coupons. The use of coupons is well advised when elasticity of demand is verified for the product category, or consumer behavior in the product category is typified by brand switching. Cents-off coupons either placed in the media or in the package provide the catalyst for brand choice among products that are viewed as essentially the same. Evidence suggests that coupons in the package stimulate greater brand loyalty than media-distributed coupons.[13] Further, it appears that particular consumer groups are more prone to be affected by such product deals.[14] The use of coupons is an effective way to gain new users for the brand and to stimulate repeat purchases with package coupons.

Premiums. Premiums are items offered free with the purchase of another item or offered at a greatly reduced price. Banks have recently employed premiums to attract new customers and increase savings deposits. Many firms offer a related product free (a razor or blades attached to shaving cream) to stimulate demand, but the use of this tactic must be carefully considered. First, the cost of offering premiums must be weighed against potential benefits. Second, the appropriate premium must be chosen so that a legitimate inducement for the consumer results.

---

[12]*Sales and Marketing Management,* February 9, 1976, p. 104.
[13]Joe A. Dodson, Alice M. Tybout, and Brian Sternthal, "The Impact of Deals and Deal Retraction on Brand Switching," *Journal of Marketing Research,* Vol. 15 (February, 1978), p. 72.
[14]Robert Blattberg *et al.,* "Identifying the Deal Prone Segment," *Journal of Marketing Research,* Vol. 15 (August, 1978), p. 369.

Courtesy of GTE Lighting Products

Illus. 11-4   Contests Help Generate Store Traffic

Contests.   Games and contests of all types can be used to draw attention to a product. Many times this tactic is implemented on a cooperative basis between a manufacturer and retail outlets. Contests can have a great effect on generating traffic in the retail outlet.

Users of the contest technique must be careful not to violate many state laws that forbid their use. Further, games and contests usually cannot require the purchase of the product for participation. In light of this fact, gaining attention for the brand or building store traffic is a more appropriate objective than demand stimulation.

Trial Offers and Sampling.   The effect of getting consumers to try the product is a powerful one. This being the case, trial offers and sampling are sales promotion devices designed to accomplish just that. Free samples of detergents, shampoos, mouthwashes, and the like are distributed free to expose consumers to a brand. Many times this tactic is used for new products, but it can also be used in weak market areas or segments to increase brand performance. Trial offers have essentially the same intent but are used for more expensive items. Appliances, watches, hand tools, and related products are often offered on a ten-day free trial to overcome consumer inertia to trying the product. Trial offers and free samples have the advantage of getting the product into consumers' hands without expense on the consumer's part. The expense to the firm, however, can be formidable and the segments chosen for this promotional device must have high potential.

Point-of-Purchase Materials.   Product displays and information sheets are useful sales promotion items to reach consumers at the point of purchase. Many times the product display is designed to draw attention to the product. Equally as often it is a technique for gaining additional shelf space and exposure in the retail setting. Hand-out materials at the point of purchase can be an important complement to the personal selling process for shopping goods. In situations where consumers are comparing brands on features and judging the product at the point of purchase, additional information at this stage in the decision process can be very effective.

Trade Shows.   Trade shows are events where several related products are displayed and perhaps demonstrated to members of an industry or industries that constitute the potential market. In conjunction with displays, company representatives are on hand to explain the product and perhaps make an important contact for the personal selling effort. The use of trade shows can be carefully planned and should be considered a part of the overall promotional program.[15]

Objectives for Sales Promotion

The technique of sales promotion and its many tactics should be implemented only after specifying the objectives for its use. The following identify basic objectives that can be pursued through the use of sales promotion.

1.   Attract new users to the brand.
2.   Stimulate repeat purchase.

---

[15]Suzette Cavanaugh, "Setting Objectives and Evaluating the Effectiveness of Trade Show Exhibits," *Journal of Marketing,* Vol. 40 (October, 1976), p. 100.

3. Stimulate larger purchases.
4. Attract attention to the brand.
5. Build store traffic.
6. Introduce a new product.

An important thing to remember regarding sales promotion is that it will rarely (if ever) be the dominant element of the promotional mix. Rather, sales promotion should function in a supportive capacity to add another dimension to the advertising and personal selling efforts. Further, objectives for sales promotion should be identified within the context of aiding these major promotional mix variables.

PUBLICITY

Relatively few discussions of the promotional mix clearly portray publicity as a major element. The reason it is included here is that the typical commercial enterprise can make good use of publicity; furthermore, nonprofit organizations may have to rely heavily on this type of promotion.

Publicity is nonpaid for media exposure for a product or firm. While this element of the promotional mix will never dominate the promotional strategy, it can prove to be an image builder and heighten consumer awareness for the product or firm.

Perhaps the most important task in the publicity area is for the firm to *be prepared*. The firm should have a comprehensive and current file of information that makes for good publicity. The file should give a realistic and praiseworthy view of the firm's products and corporate behavior.

The types of items that make for good publicity are:

1. New products
2. New personnel
3. New corporate facilities
4. Innovative corporate practices (energy-saving effort, the use of new technology)
5. Charitable activities by the firm
6. Community or service activities of the firm

Firms have typically underutilized publicity and have not been organized to take advantage of this opportunity to communicate with consumers.

INTEGRATING PROMOTIONAL MIX VARIABLES

The integration of the promotional mix variables must be achieved at two levels: (1) with the other elements of the marketing mix and (2) with one another. It is critical that advertising, personal selling, sales promotion, and publicity are coordinated and implemented in a fashion whereby synergy is achieved.

The integration of the promotional mix variables with the other elements of the marketing mix draws heavily on the factors discussed in Chapter 10 regarding the environment for promotion. Further the discussion of influences on the promotional mix in this chapter highlights areas where integration can be achieved.

The basic premise of this phase of the integration of the promotional mix is that the level of activity for each promotional element be consistent with and enhance the other activities in the firm's overall marketing effort. To this end, the promotional strategy must be incorporated with the systems approach to marketing planning discussed in Chapter 1. In this way, both the effect of promotional efforts and the contribution of promotion to the marketing effort will be optimized.

Integration of promotional mix variables with one another is a matter of planning and timing. First, the analysis of influences on the promotional mix will contribute greatly to the integration. Second, the possible conflict of promotional program elements must be identified and rectified. For example, a coupon sales promotion tactic may conflict with certain message elements (such as a quality image) proposed for the advertising effort. Third, mix variables must be evaluated for their potential to complement each other. Ideally advertising will support the personal selling effort and the personal communications will be designed to exploit the mass communications effect. Further, any sales promotion tactics employed will provide substance for the advertising message. Finally, the timing of execution of each promotional mix element is coordinated in such a way that the opportunity exists to take advantage of each prior effort. For example, point-of-purchase materials can emphasize the message theme consumers have been exposed to through advertising.

The process of integrating promotional mix variables is greatly enhanced by the systematic approach to devising the promotional mix presented in this chapter. If each phase of the development of the promotional strategy is fully developed and specified, then integration of the elements is actually an on-going and pervasive effort.

QUESTIONS AND ANALYTICAL PROBLEMS

1. When is a firm likely to rely on personal selling as the dominant element in promotion? When will advertising be the primary promotional effort?

2. When is it appropriate to establish *sales* as a promotional objective? Why are sale per se usually an inappropriate statement of promotional objectives?

3. List four intended behavioral effects that might be established for promotion. Give an example of an advertisement that ad-

dresses one of these behavioral effects.

4. What are the fundamental drawbacks of most budgeting procedures for promotion? How does the objective and task approach overcome these deficiencies?

5. Describe the difference between product and institutional advertising. Which industry is currently relying heavily on institutional advertising?

6. Identify two ways in which an ad-

vertisement can be creatively ex- ecuted? Identify an advertisement you consider creative; point out how the effect is achieved.

7. What is *flighting?* What is the main purpose of the technique?

8. What do you consider the single most important factor in media choice? Defend your position.

9. Choose a retail store in your area

and analyze the personal selling approach used by the store person- nel. How does it compare with the discussion of personal selling in the text.

10. Is there a product you are particu- larly attracted to by a cents-off coupon? Why is the use of sales promotion for this product effective?

Case 11-1 • TYLER BARON ENDORSES BARROW SLACKS

Bud Green, advertising manager of Barrow Clothing Industries, was in the process of evaluating the most recent advertising proposal from the Lear Advertising Agency. The Lear account executive had proposed building an advertising campaign around Tyler Baron, the young and flamboyant world chess champion from Menlo Park, California. Bud Green was unsure about the potential effectiveness of the campaign.

Barrow Clothing Industries is an old-line firm located in the Twin Cities area of Minnesota. The firm earned its initial reputation in the 1920s for manufacturing men's fine suits of 100 percent wool. During the 1950s the firm slowly expanded its product line into sport coats and finally into men's dress and casual pants. During the middle 1970s the firm's management decided to develop national distributors for the firm's pants and other prod- ucts. Along with this decision came the necessity to engage in national promotion. The promotion program was two pronged. First, consumer demand for the product was stim- ulated through consumer advertising on national television. Second, direct-mail and per- sonal selling were used to recruit an adequate number of retail outlets for the product. Generally one retail outlet was established for every 50,000 people in a retail trade area.

The initial consumer advertising campaign had the specific objectives of building aware- ness of the product. The second campaign, the one currently in the planning stages, was for the purpose of building secondary demand, that is, demand for the Barrow brand.

Bud Green wondered about the effectiveness of using testimonials in building brand preference. He also wondered whether Tyler Baron was the best person to give a testimo- nial. Even though the ads were creative—"When you sit as much as I do, you don't want to get 'checked' by your pants"—and effectively produced, Bud was still unsure about the testimonial concept.

How would you advise Bud Green about testimonials? Would testimonials be suitable for all types of products? Are testimonials suitable for men's pants?

Case 11-2 • THE A AND M BOOKSTORE

Linda Fowler, owner and manager of the A and M Bookstore of College Station, Texas, is considering using a different promotion tool—cents-off coupons. Specifically, she wants to increase the turnover of her Texas A and M souvenir stock. Souvenir items include beer mugs, ash trays, hats, pennants, T-shirts, and other items through which students and alumni can display their support for the college. All souvenir items are adorned with the team mascot, a Collie named Reveille, or Sarge, a cartoon character.

Linda normally has little difficulty selling souvenir items. In fact, her suppliers indicate that Texas A and M fans are some of the most enthusiastic souvenir purchasers in the United States. However, Linda had mistakenly overpurchased to take advantage of quantity discounts. Now she is faced with the possibility of carrying the inventory through the spring and summer, a possibility she does not want to turn into a reality.

Linda has never used coupons before but is considering using them because advertising in the Texas A and M student newspaper and a storewide 10 percent-off sale have not helped her excess inventory situation. The thought of using cents-off coupons came to her as she used a coupon to save ten cents on her last purchase of a pound of coffee. She realized that coupons are usually used only on food products but that they may be effective with other types of products. She has concluded that investigating the possibility of using coupons is worth the effort.

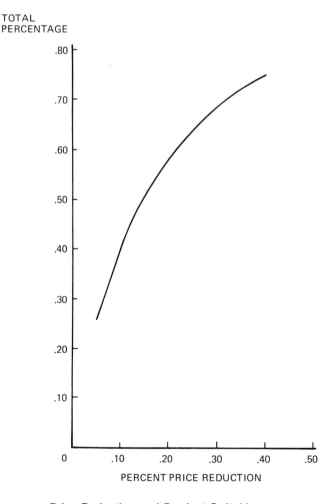

Illus. 11-A   **Price Reduction and Product Switching**

Table 11-A   **Emerging Conclusions from Sales Promotion Research**

1. Sales promotions are most effective for new product introductions or unfamiliar brands. However, except for new product introductions, substantial doubt has been raised about the ability of deal offerings to attract new consumers who will be loyal following deal retraction.

2. For immediate effects, sales promotions can induce substantial brand switching and when coupled with advertising can have a synergistic effect on total sales.

3. Repeat purchase probabilities appear higher for food than nonfood products; package coupons appear most effective for maintaining current brand franchises.

4. Consumer deal proneness is positively correlated with venturesomeness, media exposure, and gregariousness, and is inversely related to brand loyalty.

5. For those brands which do not dominate competing brands on a critical product attribute, sales promotions provide an alternative for attracting purchasers of other brands.

6. Means of distribution and value associated with promotion can have a significant impact on campaign success and coupon redemption rates.

7. Future applications of sales promotions will undoubtedly increase in response to increasing consumer price-consciousness and in efforts to fight advertising clutter and to encourage retailer support.

Linda's investigation is leading in two directions, First, she is interested in the costs and methods by which coupons can be delivered to potential users. She has learned that the local paper and the university paper can print coupons as part of an advertisement. Moreover, she was surprised to learn that coupons can be printed on handbills and distributed by a local Boy Scout troop for about the cost of a couple of newspaper advertisements.

The second area Linda is investigating is the amount of coupon discount necessary to stimulate sales. Her initial investigation of this topic led nowhere. Finally, one of her part-time employees, a marketing student at the university, showed her a research paper that he had received in one of his marketing classes. The paper contained some useful information about coupons and grocery products. The most useful information from the paper is shown in Illus. 11-A and Table 11-A.[1] Linda is unsure whether the graph relating to percentage price reduction and cumulative percentage of people willing to switch is of any value.

Should Linda use cents-off coupons to stimulate sales? If so, how should the coupons be distributed? Is the information shown in Figure 11-A and Table 11-A useful to Linda in any way?

[1]Illus. 11-A and Table 11-A were taken from a paper submitted to the *Journal of Advertising Board* by William O. Beardon, Jesse E. Teel, and Robert H. Williams entitled, "Consumer Response to Cents-Off Coupons."

12

distribution

Today, retailers sell wholesale, wholesalers sell retail, hardwares sell soft goods, department stores sell food, food stores sell appliances, they all sell toys, and discount stores sell everything.

--Donald J. Bowersox, "Changing Channels in the Physical Distribution of Finished Goods," *Marketing and Economic Development: Proceedings of the American Marketing Associated National Conference,* P. D. Bennett (ed.), 1965.

Only in rare cases does a company that manufactures a product sell it directly to its ultimate consumer. It would be a tremendous and probably unwise undertaking for General Mills, for instance, to sell and deliver each of its brands of breakfast foods directly to the more than 80 million consumer units that are its potential customers. However, some manufacturers do reach their ultimate consumers through their own retail stores; others hire door-to-door sales representatives. Direct movement from producer to consumer, however, amounts to less than 3 percent of all goods sold.[1] This means that over 97 percent of all goods sold are resold one or more times by sellers other than the original producer. Such being the case, it is clear that the success of the producer or manufacturer is dependent on how effectively these resellers do their jobs. These resellers are composed of a linkage of the different kinds of agents, wholesalers, and retailers. The manufacturer usually takes the initiative in putting together a chain of such institutions that will bridge the gap between the factory and the ultimate consumer. This linkage is called a *channel*.

---

[1] U.S. Department of Commerce, Bureau of the Census, *Census of Business, 1972.*

This chapter defines the concept of channels, briefly discusses various marketing functions performed within the channel, analyzes conventional and vertical marketing channels, presents the factors affecting channel design, explores the dynamic forces leading to channel change, and presents an overall view of the effectiveness of distribution channels. Illus. 12–1 provides condensed descriptions of the functions undertaken by middlemen. A knowledge of these functions will assist in understanding conventional channels of distribution.

DEFINITION OF A MARKETING CHANNEL

According to the Committee on Definitions of the American Marketing Association, a *market channel* is "the structure of intracompany organization

---

Retailers

    Buy goods and resell them to ultimate customers.

    Vary by size and number of product lines carried.

    Most retailing is in-store operation, but mail-order, in-home and vending machine sales are important for some lines.

    May be independent ownership of one or two stores or may be chain (multiunit) operations.

Merchant Wholesalers

    Buy goods and resell them to retailers, industrial users, other wholesalers, export markets, or government entities.

    Most handle many items—frequently of competing brands.

    Principal advantages are relatively low physical distribution cost and, because they buy the goods, they relieve the manufacturer of costs and risks of holding inventories near the point of sale.

    Most are service wholesalers, i.e., they maintain inventories, have sales forces, grant credit, deliver, and often have capability to provide maintenance and repair services. There are also limited service merchant wholesalers that provide only one or a few of the services.

    Most are independent (accounting for approximately 45 percent of the wholesale sales volumes), but some are owned by manufacturers (about 35 percent of wholesale sales volume).

Agent Middlemen

    Do not buy goods.

    Principal service is to provide aggressive selling.

    Commonly handle only a few complementary, but noncompeting products.

    Usually specialize in goods sold to one or two industries, hence, provide knowledgeable, competent sales personnel.

    Manufacturer bears costs and risks of owning inventories close to the point of sale.

Illus. 12-1   **Basic Functions of Middlemen**

units and extracompany agents and dealers, wholesale and retail, through which a commodity, product or service is marketed."[2] A market channel may also be defined as the sequence of institutions listed in the order of their participation as buyers, sellers, or holders of the physical products or services in providing the facility to move these products or services from producer to consumer.

As an example Illus. 12–2 shows the channel involved in the movement of apples from Yakima, Washington, to upstate New York. Notice that the broker did not take title or possession of the product. The auction assumed the responsibility of physical possession but did not take title. Both these institutions, however, were in the channel.

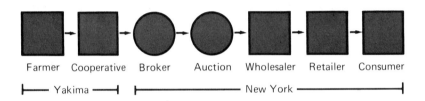

Farmer   Cooperative   Broker   Auction   Wholesaler   Retailer   Consumer

├── Yakima ──┤   ├──────────── New York ────────────┤

Illus. 12-2   **The Channel Flow of a Bushel of Apples**
                         From Washington to New York

CONVENTIONAL CHANNELS

Of the conventional routes that manufactured goods take to reach the consumer, the most common are as follows (see Illus. 12–3):

1. Manufacturer direct to consumer
2. Manufacturer to retailer to consumer
3. Manufacturer to wholesaler to retailer to consumer
4. Manufacturer to agent middleman to wholesaler to retailer to consumer
5. Manufacturer to agent middleman to retailer to consumer

The problem of selecting a channel is simple if all one has to do is select one of these routes according to the type of merchandise each one handles. Regard-
less of the classification of the institutions, however, each differs in the amount, kind, and quality of service it provides. If a company is forced to choose a designated wholesaler as a route to market, it might be wise to sell direct and not use the wholesaler. Yet, because of the kind and quality of services given by another unusually aggressive wholesaler, the company may find it more efficient to sell through this wholesaler. There are strengths and weaknesses in each of the conventional methods, and it is difficult to make broad general-

---

[2]Ralph S. Alexander and the Committee on Definitions, *Marketing Definitions* (Chicago: American Marketing Association, 1963), p. 10.

izations about them. In selecting a channel, the specific institution and its management should be considered along with the classification of service rendered.

Manufacturer Direct to the Consumer

The manufacturer can reach the consumer directly by the use of one or more of the following routes: door-to-door sales, sales through the manufacturer's own retail stores, direct selling (through an advertising medium such as television), and sales by mail order. None of these methods accounts for a very high percentage of total retail sales. Door-to-door methods account for approximately one percent; mail-order sales, one percent; sales through manufacturers' retail stores, less than one percent, and direct sales, one percent.

When a manufacturer decides to go directly to the consumer, the manufacturer assumes the responsibility of performing or directing the performance of all the marketing functions necessary to complete the flow of the good. Since the manufacturer will be applying these functions to only one product (or line of products) and must extend the services to a large number of accounts, we can see why this particular channel is reputed to have the highest marketing costs. The following conditions specifically contribute to increased costs:

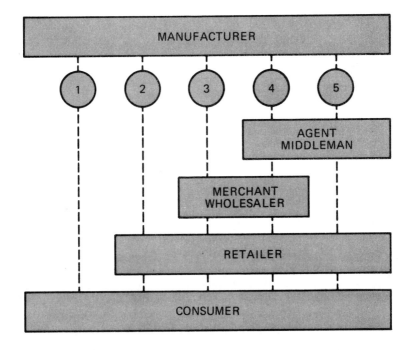

Illus. 12-3   **Conventional Channels of Distribution**

1. Building and maintaining a large, well-supervised sales staff
2. Building and maintaining extensive systems of warehouses and inventories in order to make prompt deliveries to many different customers.
3. Providing adequate financing of the additional functions
4. Assuming the risk of credit extension

The offsetting advantages that may lead to increased sales volume by direct selling are:

1. More aggressive, concentrated, controlled selling
2. A closer contact with the consumer, making it easier to determine the needs of the consumer
3. The elimination of the profits that ordinarily accrue to middlemen
4. The opportunity to provide technical knowledge in selling
5. More rapid physical movement of goods than if they have to travel through several middlemen; which is especially important in the case of perishables

Door-to-Door Sales. Under this method the manufacturer has complete control of the product and can provide the right amount of sales push at the point of sale. This method provides a means of introducing a product that retailers may be reluctant to stock and which requires considerable and complicated communication to sell. The feedback from a well-managed, door-to-door sales force should be excellent, since the salespeople are controlled directly from the home office. The entire sales force should be very flexible and sensitive to the control of management. This method places a significant hindrance on management, however, in maintaining an adequate sales force.

While a great deal of capital is not necessary to carry on this type of operation, unit selling costs are usually higher than for other types of selling.

Selling Through Manufacturer's Own Stores. Manufacturers achieve two significant advantages by selling through their own retail stores: first, they exercise greater control and influence over their product; and, second, they get a direct feedback from the consumer. With such information they can provide the control and sales push required to move the product completely through the channel. The problems of perishability and service to the company's product can be managed in a manner that will enhance the company's prestige. A considerable capital outlay is necessary to set up and operate such stores, however, and the company must have a product that sells in sufficient volume to absorb the overhead of operating a retail store.

As one alternative to high-volume sales of its own products, the company may stock complementary lines of other manufacturers. Once a company adopts this policy, however, it finds itself in the retail business, facing additional management problems. Unless the company has adequate lines in the stores, physical movement and control of stock and overhead render the method expensive. In instances where it is practiced, it is presumed that the advantages of feedback, control of product, promotion, and service outweigh costs in the judgment of management.

Mail-Order Selling by the Manufacturer. The mail-order channel from the producer to the consumer has survived against great odds. The convenience it offered, which was the main reason for its growth, is not a significant factor today. Suburban shopping centers, supermarkets, and the increased mobility of the consumer have removed the barriers to shopping which once encouraged the user of the mail-order channel. Manufacturers who have an unusual product or who can offer bargains still find some success in this type of sales, in spite of spiraling postal costs.

Direct Sales. Developing in the late 1960s, direct selling differs from mail-order sales basically in the method of delivery of the appeal to the consumer. Direct sales manufacturers market products through radio and television media to mass target markets. Consumers respond directly to the manufacturer by either mail or telephone. Subsequently the manufacturer either delivers the product or sends it through the mail. Automobile accessories, kitchen appliances, and records were early favorites in direct sales. Even though accounting for only one percent of manufacturer to consumer sales, direct selling is the fastest growing method in the manufacturer-direct-to-consumer marketing channel today.

Manufacturer to Retailer to Consumer

Some manufacturers find it desirable to bypass wholesale intermediaries and deal directly with the retailer. This channel is especially desirable when the company wishes to enjoy direct control of its products. This need for close control usually occurs if the product is perishable or highly fashionable, thereby making time an important factor. A manufacturing company may also prefer a direct contact with the retailer for strategic or competitive reasons. With products of high unit value, such as pianos, jewelry, silver, and agricultural machinery, the price of each unit is large enough to cover easily the overhead costs of selling direct to the retailer. Other circumstances that tend to encourage direct selling are: (1) when the products of a single firm constitute a substantial part of the retailer's stock and savings can be made on bulk shipments, (2) when products command a large enough market that their consumers are fairly numerous in relation to the territory that must be covered, and (3) when the product requires installation and replacement parts.

By relying on their own sales forces rather than using wholesalers to represent them, manufacturers know that they will receive the concentrated effort of their sales representatives. Manufacturers will not have to compete with other products in a wholesaler's line including, perhaps, private brands of the wholesaler. Having their sales representatives make regular visits to a store allows the manufacturers the opportunity to build goodwill with the retailer's sales personnel by passing on important sales information and helping them with point-of-purchase displays. This channel facilitates cooperative advertising and promotional campaigns between the manufacturer and the retailer without wholesaler intervention. It provides a means to resolve difficulties and to promote better cooperation.

As with direct selling to customers, the obvious disadvantages of the program are:

1. The high cost of selling and processing sales to a large number of accounts
2. Bearing the risk of credit extension
3. The physical movement of goods in small lots to widespread places
4. Maintaining adequate storage facilities and inventories
5. The small volume and distances from some warehouses

The foregoing conditions make it impractical to sell to some retailers. Yet, when a company sells to large accounts directly, it is difficult to maintain desirable relations with wholesalers on whom the company depends to sell the small accounts.

Manufacturer to Wholesaler to Retailer to Consumer

Best known of all channels of distribution is the one that utilizes the wholesaler. In fact, it is commonly known as the traditional or customary channel. In spite of its popularity, it is seldom used exclusively. Most manufacturers reserve the right to sell to chains or large retailers, to associations of small retailers, and sometimes even directly to small retailers besides selling to the wholesaler. The functions that a wholesaler performs—buying, storing, selling, making deliveries, and extending credit—and the advantages of using these services will be discussed in Chapter 15.

Manufacturer to Agent Middleman to Wholesaler to Retailer to Consumer

This channel of distribution utilizes the services of agents or brokers to contact wholesalers. The prime function of agents or brokers is selling (or buying, if they represent wholesalers or large retailers). In Chapter 15 we will discuss the contribution of the broker, the manufacturers' agent, the selling agent, and the commission merchant. Agents and brokers have found their greatest popularity among manufacturers who either are not large enough to establish profitably their own sales organizations or who wish to concentrate their efforts on production, transferring to others the major responsibility of marketing their goods.

Manufacturer to Agent Middleman to Retailer to Consumer

The last major channel of distribution that we shall consider requires that agents and brokers call directly on retailers. This channel is frequently used in the clothing industry and in other industries characterized by a large number of small manufacturers. The channel is also found in industries where the product lines can spoil quickly or become obsolete. In many cases the product lines of the manufacturer are so limited that a company sales force is too costly. When this occurs, independent agents representing more than one manufacturer will evolve in the channel.

VERTICAL MARKETING CHANNELS

The channel systems discussed so far are essentially individualistic in nature. Each member of the channel operates somewhat independently of the other channel members. In these channels some recognition exists that the welfare of one channel member is related to the welfare of other channel members. However, little planning or coordination is carried out to take advantage of this mutual interdependence.

Vertical marketing channels, on the other hand, are designed specifically to capitalize on the interdependence of each of the channel members.[3] *Vertical marketing channels* (sometimes called *vertical marketing systems*) have been defined as "professionally managed and centrally programmed networks, pre-engineered to achieve operating economies and maximum marketing impact."[4] The definition implies that channel members cooperate in some way. This cooperation in turn implies that one, two, or perhaps all channel members are better off than if cooperation does not take place. Also implicit in the definition is the idea of channel leadership. ". . . professionally managed and centrally programmed . . ." implies that people are managing and programming. Similarly, those persons doing the programming and managing must have the power or control in the channel necessary to carry out the job.

Vertical marketing channels can bring efficiencies and economies to the channel for at least three reasons. First, the performance of channel functions can be positioned at the most efficient location in the channel. For example, marking the price on each individual product can be time-consuming and expensive at the retail level. Conversely, at the manufacturer's level this task can be handled much more efficiently. Second, the duplication of various marketing functions can frequently be eliminated. For example, in corporate-owned channels, personal selling need only occur one time—between the retailer and the ultimate consumer—instead of two or more times (i.e., manufacturer to wholesaler, wholesaler to retailer, and retailer to ultimate consumer).

Finally, vertical marketing systems are usually large and therefore can achieve economies simply because of their size. One outgrowth of the size factor is the increased buying power vertical marketing channels may possess. When Sears Roebuck and Co. buys a product to stock in their stores, they enjoy a strong negotiating position because of the size of the order. Additionally, purchasing in large quantities frequently reduces the per unit manufacturing and transportation charges, and therefore the product's cost.

Vertical marketing channels are not always more efficient than individual channels. One factor that favors individual channels is the competitive necessity to keep costs low. The lack of discipline imposed by competition can, at times, allow

---

[3]The basis for this discussion is drawn from Bert C. McCammon, Jr., "Perspectives for Distribution Programming," *Vertical Marketing Systems*, edited by Louis P. Bucklin, (Glenview, Ill.: Scott, Foresman & Co., 1970), p. 32.

[4]*Ibid.*, p. 43.

costs in vertical marketing channels to rise above those found in individual channels.

Three primary types of vertical marketing channels have been identified; they are *administrative, corporate,* and *contractual.*

Administrative Channels

Administrative vertical marketing channels rely on programs developed by one or more of the channel members to achieve channel-wide economies. Frequently channel members are motivated to participate in the programs because the program-developing firm maintains some power or control over the other organizations. Channel power or control can result from a number of factors. One of the most important is a strong customer patronage for the product. If a manufacturer markets a product with a strong customer following, retailers may have to stock the product simply to satisfy customer expectations. In this situation, retailers may be willing to go along with the manufacturer's dictated plans, simply because they have no choice. As an example, "Kraftco has developed facilities management programs to administer the allocation of space in supermarket dairy cases. Kraft's power stems from the fact that the company accounts for 60 percent of dairy case volume, exclusive of milk, eggs, and butter."[5] The grocery stores need Kraft's products and are willing to cooperate to acquire and maintain the Kraft line.

Corporate-Owned Channels

Corporate-owned vertical marketing channels constitute ownership of different levels of distribution in the channel by one organization. For example, a manufacturer may *integrate forward* by purchasing or forming its company-owned wholesale and retail outlets. A retailer may also *integrate backward* by purchasing a source of supply. Numerous examples of this process exist. Singer, Sherwin-Williams, and Hart, Schaffner and Marx are examples of manufacturers who have integrated forward.[6]

Sears, in general merchandise retailing, and Safeway, in food retailing, are examples of retailers that have integrated backward. In 1974, for example, Sears maintained a financial interest in 31 of its 12,000 suppliers. These 31 suppliers provided about 28 percent of all Sears' purchases.[7] Some major wholesalers, in fact, have integrated both backward and forward.

Coordination and resultant operating economies in corporate-owned vertical marketing channels are achieved because absolute control is maintained. The division of labor in the channel is designed to be as efficient as possible. The elimination of duplicate effort is insured, and most channel members maintain an orientation and commitment to the entire channel, not to any one unit in it.

---

[5]Louis W. Stern and Adel I. El-Ansary, *Marketing Channels* (Englewood Cliffs, N.J.: Prentice-Hall, Inc., 1977), p. 395.

[6]For a discussion of the opportunities and difficulties in operating a corporate vertical marketing channel, see "A Paintmaker Puts a Fresh Coat on its Marketing," *Business Week* (February 23, 1976), p. 95.

[7]William Gruber, "Sears' Success Affects Many," *Chicago Tribune,* September 2, 1975, Sec. 2, p. 7.

Well-run corporate-owned vertical marketing channels represent one of the best methods to bring economies to the channel of distribution.

Contractual Channels

Contractual vertical marketing channels are those in which channel relationships are formalized by legally binding contracts. These contracts formalize the role that each channel participant plays in moving the product from the manufacturer to the ultimate consumer. More specifically,

> Contractual integration occurs where the various stages of production and distribution are independently owned but the relationships between vertically adjacent firms are covered in contractual agreements. . . .[8]

Contractual vertical marketing channels, like administered and corporate-owned channels, achieve economies through coordination of channel functions and the elimination of duplicate tasks.

Contractual vertical marketing channels are somewhat unique in that they combine the strong attributes of both big and small business. The dedication and profit concern of the small business owner can be combined with the marketing impact and scale economies of large business organizations. In certain situations this combination can give contractual vertical marketing channels a differential advantage over other types of channels.

Voluntary Chains and Cooperatives. Two general types of contractual vertical marketing channels exist: voluntary chains and cooperatives, and franchise organizations. Voluntary chains and cooperatives also include two general types. Wholesale-sponsored groups are developed when a wholesaler bonds together a number of independent retailers. Because of the willingness to cooperate, economies and advantages accrue to both the wholesaler and the retailers.

Perhaps the most obvious example of a wholesaler-sponsored voluntary group is the Independent Grocers Alliance (IGA Food Stores). By cooperating with a wholesaler, numerous small, independent retailers have been able to compete with large food chains. Other examples of wholesale-sponsored voluntary groups include Western Auto and Ace Hardware and Trustworthy Hardware.

Retail-sponsored cooperatives operate in a similar manner to wholesaler-sponsored voluntary groups but differ in organization. The usual practice is for a group of retailers to organize and operate their own wholesale firm. Through cooperative efforts the retailers are able to take advantage of economies of scale as well as achieve some of the market impact of large organizations. Retail cooperatives have operated mainly in the food industry, with Associated Grocers (AG) being the most notable example.

Wholesaler-sponsored voluntary groups and retail cooperatives have generally prospered since their inception in the 1930s. Especially in the food industry these

---

[8]Donald N. Thompson, "Contractual Marketing Systems: An Overview," *Contractual Marketing Systems,* edited by Donald N. Thompson (Lexington, Mass.: D. C. Heath & Company, 1971), p. 5.

forms of contractual marketing channels have succeeded in competing with corporate-owned channels. A major study of food-marketing practices conducted some years ago indicated that, nationally, the voluntary groups and cooperative chains were almost equal in total food sales to the corporate chains.[9]

In general, wholesale-sponsored voluntary groups have fared better than retail-sponsored chains. The reason for this is probably the strong leadership that an established wholesaler can provide. When the wholesale organization depends on guidance from numerous retailers, as in the case of retail cooperatives, strong action is frequently difficult to undertake.[10]

Franchise Organizations.   Franchise organizations are a second type of contractual vertical marketing channel.

> Franchising as it is generally known today is a form of marketing and distribution in which a parent company customarily grants an individual or a relatively small company the right or privilege to do business in a prescribed manner over a certain period of time in a specified place.[11]

The definition of three terms is necessary to understand franchising.

> The parent company is termed the *franchisor;* the receiver of the privilege the *franchisee;* and the right or privilege itself the *franchise.* The privilege may be quite varied. It may be the right to sell the parent company's products, to use its name, to adopt its methods, and to copy its symbols, trademarks, or architecture, or the franchise may include all these rights.[12]

The franchise itself is usually in the form of a legal contract stating what the franchisor and the franchisee will and will not do.

Numerous types of franchises exist, but four types appear to be most common.[13] First, some manufacturers franchise retailers to sell or market specific products. Examples include automobile dealerships and franchised service stations. Second, manufacturers franchise wholesalers. Coca-Cola franchises local bottling works to bottle Coke (using company provided syrup) and to distribute the product to retailers. Third, wholesalers franchise retailers. Rexall Drug franchises independent drug stores to market the firm's private label or distributor brand products. Fourth, are service-sponsored retailer franchises. In this type of franchise the franchisor authorizes an independent business person to offer various types of services. Examples include Hertz car rental businesses and Holiday Inn Motels.

Franchising offers many advantages to both the franchisor and the franchisee. A strong plus for the franchisor is the commitment of the franchisee to success. A second advantage is that the franchisor is able to expand without raising capital,

---

[9]National Commission on Food Marketing, *Organization and Competition in Food Retailing,* Technical Study No. 7 (Washington: U.S. Government Printing Office, 1966), p. 33.

[10]Stern and El-Ansary, *op. cit.,* p. 405.

[11]*Ibid.*

[12]Charles L. Vaughn, *Franchising* (Lexington, Mass.: D.C. Heath & Company, 1974), p. 2.

[13]William P. Hall, "Franchising: New Scope for an Old Technique," *Harvard Business Review,* Vol. 42, No. 1 (January–February, 1964), p. 60.

because the franchisee usually must pay a substantial sum of money to acquire the franchise.

Unfortunately franchising has received somewhat of a bad name because of practices of some unethical franchisors and because of others who have failed to use sound business practices. These franchisors concentrate on selling franchises rather than on assisting a franchisee in establishing a profitable, ongoing business.

FACTORS AFFECTING CHANNEL DESIGN

Part of the marketing manager's job is designing and activating the channel of distribution. Typically the manager may not have absolute control over what channels are used. In some situations channel members may be in a much stronger position than the producer to pick the products they want to carry and the firms they want to represent. In other situations channel alternatives may not be available. Finally, the ideal channel, as pictured by the marketing manager, may not even exist. Channels are extremely complex and varied.[14] Frequently the usual channel of distribution for a product may differ, depending on the tradition and practices in various parts of the country. The result of these factors is that a marketing manager may feel that he is being chosen by the channel, rather than the other way around. Nevertheless, the marketing manager can begin to design the ideal channel by answering some basic questions.

Basic Channel Questions

Regardless of whether designing and activating the ideal channel is possible, the marketing manager should attempt to answer a minimum of four basic channel questions. The questions relate to the type and number of of middlemen, the marketing tasks performed by each type of middleman, and the terms and mutual responsibilities of each type of middleman.[15] When these questions are answered satisfactorily, the marketing manager is in a much better position to decide whether a current channel of distribution can be used, whether a new channel must be started, or whether channel difficulties will simply prevent the product from being marketed.

What Type of Middleman Will Be Used? The first question that must be addressed relates to the institutional composition of the channel. More specifically, will wholesalers be used? Are agents or brokers necessary? Will retailers be required, or can we go direct? For certain industries these questions are answered rather easily. For other industries, a much wider range of acceptable alternatives exists. A firm manufacturing a commonly purchased food product may have no

---

[14]Phillip McVey, "Are Channels of Distribution What the Textbooks Say?" *Journal of Marketing,* Vol. 25, No. 1 (January, 1960), p. 61.

[15]The basis for this discussion is drawn from Philip Kotler, *Marketing Management: Analysis, Planning and Control* (2d ed.; Englewood Cliffs, N.J.: Prentice-Hall, Inc., 1972), p. 569.

choice but to attempt to get wide distribution through supermarket chains and wholesalers. However, even within the food industry, exceptions do exist. For example, Charles Chips, a high-quality potato chip, have been successfully marketed directly to households.

Ladies' cosmetics is one industry where many different channels of distribution are effectively used. Avon sells door to door; other firms market through mass merchandisers; and some firms distribute only to high-quality department stores.

A number of different channel structures may be available to distribute the product. The exact institutional makeup of the channel depends on such factors as customer characteristics, the financial strength and objectives of the firm, and the activities and strengths of competitors.

How Many of Each Type of Middleman Will Be Required?   This decision depends on a number of factors. The objectives of the firm, the product type, and the nature of competition can all influence how many of each type of middleman is used. The amount of market exposure desired for the product is especially relevant in this selection. Three different levels of market exposure are usually considered.

Intensive Distribution.   For many goods, especially those classified as convenience goods, a maximum exposure to the public is desirable to capture a significant share of the market. Wrigley's chewing gum, Gillette Trac II blades, Coca-Cola, Scotch tape, and Kleenex tissues are examples of goods that are found everywhere —in drugstores, grocery stores, variety stores, supermarkets, and department stores, not to mention vending machines, magazine stands, and candy counters. Because such goods could easily be replaced with another brand, the manufacturers must either arrange their channels to provide a widespread availability or must be content to service only their most profitable accounts. To obtain complete coverage generally requires the utilization of more than one type of channel. Producers may wish to sell directly to their largest accounts and to use a wholesaler to reach their widely scattered outlets.

Selective Distribution.   When manufacturers wish to build a certain class image for their products they select those outlets that identify with that class. Producers can expect better service if they cultivate a few resellers who have the same objectives the producers have in reaching preferred customers. Costs will probably be less since contacts will be limited and individual shipments fewer and larger.

Selective distribution requires a well-planned system of evaluating outlets and selecting only the most desirable. Working on the assumption that no representation at all is better than poor representation, manufacturers have been able to reduce their selling costs and increase their sales by distributing only through institutions that work closely with them in selling their particular products. Manufacturers gain the advantage of having a small number of most-preferred institutions to serve them in the promotion of their products.

Exclusive Distribution.   Exclusive distribution extends the advantages of selective distribution, but there are also some risks. By careful selection of qualified dealers, manufacturers can expect close cooperation and enthusiastic promotion of their products. They can select firms that will provide a maximum of prestige for their products—firms which will be most likely to sell to the clientele the manufacturers have designed their products to reach. The producers run the risk, however, of not having the product distributed widely enough to achieve maximum selling impact. They may also inherit the ill will of other prominent sellers by refusing them the privilege of handling their products. Manufacturers must also insure that an exclusive distribution system does not violate the law. In general, agreements between manufacturers and dealers in which a dealer is given exclusive distribution rights for a product are not illegal per se. However, when the effect of the agreement is to substantially lessen competition or to increase the tendency toward monopoly, exclusive distribution agreements are illegal.

These three methods are described to indicate a range of choices open to the manufacturer. Actually a company may adopt a policy that is a combination of the ingredients of all three. It is impossible to get complete market coverage and to enlist the promotional loyalty and full cooperation of outlets. A company must examine the possible outlets for its product and tailor a program to include as many of the desirable qualities as possible while avoiding as many disadvantages as possible.

What Marketing Tasks Should Each Middleman Perform? A number of tasks have to be performed while moving the product from the manufacturer to the ultimate consumer. Some of these tasks include transportation, storage, keeping track of inventory, finding prospective customers, making sales, and communicating with the market. The marketing manager attempts to design the channel in such a way that the tasks will not have to be performed more than necessary and that the middleman capable of performing the task most efficiently will do so.

What Terms and Mutual Responsibilities Are Appropriate? Answering this question determines "the mix of conditions and responsibilities that must be established among the channel members to get the tasks performed effectively and enthusiastically."[16] Kotler refers to this as the "trade-relations" mix.[17] Included in this mix should be policies relating to price, conditions of sale, territorial rights, and an enumeration of the services to be performed by each party.

Price policies in this context generally refer to the percentage discount off list price offered to various types of institutions in the channel. For example, retailers may receive a 40 percent discount while wholesalers receive a 60 percent discount. The differential discount is usually justified on the basis that wholesalers perform functions such as breaking bulk for the manufacturer that retailers do not perform.

Conditions of sale usually include three particulars. First, financing terms must be specified. Specifically, cash discounts for early payments and the date when full payment is due have to be mutually understood. Second, the time when the title for the product changes hands must be specified. Finally, the type of guarantees

---

[16]*Ibid.*, p. 573.
[17]*Ibid.*

the supplier offers must be made clear. For example, many wholesalers want price protection guarantees from their suppliers. These guarantees state that if the supplier lowers the price late in the year, early buyers will receive a refund.

Territorial rights refer to such items as how many dealers will be allowed to handle the product in a trade area. Also, provisions are frequently made for partially rewarding a dealer if a sale takes place in the dealer's territory but not through the dealer's efforts. A mail-order sale made directly from the manufacturer is an example of this provision.

An enumeration of other types of services to be performed by the supplier or dealer might include topics such as information collection, promotional support, and the handling of defective products. Ideally a clear understanding exists between supplier and dealer on all these questions.

Objectives Affect Channel Design

One of the most important factors affecting the design of the channel of distribution is the objectives of the firm. Firm objectives, whether concerned with such things as profit or market share or with management values, can constrain or limit the range of acceptable channel alternatives. Some of these objectives are discussed here.

Level of Potential Revenue.   For some firms certain channel alternatives are unacceptable because the revenue potential of the channel is limited. For instance, some distribution channels reach only limited markets. Other channels simply have a limited capacity to market sufficient quantities of merchandise. One of the reasons that marketers of large appliances moved from department stores to discount houses in the early 1950s was that the location and structure of department stores simply failed to create the ability to move enough merchandise.

Channel Control and Leadership.   Producers may wish to control the channel of distribution for at least two reasons. First, management may perceive that channel control leads to higher profits. Second, management may realize that conventional channels of distribution consist of several relatively independent organizations. Consequently, the advantages of central direction to the channel are absent.[18] To achieve these advantages, frequently some firm must lead the channel.

Leadership, in this context, means "the capacity to direct or command the activity or behavior of others."[19] The desire to lead or control the channel of distribution by any one firm relates directly to how the well-being of the firm is affected by other channel members.

Institutional Flexibility   The institutions selected to sell the company's product should be both progressive and flexible. Once a channel has been estab-

---

[18]Robert W. Little, "The Marketing Channel: Who Should Lead This Extra-Corporate Organization," *Journal of Marketing,* Vol. 34, No. 1 (January, 1970), p. 31.

[19]*Ibid.,* p. 1.

lished, it is difficult to change it; however, the channel should be able to adapt itself to inevitable market shifts. Progressive improvements in channel services are necessitated by the evolving nature of the product, the market, and the strategy of competing institutions. The history of marketing is a record of changing routes to the ultimate consumer. The general store gave way to the specialty store. Department stores developed and grew in importance. Then the chain store, especially in the food field, grew spectacularly during the 1920s and caused shifts in prevailing trade channels. Since World War II, the various forms of discount houses have become competitive threats to different kinds of businesses. Supermarkets, with their scrambled merchandising policies, have also been a factor.

The food wholesaler provides an excellent example of change. Chain stores, with their own warehouses and their low margins, became a serious threat to the food wholesalers. Existing grocery wholesalers had to adapt themselves to changes or go out of business. Many food wholesalers were sufficiently flexible to adapt, but many others failed. Some of those that succeeded changed their patterns of operation and reduced their expense margins from 12 percent in 1930 to 4 percent in 1969 and increased their services to retailers. They achieved this goal by several methods.

First, as a result of common interests with food retailers, food wholesalers were able to encourage the retailers to purchase large volumes at reduced selling costs to themselves. Weekly order blanks were prepared that simplified ordering without the aid of a sales representative. Second, single-story warehousing was adopted, reducing the time and energy necessary to unload and load the food products. In this connection considerable savings were effected as a result of the use of conveyors, pallets, and trucks. Third, machine accounting and better management of credit and delivery operations reduced costs. Fourth, the food wholesalers were able to hold their volume by adopting various methods of increasing the sales of their customers. They organized voluntary chain store associations, such as the Independent Grocers Alliance, by which means they guaranteed themselves a certain percentage of the retailer business. In return for this guaranteed percentage of the retailer's sales and a small fee, the wholesalers disseminated specialized price and merchandising data and prepared a cooperative advertising campaign. In some instances independent grocers accomplished the construction of a closely knit organization and set up their own wholesalers who performed all the above functions. Most of these economies were passed on to the retailer, making it possible for the retailers to compete with the chains.

Marketing Mix Factors.   How the channel complements other marketing mix factors is also important. If one of the firm's objectives is to sell at very low prices, but the current channel does not facilitate this objective, the channel may have to be changed. Three aspects of the channel-marketing mix relationship are discussed here.

Movement of the Physical Product.   Costs in terms of money and time are basic elements to consider in evaluating any method of moving goods from the producer to the consumer. For example, a city with a population of 50,000 may have 20 stores that handle the company's product. It probably is more costly for the company to make 20 calls in this and similar cities than it is to sell to one wholesaler and let the wholesaler make the contacts. Indeed, the extra cost of all the sales calls will likely be so great that it offsets other advantages that may accrue from personal contact, such as servicing the product or more intensive selling effort.

On the other hand, if the city has a population of 400,000 and the company's business is done through 20 outlets, it is conceivable that the volume of sales to each store may be sufficient to make direct contacts profitable. This is especially true if there are advantages that may accrue from more effective selling as a result of a direct contact.

In some instances, it may be desirable for one company to use two channels. A large food company may sell to high-volume stores by direct shipments; where the volume does not justify the overhead expense, the company may sell through wholesalers. There is a risk that such a policy may disturb wholesalers, who would resent the company's selling to the large accounts and leaving the units with small profit potentials to the wholesalers.

Promotion and Communication Qualities. The movement of most products requires a promotional push; they do not always move as a result of low prices or the pure force of gravity. In certain circumstances, however, the flow seems almost automatic, and little or no promotion is necessary. During World War II, when there was a scarcity of goods, few promotional efforts were required. The unsatisfied desires of customers resulted in suction that pulled products through the channels. Under such conditions the economy of movement of physical goods to the point of consumption and the number of transactions were the dominant factors to consider in choosing a channel.

Even during normal times different goods require various amounts of promotion. Raw materials change marginally over a period of time and require less promotion than consumer goods. They are pulled through the market by the sale of products of which they are a part. Steel is in demand not because a desire has been created for it, but because it is a component of the automobile. Copper has a conventional market flow, where selling by the institutions in the channel is less important than the goods for which there may be an array of alternative choices. Even under these circumstances, copper and steel companies must do some selling and advertising. On the other hand, the ultimate consumer of manufactured goods is almost constantly confronted with a multiplicity of choices. Since the ultimate consumer has so many alternatives from which to choose, the movement of each product must be aided by a positive selling story.

What is true at the consumer purchasing level is also true at the retail and wholesale purchasing levels. Wholesalers and retailers who are alert to market opportunities are sensitive to consumer desire. They stock what is asked for most frequently. They build their business by selecting from the many alternatives available those goods that are most likely to satisfy the consumer's request.

The Pull of Advertising. If manufacturers are in a position to advertise extensively, they may create a "suction force" for their products. This created desire may be so strong at the consumer level that retailers and wholesalers will almost be forced to have the stock available. Some popular TV programs carry such a demand-creating impact with little support from other advertising. The soap companies with their tremendous national advertising campaigns create such a suction force at the consumer level that a retailer is embarrassed not to have the product in stock and on display.

The Push of the Sales Representative. The pull of advertising may need to be supplemented by the push of salespeople. The nature of this need determines, more than any other factor, whether manufacturers will send out their own sales representatives, set up their own branches, or entrust the selling to wholesale institutions. Full-line wholesalers carry too many brands to make it possible for them to provide any selling/promotion push for a single brand. The most they can offer is the economy of a positive contact and some possible savings in physical distribution. Specialty wholesalers are better equipped. A limited line with a promotional focus on one brand in a certain shop enables them to give both selling and service attention to a product. Here, again, the manufacturer must answer the question of cost and satisfaction. Are the selling and service provided by the specialty wholesaler sufficient to pay for the extra margin of cost that the wholesaler exacts for the services? Or, for a similar margin, can manufacturers send out their own sales representatives who are specially trained to tell the company's story? By using their own sales forces, sellers can maintain greater control of their products, organize their own selling programs, and get a complete feedback from the market. Again, there is the question of adequate volume to absorb the costs of an extensive program of this kind.

The Cooperation of the Reseller. Almost as strategic as the push or pull of advertising and selling is the building of goodwill with the reseller. These resellers may be brokers, wholesalers, or retailers, who have the discretion and skill to provide the product with constant availability. Often they choose the site of the product display and the amount of shelf space. The maintenance of amiable relations with all institutions in the channel flow is imperative even when the demand pull is strong. Well-advertised products will experience a decrease in sales if stock is not available, exposed, and presented in a positive manner at all selling points.

The goodwill of the food retailer was so important to one of the major manufacturers that it undertook a costly program to develop positive relationships. First, the company did a great deal of research to collect cost figures for different retail operations. Then it made an extensive study of the effectiveness of shelf space and determined how profits could be increased by placing high-margin items at strategic selling points. The chief executive officer of the firm then contacted the presidents of large food chains which did a high percentage of the overall food business and made a personal presentation of the research findings. He succeeded in building excellent relations, which his sales representatives have taken special pains to maintain, with these firms.

There are infinite combinations of institutions and programs that provide for the promotional needs of a particular company. To obtain an optimum combination of the above described promotional ingredients, considered in the light of costs and potential results, is the challenge which confronts marketing management.

Feedback Information   The tempo of new product introduction and improving distribution patterns is constantly accelerating. Unless prompt and carefully designed action is taken to keep a company abreast of these changes, the newer and better products and services of competitors will steal its market. Furthermore, the growing tendency to segment markets according to the desires of individual customers, reference groups, or classes of customers accentuates the need for accurate feedback. The demands for consumer satisfaction, encouraged by the federal government's Consumer Council, provides an additional reason for securing accurate feedback from different segments of the market.

Companies such as Singer Sewing Machine, Eastman Kodak, and Avon have direct contact with customers and, therefore, are in a position to secure the feedback information they need. But when a company entrusts its products to resellers, how can it be sure that the feedback it obtains is adequate and accurate? To be helpful to a company, feedback information from institutions which sell the product should cover at least four areas: (1) the product characteristics as compared with competition, (2) inventory conditions of the channel institutions, (3) appraisal of the service provided by the company, and (4) changes in market conditions.

Manufacturers would do well to recognize two basic conditions affecting the feedback available to them. One is the number of resellers they use to reach the market. The shorter the channel, the more likely it is that the manufacturer will get quick and accurate feedback. The other condition is the degree to which the cooperation of the channel institutions is secured. Often the manufacturer can win their support by performing a service that is useful to them.

Channel Member Characteristics

One of the primary factors affecting channel design is the actual characteristics of the channel members. Channel member characteristics can limit the types of channel alternatives available. Additionally, channel member characteristics can represent opportunities that can be exploited by alert organizations.

Target Market Characteristics.   Target market characteristics affect channel design in a number of ways. One of the easiest ways to visualize this is by considering a few differences between the ultimate consumer market and the industrial market. First, there are far more ultimate consumers than industrial consumers. Generally the more customers in the target market, the higher the tendency for longer channels that involve more and different types of middlemen. Second, ultimate consumers are widely distributed around the country; industrial buyers are much more concentrated in specific geographical locations. The degree of geographic concentration is pointed out in Table 12–1 wherein states are ranked by amount of manufacturing output. Notice that few states outside the Northeast and Great Lakes region (for example, California, Texas, and North Carolina) are high on the scale. California, the leading manufacturing state, accounts for 7.32 percent of manufacturing output in the United States. Ohio accounts for 7.29 percent, Illinois for 7.14 percent, Pennsylvania for 6.74 percent, and New York for 5.95 percent.

Table 12-1   States Ranked by Manufacturing Output: 1979
(Billions of Dollars)

California	$110,188	Iowa	21,000
Ohio	109,676	Oklahoma	18,521
Illinois	107,421	Maryland	17,704
Pennsylvania	101,413	Kansas	15,795
Michigan	98,261	Arkansas	15,658
New York	89,587	Mississippi	15,282
Texas	88,988	Oregon	14,853
New Jersey	63,573	Colorado	12,540
Indiana	56,707	West Virginia	11,443
North Carolina	46,701	Nebraska	9,221
Massachusetts	41,235	Arizona	8,165
Wisconsin	38,246	Utah	7,653
Missouri	36,994	Rhode Island	7,585
Georgia	36,087	Maine	6,632
Tennessee	35,130	Delaware	5,787
Minnesota	31,152	New Hampshire	5,404
Louisiana	28,536	Montana	4,316
Florida	26,214	Idaho	3,692
Connecticut	25,866	New Mexico	2,962
Virginia	25,347	Vermont	2,457
Kentucky	25,265	Wyoming	2,096
Alabama	25,222	South Dakota	1,870
Washington	21,314	North Dakota	1,083
South Carolina	21,299	Nevada	535

Note: Data for Alaska and Hawaii were not available.
Source: "Sales and Marketing Management's 1979 Survey of Industrial Purchasing Power," *Sales and Marketing Management*, Vol. 122, No. 6 (April 23, 1979), p.4

Additionally, customers tend to purchase in different quantities and at different rates. Ultimate consumers make many small, frequent purchases. To directly satisfy the purchasers without the assistance of numerous middlemen will, in most situations, be prohibitively expensive. On the other hand, industrial purchases are made less often and in larger quantities. One factor contributing to this tendency in the industrial market is, in addition to being concentrated by geographical area, manufacturers are also concentrated by size. As shown in Table 12–2, a few large companies are responsible for a major portion of the sales in many industries. The combination of geographic and size concentration makes shorter and more direct channels of distribution more feasible in the industrial market.

Middlemen Characteristics. Different types of middlemen may generally be better suited to perform certain marketing activities. Merchant wholesalers are better able than agents or brokers to handle credit merchandise since the latter two never take formal ownership of the goods they distribute. Wholesalers are usually better equipped to deal with inventory storage than are retailers.

The relative strengths and weaknesses of *each* prospective wholesaler must be investigated. A general class of middlemen may be suited for a particular manufac-

**Table 12-2   Percentage of Sales Made by Largest Companies
in Selected Industries**

	Four Largest	Twenty Largest
Motor Vehicles	93	99+
Aircraft	69	98
Sawmills and Planing Mills	17	32
Radios and Related Products	57	96
Paperboard Boxes	19	58
Small Arms Ammunition	88	98
Tires and Inner Tubes	73	97
Footwear	26	61
Plastic Products	8	23
Paints and Varnishes	22	49
Dresses	9	18
Farm Machinery (except tractors)	46	67

Source: U.S. Department of Commerce, Bureau of the Census, *Census of Manufacturers, Vol. 1* (Washington: U.S. Government Printing Office, 1972, pp. SR2-50--SR2-156.

turing firm's needs. Nevertheless, *specific* middlemen within the general class may be unsuited. Therefore, specific middlemen must be investigated before they are included as primary channel members.

Competition's Characteristics.   The importance of competition's character-istics has previously been mentioned with respect to distributing food products. A firm attempting to get widespread distribution may have no choice other than using the same channels of distribution as its major competitors. Competitors' dis-tribution activities may also have the opposite effect. The channel may sim-ply be so dominated by competitive products that a new, different channel must be selected. Charles Chips, mentioned earlier, is one example. Certain brands of vacuum cleaners and cosmetics are also examples of firms using a direct channel in lieu of more traditional channels used by established firms.

Firm Characteristics.   Two firm characteristics are particularly relevant to channel design and selection. First, the financial position of the firm is of utmost importance. Many firms may wish to establish corporate-owned channels of distri-bution but simply do not have the financial resources for the undertaking. The usual situation occurs when a firm is so strapped for cash that brokers, selling agents, or manufacturers' agents must be used to move the product through the distribution channel. These middlemen are usually compensated by a specific percentage of the sales revenue they earn. Therefore no cash outlay on the part of the firm is required.

The nature of the firm's product is also important. If the product is highly perishable, such as fashion items or food, short, direct channels are frequently used. If the product is technical and requires high-level service or expertise to install or maintain, the channel is usually more direct. Also, items that are large and difficult to transport are frequently distributed directly.

Finally, direct channels of distribution are frequently only possible when the product is of high-unit value. The high-unit value is necessary to support the added expense of direct distribution.

THE DYNAMIC FORCES INFLUENCING CHANGE

Technology, competitive strategy, changing habits of customers, and living conditions of the people are factors responsible for change in all marketing practices. This is especially true with respect to market channels. A change in a channel does not always refer to a different combination of institutions, although such changes are often made. Rather, constant adaptations are being made in the types of services that are given by the institutions in the channel. One specialist has commented:

> Some of the most fundamental channels of trade in the United States seem to have been in a constant state of evolution for decades.[20]

The fact that retail sales are approximating $860 billion today, compared with $40 billion in 1929, accounts for many changes in the institutional flow. Increasing volumes in the flow create opportunities for new firms and force the firms already in the channel to alter their practices.

Forces affecting marketing methods are almost infinite in number and as complex as the forces that are responsible for social evolution. A discussion of four areas, however, will reveal many of the important forces for channel change. First, the innovation of new products prompts examination of new routes to market. Second, institutions adapting to new levels upset market equilibrium and encourage further change. Third, changes in buying habits of the customers create opportunities for institutional evolution. Fourth, the growth of research encourages firms to seek better methods of reaching the market with their product. It is likely that most changes in the channel are some combination of these forces. Seldom is a case so simple that it may be solved by the analysis of just one cause-and-effect relationship. Nevertheless, an integrated view of the whole will be improved by a look at each of the areas separately.

Product Innovation

A significant change in a product or in its rate of sale or a new product entering the market frequently alters the type of service required of a market channel. The frozen-food industry made it necessary for food wholesalers to expand their operations to handle frozen products. Equipment was expensive; its use increased both capital requirements and fixed operating costs. Moreover, increases in fixed costs

---

[20]Wroe Alderson, "Factors Governing the Development of Marketing Channels," *Marketing Channels,* edited by Richard M. Clewett (Homewood, Ill.: Richard D. Irwin, Inc., 1954), p. 21.

require greater volume and higher break-even points. Those institutions that cannot adapt to such changes are forced out of the market; those which remain obtain the increased volume.

On the retail side of food marketing, the increasingly higher capital investment required because of frozen foods, prepackaged meats, and other innovations restricted entry into the field in recent years. The fact that there now are fewer and larger food retailers changes the channel strategy with respect to the number and types of wholesalers necessary to reach those retailers. With larger volume outlets, direct sale to the retailer by the manufacturer is more profitable. Wholesalers are forced to adapt their costs and services to such changes or lose their volume. The entry of the frozen-food industry into the market is only one of the contributing reasons why there has been a reduction in the wholesale and retail outlets in the food trade; but it has been a typical innovation that illustrates one force influencing changes in channel flows.

Another excellent example of product innovation and the adaptation of channels is the rapid increase in the number of home appliances sold in the last forty years. A backlog of demand accumulated during World War II. Technological advances brought new appliances and improved models of established appliances on the market. How could the manufacturer keep abreast of competition in handling this increased volume? Since the unit of sale was large and the number of appliance stores was limited, direct sales from manufacturers to retailers was the prevailing method of sale. Following the war, however, the greater volume of sales and the spectacular increase in the number of outlets created new opportunities. Even though the volume increased, many manufacturers chose to sell their appliances through wholesale distributors and to concentrate on production. The volume of sales was sufficiently large to justify the entrance of many wholesalers into this field. Once established, many of them expanded to include other lines of hardware and equipment. When the backlog of demand was met, some of these firms expanded their lines or went out of business. Yet the permanence of the home appliance business had an impact on the routes that many appliances take to reach the consumer.

Another interesting, but normal, aspect of this situation is that different companies still do not agree on the most efficient methods. White-Westinghouse and General Electric decided that company-owned distributors with warehouse, sales, and service facilities would do the job better. Whirlpool, however, sells its products through independent wholesalers. Such variations are common in many fields where similar products are offered. Availability of capital funds, adequate management talent, and breadth of the line offered for sale may influence companies to sell directly to the retailer. On the other hand, the lack of such resources, narrowness of line, and limited management skills may prompt another company to allow wholesale distributors to sell and service their products. In any event, the examples cited illustrate that change in types of products sold or the velocity of their flow has an impact on the services performed by the outlets making up the channel and, in some instances, invites the entry of new institutions.

Institutional Innovation

Several impelling forces encourage changes in the institutions making up the channel. First, the tendency to modify the distributional machinery to correspond to the changes brought about by the entrance of mass production techniques into industry is growing; second, distributors have risen to such importance in the economy that they seek to become independent from the producers; and, third, evolutionary changes result from a combination of progress in technology, social evolution, and competitive strategy.

The increased flow of goods from 1929 to the business census year of 1971 was due primarily to improved technology in production and to increased efficiency in distribution. During this period retail stores increased from 1.5 million to 1.8 million, an increase of over 20 percent in the number of stores; while sales in constant dollars increased 170 percent. The average sales per store in 1971–1972 dollars increased from $55,000 to $228,000. This more than quadrupling of sales per store represents more than the sale of the same kinds of goods. It means the acquisition of additional lines of merchandise. Seldom, today, do we see a food store that does not carry meats and vegetables. Not too many decades ago combination food stores—those which sold meat as well as groceries—were quite uncommon. The drugstore also has spread its line to include sundry items not carried in the drugstore several years ago. Discount houses, another new kind of dealer, account for considerable sales volume in certain fields.

In order to meet competition from other institutions, as well as the threat of direct sale by manufacturers to retailers, wholesalers are forced to spread their line to include additional items. Food wholesalers now sell meats, vegetables, and frozen foods. Hardware wholesalers have expanded their lines to include furniture, appliances, and other sundry items that were not a part of their lines in the 1930s. Some of these wholesalers have spread so broadly that they include drug items under the same operation.

Food wholesalers have spread their activities to the extent that they perform many of the functions formerly performed by retailers. To survive in competition with chain stores and with other wholesalers, a food wholesaler frequently furnishes the capital to finance a retail store, supplies credit for merchandise inventory, prepares promotion and advertising, and provides information on merchandising and layout fundamentals. The wholesaler must innovate or discontinue business. Such innovation creates still new opportunities for the flow of goods and stimulates reappraisals of channels by sellers. Thus, channels are in a constant state of innovation and flux.

For example, one comparatively large food chain has departed from the traditional chain-store policy of doing its own warehousing. This chain buys in large volume from established wholesalers in the location in which it operates. Its large volume account is sought by wholesalers. But to satisfy the demands of this chain and others in the same category, competing wholesalers have had to reduce their margins of cost and increase their volume. They have also been forced to expand their offerings in order to match the lines sold by the supermarket chains. In one locality, competition to obtain the business of these stores has motivated two wholesalers to add meats and other products to their offerings.

At present this chain of supermarkets is offering specials in boys' wear. The wholesalers now are debating whether they should add a line of dry goods and drugs. The issues at stake are: Will the volume of such additions be sufficient to compensate for added costs of supervision, overhead, selling, and other expenses? What facilities will they require that they do not now possess? To what extent can their present excess capacity in plant and facilities be absorbed by such addition? Will the adoption of these lines provoke retaliation by drug and dry goods wholesalers? Is it possible that the other institutions may increase competition by invading the food lines? Is it likely that the wholesalers will attempt to spread their offerings to include products to supply the outlets they serve, provided the demand is sufficient to justify such innovation? This is only one area of institutional change; similar forces are at work on practically all marketing fronts.

Changing Buying Habits of Consumers

The final test in the dynamics of change rests with the decisions of the consumer. If the consumer chooses to buy drugs and dry goods in volume from the supermarket, the wholesaler will stock these goods and seek the business. This movement creates a new focus of competition among the food wholesaler, the rack jobber, and established wholesalers in dry goods and drugs. It is true that many changes in the manner of consumer response result from the overtures of the seller to win consumer favor. Yet changes arise independently of the seller's efforts. The automobile is largely responsible for shopping centers and one-stop shopping. This change is partly the result of the increasing number of wives who now work and share shopping responsibilities with their husbands. Suburban living has given rise to new customs, new habits, and an entire array of new products and types of selling. Increasing the amount of discretionary spending money has changed the proportions in which goods are sold. Travel, both domestic and abroad, has influenced business and consumer preferences.

These are a few of the factors that have altered patterns of consumption, and with each change in the pattern of consumption come new opportunities in retailing. Changes in retailing are reflected in wholesaling and agency firms. Indeed, they influence the entire channel policy of manufacturers.

Influence of Research

Effective channel strategy emerges as an integrated process evolved from a plan that recognizes all the forces that influence change. It is usually impossible to determine exactly what changes ought to be made and when they should be implemented. Yet, if the business executive postpones action too long, it may be too late.

Specific questions which puzzle typical business executives are: What channel changes should be made, and when? These are also the questions they must act upon. They cannot postpone decisions until the "best" method of arriving at answers is devised. Consequently, they act. By methods they themselves admit are imperfect, they arrive at decisions which, even when proved workable, cannot be proved correct. They wish they knew more about how to make the decision and how to appriase the results.

Today's business executives can take a less fatalistic view of this problem than could their counterparts two decades ago. Business research tools have been developed to remove some of the guesswork. For example, one large food manufacturer added a line of cereals to its offerings. The company did not have sufficient facts to determine which marketing channel it should use. It had a distribution system of branch warehouses for its present line, but it would have had to expand those facilities considerably to sell the new line of cereals. According to the findings of a consulting firm hired to analyze the problem, distribution costs through established wholesale channels would be 16 percent of the retail price. If the company sold the products through its own branch houses, it would cost 21 percent. Hence, the company chose to channel the new product through wholesalers. This cost differential raised the question as to whether the company was wise in retaining its branch distribution system for its main line of products. The system already was established and functioning efficiently, the company's product was a delicacy that was perishable, and competition was keen. In order to exercise greater control over the product and to provide the necessary promotion push all the way through to the consumer, the company chose to retain its branch warehouses and to increase its staff of salespeople.

Another analytical pattern that is much too frequently neglected is the analysis of customers to determine whether all are being reached by the most effective, as well as the most economical, channel. In one case an analysis showed that 95 percent of all sales in one geographic area were unprofitable. By applying this test to the overall company market, two thirds of the customers were estimated to be unprofitable accounts. These accounts were transferred from the direct sale list to those that it could serve through its dealer organization. The company was encouraged by the results. The inventory, break-even points, and overhead costs were lowered. There was a 15 to 30 percent decrease in expenses and a 20 percent increase in net profits.

Another means of determining the relative efficiency of different channels is to experiment. Representative test divisions of the market may be selected using prospective channels to reach each division. Costs and advantages in each area can then be compared. Careful control must be kept to see that adjustments are made so that the different divisions are comparable.

Research and analysis assist in clarifying issues and point the way for action. As the skills and machinery for analysis improve, solutions will become more reliable and available. With the multiplicity of forces operative in the marketplace, however, *best* and *sure* solutions are goals that may only be approached.

AN OVERALL VIEW

The problem of channel selection must be a part of the overall planning of the company. It cannot be separated from production, pricing, transportation, or promotion. As an example let us examine the case of the Polaroid Land Camera, a

product that entered the market in the early 1950s and has been unusually successful because the company's marketing program has been innovative and alert to the
problem of channels.

In spite of the customary method of selling cameras through distributors,
Polaroid chose to employ a sales force adequate to sell through retailers. Why was
this method chosen? In terms of the cost of moving the physical volume of goods,
this method was consistent. The camera was not bulky; the unit value was comparatively high. At the outset the company chose to sell through only 5,000 selected
outlets. This number could be called on and serviced without excessive outlay in
making contacts and completing transactions. If the product had been of lower unit
cost, greater bulk, and sold to 50,000 retailers, direct sale to retailers might not
have been the answer.

The strategy of selling directly to retailers was also consistent with the promotional potential of the product. The company, in the early stages, faced a market
in which the photographic trade was both hostile and doubtful. Photographic
equipment dealers were fearful that if the product were too successful, it might
hurt their film-developing business. On the other hand, they were doubtful that
the process would be as successful as the company claimed. Both these factors
tended to create resistance at the retail level, resistance of a nature that required
the explanation and selling of a person with adequate training. Such a person had
to specialize solely in selling the camera and in demonstrating its operation. Distributors could not be trusted to provide the promotional zeal for the product to
achieve this goal. On the other hand, the company had faith that its product would
become a mild sensation at the consumer level. The strategy, then, was to adopt
a promotional program at the consumer level that would provide the suction to
draw the product through the channel to the consumer.

If the company's assumptions were correct and the product did become a mild
sensation, it would have an added advantage. Retailers who handled the product
would buy from the company with little selling and servicing. In view of the small
bulk and high unit value, minimum warehousing would be necessary and the
company could distribute directly to the retailer at little cost. Because of the great
popularity of the product with the public, the company could exact a high price.
It could also expect the retailer to sell at a comparatively low margin, since much
of the retail selling cost was the result of national advertising and the nature of the
product. The company provided encouragement to its dealers by offering them
selective contracts and agreeing not to sell to any who would not sell at a price
that would provide the retailer with a satisfactory margin.

The company's projected plans were realized. Once the camera was on the
market, the selling and advertising campaign brought it enthusiastic consumer
response. Dealers who were doubtful and hostile at the outset eventually stocked
the product, first because consumers demanded it and second because the camera
and the film brought them profit. The manufacturing company's profits and stock
have risen steadily.

This example illustrates many of the forces that must be considered in selecting
a channel. The wholesalers and agent middlemen who may have played a part in
the traditional distribution of cameras and camera equipment were not used

because of special circumstances in the nature of the product. We also note the interrelationship of product, price, promotion, and place as factors that enter into channel consideration.

Effective Utilization of Distribution Channels

The selection of the distribution program that manufacturers prefer to use does not end their distribution problems. On the contrary, it places them in the position where they can turn their factually supported suppositions into real profits by executing well-laid plans. The thoroughness and care that have gone into planning must continue in the execution of their plans. Efficient handling of their channels will be more a determinant of their volume than the market potential inherent in any particular marketing channel. Just as wise and effective selling helps answer their sales volume problems, so will such selling help activate the channel institutions they have chosen.

No organization can, in and of itself, accomplish anything. Accomplishment comes from live men within the organization. The manufacturer's problem now becomes one of establishing better-than-favorable relations with the individuals who comprise the institutions in their channels and of supplying the oil that will make the machinery run smoothly. Adequate profit margins, of course, will inspire the basic movement, but beyond profit there must be a recognition of long-term goals and conditions rather than a concentration on the immediate; there must be the integrity that inspires confidence; there must be the regard for the well-being of others that assures their satisfaction.

Constant Review

With the execution of their programs, manufacturers still find their jobs unfinished. Just as they constantly review their production processes and and analyze them in the light of technological improvement, so must they constantly consider the changes that occur in the dynamic area of marketing. Besides bringing new and progressive methods, the movement of time also brings altered conditions in markets, in consumers' habits, and in the availability of resources. Each requires a review of the existing institutions and an evaluation of the distribution program as a whole.

Such an evaluation program was initiated by General Electric Company in 1954.[21] At that time sales of appliances were very uneven throughout the year. This condition made it necessary to follow a widely fluctuating production schedule. Since such "jerky" production was expensive in terms of overtime, delays, lost sales, and high shipment charges, the company conducted a major survey and took a new look at the consumer. The survey revealed that the fluctuations were not the fault of the consumer but resulted from a weakness in the company's linkage with its distributors. So, the company conducted a two-year program to educate top and middle management on improving relations with its distributors. As a

---

[21]"GE Seeks the Answer in Its Distribution System," *Business Week* (October 2, 1954), p. 68.

result of this program, General Electric achieved a leveling of its production schedule as well as a much closer communicating relationship with all the institutions in the distribution channel so that the distributors would respond effectively to the introduction of new products. For example, the company succeeded in marketing the electric toothbrush and the electric carving knife. In connection with new products, General Electric's marketing management found that its distribution system could handle about five new products a year. The company learned that if more products were introduced, the distributors would tend to neglect already established products which were maintaining a strong profit potential.

QUESTIONS AND ANALYTICAL PROBLEMS

1. Define channel of distribution.
2. Why does the door-to-door sales method almost always cost more than the method of selling products through the channel of manufacturer-wholesaler-retailer-consumer?
3. How do direct sales differ from door-to-door and direct-mail selling?
4. Under what conditions might manufacturers successfully and economically sell their output through the channel of manufacturers' sales force-retailer-consumer?
5. Well under 10 percent of manufactured consumer goods go directly from manufacturers to ultimate consumers, while probably as much as 70 percent of manufactured industrial goods go from manufacturer directly to industrial consumers. Explain why the difference exists.
6. Define and clearly distinguish intensive distribution, selective distribution, and exclusive distribution.
7. What are the most important considerations in selecting a marketing channel? What effect does each of these considerations have on the structure of a marketing channel

for a widely used, low-priced consumer good and a technical, complex, high-priced industrial product?
8. What marketing channel changes take place when consumers show that they will purchase kitchen items in large quantities from grocery stores? The goods formerly were sold only by hardware and department stores.
9. Why would a supermarket operation that owns five food stores, each selling approximately $1.5 million annually, decide to use regular wholesalers? Why not set up its own warehouse operation?
10. Give two examples of products that lend themselves to successful intensive distribution. Explain clearly why you would choose to market these products in the widespread manner suggested by intensive distribution.
   (a) Do the same for selective distribution.
   (b) Do the same for exclusive distribution.
11. A young man invented a product that had ready acceptance at service stations in his city. The product can be manufactured for 85 cents each with his present facili-

ties. He has been selling the product for $2.10, which pays his present sales costs and returns him a net profit of 27 cents each. Assume that his manufacturing and sales costs are properly calculated. How do you suggest that he sell the product in an area covering the Rocky Mountain and Pacific Coast states?

Case 12–1 • GRADE MANUFACTURING COMPANY

The Grade Manufacturing Company sells its line of hay mowers, rakes, and bailers, as well as replacement parts, to about 20 wholesalers, many of whom also distribute the farm equipment of other larger firms. In 1975 executives of the company decided to evaluate the company's distribution policy to determine whether it would be more profitable to sell direct to retail outlets. This move was prompted by the fact that company sales, which had remained stable for the preceding five years, were expected to finish less for the current fiscal year than the previous year.

Grade products are not as competitive on the market as the equipment of most large companies (International Harvester, Case, John Deere, etc.) because Grade equipment is of extremely high quality and is consequently high priced. Therefore, company officials believed that, since Grade products are slow-moving items, the distributors were devoting their principal efforts to selling the products of larger manufacturers and were not giving proper emphasis to Grade products.

The sales division of Grade Manufacturing Company consisted of the sales manager, Mr. Bohn, and four sales representatives. All five tried to spend most of their time working with the wholesalers. However, since they were often called on to do missionary work with the retail dealers (of which there were 250 in ten states) and with farmers, very little time was left for them to do an adequate selling job. Mr. Bohn therefore recommended that the company establish five strategically located warehouses to service its retailers. He stated that, even though such a move would require an immediate financial outlay, the company would receive benefits from it very shortly. He pointed out that the 20 percent allowance which Grade was giving to its current distributors would be adequate to cover the expenses of a large company sales force and several company distributing outlets.

Do you agree with Mr. Bohn in recommending a more direct contact with the users of Grade products? If you were the general manager, what additional information would you ask Mr. Bohn to supply in support of his recommendations?

Case 12–2 • THE SUN VALLEY SKI COMPANY

In 1974, Bob Manning and Brad Barron, both of Sun Valley, Idaho, entered into a partnership to manufacture and market the Sun Valley Ski. Bob was a well-known ski instructor in Sun Valley. He had moved to Sun Valley in 1966 from Greenriver, Wyoming. Brad, also from Greenriver, moved to Sun Valley in 1970.

While a ski instructor, Bob spent about six months a year on skis. He had skied on every available make and model of ski. Eventually he designed what he thought was a superior recreational ski, which was a combination of wood, fiberglass, metal, and graphite. The ski tracked well and performed excellently on both pack and powder snow. After Bob had developed a manufacturing process for the ski, he began to contemplate how to market his product. It was at this point that he realized he needed help. Brad, who was managing a retail ski store at the time, was offered a 30 percent share of the profits if he would be in charge of marketing. Brad accepted and immediately began developing a marketing plan.

Brad had developed good marketing sense through practical experience. He first worked out a description of the target market for the ski. Next, he decided that the potential target market would most likely purchase the product at specialty ski shops. Finally, he thought that distribution of the ski should be limited to the western portion of the United States, at least until the product was better established. The problem was how to get the specialty shops to carry the product. A further complication was the necessity to conserve cash, since the Sun Valley Ski Company was undercapitalized.

What channel of distribution do you recommend for the Sun Valley Ski Company. Why?

13

logistics

There is no question about the importance of transportation, handling, and storage in providing a wide range of products to markets throughout the world. It is quite common to find as much as 25 to 35 percent of the total costs of a manufactured product accountable to physical distribution of the goods.[1]

Consequently, a great deal of effort is expended to improve physical handling and distribution, Most modern factories are well organized, with little waste in time and materials. When products reach the shipping dock, however, ". . . chaos begins. In many cases the product moves by inappropriate means of transportation and often in undesired quantities. It may well be protected by the wrong kind of package. It is almost sure to be picked up and put down needlessly. It is stored in warehouses that may be badly located for today's shifting markets or not needed at all, and it is likely to be controlled by the wrong kind of paper work."[2]

---

[1]John F. Magee, *Industrial Logistics* (New York City: McGraw-Hill, Inc., 1968), p. 20.
[2]"New Strategies to Move Goods," *Business Week* (September 24, 1966), p. 120.

A systems approach to physical distribution, which we can call marketing logistics, is gaining attention. *Marketing logistics* can be defined as the development and management of a physical distribution system that will assure optimum inventory levels at all stages of the distribution process to enhance overall marketing efficiency.

The term *business logistics* includes flows of goods *to* the manufacturer or marketing institution as well as the delivery of goods and services *from* there to customers. This discussion is concerned with logistics as a marketing aid and is, consequently, confined to outflows, as indicated in the foregoing.[3]

The principal features of marketing logistics discussed in this chapter are the customer service level as a measure of performance—based on the concept of a total package of value—the role of inventories, the components of a physical distribution system, and logistics management in the firm.

This is a relatively new field for organized study; hence, terms have not been standardized. To reduce confusion for your study of this chapter, we will say that *physical distribution*—that is, movement and storage—is a major part of *marketing logistics.*

LOGISTICS CONCEPT

The importance of the logistics concept arises from the way goods are manufactured and distributed. Take, for example, a food manufacturing company that produces many items under one brand. This company has several plants; however, not one of these plants manufactures all the company's products. Some customers want to place one order for various items which are produced at several locations. At this point the company's problem is how to ship in a single truck or a railroad car the full range of items ordered by one customer. This constitutes a marketing logistics problem for the company.

Let us further say that this company maintains 128 warehouse facilities to which each manufacturing plant sends its products. These warehouses are used to receive, mix, and ship the products. Although the company is aware that it is using a costly procedure, it believes that the better service provided by having full-line stocks near each market center is worth the extra cost. Moreover, the company exercises care to assure that each shipment from a plant goes by the lowest cost means; it also attempts to keep the inventory at each of the 128 warehouses at a minimum level consistent with minimizing out-of-stock conditions.

For maximum effectiveness two factors are still missing in the control exercised by this hypothetical company. First, the company has failed to realize that maximum efficiency in one activity frequently may not support the total effectiveness

---

[3]For an overview of the whole field, see Magee, *op. cit;* Ronald H. Ballou, *Business Logistics* (Englewood Cliffs, N.J.: Prentice-Hall, Inc., 1973); or John J. Coyle and Edward J. Bardi, *The Management of Business Logistics* (St. Paul: West Publishing Co., 1976).

of a marketing organization in view of conflicting objectives in a typical manufacturing company. The marketing department, for instance, would like large inventories; whereas, the finance and accounting departments would like to see minimal stock levels. In another instance, the marketing department would like to be assured of frequent short runs on production lines; whereas, the production department would like long production runs. Or the marketing department would push for fast order processing; whereas, the finance department would settle for a slow, inexpensive system for order processing. Again, the marketing department would like to have warehousing facilities near all customers; whereas, the finance department would be content with less warehousing and the production department would prefer in-plant warehousing. When the major emphasis is on maximizing efficiency in each functional area it is likely that overall effectiveness will be reduced, or at least there is good reason to believe that it will not be maximized.

The other factor overlooked by the hypothetical company is that it is difficult to measure all costs when accounting for each separate function. In the above example the company ignored the cost of the extra inventory investment. Although inventory level at each of the 128 warehouses was relatively small, when added together it proved to be startlingly large. The effort to meet the demand for slow-moving goods required transporting goods from one warehouse to another, a cost which the company did not consider.

In the logistics approach the first concern should be the total package of value as seen by the customer. *Total package of value* includes the properties, desirability, and availability of the goods. It must be observed that customers do not buy a group of well-managed activities but rather an end product that meets needs when and where they are desired. This may require regrouping activities and coordination not possible under traditional organizational structure. Even where there is no reorganization of duties, there can be an understanding by all executives that changes may be required in product design, methods of shipment, warehousing policies, and calculating costs of activities at various stages of distribution. It is necessary to be always aware that, to the customer, worth is the quality provided by manufacturing, the attraction generated by selling, and the service provided by distribution.

CUSTOMER SERVICE LEVEL

Customer service level is a standard against which performance of the logistics function can be measured. The narrow definition is stated as follows: Service level equals the percentage of orders that can be shipped within a specified time. A firm has a service level goal of 95 percent, meaning that it will ship 95 percent of orders within 24 hours (or other specified time), for example.

That standard can be misleading unless managers understand that service level includes more than just speedy shipment. The vendor is obligated to provide reliability, consistency, and quality. *Reliability* means that the seller works with the buyer and, if necessary, with carriers (truck, rail, air or barge) to assure that the order will arrive at the customer's location at the expected time. *Consistency* is the ability of the seller to provide the stated level of service all the time or with only slight variation. *Quality* of service is the capability to assure that the right product is delivered in good condition, prepared and packed according to the customer's needs. For example, palletized loads or other material handling requirements are included in quality.

Service Package—Cost Management and a Marketing Tool

A marketing logistics system offers opportunities for cost savings, and, at least equally as important, it provides marketing opportunities for competitive advantages.

Cost Management.   As was pointed out, physical distribution is a considerable cost of doing business. The most recent comprehensive studies of which we are aware are about ten years old, but the magnitudes still appear to be reasonably valid. Heskett and others computed physical distribution costs as being approximately 24 percent of gross national product.[4]

Cost studies of various industry groups calculated physical distribution costs as a percentage of net sales and found the following:[5]

Food and food products	34.5%
Chemicals, petroleum, rubber	26.0%
Wood products	16.8%
Textiles	16.2%
Machinery	11.4%

When one considers that total advertising costs are slightly over 2 percent of Gross National Product and for food products companies range from around 4 percent (General Mills) to 8 percent (General Foods) of net sales, one can see why managers began to look at physical distribution as an area for possible cost savings.

If physical distribution costs in the food industry can be reduced by only 1 percent, $3.40 has been saved on each $100 of sales. To make $3.40 added profit by increasing sales, a company has to sell $233 more (assuming a net profit of 1 percent on sales).[6]

Savings can be made by decreasing the customer service level, as well as by better management of all activities connected with shipping and storing goods. It is, however, more important to engage in cost management than in cost reduction only.

---

[4]J. L. Heskett, Robert M. Ivie, and Nicholas A. Glaskowsky, Jr., *Business Logistics* (New York City: The Ronald Press Company, 1964), p. 17.

[5]Richard E. Snyder, "Physical Distribution Costs: A Two-Year Analysis," *Distribution Age*, Vol. 62 (January, 1963), p. 50.

[6]See James A. Constantin, Rodney E. Evans, and Malcolm L. Morris, *Marketing Strategy and Management* (Dallas: Business Publications, Inc., 1976), p. 309, for a more detailed, similar computation for several industries.

One approach is to consider and measure what is involved in implementing a specific customer service level.

A Marketing Tool A recent study determined that, when making choices among competing suppliers, physical distribution service was second only to product quality. Price, supplier management, and other considerations were of less importance in ratings provided by over 200 purchasing offices.[7] That does not mean that every buyer would give the same ranking for every purchase. It does, however, indicate that the logistics area provides an opportunity for a seller to gain a competitive advantage.

Identify Customer's Service Requirements. Not all customers will have the same perception of quality of service, and within one firm the importance of service level will most likely vary among product classes (see "Purchase Weight Segmentation" in Chapter 5, page 90).

The marketing manager should determine the value placed by customers on the following:

- Time elapsed from placing order to receipt of goods by product class, time of year, or other important variables
- Consistency in time elapsed and allowable variation
- Percentage of back orders because of out-of-stock conditions
- Any limits placed on frequency of orders and size of acceptable orders (Is there an extra charge for small orders, for example?)
- Ordering methods, billing procedures, order status information, and other information/office procedure matters
- Returns policy
- Accuracy (percentage of errors in order filling)
- Action on complaints

Properly monitored internal records provide much of the information. If orders for a particular product or from certain customers or geographic areas are declining or not growing, the customer service ingredients should be examined. Some of the warning signals that indicate a need for service correction are (1) stockouts are increasing; (2) stockouts are more frequent on orders from major customers than from small-volume customers; and (3) complaints of slow delivery, damaged goods, and errors in filling orders are increasing.[8]

It is also recommended that the marketing department query customers about their service needs ranked in order of importance. Sales representatives are frequently instructed to gather that information

One firm learned that only a few products in its large line needed a 95 percent service level and a 75 to 80 percent level was satisfactory for other products. Cost

---

[7]William D. Perreault, Jr., and Frederick A. Russ, "Physical Distribution Service in Industrial Purchase Decision," *Journal of Marketing,* Vol. 40, No. 2 (April, 1976), p. 3.

[8]Robert E. Sabath, "How Much Service Do Customers Really Want?" *Business Horizons* (April, 1978), p. 27.

savings from lowering customer service resulted in lower prices, giving the firm an advantage.

A manufacturer of perishable food items had a 98 percent service level defined by the firm only in terms of speedy shipments—98 percent of orders were shipped on the same day that orders were received. It was costly to maintain that level. The firm maintained stocks at 170 public warehouses. Inventories in those warehouses were not carefully monitored. Consequently, there were many shipments of out-of-date merchandise. Naturally, customers were dissatisfied and sales fell. Customers defined service as *both* rapid order filling and high product quality.[9]

Trade-Offs.   Trade-offs will be required. For example, a firm finds that it costs $58 in office and warehouse procedures to fill an order. It then calculates that the break-even size order is $600. Should it refuse orders of less than $600? Should it refuse frequent reorders of almost $600? To answer those questions, the firm's managers must consider whether filling small, frequent reorders will help them keep a customer whose several large orders make that a major account. They must also consider whether the small-order customers have the potential to become large, valued customers.

A decision to increase a service level of 75 percent to 85 percent will require larger inventories, more warehouses, perhaps different data processing equipment, and maybe a change in organization. Will sufficient sales increases result that will justify the increase?

Environmental Analysis of Customer Service

One should analyze the current state of the external environments. Especially examine the economy, including financial institutions and stockholder postures, the competitive environment, and the political-legal environments. Evaluate what is learned to determine what marketing policies are desirable and possible.

Internal Environment—Integrated Effort Required.   Examine the internal environment by a systems approach. The purpose of the examination is to reveal the effect on each functional area of a proposed change in customer service.[10] Assume that we are proposing a change in customer service from the 80 percent level to a 90 percent level. What is the effect on each functional area? Sales volume, working capital, transportation, inventories, data processing, and production rate will all be affected. The following lists include some of the important items to consider.

---

[9]*Ibid.,* p. 27.

[10]See Martin Christopher, "Marketing and Logistics—A New Area of Management Concern," *Industrial Marketing Management,* Vol. 2, No. 2, (February, 1973), p. 136, for a discussion of out-put budgeting to measure costs of a "mission" that cuts across functional lines.

Marketing	Finance	Production
Projected sales	Working capital requirements	Effect on production
Prices–will they increase?	Budget for transporting	costs if production
Promotion to take advan-	and handling equipment	runs added
tage of this added	Data processing budget	Requirement for
service	Equipment and possible	workers and equip-
Distribution policy	change in methods and ex-	ment
	tent of accounting	Warehouse space

Background for Trade-Offs   Knowing how some firms handle physical distribution and discussing what must be considered before a change is made in customer service will help you see how the distribution process is integrated with other functions of the organization and what some of the necessary trade-offs are.

Contribution of Physical Distribution

In their transformation from raw materials to finished products goods are either in transit or in storage. Frequently storage is necessary at both ends of a transportation link to achieve maximum economies. Wholesalers of canned goods may have to store their products for a period if they buy them in carload lots, but their savings in freight costs would be greater than their storage costs. Also, a canner may store and defer transportation until the economies of carload rates can be achieved. Transportation and storage are interdependent and become a single problem of costs in achieving the goal set forth in our discussion of logistics.[11]

Transportation and storage are important marketing functions. They (1) increase the variety of goods available, (2) broaden the area of competition, (3) increase specialization, and (4) increase satisfactions and reduce costs for the buyer and the seller.

Increase Variety of Available Goods.   As we gain more skill in providing economical transportation and storage, the area of the firm's market broadens. A greater array of goods is available for our convenience. It may be South American caronoba wax, Australian wool, Indian spices, or Libyan rubber. Domestically the Seattle housewife can buy Tide detergent at the same price that is paid by a consumer in Cincinnati, where Tide is manufactured. The San Diego factory worker can buy Arch Preserver shoes for the same price that he will pay for these

[11]David E. Lilienthal, *Big Business: A New Era* (New York City: Harper & Row Publishers, Inc., 1953), p. 88.

shoes in the city of their manufacture—Beverly, Massachusetts. Economical movement greatly increases the variety of goods available to American consumers and enhances their standard of living. By the use of improved methods of transportation, a business manager broadens markets, reduces costs, and increases sales volume and profits.

Broaden the Area of Competition.   Were it not for low-cost transportation and storage, we could have no competitive national market. Continental Can would not be in competition with American Can; Colgate would not be concerned with the share of the market gained by Crest; nor would National Biscuit Company in New York City be anxious about Purity Biscuit selling as a competitor in the West. Yet, because of transportation and storage, competition is effective throughout the nation. Every company operating a plant within the borders of the nation must be keenly alert to the activities of its competitors. The fact that they are miles apart geographically does not insulate them from the necessity of providing equal or better values at comparable costs. Indeed, innovations in transportation and storage facilities have improved competition by making location monopolies more difficult to accomplish.

Increase Specialization.   Transportation and storage are necessary for specialization—specialization is necessary for mass production—mass production is necessary for low prices. If Eastman Kodak were forced to sell its entire output in Rochester, the volume would not be large enough to justify the degree of specialization necessary to maintain the efficiency of the production line. A decrease in specialization could result only in increased costs. Furthermore, transportation and storage make it possible for the entire nation to enjoy the benefits of California and Florida citrus fruits, Washington apples, Illinois corn, Maine and Idaho potatoes, and Seattle salmon and tuna. If each locality were to train its own people to manufacture the goods they used and to grow the products they consumed, their supply would be diminished and their variety would be restricted. Transportation and storage make specialization by task and locality possible. Specialization in both of these areas is fundamental to low prices, maximum variety, and high volume.

Immediate Availability of Goods.   Storage is necessary because buyers do not wish to wait for merchandise to be shipped from its point of production when they choose to buy. They want the goods now. Consumer wants cannot be anticipated daily or weekly or even monthly with perfect accuracy. Retail stores find it necessary, therefore, to store goods in order to have them available when they are wanted. A typical food store carries enough food in storage, measured in terms of dollars, to carry it for about 22 days of sales. The drugstore carries a 60-day supply. Department stores carry about a 90-day supply of goods. The aim of the management of each of these institutions is to decrease the stock necessary to meet its demands or to increase the demands and in this manner shorten the period of time stock is kept in storage.

There are three dangers in avoiding storage costs by decreasing the size of the inventory. The first is that the store will not carry the specific goods desired by customers. The second danger is that, even though the store might carry the goods as a part of its line, it may run short of desired goods temporarily. Both of these situations result in lost sales, and the store is not able to satisfy its customers. A third reason is that such a policy requires more frequent delivery of a small volume of goods. This, in turn, results in an increase in transportation rates and extra administrative costs. Thus, at the retail level, storage is necessary to give the customers the satisfaction they desire and to achieve economies of transportation.

At the wholesale level the same factors apply. A wholesale establishment is an assembly point and a storehouse. Thousands of manufacturers send their goods to hundreds of wholesalers to be re-sorted and stored until ordered by the retailer or other wholesalers, or possibly by manufacturers.

If the wholesaler does not have goods available for the retailer in a short time, the retailer must carry heavy stocks at a point where rent and storage costs are high. The wholesaler can also buy in carload lots more frequently than the retailer can and realize savings in transportation costs. As is the case of the retailer, wholesale management attempts to reduce its stock to as low a point as possible, thus reducing storage cost and danger of obsolescence. At the same time, wholesale firms wish to carry lines that enable them to compete successfully and to have enough of the right goods on hand when they are required.

Similarly, manufacturers must coordinate production with the anticipated orders of the wholesaler and others. These firms give the product its final form. Once Brown Shoe Company, in St. Louis, makes a piece of calf hide into a lady's shoe, it cannot be recast. If fashion changes before the supply is sold, some sellers will suffer a loss. On the other hand, if the shoe style continues to be popular, the company must have the shoe in stock or lose sales. As has been pointed out, the coordination of goods produced with the current demand is the function of merchandising. In examining the flow of goods from manufacturing through retailing, it is evident that storage is important to the proper function of merchandising.

Each of the stopping places in the channel of any material requires a certain amount of storage. Indeed, while marketing has been described as a vast system of tributaries, the flows must, in nearly all instances, emanate from reservoirs of stored goods. In but few instances is there a daily movement of goods in and out of the reservoir in uniform amounts. Rather, the purchases on the consumer markets trigger the movement back through every channel. Goods move into the retail store when its stock dwindle as purchases occur. Reservoirs of goods at all levels must be adequate to meet the immediate needs of the consumer market, which cannot be perfectly predicted.

Using Elements of the Physical Distribution Process for Competitive Advantage

The manufacturer who finds a way to make fast, dependable deliveries can thus gain a big competitive edge. Many manufacturers are gaining that edge by a total overhaul of their distribution system. Sometimes the way to greater profits is to increase warehousing costs. As an example, let us consider the Hammond Valve Corporation, a company in Chicago that makes bronze valves. The company formerly distributed its products through jobbers. In the mid-1960s management decided that profits could be increased by improving service to customers. The company opened six regional warehouses. Now it takes two days to service a customer's orders instead of six weeks. Sales have more than doubled in the past five years, and the greatly increased volume and lower unit production costs have far outweighed the added costs of operating warehouses. For other companies the analysis of physical distribution can mean fewer warehouses. It can mean, for example, going to air freight, as Raytheon and American Optical Company have done.

When Gillette introduced a new blade, air freight was used to rush the blades to market, but this added to cost. Finally, a management study group, by the use of a computer model of a distribution system, found that by revamping the paper work it could cut down the number of days it took to process an order. The company then could return to low-cost surface freight for routine shipments and still keep up delivery schedules.

What is best for one company is not necessarily best for another, as illustrated in the following two examples. Johnson and Johnson, the surgical supply manufacturers, used to ship to every part of the country every day. They now hold back shipments to take advantage of full truckload rates and find the service just as fast. By proper order-handling procedures they can ship whole truckloads at a time and avoid repeated intermediate handlings that cause delay, soiling, or loss. They ship on a scheduled basis. Now, when they have a true emergency, they can handle it efficiently. On the other hand, Singer Sewing Machine Company used to ship machines once a month, but now it ships four times a month. The company now pays less-than-truckload rate which is almost double the carload rate, but this is more than offset by lower inventories in stores. Most of Singer's 1,600 Sewing Centers are in high-rent districts, making inventory costs relatively expensive; hence, the somewhat higher freight rates are offset.

INVENTORY MANAGEMENT

An examination of the nature of inventory costs and the role in logistics of inventories provides a base for inventory management.

Inventory costs are typically classified as (1) carrying costs, (2) procurement costs, and (3) stockout costs.

Carrying Costs[12]

Carrying costs are those incurred in holding an item in inventory. To carry goods for a year is expensive. It is generally estimated that carrying costs, as a percentage of inventory value, average 20 to 25 percent. A recent study of six companies disclosed carrying costs ranging from 14 percent to 43 percent.[13] This includes (1) opportunity cost or the interest on capital tied up in inventories, (2) obsolescence, (3) protection against damage or deterioration provided by proper warehouses or other storage areas, (4) handling costs required to move goods in and out of storage, and (5) taxes and insurance.

Procurement Costs

Procurement costs, or *order costs,* consist of (1) records of inventory levels and determination of order points (*order point* is the level of inventory at which a reorder is placed); (2) selection of suppliers, and (3) office work to prepare requisitions, receiving reports, processing payment, and posting to inventory records.

Stockout Costs

Stockout cost is the cost of not having an item available when it is required. Stockout costs are difficult to measure accurately, but they can be large. They include three possible costs to the firm; cost of back ordering a requested item, a lost sale, or a lost customer as a result of inability to fill orders.[14]

Logistics View of Inventory Levels

A more effective inventory management results if there is complete understanding of the reasons for inventories and of the functions they perform. Inventories exist because (1) customer demand is not uniform nor is it completely predictable, (2) it takes time to make or to move a product, (3) it is usually inordinately expensive to manufacture and distribute items unit by unit in response to individual orders, and (4) some products require seasoning until they reach a certain quality level—products such as ice cream, wine, and lumber.

Logistically four functions are performed by inventory, and a certain stock level must be maintained for each. These functions are:

1. For efficiency in manufacturing, *process stocks* or certain items must be on hand because of the time required for some manufacturing processes and because of the time required to move raw materials, goods in process, or finished goods from one place to another.

---

[12]See Coyle and Bardi, *op. cit.,* Chapters 3 and 4, for calculations of costs and for inventory control methods.

[13]Bernard J. LaLonde and Douglas M. Lawbert, "A Methodology for Determining Inventory Carrying Costs" (In proceedings of the Fifth Annual Transportation and Logistics Educators Conference, Chicago, October 12, 1975).

[14]Donald J. Bowersox, Edward W. Smykay, and Bernard J. LaLonde, *Physical Distribution Management* (New York City: Macmillan, Inc., 1968), p. 212.

2. *Lot sizes* are required because one produces, ships, or buys in larger lots than are immediately required. A consumer may buy several cans of fruit at one time, while the grocer finds it convenient to buy 30 cases at a time and to stock his shelves a case at a time.

3. *Safety stocks* are required to assure proper levels of inventories in the face of variations in demand or delivery.

4. *Seasonal stocks* must be available. These stocks arise from uniform production and seasonal demand, such as garden tools or Christmas items, or those stocks developing because of seasonal production and near-uniform demand, such as canned fruits and vegetables.

Ideally each inventory should be at absolute minimum for maximum efficiency of the distribution process. This goal is clearly impossible to achieve because of unforeseen delays due to weather, production breakdown, and the like.

Inventory control systems are designed to maintain an optimum level of inventory. If the level is too high there are excessive carrying costs and if too low sales are lost. Essential features of a control system are (1) the order quantity—how many units to order at one time, (2) lead time—how much time elapses between placing the order and receiving the goods, and (3) reorder point—the stock level which signals you to reorder. For example, if lead time is three weeks and demand is 100 units per week, reorder point is $3 \times 100 = 300$ units.

A complete inventory control model is beyond the scope of this book.[15] It is instructive, however, to examine a common phenomenon in stock control known as the 80–20 principle; that is, about 20 percent of items in an inventory will account for approximately 80 percent of sales volume.[16]

This will be evident if the contribution to revenue of each product is monitored. A simple method is to prepare control cards as follows:

Item Code	Unit Price	Units Sold	Annual Sales
1234	$ 20	9,700	$194,000
0789	$400	380	152,000
⋛	⋛	⋛	⋛
5432	$280	0	0

That was done for a distributor who carried approximately 700 items, and from an analysis of unit sales Illus. 13–1 was prepared.

---

[15]For examples of inventory control systems see Ronald H. Ballou, *Basic Business Logistics* (Englewood Cliffs, N.J.: Prentice-Hall, Inc., 1978) Chapter 10, or Coyle and Bardi, *op. cit.,* Chapter 4.

[16]See Coyle and Bardi, *op. cit.,* p.54, for the ABC analysis which is used to classify items by cash flow, lead time, and stockout costs–the 80/20 principle obtained for many companies.

PERCENTAGE OF SALES

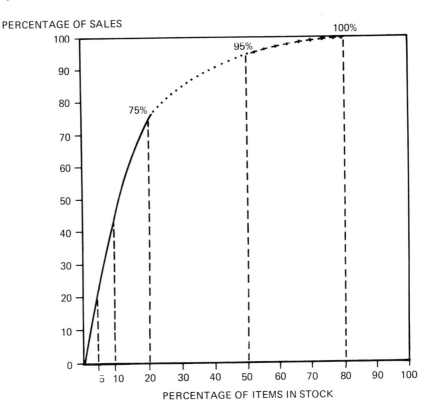

Illus. 13-1   **Analysis of Sales and Items in Stock**

Notice in Illus. 13–1 that 5 percent of the items carried in stock accounted for 19.4 percent of annual sales of the company; 20 percent of items provided about 75 percent of sales; the next 30 percent of items accounted for approximately 20 percent of sales; the next 30 percent of items brought 5 percent of sales; and there were no sales of the final 20 percent of items.

The manager of that firm made the following decisions:

1. Dispose of the no-sale 20 percent of items.
2. Reduce inventory levels in the 30 percent of items that accounted for only 5 percent of sales.
3. Use the money saved in reduced carrying costs to improve customer service level in the highest sales volume items and provide some price reductions.

In addition to knowing whether the right items are being stocked, it is necessary to calculate the costs of adding items.

Assume a probability distribution of demand (use Poisson distribution). Assume further that we add one model—for example, in addition to black typewriters we now offer one other color. The reserve requirement will increase by 81 percent (see any statistics text for the computation). The manager must estimate whether sufficient extra business will be generated to offset the cost of the added item.

COMPONENTS OF PHYSICAL DISTRIBUTION SYSTEMS

Principal components of a physical distribution system that must be designed and integrated for maximum effectiveness are:

1. *Information system.* An information system is needed to assure that proper inventory levels are maintained at all stages of the system. This includes a communications and order-processing system to facilitate integration of all components and provide facilities for controlling the entire distribution system.
2. *Storage facilities.* Particular attention should be paid to the design of storage facilities (both internal and external) to assure proper handling and reduce the cost of moving goods into and out of the inventory-holding points.
3. *Transportation.* Principal considerations for judgment relative to this component are speed, reliability of performance, and cost.
4. *Materials handling and packaging.* These components involve considerable capital and also directly affect all other elements of the system.

Information System

Marketing executives have for a long time had an awareness that marketing effectiveness is limited by information gathering and processing capability. Wholesalers were among the first to use electronic data processing equipment to provide information for the establishment of reorder points. Alcoa and others have communication networks which tie together regional sales offices and manufacturing plants in order to facilitate control of inventory. A goal of some manufacturers and retailers is a system that includes a device attached to every cash register in the country that will transmit information on sales simultaneously to each supplier and transporter of the store's merchandise.

One of the most elaborate existing systems is the Pittsburgh Tele-Computer Center of Westinghouse Corporation. All 53 industrial products warehouses of Westinghouse are connected with each company sales office. Each order obtained by a sales office is teletyped to the Pittsburgh Center computer. The order is processed, and shipping orders are prepared and sent over the wire to the warehouse closest to the sales office. Total time for the entire process is under two minutes. In the computer memory are stored the levels of each item in inventory in each warehouse. The computer is also programmed to signal each reorder point. The company reports that shelf stock has been lowered from inventory valued at $33 million to $18 million. Savings are worthwhile since the cost of carrying industrial electrical products at Westinghouse is about 20 percent of sales.

Limited Stores emphasizes inventory turnover. Each store transmits, through electronic cash registers, daily information on merchandise sold by classification, style, color, size, and price to its distribution center at Columbus, Ohio.

A few other companies have similar systems for processing orders for consumer goods. Sears Roebuck and Co. maintains a fashion goods warehouse in New Jersey where, in addition to order processing, the computer is connected to an automatic warehouse so that goods ordered are selected and moved to the shipping dock without being handled manually. The merchandise controller for Sears reports savings from the system but stresses the fact that it is not possible to compute judgment. Buyers must exercise judgment to assure that proper goods are in stock.

Important to the logistics concept of physical distribution is linking a physical distribution information system with other information systems of the business. Several of the available business data systems are designed to allow integration of operational control systems so that production, shipping, stock ordering, and cost accounting information can all be served from a single input. Information can then be fed out to whatever operating function requires it.

Storage

For proper integration into the physical distribution system, storage facilities must be properly located and must function efficiently in the processing activities of warehousing.

Location of Storage Facilities.   Any supplier has one of two choices to make regarding warehouse location. A centralized storage policy can be adopted. This means that all shipments to customers are made from one location. For some basic materials and products such a policy is feasible. If a steady flow of the product is required, provision can be made to ship in such quantities and on such schedules that the customer will always have the product when it is required. For example, an iron mine in Peru owns its fleet of ore carriers and makes regular shipments to Japan. This requires loading facilities and stocks in Peru sufficient to meet shipping requirements at all times. It also requires large storage facilities in Japan to receive the large quantities of ore carried in each vessel. As long as the shipments are made regularly, the time required to cross the Pacific Ocean is of concern only as regards cost of the vessel and crew and the investment in ore during the time of shipment. Many manufacturing plants operate with supplies coming from one distant point. This is possible so long as the supply comes in a steady flow.

When, however, requirements of customers fluctuate in volume and in particular items needed, it is necessary to provide supplies close enough to the customers so that undue delay is not encountered. The growth of steel and copper wholesale operations in or near developing manufacturing centers exemplifies this kind of requirement. Manufacturers of many types find it impossible to make continuous and uniform production runs and must, therefore, depend on having needed raw materials and components readily available. At the same time it is uneconomical for them to build up large inventories of such goods. Hence, the other choice for a supplier is to establish warehousing facilities close to manufacturing centers.

Location Studies. Application of mathematical methods made possible by computers are now common in studies to determine optimum numbers and locations of storage points. Typical computations that must be made include the following:

1. Costs incurred from lost sales because of the distance from storage points
2. Costs of operating storage facilities
3. Transportation costs from manufacturing facility to branch warehouses
4. Transportation costs from branch warehouses to customers
5. Costs of maintaining inventories at branch warehouses

To determine these costs, it is necessary to know the quantities required in storage and in transit, usual order quantities, speed of supply desired, and product mixes required at each location. From these requirements it is easy to see why simulation models and statistical techniques have interested large suppliers.[17]

Processing Functions of Warehousing. Warehouse design obviously depends on the job to be done. Consequently, it is worthwhile to decide in detail just exactly what is to be accomplished. The following list looks simple, but unless provisions are made to assure that each activity fits well in the system of physical distribution, it can be a hindrance to overall effectiveness. Such functions are receiving goods; identifying and sorting; dispatching goods to storage, holding, and recalling; selecting and picking goods; marshaling shipments; and dispatching shipments. It is presumed that proper material handling equipment for palletized as well as loose items will be provided.

Transportation. Transportation is the link between sources of supply and points of demand. It creates time and place utilities. Time has, in a logistics system, a dimension beyond getting goods to a place when desired.

An important element is the cost of capital tied up while time passes. The marketing manager of a motor freight line tells of a publishing company that has much of its printing done in the Far East. Most of the publisher's customers are in states east of the Mississippi River. The company had shipped the books by water from the printing plant through the Panama Canal to a port on the East Coast. The motor freight representative suggested that the books be unloaded at a West Coast port and then shipped by truck to customer locations. That did not appear attractive to the publisher, since freight costs would be increased by almost 56 cents per hundred pounds. The sales representative demonstrated that the publisher could save, on the average, 18 days on each shipment. Savings on the value of the inventory during that time would not only offset the extra freight charges, but would be worth almost 10 cents per hundred pounds in addition. Hence, it is total time costs that must be calculated, including costs of capital, storage, risks, and chances of lost sales.

---

[17]For examples see Ronald H. Ballou, *op. cit.,* Chapter 8.

Means of Transportation

The means and relative importance of transportation in the United States are shown in Table 13–1.

Railroads. Railroads still are the most important means of moving cargo. This is because there is no more efficient use of power in transportation over land.

Recently railroads have been introducing innovations to provide better service and regain some of the business they have lost, as well as to share in the increasing tonnages hauled. One of the profitable railroads in the country is the D&RG which has a rigorous road through the Rocky Mountains. D&RG has reduced the number of cars in each train. By increasing the speed and decreasing the handling required for making up and distributing trains, the railroad is recapturing business that had been lost to other handlers.

Many lines have built larger cars which have brought savings to shippers. Railroad costs do not go up proportionately with the volumes they carry; hence, rates are often less per ton when big volumes are shipped in the new large cars. In the meat-packing business savings have been made by using the larger cars. The vice-president for distribution and transportation of Armour and Co. says:

> For many years, meat moved in refrigerator cars kept cool by ice and salt. The normal weight of the load on which rates were based was 21,000 pounds. Now meat moves in far larger cars cooled either by mechanical or chemical means with much better insulation and is moved at the rate of 100,000 pounds per car. The difference in rates is about one cent a pound or $1,000 a car.

To Armour, which ships about 8,000 tons of pork a week, one cent a pound is a substantial amount. It has meant that to take full advantage of these savings, Armour and other meat packers have moved their stockyards and slaughterhouses away from consuming areas and closer to growing areas.

The rack cars on the railroad which handle automobiles (12 per car for a standard size automobile, and 15 per car for a compact size) have recovered

Table 13-1   **Freight Shipments by Type of Carrier Percentage of Total Ton-Miles**

	Rail	Motor Vehicles	Inland Waterways	Oil Pipelines	Airways
1950	57.4	15.8	14.9	11.8	0.03
1960	44.7	21.5	16.6	17.2	.06
1970	39.8	21.3	16.5	22.3	.17
1975	36.4	23.5	16.5	23.5	.19

Source: Statistical Abstract of the United States, 1977 (98h ed.; Washington: U.S. Government Printing Office, 1977) No. 1042, p. 627.

automobile shipping business for the railroads by reducing shipping costs per automobile.

Trailer-on-flat-car shipments, commonly called piggyback, have brought some business back to railroads. Joint motor-rail rates are now established to most parts of the United States. There are only rough estimates of the volume of cargo handled by the method of hauling motor trailers on railroad cars, but it is worthwhile business for some lines.

For some of the bulk commodities, such as coal and grain, there are *unit trains,* which are semipermanently coupled trains that shuttle back and forth between one shipper and one consignee. They avoid intermediate freight yards, improve dependability, and cut costs. Savings are sizable over ordinary freight since a loaded car on the average spends 20 hours of each 24 on a siding or a freight yard.

By promoting a long-existing rate device, railroads have made the use of distribution centers even more attractive. This rate is the *intransit rate.* Inventories can be reduced through intransit storage and transloading. To make use of *intransit storage* shippers forward carload lots directly to a centralized storage facility from their manufacturing plants. Goods are then stored until orders are received from customer outlets. In some cases the goods may be repackaged or even assembled. The carload of mixed goods then can be forwarded to the final destination. The manufacturer thus provides maximum flexibility and still pays only the standard transcontinental through rate, with a small charge for instransit storage.

In the second method of inventory reduction called *transloading,* a car of merchandise starts out from a manufacturing plant destined for either a shipper transloader or a railroad transloader, not a centralized facility. If the shipper transloads, the car can be shipped to a central location where the goods can be unloaded and stored. At a later date a portion of the car can be mixed with other goods and sent to any location. The shipper is charged only a small additional intransit fee for the service. If the railroad transloads, full cars are sent to a central location where they are separated into three or four car groups, each of which is then shipped to a different customer. In effect, through transloading either by the shipper or by the railroad, a shipper can receive less than carload service and still pay the cheaper carload rate.

Motor Carriers. The motor truck brought a new mobility to goods. It brought productivity to areas that had been unproductive and greater productivity to areas which had been productive. Two examples illustrate the point.

The towns in southwestern Colorado and southeastern Utah were farther away from a railroad than any cities in the United States. Like the upstate dwellers in New York in 1820 before the Erie Canal, they were merely self-sustaining. With the coming of the truck they were able to specialize in the production of wheat, beans, sheep, and cattle, and to accommodate tourists. Many grew wealthy. But most significant was the discovery of uranium. This area became the center of the nation's uranium boom. It would have been a costly and slow process to build railroads to all points where productive mines were established. Trucks, however, served the purpose well. Even with makeshift roads, it was possible to get ore out. The industry grew with facility and without handicap.

Now let us view the west side of Manhattan Island, either early in the morning or in the evening. This is the time when trucks are either beginning or terminating their day's travel. Some of this traffic is within the city, but much of it is awaiting the turn to go through the tunnels. Thousands of trucks pass through these tunnels daily carrying millions of pounds of goods. Without trucks to make the deliveries and pickups on this island, it is possible that trade would be restricted by at least one third.

Thus, both in areas having a sparse population and in heavily populated sections, trucks provide place utility that increases market areas, intensifies competition, and increases the volume of marketing activity. Not only have motor trucks increased the amount of traffic they have hauled, but also their share of the transportation business has increased from 15.8 percent in 1950 to 23.5 percent in 1975 (see Table 13–1 on page 289). There are several reasons for such an increase.

On most short hauls trucks can save the shipper time, and time is a significant factor in merchandising, since it is closely related to cost. Even on long hauls trucks frequently can save a shipper some time. Railroads move faster than trucks, but the switching, unloading, and picking up of cars enroute slows up the freight train considerably.

Truck schedules are so flexible that they can meet unusual time requirements of a shipper. They can go out of their way for a pickup or a delivery. They can vary a time schedule for the convenience of an order. The shipper can also send a smaller load than a railway carload and get a full-truck rate. Furthermore, the packing expense is less than with the railroad.

As for rates, for a specific shipment a comparison may favor trucks slightly or truck rates may be higher than rail rates, depending on the product and the haul. In terms of overall cost of moving goods from factory dock to destination, the truck usually is cheaper for short hauls because the truck rate includes pickup and delivery, and there is usually little or no packing cost.

At this time it is impossible to predict what effect the energy crisis will have on motor carriers. Reduced speed limits and the possibility of fuel rationing certainly could shift a significant amount of the goods that trucks haul to railroads. The policies set by the Energy Department could accelerate the decline of some agricultural truck farming operations that are dependent on trucking for their survival.

Water Transportation. The principal items of shipment on waterways are raw materials—iron ore, grains, coal, chemicals, sugar, coffee, cotton, and rice. The areas where inland shipping via water is most extensively practiced are the Great Lakes, the Mississippi River and its tributaries, the coastal rivers, and the canals. The principal canal is the New York Barge Canal, formerly the Erie Canal.

Improvements in water transportation continue to be made. The St. Lawrence Seaways plan, which opened the entire Great Lakes area to seagoing vessels, and navigation projects by the army engineers are examples. It appears that this method of transportation will become more important as such developments continue.

There is increasing interest in facilitating movement of goods between inter-continental and intracontinental carriers. A substantial part of all surface transportation cost is accumulated in terminals. This is particularly true of water transportation. Costs are incurred in loading and unloading, in transfer to ground transportation, and in serious losses due to pilferage and damage. Much work is now being done on containers that are interchangeable between carriers which are expected to reduce these terminal costs.

Waterway travel is not as rapid as the railways or the trucks. In some instances, depending on the arteries, it is seasonal, since there must be sufficient water depth to carry the vessels. Floods are also a factor that may interfere with, or even destroy, the movement of goods. These factors must be balanced against economies of the waterways.

Pipelines.   Pipelines are not often recognized as a significant part of our transportation system, but they carry over one fifth of the tonnage that moves through the transportation arteries of the United States.

The versatility of pipelines that makes it possible to transport at different intervals crude oil, gasoline, kerosene, fuel oil, and gas has increased the usefulness of the lines. They provide low-cost transportation. Crude oil cost per ton-mile shipped via pipeline was estimated by the Interstate Commerce Commission as 1.98 cents as compared to 10.62 cents by the railroads. For refined products, such as gasoline, kerosene, and fuel oil, the rate was 4.39 cents per ton-mile by pipeline and 11.19 cents by rail. Pipelines would be much more widely used if they were more numerous and were accessible to all the areas where petroleum products are used and produced. The great differential in cost is encouraging such extensions.

Air Transportation.   Only goods that have a comparatively high intrinsic value can be carried by air freight. The rates average approximately 22 cents per ton-mile as compared to 1.3 cents for railroads and 6.5 cents for trucks. Several factors are important in setting rates on air freight. On the cost side of the analysis are the bulk and weight of the product. On the demand side, the desirability of the product ascribed to it by the buyer or consumer must be considered, as is the case in all other price-determining calculations. Further, there is the dimension of time that often makes a product a prospect for air transportation. Some products are shipped by air because of a quality of perishability. Fashion goods, flowers, and some vegetables and fruits are in this category. Time also is strategic in the case of repair products that may be vital to the operation of a plant; or it may be an important competitive factor, as, for example, a merchandising establishment that wishes to offer a new product first to its clientele.

It is also possible that quick deliveries by air transportation may make it unnecessary for businesses to carry large stocks. It is costly to manufacturing and merchandising establishments to maintain inventories to meet contingencies. A manufacturer may be required to stock a supply of spare parts to guarantee the continued operations of its own machines or those of its customers. In a merchandising establishment extra investment may be required for items within unpredictable rates of sale. If supplies run short, air freight can supplement them without impairing the efficiency of the operations.

An instance of this kind was reported when an airline flew a 20,000-pound steel rod from Philadelphia to Los Angeles. The shipment could have required two weeks by rail. Furthermore, no elaborate and expensive packing was necessary. Certainly this plant would have found it expensive to have been idle during the period required for the product to come by rail. Plant operators never know when a repair part is going to be needed; thus, a large store of various products would otherwise have to be available.

Proponents of air freight agree that the cost factors are such that it is unlikely that a high percentage of freight tonnage will be directed to air travel in the near future. They suggest, however, that in the areas which we have described there are still many savings possible that business firms are not exploiting to their most profitable potential.

Products that are transported now are machinery (much of which is made up of automobile and airplane parts), women's wearing apparel, drugs, printed matter, sea food, cut flowers, and perishable food products. With improved technology and the continuation of the educational program, air transportation probably will become even more widely and intensively used.

Materials Handling

Methods and equipment for improving materials handling can contribute to savings in distribution costs as follows:

1. By increasing the usable capacity of storage space. By using the height available and by minimizing aisle space as much as possible, the effective capacity is maximized.
2. By improving operating efficiency. Effective design and proper equipment reduce the number of times goods are handled. For example, it is costly to handle a case of goods manually from a stack to a hand truck and from the hand truck to another stack. A conveyor system or palletized loads reduce that handling.

Also, by improving the flow of goods, materials handling facilitates getting goods to customers on time and in proper condition—a contribution to the customer service level.

Packaging

The size and shape of packaging influences costs, type and design of materials handling equipment, and transportation methods.

One purchasing agent for a large concern that buys many millions of dollars worth of goods each year states that nearly 100 percent of the materials received from the many suppliers are improperly packaged. Common packaging faults are excessive weight per unit; improper protection; difficulty of handling, loading, and transporting with available facilities; and waste of time in packing and unpacking the product due to excessive packaging. One supplier was advised that it was not necessary to use a package which included an outside wooden crate, a heavy cardboard box, and an inner wrap of grease-resistant, waterproof paper. Elimination of the cardboard box and some of the wood reduced the weight by 30 percent and the cost of packaging by nearly 50 percent with no consequent danger of damage to the product. It also increased the ease of packing and unpacking.

Packaging has both marketing and logistics connotations. Consumer or *interior* packaging is important in marketing as it provides information and visibility to the product in retail displays. Industrial or *exterior* packaging has to be designed to provide protection to the goods, effectively use storage space in warehouses and transport carriers, and assure ease of handling.[18]

PHYSICAL DISTRIBUTION MANAGEMENT

An effective system of physical distribution can never be built if concern begins only at the shipping dock. Norge Division of Borge-Warner Corporation exemplifies organizations that utilize the concept of marketing logistics. For that company all distribution functions (starting with forecasting, production scheduling, and continuing through warehousing, order processing, and shipping) have been consolidated into one department under a director of physical distribution. The following changes have been effected as a result.

Until 1964 the price of Norge's home appliances practically doubled from the end of the production line to the hands of the consumer. There were six departments at Norge (in addition to distributors at the Norge plants and to distributors at the wholesale and retail levels), all of which had a hand in distribution but without common direction or common policies. The traffic department shipped the best available way so that shipping was a matter of expediency of the moment.

According to the president of the company, sometimes warehouses were underutilized and sometimes it was necessary to rent outside space to take overflow. An excess of one product sometimes forced Norge into what the industry called a "loading program," which is pushing surplus products off onto dealers

---

[18]See Coyle and Bardi, *op. cit.,* Chapters 5 and 6, for a good discussion of warehousing, type of materials handling equipment, and packaging.

with special concessions that boost accounts receivable and cut profits. Now, under the director of physical distribution, the company has ceased loading distributors. The company has substantially reduced plant inventories, distributors' inventories, and accounts receivable. This has resulted in the reduction of overall investment and, at the same time, in an increase in profitability. A specific step was the establishment of a regional warehouse at Utah's distribution center for Norge's West Coast distributors. Norge plants around the United States ship their complete lines of appliances, mostly in carload lots to the distribution center. From there Norge can make deliveries to West Coast dealers in four or five days instead of twenty, which was the prior average. The new system has achieved a 50 percent reduction in dealer inventories and accounts receivable.

Norge's approach was to have a logistics manager at a top management level. Others use a logistics coordinator, a coordinating staff, a matrix organization in which managers of manufacturing, engineering, marketing, accounting and transportation share logistics authority responsibility.[19]

A McKinsey Company Survey on physical distribution reported that firms which rated high on their scale of excellence in logistics developed the following information:

1. Transportation costs
   a. Total costs for the company and each operating division by rail, common-carrier truck, and company-operated truck
   b. A comparison of those costs to sales this year versus last
   c. Total transportation from plant to warehouse and total transportation costs from warehouse to customer; inbound freight figures and penalty cost figures for partial shipments
2. Warehousing costs
   a. Total
   b. Public warehouse costs per square foot per dollar of product handled
   c. Company operated total costs (in the plant and in the field) per square foot per product per dollar of product handled
3. Inventory performance, actual versus planned
   a. By location
   b. Low-volume items
   c. Cost of carrying inventories
4. Quality of service on time-order performance
   a. Percentage of orders shipped on time
   b. Severity of late orders and customer problems
   c. Comparison with competitive service on liability, speed, time, and delivery[20]

---

[19]"Overhaul at Norge Speeds Deliveries—and Profits," *Business Week* (September 24, 1966), p. 126; Göran Persson, "Organization Design Strategies for Business Logistics," *International Journal of Physical Distribution and Materials Management,* 1978, Vol. 8, No. 6, p. 287, provides development of and evaluation of various organizational designs for handling the logistics function; Robert G. House and Jeffrey J. Karrenbauer, "Logistics System Modelling," *International Journal of Physical Distribution and Materials Management,* 1978, Vol. 8, No. 4, p. 189.

[20]John F. Stolle, "How to Manage Physical Distribution," *Harvard Business Review* (July–August, 1967), p. 43.

It can be said that the logistics approach calls for intellectual rather than mechanical changes. A real systems approach to physical distribution will almost certainly require some shifting of duties and responsibilities. This is due primarily to some of the conflicts noted earlier among a marketing executive, a finance executive, and a production executive, who try to achieve maximum efficiency in their respective tasks, but at a cost to the overall effectiveness of the firm.[21]

QUESTIONS AND ANALYTICAL PROBLEMS.

1. Define *marketing logistics.*
2. What is meant by the statement that customers buy a total package of value?
3. Select one industrial product and one durable consumer product and list what would be included in the package of value of each of those products.
4. Define *customer service level.* What is meant by reliability, consistency, and quality as they apply to customer service level?
5. Describe a company and a product for which a low customer service level would be tolerated.
6. Refer to the lists under the heading "Internal Environment— Integrated Effort Required" on page 278. If a firm increases the customer service level from 80 percent to 90 percent, what specific effects will that have on distribution policy, the data processing budget, warehouse space, and working capital requirements?
7. Specify how physical distribution (a) increases availability of goods, (b) broadens competition,

and (c) increases specialization.
8. What is included in inventory carrying costs, procurement costs, and stockout costs?
9. A retailer of unfinished hardwood furniture is located in a shopping center that has a large number of shoppers every day. Another retailer of the same kind of furniture is in a warehouse-type structure several blocks from any other retail outlets. What logistics trade-offs has each of those retailers made?
10. What are the major components of a physical distribution system? What contribution to the system does each component make?
11. What makes a logistics concept of more value than operating, transportation, and storage as discrete functional operations?
12. What trends do you see in the percentage of freight hauled by each of the types of carriers identified in Table 13–1, page 289? What causes those trends? In your answer include a statement of the critical advantage of each type of carrier.

---

[21]See Walter F. Friedman, "Physical Distribution: the Concept of Shared Services," *Harvard Business Review,* March–April, 1975, p. 24, for illustrations of use of facilities of distribution centers and public warehouses to reduce costs and increase logistics efficiency.

13. How can intransit storage be used to improve customer service and reduce logistics costs?
14. Will each of the components of a physical distribution system have the same importance for all compa-

nies? Provide two examples to support your answer.
15. What, if any, organizational changes are required for a company that adopts a logistics concept?

Case 13–1 • THE MAIL-ORDER TOBACCO COMPANY

The Mail-Order Tobacco Company has traditionally specialized in the custom blending of fine pipe tobaccos. Customers usually try several of the firm's offerings and eventually choose the ones they like. Once the selection is made the company automatically sends the smoker a new supply on a regular basis, usually monthly. The customer is billed monthly for the tobacco purchased the previous month. The billing statement also includes order blanks and announcements of new tobacco blends and special sale items.

The Mail-Order Tobacco Company has been very successful using the automatic delivery system. The company president and founder, Lewis Gaither, credits his success to the high level of customer service provided. Customers don't have to leave their own home to try various blends of tobacco and to be constantly replenished with a fresh supply. However, Mr. Gaither is not entirely happy.

In the past few years sales to college-age customers have declined. Mr. Gaither credits this sales decline to a number of factors. First, the number of college-age youths is declining. Second, the publicity about health problems and cigarette smoking has had a carry-over effect on pipe smoking. Finally, more and more college-age people (primarily men) are chewing tobacco or using moist tobacco products such as Skoal or Happy Days Mint. Mr. Gaither commented with envy that "sales of chewing tobacco products had grown at the rate of 11 percent a year since 1974."[1]

Because of the growth in chewing tobacco products, Mr. Gaither has firmly committed to expand his product line to include a wide variety of chewing tobacco. But questions about the marketing of the product were still undecided. First, he wondered whether the automatic delivery system would be as effective for tobacco chewers as for pipe smokers. Second, he questioned whether the special packaging and storage requirements of moist tobacco would make direct-mail distribution too expensive. Finally, he wondered whether a large enough market for specialty chewing tobacco existed. To answer these and other questions, Mr. Gaither considered having a marketing research study conducted.

If you were Mr. Gaither, what specific types of information would you like to have before going ahead with the chewing tobacco program?

---

[1]Julie Salamon, "Many College Men New Get Something Worth Chewing On," *The Wall Street Journal,* May 22, 1979, p. 1.

Case 13–2: WABASH DOORS AND BUILDING MATERIALS

Freda Fields, the general manager of Wabash Doors and Building Materials, was analyzing the firm's distribution system. Specifically, she was concerned about the fact that physical distribution was not handled by any one department but was a joint responsibility. Although no evidence was immediately obvious that distribution was not effective and efficient, Ms. Fields was still not sure.

The company manufactures pressed particle board doors and particle board siding. The particle board material is a combination of wood fiber and fiberglass resin which have been bonded together under tremendous heat and pressure. The material can be made to look much like wood, depending on the coloring and type of mold used.

The current practice is that the production manager receives orders directly from the sales manager. Production is scheduled on an order basis, with jobs being completed on a first-in, first-out system. When the production of an order is completed, it is packed by any available production people and moved to a holding storage area. The merchandise is supposedly then under the operational control of the traffic manager who arranges the transportation for the product. At times the merchandise may remain in the holding area for five to seven days, depending on how busy the traffic manager is. The traffic manager arranges transportation for the order based on train or truck availability and upon cost. Considering all aspects of the process, Ms. Fields estimates that order lead time (time from order placement to order receipt) is about three weeks.

Ms. Fields wonders whether combining all physical distribution activities under one person will reduce lead time. She also wonders whether she should attempt to set a customer service objective in terms of lead time and then implement a physical distribution system to meet the objective. Finally, Ms. Fields wonders whether economies in production can be achieved through establishing an inventory of products rather than through the manufacture of each order on an individual basis.

What do you recommend to Ms. Fields?

5

Marketing Institutions

14

retailing

--Louis Epstein,
founder of Pickwick Bookstores

A *retail transaction* is a sale to an ultimate consumer. Already discussed in this text are the motives for purchasing and the bases which marketers use to establish product mixes to meet the needs of various market segments. But what of the retail sale itself and the environment in which it takes place? J.C. Penney, founder of the chain of stores that bear his name, enjoyed frequent talks with student groups—talks in which he was fond of reflecting on what he called the "Golden Three Feet." That space between the customer and the salesperson, or the customer and a self-service display, he said, is where the planning, production, promotion and distribution of goods meet their test. No matter how much satisfaction value the producer of consumer goods builds into the product and how well that value is communicated to potential users, it is the retailer who either consummates or obstructs the sale.

A few definitions must be kept in mind to fully comprehend retailing. First, *retail stores* are establishments engaged primarily in retailing.[1] Also, *retailing* is an

---

[1]*Primarily engaged* is defined by the Census of Business as "deriving over 50 percent of revenue from retailing." Almost all retail stores are engaged close to 100 percent in retailing. Exceptions are retail establishments that sell and service products and sell some parts to repair technicians, such as automobile and some television dealerships.

activity that includes all retail transactions, including both store sales and nonstore retail sales. Nonstore retailing is accomplished by mail order, from catalogs, via in home purchases aided by salespeople, at vending machines or, in some cases, the place of manufacture, such as a craftsman's shop. All such transactions are retailing.

The majority of retailing is done through retail stores. As evidenced in Table 14-1, 97 percent of the 1978 retail sales of merchandise were store sales; 3 percent

**Table 14-1   Retailers Classified by Principal Lines Handled
Percentage Distribution of Total Retail Sales (1977)**

Durable Goods

Building materials, hardware, garden supply, and mobile home dealers	10
Automotive dealers (motor vehicles and auto supplies)	20
Furniture, home furnishings, appliances, and radio and TV stores	5

Nondurable Goods

General merchandise group (department stores and variety stores, including general merchandise discount stores)	13
Food stores	22
Gasoline service stations	8
Apparel and accessory stores	5
Eating and drinking establishments	9
Drug and proprietary stores	3
Liquor stores	2
Nonstore (mail order, direct selling, and vending machines)	3*

*When catalog sales by mass merchandisers such as Sears, Montgomery Ward, and some major discount chains are subtracted from the general merchandise group and added to nonstore volume, this sales volume approaches 10 percent.

Source: Derived from *Survey of Current Business,* December, 1978, pp. 5–12.

were nonstore sales. (Retail service sales such as medical services, education, and repairs are not included here. They are the subject of Chapter 17.)

MERCHANDISE LINES HANDLED

A *merchandise line* is a group of related products. *Merchandise assortment,* or *product mix,* is the range of goods offered by a firm. Retailers must determine the *width* and *depth* of the assortment to handle. Width refers to the number of lines and depth to the selection within a line. A supermarket may have several nonfood lines, including a few tools—giving it a wide assortment. Within the department that offers tools, supermarkets are likely to have one kind of hammer—a shallow selection. A hardware store, on the other hand, will have a narrow assortment but more depth in each line—nine types of hammers, for instance. Table 14-1 displays a broad classification of store types according to the principal merchandise lines sold.

In the Census of Distribution retailers are classified according to the product line which provides the major portion of a store's sales. You know that some retailers handle several lines and others specialize in products within one line. Further, *mixed merchandising*—sometimes called *scrambled merchandising*—arises. That term means that a store adds width to its assortment by adding lines not traditionally related to each other or to the store's original product assortment.

To understand how retailing operates it is convenient to classify retailers not only by the type of products they sell but by categories that explain the different strategies or methods of operation employed.

CLASSIFICATION OF RETAILERS

It is useful to classify retailers as follows:

1. By strategies employed
2. By firm size and form of ownership
3. By location

Keep in mind that those are not mutually exclusive categories.

Strategies Employed

The strategy elements employed, you will recall from Chapter 2, are *product* type, quality, features, and diversity; *price* level and emphasis on price as a competitive weapon; type and amount of *promotion* employed; and *distribution* methods, including the number and type of retail outlets used.

Reasonably distinct categories of retailers can be identified according to how those strategy elements are used, as in the following classifications:

Department stores
Variety stores
Full-line discount houses
Supermarkets
Single-line stores
Specialty shops
Convenience stores
Some emerging types
Nonstore retailers

Department Stores. Department stores began in Europe. By the mid-1880's Wanamaker's in Philadelphia, ZCMI in Salt Lake City, and Macy's in New York City were established in the United States. Today department stores account for approximately 10 percent of all retail sales in the United States. Their operations have increasingly shifted away from downtown dominance in many areas.

Downtown department stores do about 1 percent of total retail business now, as opposed to 8 percent some years ago.

Department store development and dominance reflect influences in the external environment, as was pointed out in Chapter 2. First, growing incomes and population during the stage of booming department store growth increased the potential for sales volumes of marketing institutions. Second, the urbanization of population tended to concentrate purchasing power and buying in the shopping areas of cities. Third, the growth in the manufacturing and industrial structure was geared to turn out an increasing flow of manufactured goods. Fourth, the progress of scientific management pointed up the importance of getting maximum volume under one set of overhead costs and under one group of skilled managers. Fifth, the integration of the buying function made it possible for the store to bypass the wholesaler and buy directly from the manufacturer.

Advantages and Limitations of the Department Store. The department store is characterized by its wide offering of merchandise, divided into departments. On the average its sales exceed those of other stores in its operating area, and its clientele is predominantly made up of women. Department stores usually offer a considerable number of free services, including credit, layaway plans, delivery, and parking.

The department-store type of operation has its limitations. It is difficult for a large store to convey an atmosphere of warmth and personality usually found in small stores. In past years men were especially reluctant to patronize department stores. Many people preferred—and some still do—the personalized service that a clerk renders in helping them make their selection. This service is more likely to be available in a specialty store.

Further, active management of a department store is far removed from the point of the sale. Management influence that reaches to the floor of the store and motivates the clerk to respond with the same enthusiasm and interest that are found in the specialty shop is difficult to achieve. This is the weak link in the marketing flow. Additionally, department stores have frequently employed low-paid, part-time clerks who are not properly trained to give superior service.

Department stores are also plagued with high operating expenses. Although such stores achieve a high volume of sales, approximately 50 percent of their employees and 40 percent of their floor space are devoted to nonselling activities and functions. Thus, the average expense ratio for department stores ranges from approximately 35 percent to 40 percent. While such figures may be slightly lower than those of specialty stores handling similar merchandise, no distinguishable or marked savings are consistently evident.

Organization of the Department Store. One of the reasons for the development of the department store is specialized management. Most department stores follow a pattern of dividing responsibilities among four major functional areas—merchandising, store operation, financial control, and publicity.

Merchandising. Probably the most significant functional area is merchandising. This function is administered by a merchandise manager who is one of the four top executives of the store under the general manager. In this capacity the merchandise manager directs the activities of all who are engaged in buying.

Store Operation. Another significant area of organization responsibility is the maintenance of store plant and personnel. The selling floor must be attractive and presentable to the public. Constant innovations in layout arrangement are necessary. A nonselling staff numbering over half the total employees must be maintained and supervised. Service departments such as those receiving and marking merchandise and those which maintain, for instance, parking areas are significant operations in their own right in the large store.

Financial Control. Another significant function in a department store is that of financial control. A store is successful only if it shows a profit. The statements prepared by the controller's department provide information which enables management to analyze the operation of each segment of the business. The expenses and profits of each department are available in a separate statement.

Similar problems and standard accounting procedures make it possible to compare financial ratios and operating data among many stores. Such comparisons are useful because the success of merchandising methods and innovations can be tested by some stores, and reports of successes and failures can be shared with a group of stores. This is vital because most department store sales are now made by chains.[2]

Publicity and Advertising. One of the great challenges of the department store is the establishment of institutional prestige. Furthermore, it must communicate its merchandise values to the public in an effective manner. So important is this selling and communicative function that one of the four divisions of the department store management devotes itself entirely to its performance.

Variety Stores. The F. W. Woolworth Co. was the original variety store. Its founding arose from Frank Winfield Woolworth's experience while he was a young clerk in a dry goods store. A table of miscellaneous small wares over which he had placed a sign reading, "Anything on this table for five cents," was nearly cleared the first day. Succeeding trials of other experiments with some successes and failures taught Woolworth that location, large-scale buying, and careful monitoring of customer needs for low-priced household necessities were essentials for his kind of business. Imitators followed, and variety stores accounted for a considerable share of retailing for some years. Cultural and social changes, in addition to income shifts and changing downtown patterns, have resulted in the diminution of variety store influence.

Woolworth is the major factor in the variety store field. Its best selling products are sewing notions, candy, toys, plants, and men's and boys' clothing.[3] The

---

[2]See Malcolm P. McNair and Eleanor G. May, *The Evolution of Retail Institutions in the United States* (Cambridge, Mass.: Marketing Sciences Institute Report 76-100, 1976), Chapter 2, for an explanation and description of the development of department store chains.

[3]Woolworth: "The Last Stand of the Variety Store," *Business Week,* January 9, 1978, p. 85.

stores continue to offer convenience and slightly different merchandise than do discount stores. Location continues to be important. Over half of all variety stores are in downtown areas, and the most profitable ones are in rejuvenated downtown retail districts.[4]

The Full-Line Discount Store. Reduced prices have been widely used as a competitive weapon and, consequently, there have always been merchants who attempt to discount prices on some items. The name *discount house,* however, is attached to the type of operation that began immediately after World War II. The usual beginning was to advertise and sell brand name appliances at discounts as great as 40 percent lower than the usual price in other stores. The discounters gradually added to their lines and eventually offered almost everything found in department stores. The discount house entered the mass market with a low-status image, and its margins and prices have also been low.

There is no specific classification for the discount house in the census reports or other published organs. Official figures, therefore, are not available. The trade paper, *Discount Store News,* however, defines the *discount store* as one that contains (1) over 10,000 square feet, (2) sells both hard and soft goods, and (3) maintains a cost structure below that of a traditional store.[5] This definition does not permit drawing a sharp line of demarcation between a department store and a discount house. The offices of the F. W. Woolworth Co., for example, would rather have their Woolco stores considered as department stores, yet the *Discount Store News* lists Woolco as a discount store.

In the late 1940s and early 1950s the discount house entered the marketplace quietly by passing out membership cards to selected groups such as trade unions and government employees. It featured hard goods of respected brands and sold them below the existing fair-trade prices. At that time the discount house was not a low-status store. It was a mark of distinction for a person to hold a discount store card and buy at prices which were significantly lower than were legal under the resale price maintenance law. However, this period was short-lived. The idea spread throughout the nation—first in the large cities, then in smaller ones.

The rapid growth of the discount house provides evidence of the difficulty of maintaining a price structure based on law when it is contrary to the laws of supply and demand as expressed in the marketplace. For example, a 40 percent markup on refrigerators was not uncommon under the resale price maintenance law, and such a markup presumed a certain number of services. Such a margin, however, would make it possible for retailers to buy a refrigerator for $210.00 and sell it for $350.00. The discount house, if it could acquire sufficient volume, could sell the refrigerator for $262.50—a difference of $87.50. Other products were marked proportionately low. Such a savings was of sufficient magnitude to offset the services provided by the conventional store.

---

[4]For some causes of the decline of variety stores, see Rush Loving, Jr., "W. T. Grant's Last Days —As Seen from Store 1192) *Fortune,* April, 1976, p. 108.

[5]*Discount Store News,* Vol. V, No. 7 (August 22, 1966), p. 1.

This explanation should not be understood to mean that discount houses sell all their merchandise significantly below competing department stores. Like most other marketing institutions, discount houses have price leaders and also products whose margins are comparable with department stores in the same city.

As is usually true with innovations in retailing, there was a great expansion in discount stores. The expansion was followed by considerable numbers of failures. Those that have proved successful keep stores physically attractive, carefully follow consumer preferences, stress known brands, have credit facilities, provide for exchange or return of items, and staff the stores with people who can provide assistance and information.

Retail consultants point out that the discount chains that fail or are in trouble have not traded up in quality and fashion to meet the needs of consumers who are better educated and have more disposable income than did the customers attracted to discount stores two decades ago.

Despite present difficulties of some of the discount chains, there are approximately 3,600 discount stores in the United States, according to the Massachusetts Merchandise Institute—the trade association of discount stores. Their sales volume in the aggregate is probably two thirds that of all department stores.

The comparison of basic financial data of department stores and discount stores shown in Table 14-2 indicates their basic strategy differences. The higher gross margin and operating expenses of department stores is indicative of the services they provide and the higher cost locations of department stores.

Table 14-2   Department Stores and Discount Stores Gross Margin, Expenses, and Profit as a Percentage of Sales

	Department Stores	Discount Stores
Gross Margin	39.07	28.89
Operating Expenses	34.46	24.06
Profit before Tax	4.61	4.83

Source: "Retailing: Department, Mail Order, Variety, and Drug Chains: Basic Analysis," *Standard & Poor's Industry Surveys,* August 18, 1977, pp. R130 and R133.

Supermarkets.   Supermarkets differ in operations and, consequently, there is no recognized precise definition for what they are. It is safe to consider them as large stores whose main product line is food, including meat, produce, and dairy products, as well as packaged groceries. Method of operation is largely self-service, and no credit is generally offered (there are a few exceptions); they feature price promotions and provide large parking areas. Most supermarkets offer a considerable array of nonfood items.[6]

In Chapter 2 the development of supermarkets was used to illustrate the influence of external environments on marketing strategies. Review that discussion to help you explain the success of mixed merchandising by supermarkets. Merchants wanted to cater to a large portion of household requirements to take advantage of store traffic. The addition of high-margin or fast-selling merchandise, such as personal care items traditionally sold in drugstores, offered such an opportunity. (Years ago some drugstore publications referred to those additions as *merchandise piracy.*) Consumers responded favorably because they like one-stop shopping.

Single-Line Stores.　The strategy of this type store is to offer depth in one line. They prosper best when inventories are tailored to a specific market segment and when they have merchandise buyers and salespeople who can provide assistance, make recommendations, and thus make a good "fit" of the customer's need to the product. Examples of single-line stores are those handling men's clothing, women's and misses' apparel, hardware, furniture, and pharmaceuticals.

Home improvement stores sold about 25 percent of hardware and building supplies to ultimate consumers in the late 1970s.[7] They exemplify single-line stores which apply mass-merchandising strategies of price appeal, wide and frequently deep assortments, and self-service.

Do-it-yourselfers, who like the change in activity from their regular employment, who appreciate displays and explanations that show how to do a job, and who are attracted by the prices, appear to be major customers. This is another example of an innovation that came at the right time because the environment was right. Projections indicate that home improvement stores will capture 35 percent of the market in their lines by 1980.

The strategies of single-line stores and specialty shops can be considered together because they are so similar.

Specialty Shops.　Florists, jewelers, leather goods shops, bookstores, specialty food stores, such as meat markets, cheese shops, and bakeries, as well as distinctive-line shoe stores, are specialty shops. They carry a limited, narrow, but usually deep, assortment of goods in that part of a merchandise line in which they specialize. Note that specialty shops do not necessarily sell only specialty goods as such items are classified in the consumer goods classification in Chapter 4.

Several specialty chains geared to life-style segmentation are developing. Ski apparel and equipment stores in New England and the Rocky Mountain states, a large western apparel store in Denver, and jogging equipment shops are examples,

---

[6]See "Safeway: Selling Nongrocery Items to Cure the Supermarket Blahs," *Business Week,* March 7, 1977, p. 52.

[7]William R. Davidson, Albert D. Bates, and Stephen J. Bass, "The Retail Life Cycle," *Harvard Business Review,* November-December, 1976, p. 89.

as are Petrie stores, The Limited, and Miller World, which feature general fashions that appeal to specific life-styles.[8]

Response to affluence, flexibility, and new interests by specialty shops which appeal to that group of buyers who are not satisfied with offerings of the mass merchandisers accounts for the success of specialty shops. Their strategy usually emphasizes the product mix and location.[9]

An excellent example of identifying needs of a behavior segment is found in the inception and rapid growth of stores that sell only computers. Computerland, Inc., and the Calculator Shops, both operating several stores, have great depth assortments and trained salespeople to match almost any small computer need to an individual or firm.[10]

Convenience Stores. Convenience stores stock mainly food items with a few household necessities that are frequently purchased. These stores, typified by Southland Corporation's 7-11 stores and the Circle K outlets, illustrate how one can identify and take advantage of an opportunity that arises when competitive, cultural, and economic environments provide an opening. When large grocery supermarkets became the principal outlets for foods, customers who wanted to avoid check-out lines when they needed only one or a few items provided an opportunity. A typical 7-11 shopper spends three-and-one-half minutes and $1.01 per visit.[11]

Convenience stores are located near residential areas. They are small—about 1,000 to 3,000 square feet (the average supermarket is 20,000 square feet)—open long hours, and stock narrow and shallow assortments of fast-moving items.

The small inventory must be constantly checked to maintain balance in dairy, bakery, beverage, limited frozen food, grocery, and nonfood inventories. Central office management must be well organized and alert to maintain the standard operating procedures.[12] Despite failure of some chains of convenience stores in 1976, gross profit of these stores was nearly 31 percent as compared to 19 percent for supermarkets, and net profits were slightly over three times the one to one-and-one-half percent of sales in supermarkets. Customers are evidently willing to pay 12 to 15 percent more than supermarket prices for the convenience.

Some Emerging Types. Retail catalog showrooms, warehouse furniture stores, hypermarkets, and superstores are relatively new arrivals in retailing.

---

[8]Eleanor G. May and Malcolm P. McNair, "Department Stores Face Stiff Challenge in the Next Decade," *Journal of Retailing,* Fall, 1977, p. 54.

[9]For further discussion of the "new" specialty shops, see Joseph Barry Mason and Morris Mayer, "Insights into the Image Determination of Fashion Specialty Outlets," *Journal of Business Research,* Summer, 1973, p. 73.

[10]Gene Bylinsky, "The Computer Stores Have Arrived," *Fortune,* April 24, 1978, p. 52, describes Computerland, Inc.; and Marilyn Nason, "Calculators—Only Store Chain Scores Instant Hit in Boston," *Merchandising Week,* March 11, 1974, p. 20.

[11]Allen Liles, *Oh, Thank Heaven!,* The Story of the Southland Corporation (Dallas: The Southland Corporation, 1977) p. 231.

[12]Philip D. Cooper, "Will Success Produce Problems for the Convenience Store?" *MSU Business Topics,* Winter, 1972, p. 40.

Catalog Showrooms. The name describes the operation. A customer consults a catalog—which has been widely distributed by LaBelle's, Dahnken's, or one of the other retailers of this type—goes to the showroom, sees the catalog items displayed, consults with a salesperson if further information is desired, places an order, waits a few minutes for the item to be brought from the stockroom, and takes it home. These stores use catalogs and other advertising, in addition to discount prices. They keep costs down by warehouse stocking and using a relatively small display area. Usually they feature high-markup goods such as small appliances, luggage, jewelry, and sometimes cameras and outdoor products.

Warehouse Furniture Stores. Levitz Furniture Corporation, the pioneer in this retailing method, and Wickes Corporation are sizable chains. In most large cities an independent merchant with one or two outlets also uses this supermarket approach to selling furniture. Buildings of around 150,000 square feet, with not over one third of that space used for showrooms, are fairly typical. Most of these stores stock furniture whose price and style appeals to lower-middle income families, although Wickes is successfully catering to upper-middle and upper income segments.

Hypermarkets and Superstores. Hypermarkets, first appearing in France (Hypermarche) and Germany (Grosmarkts), with a few now in North America, are large in size, sales volume, and assortment. One located on the outskirts of Montreal consists of 250,000 square feet in the main store, plus a gallery containing a travel agency, an audio components store, other small specialty services, and a warehouse-type furniture outlet. There are 49 check-out counters and the annual sales gross is more than $35 million.[13]

Superstores, also built around product assortment and price strategies, are usually one fourth to one third the size of hypermarkets. They also provide all supermarket items plus large apparel, hardware, garden supply, outdoor activity, personal care, and housewares departments.

It is estimated that these stores accounted for 20 percent of all sales in food retailing in the late 1970s.[14]

Nonstore Retailing. Mail-order, individual or group (party selling) in-the-home, and vending machine sales are nonstore retailing methods.

Mail Order. Mail-order selling through catalogs or brochures sent to homes accounts for most nonstore retail volume. Mail-order retailing includes:

1. Sales by the general merchandise chains that distribute catalogs and have catalog order desks in their stores, as do Sears Roebuck and Co. and Montgomery Ward.
2. Specialty or novelty operations that present nicknack and decorator items or those such as Chris Craft which sell sporting goods and apparel to a special

---

[13]For descriptions of these stores see E. B. Weis, "Department Store and Hypermarché Competition," *Stores,* June, 1974, p. 40.

[14]"Can Jonathan Scott Save A & P?" *Business Week,* May 19, 1975, p. 134.

segment, as well as catalogs that feature holiday goods—fruit and candy assortments for Christmas, for instance.

3.   Individual stores that send catalogs or invite mail orders in their newspaper advertising.

Mail-order retailing has grown faster in recent years than has total retailing. From 1976 to 1977, mail-order sales increased 12 percent. Total retail sales growth was 9 percent in the same period. The increase in mail-order sales includes phoned-in as well as mailed-in catalog sales by Sears Roebuck and Co., J. C. Penney, and Montgomery Ward.[15]

Items sold include "hard cover books, $966 million (more than all bookstores combined); food, $230 million; ready-to-wear, $2 billion; records and tapes, $498 million."[16] Most mail-order sales are to city dwellers, and you can determine why from the external environmental changes, especially social and cultural, in Chapter 2.

In-Home Buying.   Direct sales, in-home or door-to-door methods account for less than one percent of retail sales but are important for Avon, Fuller Brush, Amway, and a few other companies. Direct sales merchandising is an expensive way to market something because (1) a large number of people are approached to find the few interested in the product and (2) goods are handled in small quantities, making the costs of inventory, storage, and shipping per sale higher than in usual channels. Some of those costs have been reduced by party plans, whereby a group of people is introduced to the product at one time.

Nonstore retailing has increased in recent years because shopping as recreation has been somewhat displaced, for many people, by other activities. The growing numbers of families with both parents working, families with small children at home, and elderly people who find it difficult or inconvenient to get to stores also encourage in-home shopping.[17]

Retailing by Size of Firm and Type of Ownership

On the average, retail establishments are growing larger while the proportion of stores to population is diminishing in the United States. In 1940 there were 132 million people and 1,770,000 stores, or 1.3 stores for every 100 people. In 1977 population was nearly 220 million served by 1,900,000 stores, or 0.8 stores per 100 persons. There are still, however, a large number of small retailers.

Types of Ownership.   Ownership classification is by (1) *legal form*—sole proprietorship, partnership, or corporation and (2) control of units—(a) indepen-

---

[15]"Mail-Order Sales Topped $21.5 Billion, up 12%: Sroge," *Marketing News,* December 1, 1978, p. 4.

[16]Maxwell Sroge Company, Inc., *Newsletter,* undated.

[17]Peter L. Gillett, "In-Home Shoppers: An Overview," *Journal of Marketing,* October, 1976, p. 81.

Table 14-3   **Percentage of Distribution of Stores and Sales**
                     by Legal Form of Organization (1948 and 1977)

	1948		1977	
	Percentage of Stores	*Percentage of Sales*	*Percentage of Stores*	*Percentage of Sales*
Sole Proprietorship	70	35	77	19
Partnership	18	18	7	5
Corporation	12	47	16	76

dent ownership of one store, called a *single-unit* operation, or (b) a chain of stores, called a *corporate chain,* or *multi-unit* operation.

A corporate chain is a centrally owned and usually centrally managed group of stores, all of which handle essentially the same kind of merchandise. Each of the types of stores discussed in the previous section can be either a single-unit or chain operation; although, as is noted in the following discussion, some types of merchandise and operations suit chain control and management better than others.

Legal form concerns us here only as a measure of size. Because data on retailing by store size are insufficient, we use legal form of ownership as a surrogate, because most sole proprietorships are small.

The proportion of sole proprietorships has actually increased, but the share of total retail sales they enjoy has decreased from 35 percent in 1948 to 19 percent in 1977. In that same period, corporations have increased their share of sales from 47 percent to 76 percent.

Eighty-seven percent of all retail establishments in the United States are independent (single-unit) operations. Together they account for slightly more than half, 54.8 percent, of all retail store sales. The most recent, accurate tally of retailing by independent and chain organizations is displayed in Illus. 14-1. Notice that the information is from the 1974 Census of Distribution, which is based on 1972 data. We expect that when 1976 data become available we will see that the portion of retailing enjoyed by independents has diminished further, even though the proportionate membership of the establishment remains about the same. In the past two similar census, independents owned 87 percent of the stores while their share of total retail sales declined from 66 percent to 54.8 percent, as shown in Illus. 14-1.

Notice in Illus. 14-1 that the portion of sales by chains and single units varies according to the types of stores. Chains dominate department and variety store sales, but for furniture, women's wear, and drugstores, the largest portion of sales accrues to single-unit operations. There is an explanation of why that occurs in the following section.

Competitive Position: Small versus Large Retailers. Unquestionably small retailers in the aggregate have suffered from large-scale operations. One

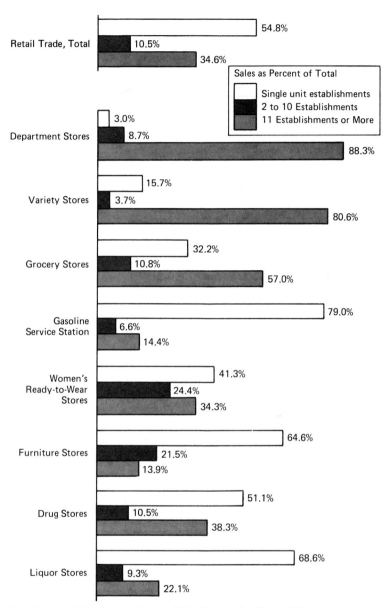

Source: U. S. Bureau of the Census, *Census of Distribution—Retailing*, 1974, pp. 1–2.

Illus. 14-1   **Percentage of Sale by Single-Unit and Multi-Unit (Chain) Firms (1972)**

should not, however, draw a trend line based on the numbers in Tables 14-2 and 14-3 and predict the demise of small-scale retailing.

There is tremendous variation in the capabilities of people who engage in retailing; hence, a quantitative study to determine factors affecting success would almost be meaningless here. We can, however, examine why small-scale retailers do better in some fields than in others, thus illustrating the comparative strengths of small and large operations. The discussion includes the areas of retail management, buying, operational expenses, promotional activities, and financing.

Retail Management. A one-store, small-sales-volume merchant cannot hire experts and specialists in management. Consequently, many merchandise and sales promotion activities suffer in comparison with those of large-scale competitors. Further, many small merchants are so engrossed in details that they have no time (even if they have the inclination) for basic management planning. Because of lack of merchandise budgets and other planning devices, they are often induced to overstock merchandise. Again, due to lack of planning, they often do not readily take markdowns to facilitate the disposal of slow-selling merchandise, with the far too common result that operating capital is tied up in unsalable inventory. Poor management is not, however, a necessary corollary to small-scale retailing.

If the independent merchant is somewhat lax in customer services and modern merchandising methods, there is no supervisory staff to improve store operations. On the other hand, there is flexibility and freedom of action precisely because the owner is not responsible to any higher management authority and can take action immediately. Flexibility and fast response to change can be a strong competitive weapon. Supervision, then, is necessary in large organizations to assure that all members of the organization conform to company policy. This is a cost that the small independent merchant can escape.

Although large-scale research and expert advice are not so readily available to the independent as to the unit manager of a chain, for example, the alert small merchant finds an increasing number of sources of managerial aids available. Trade organizations and federal government agencies provide information designed to assist nonspecialized operations. An excellent example of materials available through trade organizations includes those provided by the Independent Retail Hardware Association. IRHA, as it is commonly known, provides store layout help, merchandising aids, promotion kits, accounting advice, and other services that an independent hardware merchant might need. The United States Department of Commerce has available published materials of varying degrees of excellence on practically all management problems. The Small Business Administration has been formed to provide help structured specifically to small business of all kinds. Also, the National Council for Small Business Management Development can offer valuable training programs to managers of small businesses. Very likely there is a member of the council in the nearest university college of business and in large cities in the public school system.

Buying. The small merchant generally is at a comparative disadvantage in buying compared with department stores and chains; since he or she seldom buys in quantities large enough or regularly enough to gain preferred treatment, which might include first choice of materials and favored discounts and terms. Consequently, costs of goods sold will be relatively large in the small store. Whereas a department store or chain may have an initial markup of 42 to 45 percent on a man's suit, for example, the independent may well have an initial markup of only 30 to 35 percent. Yet the suit will carry the same retail price in both stores because of the higher cost to the independent.

Large retailers have access to research facilities that help them buy according to their customer demands. While such stores often do not have as wide a variety of goods available to customers as do independent merchants in the same field, customers often believe that the chain store and the department store provide them a wider selection because their research facilities have helped them decide what the majority of their customers want. Also, many manufacturers give preferential treatment to well-known department stores because they want their goods to benefit from the prestige of those stores.

On the other hand, a well-managed small independent, even with a limited merchandise budget, can buy selectively. With careful records and knowledge of the market, a small merchant of fashion goods, for example, can build customer loyalty because of attention to individual demands that is seldom accorded by any large organization. Selective buying and highly personalized selections from the market have built solid places in the retail community for many small retailers.

Operating Expenses. At this time there is no study that shows precisely how chain stores and independent stores compare in their operating expenses. Department stores, we know, tend to have relatively high operating expenses. Both chains and department stores effect much of their buying economy through performance of some of the wholesaling functions. Consequently, if we see only retail operating statements without evidence of how much transportation, storage, packaging, and other usual wholesale expenses are included, we do not have a valid comparison.

In general, it is safe to say that many small merchants survive because their out-of-pocket expenses are low. The owner-manager may not allocate any funds for salaries, for example. Members of the family divide the chores of store operation, and the entire household lives from whatever profit the store can make. Strict accounting might show not only a a high cost of goods sold but also a relatively high operating expense if a reasonable salary is allotted to the small store proprietor and if overtime, car expense and depreciation (when a car is used for deliveries), and similar assessments are made for all operating costs.

Sales Promotion. The small store cannot use newspaper advertising as effectively as the retail establishments with a large trading area, since the neighborhood grocery store, for example, draws its customers from an area of only a few blocks. It is not economical for such a merchant to advertise in the newspaper or on television, thus being charged for reaching all the potential customers in a large retailing area. Further, the small store has a high risk in experimenting with innovations that may attract new customers. A large department store or a unit of a chain, on the other hand, may limit experiments to a small segment of its business; and, if the new idea should prove ineffective, the entire company will not fail, since the bulk of its business goes on as formerly.

While it is true that small establishments do not have the full advantage of well-trained advertising and display personnel, they have a strong promotional device in their opportunity to establish pleasant personal relations with their customers.

Financing.　Again, department stores and chain organizations enjoy financial advantages over small stores. There are many individual exceptions, of course. Large retail enterprises receive more credit from manufacturers because they are large-quantity customers and because they usually have financial resources equal to their merchandise requirements. It is also easier for large-scale retailers to borrow from commercial banks or other lending institutions—often at more favorable interest rates than those required of small retailers. They can more readily acquire the financial resources for credit selling. These advantages place them in a position to effect better deals in buying, which in turn adds to their financial edge.

The growth and economic development of the nation favored large establishments. Improved roads, convenient transportation, and good postal and telephone systems minimized the advantage of convenient location enjoyed by such retailers as the cross-roads general store and the neighborhood grocery store.

Small Retailers Can Compete.　An examination of various business census since 1929 reveals that multi-unit firms have not made the same inroads into all retailing lines.

Illus. 14-2 is a list of selected lines of businesses in which single-unit firms account for over 75 percent of total annual sales volume. The dominance of single-unit operations can be explained by the brief analysis that follows. Further, identification of the areas of strength of small firms should suggest that effort be applied in those areas to provide competitive advantage to the single-unit firm.

In previous paragraphs it was pointed out that personalized services are a strong, competitive weapon for small stores. Does this hold true for all small stores? Consider those stores in which the selection of merchandise to fit particular tastes or requirements cannot be made in a routine manner. For example, slightly over 80 percent of sporting goods sales are made by independent (one- or two-unit) firms; whereas over 80 percent of discount house sales are made by multi-unit firms. Some of the merchandise handled by discounters is sporting goods. Can we

Passenger Car Dealers Drinking Places Florists Gift, Novelty, Souvenir Stores	Single-unit firms account for 90-97 percent of total annual retail sales of these types of stores.
Sporting Goods Gasoline Service Stations Meat and Seafood Markets Camera, Photographic Supply Stores Eating Places Book, Stationery Stores Hardware Stores	Single-unit firms account for 75-89 percent of total annual retail sales of these types of stores.

Illus. 14-2　　**Kinds of Businesses Dominated by Single-Unit Firms**

then postulate that the particular reason for the strength of independent operations in special sorts of items is the need for personalized services in such purchasing? If you will observe purchases of the items in discount stores and also in sporting goods stores, you will notice that a high proportion of the transactions in sporting goods stores involves consultation—i.e., the customer goes in with a problem and depends on the store people to help solve it. In discount store transactions, frequently not one word is exchanged.

It has been suggested that the central reason for the growth of chain stores in a certain field is that decision making can be routinized.[18] When the decisions of what to buy, of promotion and display, and of credit and pricing can be made routine, centralized management of several outlets is feasible. Holton suggests that mass distribution can be a means of reducing the cost of decision making per dollar of sales.[19] This thought can be extended to postulate that for certain kinds of businesses there will generally be a high cost of decision making per dollar of sales volume. Personalized service is necessary because the transactions cannot be made routine. Hence, in order to assess the probable strength of independent, single-unit firms in a given line or with a given group of customers, one may consider the extent to which all the transactions can be made routine.

Even in the fields dominated by multi-unit firms, there still exist sizable sales volumes enjoyed by single-unit firms. There will always be a portion of the market that demands, or at least desires, personalized service. Further, there exist sizable numbers of customers who do not respond to price or even to nonprice competition in a way that the majority does. For a number of customers for any kind of merchandise, personal service at the point of sale is critical, and the price elasticity of demand is small. Where there are sufficient numbers of these people, an independent small store can thrive. This group of customers becomes larger as personal disposable income increases. Hence, it should not surprise us that small stores are increasing their share of the market in some sections of cities, as well as in suburban centers.

Economic and sociological changes in the United States have favored concentration of retailing in many instances, and large-scale retailers have financial and promotional advantages over small merchants. Small-scale retailing is, nevertheless, certainly not doomed. Independent merchants who have reassessed their positions have found competitive weapons with which to strengthen their standing. Primarily the competitive position of independent retailers rests upon the cost-versus-satisfaction formula.

Small Store Niche. A small store's niche is found in providing satisfaction not available from the large mass-merchandising organizations. Small retailers cannot usually compete on price or massive promotion expenditures. Hence, they should consider the following sources of satisfaction: quality of the product itself; atmosphere and surroundings for shopping; attitude of the public toward the product

[18]Richard H. Holton, "Dynamic Marketing for a Changing World," *Proceedings of the 43rd National Conference of the American Marketing Association,* edited by Robert S. Hancock (June, 1960).
[19]*Ibid.*

(prestige or satisfaction from possessing a well-known product from a well-accepted outlet).[20]

Cooperative and Voluntary Groups.   The retailer-owned cooperative groups and wholesaler-sponsored groups described in Chapter 12 developed in response to the need for small merchants to gain or offset some of the advantages open to large-scale retailers. Ideally such organizations offer management, purchasing, and promotional strengths that allow the independents to maintain their inherent qualities of personal service, advice, and location to best serve those customers who are averse to mass merchandising.

LOCATION

Retail trade centers develop where it is convenient for customers to buy: first, at crossroads and harbors, then, with developing cities, in the central downtown area. As transportation and other changes facilitated urban sprawl, retail convenience stores followed into neighborhoods, and, finally, large clusters of stores developed away from downtown areas.

Downtown versus Suburbia.

During the period of rapid suburban growth from 1930 to 1960, the population living in outlying areas increased from 17 to 55 million—an increase of over three times. During this period the cities themselves increased in population from 37 to 58 million, or less than double. Retail trade followed the population from inside the cities out to the suburbs. In the decade 1960–1970 the central city population fairly well stabilized, but incomes increased somewhat more in the suburbs. Hence, downtown business districts throughout the country continued to lose retail trade relative to sales in the suburbs. The 129 major metropolitan markets' central city business districts had a 4 percent increase in retail sales in the Census of Retail Trade for the period 1963 to 1967. In the same period retail trade in suburbs of those metropolitan markets gained 34 percent. That 4 percent gain, small though it was, marked a reversal of declines for central city retailing that began in the 1940s.

Planned Shopping Centers.   Shopping centers appeared in significant numbers in the early 1950s. A shopping center is a group of stores contiguously located and developed under a master plan. Its success is based on convenience and a county fair atmosphere. The shopping center is the result of a promotion which has as its objective the housing of a variety of retail stores together. It usually includes at least one, and usually two or more, large and prestigious department stores. These institutions are described as power units since they have the power

---

[20]See John F. Cady, "Structural Trends in Retailing: The Decline of Small Business?" *Journal of Contemporary Business,* Spring, 1976, p. 11, for another viewpoint.

to attract the customer by their established prestige, broad lines of merchandise, and effective advertising programs. Small specialty stores, financial institutions, and service units are located strategically on lines of traffic between the power units and along the egress and ingress routes. Thus, within the shopping center itself, there is nearly every good or service that one would find in the city.

Now most shopping centers are covered malls, with a complementary and competitive cluster of stores arranged according to a master plan. This covered mall type of retail structure began to appear in America in the late fifties and early sixties. It has reached such popularity that most retail organizations indicate that they will build no new branches except as a part of a covered mall structure.

Downtown Malls   Detroit, Chicago, Boston, and Philadelphia, among other cities, have large developments that replaced deteriorated downtown areas with complexes of stores, restaurants, theatres, and offices. The Gallery in Philadelphia is built on land that housed a strip of cheap discount outlets, porno shops, and decaying, half-empty department stores.[21]

Some cities have built malls and park-like business district streets to maintain, or increase, downtown retailing before deterioration sets in.

Theme Shopping Centers.   Across the United States, Ghirardelli Square in San Francisco, Trolley Square in Salt Lake City, and Faneuil Hall in Boston, are illustrative of a development to induce a pleasant shopping experience. Abandoned railway stations, warehouses, street car barns, and other old structures are made into combination recreation and retailing areas.

In 1829 in Cincinnati, Frances Trollope (mother of the novelist, Anthony Trollope) built the Bazaar to house under one roof public places where men and women could mingle and "find leisure and intelligent amusement." The Bazaar contained retail shops, a coffee house, bar and a ballroom. Concerts and art exhibits were featured. It failed because it "was totally dissimilar to any other building in the country" and because it "was too far—one-quarter mile—from the center of business."[22]

The external environments were not right for the innovation.

Downtown Future?

The slight nationwide increase in retail business of downtown areas has resulted from quite large increases in a few cities. Among them were Buffalo, New York, which enjoyed a 13 percent increase in retail sales in its central business district; New Haven, Connecticut, a 32 percent gain; and Washington, D.C., 14 percent. In each case significant action was taken, such as improvement of public transportation, traffic-free malls, remodeling, or changes in merchandise offerings.

---

[21]Gurney Breckenfeld, "Jim Rouse Shows How to Give Downtown Retailing New Life," *Fortune,* April 10, 1978, p. 84.
[22]Helen Heineman, "The Angel of Faneuil Hall," *Harvard Magazine,* March–April, 1979, p. 50.

Much of the retail gain in central business districts results from changes involving shifts to specialty shops geared to pedestrians, public transit riders, and those persons who can shop during lunch breaks or in the evening when they visit downtown for cultural and entertainment events.

There may be, however, a return of regular shoppers to downtown. Increasing awareness of costly land, costly and finite limits on energy, smaller families, and desirability of fashionable and convenient in-town living will probably accentuate such developments. Edmund Faltermeyer, an editor of *Fortune,* reporting on a study tour by American real estate developers, city planners, and architects of Paris, Stuttgart, and Munich, emphasizes the livability and pleasure that can be enjoyed by inhabitants of cities. When easy access by convenient, comfortable mass transportation is provided to superb shopping malls, such as that surrounding the neo-Gothic City Hall on Munich's Marienplatz, shopping downtown gains favor.[23] The planned communities in the United States and elsewhere and the success of the best suburban shopping centers result from a recognition by alert retailers that many households "now want shopping to be part of an experience involving interesting crowds, food, and entertainment—not just buying and loading up the car."[24]

RETAILING'S DYNAMISM

The retailing methods that have succeeded are those whose introduction and innovations have fit the economic, cultural, technological, and physical environments at the right time.

Wheel of Retailing

Early department stores and, later, variety stores, supermarkets, and discount houses fit what Professor McNair described as the "revolving wheel" of retailing. An innovator attracts buyers with low prices made possible by low operating costs inherent in the innovation—low status physical facilities and few services. As the innovator prospers, others enter the field; then to maintain the business, the competitors offer services, nicer surroundings, and better location which add to costs of doing business and, consequently, increased prices. That leaves an opening for another innovator to start a business on a low-cost, low-price basis.[25] This does not explain all innovations, of course. Some of the specialty shop chains began as high-price operations, for example.

[23]Edmund Faltermeyer, "We're Building a New Kind of Togetherness," *Fortune* (October, 1973), p. 130; and "For a Glimpse of the Future, Look at the Old World," *Fortune* (October, 1973), p. 134.

[24]"Fortune's Wheel," *Fortune* (October, 1973), p. 2.

[25]Albert B. Smith (ed.), *Competitive Distribution in a Free High-Level Economy and Its Implications for the University* (Pittsburgh: University of Pittsburgh Press, 1958), p. 17.

Mixed Merchandising

When a supermarket, for instance, scrambles or mixes the grocery line by adding nonfood items, such as traditional drugstore items or hardware goods, then those stores, for survival, add to their lines. Hence, toys, housewares, and home improvement items are found in drugstores and on through the existing outlets who must adapt or fail. Mixed merchandising can result in the so-called accordian effect. Some retailers claim that lines can be scrambled, or stretched, only so far before they have to contract.

Increasing Polarity in Retailing

The moves for survival are reflected in two trends. One is toward limited-line specialty stores, some of which were described here, which provide personalized services and deep assortments. Another kind of limited-line store is the limited assortment food stores which have neither depth nor breadth of line, stocking, in a small building, about 600 items (supermarkets have 8,000 to 10,000 items), most of which are private label.

The other growth area is in mass merchandising, with economies of scale reflected in price appeal, large assortments, and self-service. The discussion of marketing logistics, pages 273–296, explains some of the management controls that enhance such operations.

Mass merchandising reaches a high point with *conglomerchants.* These are "multiple-line merchandising empires under central ownership, usually combining several styles of retailing with behind-the-scenes interpretation of some distribution and management functions."[26] As examples, J. C. Penney owns the Treasure Island stores and has added an income tax preparation service in some of its outlets. Sears Roebuck and Co. offers car rentals, insurance, and an income tax service. The Dayton-Hudson Corporation owns the Target discount chain, J.L. Hudson department stores, and B. Dalton bookstores.

THE FUTURE OF RETAILING

It is certain that by the time you read this there will be an innovation not mentioned here.

The stories of independents who have taken over grocery stores which grocery chains abandoned as failures should be encouragement to look for opportunities. In Washington, D.C., and Minneapolis, for example, independent merchants moved into locations where major chains pulled out. The areas contained many single-person and elderly couple households. Small-portion packages, single-serving cans, and pint or one quart cartons of milk met a need not filled by the chains. In Rochester, Minnesota, the new owner carpeted the store, keeps it open 24

---

[26]Rollie Tillman, "Rise of the Conglomerchant," *Harvard Business Review,* November–December, 1971, p. 44.

hours, installed two delicatessens, a restaurant, two meat markets—one with butcher service and one that is self-serve—and a large bakery. He also stocks a large department with gourmet items.[27]

As one type of retailing grows large, it almost inevitably creates an opportunity for an innovator, or a careful manager, to provide services or products that either ultra-specialization or mass merchandising eliminate.

Changes in the external environments, such as higher fuel prices or a restriction on using fossil fuels in private cars, further changes in family roles, in addition to the other shifts suggested in Chapter 2, may pose a threat to one kind of retailer but suggest opportunities to others.

QUESTIONS AND ANALYTICAL PROBLEMS

1. Define
   (a) Retail transaction
   (b) Retail store
   (c) Retailing
   (d) Nonstore retailing
   (e) Durable consumer goods
   (f) Merchandise line
   (g) Assortment width and assortment depth
   (h) Mixed, or scrambled, merchandising
2. What advantages are evidently unique to department stores?
3. What distinguishes a department store from a specialty shop?
4. Variety stores sell a smaller portion of total retail sales volume than they did several decades ago. How can you account for this relative decline in importance?
5. Many discount stores failed in the period between the mid-1960s and mid-1970s while other discount chains flourished. What basic retailing strategies evidently accounted for those failures and successes?
6. Examine Table 14-2, page 307. What can you tell from the data about methods and strategies

of department and discount stores?

7. Why do supermarkets exist? Explain fully why supermarkets flourished when they did—not 50 years earlier. Base your answer on the external environments.
8. What retailing strategy is exemplified by the addition of no-name grocery items in supermarkets?
9. From a consumer point of view what advantages and what disadvantages are there to shopping for an item in a specialty shop as compared to shopping for an item in the same merchandise class at a discount store?
10. List reasons accounting for the growth of home improvement stores.
11. Superstores are increasing in number and in relative importance at the same time limited-assortment, small retail outlets are successfully entering several markets. What lies behind the apparent success of each of these two divergent types of retailing?
12. Review the discussion of the economic and cultural external envi-

---

[27]Paul Ingrassia, "Retailing Rivalry; Independent Grocers Outsell the Big Chains by Adapting to Markets," *The Wall Street Journal,* November 28, 1979, p. 1.

ronments in Chapter 2 and then explain why mail-order retailing is growing at a rate that exceeds the growth rate of total retail sales.

13. Explain why corporate chains dominate sales of department stores and grocery stores and why single-unit operations are dominant for florists.

14. Compare a specialty food store, for example a delicatessen or a cheese shop, with a supermarket on the bases of (a) management, (b) buying, (c) operating expenses, and (d) promotion.

15. Over 75 percent of total sales volume of camera and photographic supply stores is done by independent operations, according to the most recent Census of Business. From observation we know that chains of camera stores are appearing. Explain why single-unit operations dominated that field for a long time; then explain why chains

16. Apply the maxim, play from strength, to explain what a small retailer can do to succeed.

17. Is downtown dead? dying? rejuvenating? Explain your answer and substantiate your explanation.

18. Why did Mrs. Trollope's Bazaar in Cincinnati fail? What retail management and strategy lesson is illustrated by that failure?

19. Provide three examples from your community of evidence of the revolving wheel of retailing. Also, find at least one example of an innovation that does not appear to fit the wheel theory.

20. A promoter asks you to invest in a hypermarket development in a city that has a population of 500,000. What questions are you going to ask before you invest?

21. What retail innovation have you seen that has not been mentioned in this chapter?

Case 14–1 DOUBLE J TIRE AND WHEEL ALIGNMENT

Harry Allen, the current manager of Double J Tire and Wheel Alignment, is contemplating a difficult question: how to increase the profitability of Double J. He is concerned about this for several reasons, the most important of which is his own job security.

Double J was started by two brothers, Jim and Keith Atwood, in 1955. Jim and Keith had both worked in the automotive repair business for some time. Finally, with a loan from Keith's father-in-law, the brothers rented a building and went into business for themselves. Jim generally ran the service desk and supervised the shop and shop personnel. Keith kept the books, did the buying, and sold most of the tires. An expert wheel alignment man was hired as an independent contractor. He was paid 50 percent of the revenues he produced.

Double J was successful immediately. In fact, it was so successful that by 1965 the Atwood brothers had retired from the business and had hired Harry Allen to run the shop. Under Harry's direction, Double J continued to prosper until 1975, when the competitive environment suddenly changed. In 1975 a large national franchise tire service center was constructed only three blocks from Double J. From that point on, life became more difficult for Double J and Harry Allen. In fact, Harry had been notified that unless the profitability of Double J increased by 20 percent in 1978, he would be replaced as manager.

In response to the pressure, Harry began to investigage why Double J was not as profitable as in prior years. His investigation led to the conclusion that his inventory of tires was not turning over as rapidly as before. A consultant from the Small Business Administra-

Table 14-A

Tire Lines	1968	1971	1976	1978
Radials	9.3	8.9	7.7	5.5
Belted	12.5	12.0	11.3	10.7
Truck	8.2	8.0	7.8	6.9

tion helped him compute the stock turn rate for his major tire lines for selected previous years. The consultant computed the stock turn rate by dividing cost of goods sold by average inventory at cost. The figures, shown in Table 14-A, showed a definite decline. Harry is unsure why the stock turn rate has dropped. The only thing he is sure is that his prices are competitive with other tire firms.

What are the probable causes of the drop of his stock turn rate? How will increasing the stock turn affect profit?

Case 14-2: JODY'S TEXACO

Jody's Texaco is a small self-service gas station and corner store. The station and store are operated by Jody Jones and Thelma Everest. The station and store are located on a major highway leading to a fairly large recreational area. The gasoline and petroleum product business results in $10 to $15 profit per day. Overhead costs alone are about $500 a month. Consequently, the store must pay for the remaining amount of overhead and living wages of Jody and Thelma.

Jody and Thelma are both in their 50s. Both have been married and widowed. Prior to taking over the gas station, they ran an apartment house in Southern California. Because of growing congestion, smog, and crime in Southern California, they moved to Clayton, Idaho, in 1975. Jody generally worked a shift and hired and trained others to handle the store. Thelma did all the store buying and supervised the operation of the gas station.

Jody's Texaco initially broke even. However, a large local following soon developed. Slowly the store and gas volume increased; within two years Jody and Thelma were prospering. During the third year, however, things changed. A Circle K convenience store was built on the same highway, a block from Jody's Texaco. When the Circle K opened, store and gas sales at Jody's dropped 40 percent. However, volume slowly came back and within a month stabilized at 80 percent of pre-Circle K days. The 80 percent figure applied both to gasoline and store sales.

Jody and Thelma analyzed the situation and believed that they should still be able to compete. They thought that a brand-name gasoline, flexibility in store merchandise buying, and friendly down-home service should give them certain advantages over the convenience store. The question they asked themselves was, How can these advantages be emphasized through the use of marketing tools?

With respect to pricing practices, promotion, product selection, and customer service, how can Jody and Thelma differentiate themselves from the Circle K and insure the long-run survival of the gas station and store?

15

wholesaling

Wholesaling, in its broadest sense, involves all sales transactions except those made to individuals or families for their personal consumption. Thus, it includes all sales of raw materials, sales of industrial goods from one producer to another or to an intermediary who resells to another producer, sales of all import and export items, and all sales to retailers.

Wholesaling evolved, and continues to exist because of certain characteristics of production and use. Goods are seldom consumed in the place and at the rate they are produced; certain geographic areas have a comparative advantage in product, but they are not always the areas of high consumption of their product; and industrial users do not always have local access to the variety of goods they want or need. Also, the most efficient rate of production seldom coordinates with the most desirable rate of purchase and consumption. Hence, provision must be made to have the required assortment of products at the place and the time they are needed or desired. The wholesaler serves both manufacturers and retailers or industrial consumers in the performance of this function. In the following discus-sions of some of the economic tasks performed by wholesalers, the explanation of the role of wholesaling will be restricted largely to consumer goods; but the principles will apply in some measure to the marketing of industrial goods as well.

MAGNITUDE OF WHOLESALING

The wholesale firm is not fronted with brilliant lights, nor does it dazzle with frequent double-page spreads in the daily newspaper or in the national magazines; seldom do we see wholesalers advertise on our television sets. Yet if we contemplate the institutions that make up any city, we become much more aware of the significance of this type of business. In 1972, 370,000 wholesale establishments did $695 billion worth of business, compared with $459 billion for 1,900,000 retailers during the same period.[1]

ADVANTAGES OF WHOLESALERS

Because of the conditions stated in the preceding introduction, there are certain economies inherent in wholesaling. In the following seven sections are summaries of each of the economic activities that allow efficient wholesalers to maximize their advantages.

Economies of the Re-sorting Function

Probably the most significant contribution of the wholesaler is economizing the time and energy required in the movement of goods and in the number of transactions that control them. The goods of a single manufacturer are sold by many retailers, and the goods sold by an average retailer are produced by many manufacturers. When manufacturers concentrate their sales on a few wholesale accounts instead of selling directly to the many retailers who sell their products, the number of orders that the manufacturer must process and the number of accounts that must be serviced are greatly reduced. To illustrate, if a producer of breakfast foods wishes to serve 2,000 stores in a wholesale region, the producer probably will be able to achieve complete coverage of these stores by dealing with ten wholesalers. Instead of 2,000 transactions there would be only ten, with consequent savings in sales calls, bookkeeping, credit expenses, and transportation.

Savings also accrue to the retailer. The average grocery store carries 6,000 commodities manufactured by at least 200 firms. If the manager of a grocery store had to make intelligent selections from all these varieties, he or she would have to allow time for a representative of each of the manufacturers. That would leave little time for other management functions. Furthermore, the retail buyer is not specialized in the purchase of the different commodities as are wholesalers who have specialized buyers of the several lines they handle.

---

[1]U.S. Department of Commerce, Bureau of the Census, *Statistical Abstract of the United States: 1977,* p. 829.

Savings in Transportation Costs

Total transportation costs for a given supply of goods depends on the number of shipments made by the buyer and the seller and the rate charged on the product being shipped. The rate tends to decrease as the size of the order increases. A manufacturing firm may ship enough of its entire line to a wholesaler to serve several hundred retailers. The wholesaler will then re-sort this merchandise into the goods demanded by each retailer, possibly delivering a full load of merchandise, representing the products of many manufacturers, to the retailer. By this operation a large-volume shipment of merchandise moves in both instances, and the number of shipments also is reduced.

To illustrate the economies possible in re-sorting and transportation, assume that ten retailers carry the products of ten manufacturers. If there is no intermediate wholesaler, each manufacturer must make a shipment to each of the retailers, a total of 100 shipments. Each manufacturer must keep an account and enter transactions for each retailer, which means keeping 100 accounts receivable. At the same time each of the retailers must receive ten sales representatives and keep ten accounts payable. This represents a total of 100 sales representatives' contracts and 100 accounts payable.

Now assume the presence of the wholesaler. Each of these manufacturers needs to make only one call and one delivery and carry one accounts receivable account, a total of 10 rather than 100 of each of these costly operations. Similarly, the retailer receives only one sales representative and keeps one accounts payable, reducing the total accounts payable to 10 instead of 100. The wholesaler makes 20 contacts, one each with the retailers and the manufacturers.

Without the wholesaler there were 200 contacts; with the wholesaler there were 40 contacts. Without the wholesaler 100 shipments were necessary to make contacts; with the wholesaler only 20 shipments were necessary, and these shipments were made in volume at lower rates. Thus, the savings in time, bookkeeping, wages, carrying costs of inventory, and transportation costs are what make wholesalers economically feasible.

Improved Sales Coverage

For a number of reasons, the wholesaler has a distinct advantage in performing the selling function. First, the permanence of the relationship that exists between the wholesaler and the retailer provides a reliable contact; second, the maximum degree of coverage of all types and sizes of retailers to which the wholesaler sells cannot be achieved easily by the manufacturer; third, wholesalers and retailers have a common tie, especially since the prosperity and the existence of both have been challenged by the growth and development of integrated distribution systems. In some instances this competitive pressure has forced the wholesaler into legal partnerships with voluntary and cooperative groups. Such a common challenge makes the wholesaler welcome in a store in which it would be difficult for the manufacturer's sales representative to develop a trusting relationship.

In the matter of coverage, the wholesaler enjoys an advantage. When the wholesaler's sales representative visits the small store, some kind of order is usually received because of the trusted relationship and because of the wide range or products that the sales representative carries. The order will probably be quite large compared with that given the manufacturer's sales representative, who may not even receive an order because of the narrow product line he or she represents. This fact makes it profitable for wholesale sales representatives to call on stores that would not purchase enough from the manufacturer's sales representative to make a call pay for itself. These small stores individually may not handle a significant percentage of the total merchandise that a manufacturer sells, but as W. C. Dorr wrote regarding such stores:

> (1) . . . for many manufacturers it is not small potatoes. In the aggregate, it runs as high as 50 percent of the total retail business of the country; (2) it's often the extra value that gets the sales department over the break-even point, where the headache stops and the profits begin; (3) it has been pretty well established that the wider the distribution in the secondary and third line stores, the greater are the sales in the major outlets. On many items people buy what territory-wide displays make them remember.[2]

Facility of the Merchandising Function

Being out of stock is evidence of failure in merchandising. Retailers find themselves out of stock because they do not order enough of the right stock at sufficiently frequent intervals. With the wholesaler's cooperation, the retailer can purchase small amounts because the wholesaler makes it possible for the retailer to reorder and accept delivery at short intervals.

In addition to this assistance, the wholesaler, by being a specialist in each classification of goods and by being in contact not only with many sources of supply but also with a wide field of retailers, is able to advise the retailer on lines that are selling fast and products that are new and that have shown promise. This is especially valuable for a small retailer whose own staff cannot specialize in buying areas.

Time and Place Utility

Manufacturing economies are frequently achieved if the manufacturer can produce goods at an even rate; but sales, especially consumer sales, typically vary throughout the year. Some manufacturers sell an entire year's output for a special season. A combination of storage by manufacturers and by wholesalers in anticipation of peak sales periods relieves producers and retailers of the entire burden of carrying inventories.

On the other hand, the wholesaler adds one additional stop for a product en route to the consumer. If the product requires consumption as soon as possible

---

[2]W. C. Dorr, "Direct vs. Jobber Distribution; An Appraisal of the Pros and Cons," *Sales Management* (February 1, 1949), p. 37; (February 15, 1949), p. 56; (March 1, 1949), p. 92.

after it is produced, the delay caused by this extra stop may be serious. Avoiding this delay may be sufficiently important to merit the additional expense entailed in direct sale. Perishable food and fashion items must reach the point of sale in the shortest time possible. If the wholesalers cannot streamline their operations, the advantage that they gain by providing time utility will be diminished. Instead the producer may go directly to the retailer.

Economy of Storage Services

By keeping a supply of goods available in the vicinity of the retailer, the wholesaler reduces the inventory that the retailer must carry to maintain an adequate assortment. The wholesale warehouse is a stock reservoir on which the retailer may call in case of need. If all the goods held as wholesale warehouse stock were stocked in retail stores, carrying costs would soar, since retail stores are located in high-rent districts. Ultimately such costs would be passed on to the consumer. Manufacturers can also warehouse their goods in the vicinity of the retailer. Because of the large volume resulting from carrying many lines of merchandise, however, the wholesaler can perform this function with less cost. There are exceptions that we shall discuss later.

Time utility is closely related to storage. Stock held in the vicinity of retailer demand would not be necessary if customers were willing to wait until the goods could be ordered and shipped a distance. It is also important to note that during the period of time when stock is in transit and in storage, it is the property of the wholesaler. Thus, the wholesaler assumes the risks. If the products are damaged or the price drops, the wholesaler bears the loss.

Facility of Credit

On many occasions the wholesaler makes a merchandise advance to a new business to help it get started. The wholesaler also carries the running account credit of most firms. It would be highly difficult for the manufacturer to perform this credit function as efficiently as the wholesaler. A firm that is on the scene of the retailer's activity and has a personal acquaintance with management can act with wisdom and skill in credit administration. Often, because of factors that the distant manufacturer cannot know, the wholesaler extends credit when not to do so would mean the failure of a firm that otherwise could become successful. On the other hand, investments have been saved as a result of the same wisdom in withholding credit or in collecting an account—decisions that might have been difficult if handled from a greater distance.

DISADVANTAGES OF WHOLESALERS

Even with these advantages, in many instances there are difficulties which render the wholesaler less effective in achieving the kind of selling effort that is desired by manufacturers. In the areas of business where the wholesalers are strongest, they usually carry several lines that compete directly with one another.

Under these circumstances it is difficult for the sales representative to emphasize one line of goods because (1) in a single interview the sales representative can aggressively sell only a few products since sales efforts must be divided over many lines and (2) the sales representative cannot, in justice to all suppliers, afford to push one line above others.

It is a great advantage for some products to receive direct, continuous, and active promotion from the time they leave the manufacturer until they reach the consumer. Hence, some manufacturers find it beneficial to control their products and to sell vigorously at every point along the channel.

WHOLESALERS VERSUS MANUFACTURERS

The conflict of interest between the manufacturer and the wholesaler is significant. The wholesaler has borne the brunt of a popular appeal to cut distribution costs. Our purpose in setting forth the case for the wholesaler so carefully at the beginning of the chapter was to make clear some obvious facts that may have been forgotten in debates about marketing costs.

During the decade of the 1930s, the eyes of the public were focused on distribution. It was easy to conclude that marketing cost too much because there *were,* in many cases, too many middlemen. It was also true that the impact of the competition which the chain store introduced into the retail field was not completely understood by the wholesalers. However, a change had to come. Chain stores began using their own warehouses. The development of highways and trucks revolutionized transportation; the means of communication via telephone and telegraph improved. With decreased travel and communication barriers, new routes to market became less costly and more convenient both in terms of time and trouble. These developments, accumulating over the years, converged on the wholesaler in the 1930s.

The Manufacturer's Case Against the Wholesaler

One of the problems that wholesalers had to meet during this period of challenge was declining enthusiasm on the part of the manufacturer for their services. Manufacturers began seeking a more effective route to the retailer. Some of the specific reasons for the manufacturer's attitude follow:

1. Failure to sell aggressively. Every manufacturer is strongly motivated to get the product to the marketplace first. Frustration results from the failure of the manufacturer to motivate the wholesaler to share the manufacturer's enthusiasm for the product. It has been mentioned that the promotion of individual products is difficult for the wholesaler.

2. The fact that some expenses may be eliminated by going directly to the marketplace. This statement has seemed obviously true. Many firms have found from costly experience, however, that the reverse is true. We have pointed out that, when all other things are considered equal, cost reductions favor the wholesaler because of re-sorting, transaction, and transportation savings. In some situations size of unit sales, volume of business, or location of outlets favor direct or branch sales.

3. Wholesalers promote their own private brands in competition with the manufacturer's brands. Usually the wholesaler's brands offer retailers better margins and, when all else is equal, wholesalers will sell their own brands. Such competition within the same company puts the manufacturer's promotional program at a disadvantage.

Wholesalers have a small gross margin to cover all operating expenses and profit. They must then buy carefully, since they cannot afford to carry obsolete or slow-moving stock. As mentioned previously, however, the market life of many products is short, increasing the risk of obsolescence. The wholesaler attempts to achieve maximum sales with an inventory investment as low as possible, and this in turn means that much of the burden of carrying adequate stocks still rests in large part with the manufacturer. All these factors have motivated manufacturers to seek further the practicability of setting up their own system of distribution. Other conditions, such as failure to service the product and to provide more rapid distribution to retailers, would be possible but most difficult.

The Wholesaler's Answer

The wholesaler has an answer to many of the charges made by the manufacturer and some accusations that can be lodged against the manufacturer. Like many other businesses, the wholesaler requires a volume operation to be successful. Wholesalers claim they cannot vigorously sell a product when a manufacturer deals directly with the large accounts, leaving only the small ones for the wholesaler. Such a line may be carried if there is any popular demand for it, but the promotional effort will be given to the firm whose products are sold by the wholesaler to large and small outlets alike. Volume is important to the wholesaler's profit, and it is difficult to achieve if the large accounts are serviced by the manufacturer.

Wholesalers also maintain that manufacturers must take a long-time view in their relationships with wholesalers. Such a relationship will be disturbed by the manufacturer's developing a new product and package for a certain line of products and then unloading the surplus of the old products before announcing the new one. Manufacturers who win the support of wholesalers must show a common interest in them, taking them into confidence on the development of new products, even before they are announced to the public. One example of this confidence occurred when a major drug manufacturer discovered a method of manufacturing penicillin at a greatly reduced cost. When the price reduction was announced to the trade, the company absorbed the losses that accrued on inventories held by wholesalers. Such a relationship results in sound wholesaler-manufacturer relationships and is the only type that will endure to the advantage of both parties.

Economizing Innovations. Following the lead of the retail field, wholesalers have sought means of economizing by using modern techniques and streamlining their operations. A food wholesaling firm, for instance, failed to make money because it did not have sufficient volume. The company had reduced its expenses from 10 percent of sales to 7 percent, but it continued to suffer a loss of volume. The consulting team that studied the situation discovered that two of the company's strong competitors, operating at margins of approximately 4 percent of sales, were winning the big accounts with their reduced prices. Significant, too, was the fact that the losing wholesaler was unaware of this price differential. Single-story operation, pallet and truck movement of merchandise, and machine accounting and control of stock and accounts receivable had been adopted by the wholesaler's competitors. These are but a few of the economies that wholesalers have made to meet competition.

Increased Aid to Retailers A hardware wholesaler once stated that he could increase the sales of practically every store he served by 33 percent, and some of them as high as 50 percent, by teaching the outlets merchandising techniques and layout fundamentals. This wholesaler had a model retail store set up in the showrooms of his establishment that he used as an instructional device for retailers. The same practice has been adopted by voluntary chains in the food field. Throughout the wholesale business, wholesalers have found it desirable to give aid to the retail accounts that they serve.

Increased Specialization. In some instances wholesalers have become specialists. In those areas where aggressive selling and promotion are important factors in the distribution of a line of merchandise, some wholesalers have taken exclusive distribution responsibility for the line and have sold the product aggressively. Look in the Yellow Pages under radio, stereo, TV, or kitchen appliances, and notice that certain wholesalers have exclusive distribution for certain brands. These listings indicate that where necessary and where the volume possibilities are adequate, a wholesale firm can distribute products in the same manner as a manufacturer's branch.

Improved Inventory Control. Increasing use by wholesalers of electronic data processing has improved stock control. Better inventory balance, anticipation of demand, and fewer stock-outs have resulted.

These examples of adjustments suggest that there are many other methods by which wholesalers can improve their operations. They will always have three fundamental factors in their favor: first, the economies that arise from the re-sorting process; second, close acquaintances with retailers and their problems through constant contact in a service capacity that is vital to the retailers; and, third, the complete coverage of retail firms—large and small.

WHOLESALING INSTITUTIONS

Wholesaling institutions include "establishments or places of business primarily engaged in selling merchandise directly to retailers; to industrial, commercial, institutional, or professional users; or to other wholesalers; or acting as agents in buying merchandise for, or selling merchandise to, such persons or companies."[3] Establishments of varying size, function, manner of business, and type of service are included within the scope of this definition.

The wholesale establishment did not spring into existence full blown. Each type evolved to meet specific needs of the period in which new opportunities became evident. Those institutions (middlemen) which have been able to move goods through market channels most efficiently have prospered. In their constant adjustments to meet requirements of a dynamic economy, many mutations and combinations have taken place, and still others are in process. Hence, it is difficult to phrase precise definitions of various types of wholesalers and to place each in a well-defined, clearly labeled category. Almost always some areas overlap. A manufacturer's agent, for example, may be difficult to distinguish from a broker because many of their operations are similar. Further, it must be remembered that census classifications are based on the principal business of an establishment. Hence, if 51 percent of a firm's volume derives from brokerage operations, it will be counted as a broker even though part of its effort is in another type of operation. Therefore, almost every description of a middleman that follows must either include or imply such qualifying words as *generally* or *usually.*

Table 15-1 lists the principal types of wholesale institutions now counted by the Bureau of the Census. Notice that merchant middlemen are by far the most numerous, totaling 91½ percent of all wholesale establishments. They also account for approximately 87 percent of total wholesale sales.

Table 15-2, derived from the *Census of Business*[4], portrays the principal customers of each of the broad classes of wholesalers. Notice that retailers, industrial and commercial users, and other wholesalers are the principal customers of wholesalers.

A brief description of each of the major types of wholesalers assists in understanding the role and importance of wholesaling. Only categorization and description by type of operation are presented here. One may refer to the Census of Business for classification by line of business, location, and ownership.

Merchant Wholesalers

Previous reference was made to merchant middlemen and agent middlemen. The principal categories of each type are presented in Table 15-1. The first category, merchant wholesalers, includes those who are referred to as

---

[3]U.S. Department of Commerce, Bureau of the Census, *Census of Business: 1967.*

[4]A *Census of Business* is made for each year ending in two and seven. Complete data from the 1977 census—completed in 1978—were not available at the time this text was prepared. Hence, 1972 data, the most recent data available at that time, were used to portray the relationships between the classes of wholesalers.

Table 15-1   **United States Wholesale Trade by Type of Operation**

Type of Operation	Percentage of Total Wholesale Establishments	Percentage of Total Wholesale Sales
Wholesale Trade Total	100.0	100.0
Merchant Wholesalers, Total	68.4	44.8
Wholesale Merchants	6.6	39.6
Importers	1.7	2.3
Exporters	0.7	2.1
Terminal Grain Elevators	0.2	0.9
Manufacturers' Sales Branches, Total	9.8	34.2
Manufacturers' Sales Branches—with stock	5.4	14.6
Manufacturers' Sales Branches—without stock	4.5	19.5
Petroleum Bulk Stations	9.7	5.4
*Merchandise Agents, Brokers, Total	8.5	13.4
Auction Companies	0.5	1.0
Merchandise Brokers	1.4	3.1
Commission Merchants	1.7	3.1
Import Agents	0.1	0.4
Export Agents	0.2	0.7
Manufacturers' Agents	3.9	3.3
Selling Agents	0.6	1.4
Purchasing Agents, Resident Buyers	0.1	0.2
Assemblers of Farm Products	3.6	2.2

*Agent middlemen—all others are classified as merchant middlemen.

Source: U.S. Department of Commerce, Bureau of the Census, Census of Business: 1972, and "Current Business Reports," Monthly Wholesale Trade: 1974.

service or full-service wholesalers and others who are called limited-function wholesalers.

Usually wholesale merchants are full-service wholesalers. They provide storage, sales representatives, delivery, order desks, credit, and usually, where required, repair services. They can provide wide retail outlet coverage and the full range of services because they can spread the cost of each sale and delivery call over a wide range of products.

A particular type of full-service wholesale merchant is the industrial distributor. The Census Bureau has defined an industrial distributor as an establishment that "handles a general line of industrial goods and sells largely to industrial users . . . establishments dealing in a more or less complete line of materials and/

Table 15-2 **Percentage Distribution of Sales by Type of Operation and Classes of Customers (1972)**

Classes of Customers	Merchant Wholesalers %	Agents and Brokers %
Retailers	36.8	20.8
Industrial and Commercial Users	40.8	41.0
Other Wholesalers	14.8	27.3
Consumers	1.3	0.3
Export	5.2	8.1
Federal Government	2.3	2.2

Source: U.S. Department of Commerce, Bureau of the Census, *Census of Business, Wholesale Trade,* 1972 pp. 4–5.

or supplies for mines, factories, oil wells, public utilities, and similar industries. Establishments engaged primarily in selling machinery are not included." For general purposes it is usually convenient and accurate to include organizations that buy and sell such equipment as machine tools and special screening and filtering equipment, even though such establishments would not maintain large general warehouse stocks and otherwise specifically meet the census definition.

As is the case with other full-service wholesalers, the industrial distributor usually can be classified as either (1) a *general house,* which carries a wide line of supplies and tools used by many types of businesses; (2) a *product specialty house,* which carries a rather complete assortment of each of a limited number of lines; or (3) a *trade specialty house,* which serves the needs of a particular type of customer and carries a full line of goods required by such customers—hotel and restaurant supplies, oil field supplies, and similar items. The range of services, reflected in their operating costs, average 14 percent (see Table 15-3). One must remember that those costs are average. Food wholesalers' costs are frequently as low as 3 to 4 percent.

Importers and Exporters. Merchants who largely confine their operations to buying primarily from foreign sources are classified separately from other wholesale operations even though they may be similar to other purchasing merchants. They are described in census publications simply as importers. Merchant wholesale establishments that are primarily engaged in selling to foreign markets are likewise separated in wholesale trade statistics and are classified as exporters.

Table 15-3   Selected Middlemen Operating Expenses

Type of Operation	Operating Expenses as Percentage of Sales
Merchant Wholesalers	
Service Wholesalers:	
Wholesale merchants, distributors	14.4
Terminal grain elevators	4.5
Importers	10.3
Exporters	4.1
Limited-Function Wholesalers:	
Cash-carry wholesalers	8.8 est.
Truck, wagon distributors	14.2 est.
Manufacturers' sales branches with stocks	11.3
Manufacturers' sales branches without stocks	4.1
Merchandise Agents, Brokers *	
Auction companies	2.9
Brokers	3.2
Commission merchants	3.4
Export agents	1.9
Import agents	2.2
Manufacturers' agents	6.4
Selling agents	4.2
Purchasing agents, resident buyers	3.6
Assemblers of Farm Products	8.6

*For all types of merchandise agents and brokers, the data represent the amount of brokerage or commission received rather than total expenses incurred.

Source: U.S. Department of Commerce, Bureau of the Census, *Census of Business: 1972, Wholesale Trade.*

Limited-Function Wholesalers.[5] Among the limited-function whole-salers are truck distributors, rack jobbers, drop shippers, retail-cooperative warehouses, and wholesaler establishments operated by and for consumer cooperatives.

Merchant wholesale establishments, distinguished by the fact that they combine sales and delivery functions and that they normally carry a limited assortment of fast-moving items of a perishable or semiperishable nature, are commonly called *truck distributors.*

These establishments commonly carry relatively small stocks in storage; indeed, in some cases, they buy only enough for one day's operation. The driver of the truck is also the sales representative, making sales calls and deliveries at the

---

[5]*Limited function* here means wholesalers who do not provide all the services commonly associated with large merchant wholesalers—services such as sales representatives, delivery, granting of credit, an order desk in the warehouse, large stocks in a warehouse, and repair facilities.

same time. Such operations are among the most costly of the various types of wholesaling because a truck is an expensive warehouse and because representatives make relatively small sales per call, usually sell in small quantities, and provide frequent delivery service. (See Table 15-3 for comparative cost of operation data.)

Snack foods, fresh coffee, salad dressings, some dairy products, and other goods that sell best when they are fresh and frequently restocked are the main stock in trade for truck distributors. Grocery stores, restaurants, and taverns are the chief customers of this type of wholesaler.

Not all trucks that deliver small quantities to such stores are truck jobbers. The classification is reserved for merchant wholesalers who buy for their own account and attempt to sell at a profit. Quite commonly such institutions are small business enterprises; the owner handles one truck and two or three other driver-sales representatives service accounts in the owner's trucks.

A recently developed class of wholesale establishment is the *rack jobber,* actually an extension of the truck distributor. Rack jobbers are merchant middlemen who sell mainly through grocery stores of the self-service type. The rack jobber arranges with the store owner for display space, which the rack jobber then supplies with various items. As a rule, rack jobbers specialize to some extent and generally confine their sales to one brand in a line such as drug items, household and kitchenware, or inexpensive clothing—socks, children's underwear, ladies' hose, and the like.

The rack jobber keeps stocked and in order the display rack on which his or her merchandise is arrayed. The rack jobber prices, displays, and sets up whatever point-of-sale material is appropriate. On the rack jobber's periodic visits to the outlet, the rack jobber restocks and bills the store for the amount replaced, thus, in essence, dealing with goods on consignment. Because of the services performed by the rack jobber, such as stocking, arranging displays, and pricing, retailers are generally willing to sell items that normally carry a 30 percent markup, for example, for a markup of only 20 percent when they are put in the stores by rack jobbers.

A *drop shipper* is a wholesaler who buys and sells goods but does not store them. Rather, a drop shipper arranges for the shipment of goods directly from the producer to the buyer. Drop shippers deal in bulky goods—bulky in the economic sense of being inexpensive per pound. Generally these goods are easily graded and are sold by grade; they usually are sold in large quantities and are most often available from several sources. From a sales volume measurement, coal and lumber are probably the most important items. An example of drop-shipper operations is found when a building contractor desires lumber of certain specifications. It is much easier and, in the long run, more economical for the contractor to buy from a drop shipper than it is to make all the arrangements alone. The drop shipper takes the order, finds lumber to meet the required specifications, buys it, arranges for its handling and shipment, and sees that the contractor receives the right goods at the time and place desired. The drop shipper may not actually see the goods but bears all entrepreneurial risks involved in buying and selling goods. The drop shipper owns the goods from

the time they are purchased until they are delivered and sold to the drop shipper's customers

The nature of the goods in which this type of wholesaler deals makes such
storage and handling prohibitively expensive. Because of an absence of storage
expenses and minor handling expenses, the drop shipper operates on a close
margin—a much smaller gross than does the typical regular full-service wholesaler.

Other limited-function wholesalers, such as retail-cooperative warehouses
and wholesale establishments of consumer cooperatives, are discussed with
their retail counterparts; hence, no further explanation of them will be made
here.

Noticeable trends in merchant wholesaler statistics illustrate how marketing
institutions respond to changes in the economy. The census of 1939 showed that
retailers were the customers for 59 percent of merchant wholesaler sales. In 1972
that figure was 37 percent. This is understandable since, as retail institutions
expand, they tend to do more direct buying from producers and manufacturers or
through resident buyers.

Another development is that there are more small specialty wholesalers in this
group than in 1939 and previous years. As more people move to urban centers
and as average incomes increase, markets for specialized products grow sufficiently
large to support specialty stores and specialty departments. Hence, wholesalers
specialize in order to provide better information and more depth in certain types
of merchandise. Large, general-line wholesalers who provide a wide range of
products have almost disappeared.

Manufacturers' Sales Branches

A succinct description of activities of manufacturers' sales branches is found
in the Census of Business definition:

> Manufacturers' sales branches are establishments owned by manufacturers or
> mining companies and maintained apart from producing plants primarily for sell-
> ing or marketing their companies' products at wholesale. (Branch stores selling to
> household consumers and individual users are classified in retail trade.) Sales
> branches or sales offices located at plants or administrative offices are included
> when separate records were available.

It should be noted that in the *Census of Business* manufacturers' branch houses which
sell appliances to retailers and builders are counted as merchant wholesalers.

Petroleum Bulk Plants

This is a category that does not differ greatly in type of operation but is counted
separately because of the special and restricted nature of products handled. Inventories are usually restricted to gasoline, kerosene, fuel oils, lubricating oils, and
other bulk petroleum products. The principal customers of bulk plants and terminals are retail outlets, service stations, industrial accounts, and other wholesalers.

Merchandise Agents and Brokers (Agent Middlemen)

The diversity and overlap of the services rendered and methods of operation employed by agent middlemen render accurate, distinct classification an impossibility. Hence, data on these establishments are often approximations, and those who measure them occasionally must use arbitrary definitions to determine where sales and establishments are to be counted. Within those limitations the following descriptions of operations are presented.

Merchandise Brokers. Merchandise brokers negotiate transactions—effect a meeting of minds—rather than consummate sales as do regular wholesalers' sales representatives. In a strict definitional sense, brokers never take possession of goods, assume title, or take the risk of price fluctuations. Normally brokers neither handle invoices nor finance either principal or customer. Producers who make use of brokers generally limit brokers' powers regarding prices and terms and require confirmation by the principals to make a bona fide transaction. Brokers are paid a commission based on, in most cases, the value of merchandise moved, but in some lines the commission or fee is based on the physical quantity of goods.

Brokers deal principally in food, farm products, and related trades, although they are found in some industrial lines. Since brokers assume none of the risks of price fluctuation or physical damage to goods, their fees are, of course, relatively low. Some high-volume brokers handle their business from home or hotel rooms without maintaining a regular office. This is possible because the brokers' most valuable product is their knowledge of market conditions, sources of supply, and other general market information. This is illustrated by examining the brokers' cost of doing business shown in Table 15-3. The average brokerage fee is 3.2 percent of sales.

Commission Merchants. Commission merchants are not merchant middlemen because they do not take title to goods. *Commission merchants* are distinguished from other agent middlemen in that commission merchants regularly take possession of the goods they handle, even though they do not take title to them. The type of commission merchant most familiar to readers is probably that found in large city produce markets. The commission merchant accepts goods on consignment and undertakes to sell them at the most favorable price and terms that can be negotiated.

The sales of commission merchants have declined in volume relative to other wholesalers of produce and basic commodities. Formerly, when farm goods were distantly removed from consumer markets in terms of time and information, there was so much risk attendant upon handling produce that wholesalers were not generally eager to purchase for their own accounts. The risks of price fluctuation and physical deterioration that followed when goods took a long time reaching the market and when market information was not readily available were too great. Farmers also found it difficult to follow price trends in central markets and, hence, had to rely on someone else to dispose of their produce. Commission merchant establishments developed to fill the needs created by these conditions. Today produce is sent to them on consignment; they receive and display it to the best of their ability. A commission, agreed upon as a percentage of the sales price received, is deducted by the commission merchant from the cash receipts, and the balance is sent to the producer.

Commission merchants handle a limited amount of merchandise other than agricultural commodities, but they are not major outlets for any such goods. Under the generally accepted definition, *factors* who specialize in such raw farm products as cotton are commission merchants and are counted as such by the *Census of Business*. [6] Even though commission merchants appear to provide a fairly wide range of services, the fees and commissions they charge are, on the whole, roughly equivalent to those received by brokers. This indicates that receiving and holding goods cost about the same as the seeking out that brokers do.

Manufacturers' Agents.   According to the *Census of Business* definition of *manufacturers' agents,* they are "establishments selling, on an agency basis, a part of the output of manufacturers, usually two or more, whose goods are noncompeting. Their principal duty is selling, although some of them warehouse goods for their principals." Manufacturers' agents are found principally in industrial and durable goods lines, but they also handle a relatively small volume of such lines as housewares, commonly found in grocery and limited-price variety stores.

The value and use of manufacturers' agents can perhaps best be explained by a hypothetical example. Let us suppose that the Agnew Company manufactures a high-quality industrial pump. For several years Agnew has enjoyed considerable success in markets close to the plant by selling direct, with one or two company sales representatives. The firm decides to expand operations into West Coast, Southwest, and Southeast markets. The company is not financially able to set up company outlets in centers of each of those markets; and even if it were, it is doubtful that its specialized product would achieve a sales volume sufficient to support an entire sales office in any of the areas. Manufacturers' agents, one in each of the market areas to be covered, who handle lines of goods that go to potential users of Agnew pumps, can be utilized. By spreading costs over several other lines in one or two industries with which they are intimately acquainted, manufacturers' agents can give good coverage for the Agnew product.

Characteristics of manufacturers' agents make them reasonable outlets for this type of distribution. These agents restrict their activities to a specified geographical area, handle part of the output of two or more noncompeting, but complementary lines, and are usually somewhat restricted by their principals as to sales and price policies. These agents generally have thorough knowledge of one or two industries that use the type of products in which they specialize.

---

[6] *Factor*—(1) A specialized financial institution engaged in factoring accounts receivable and lending on the security of inventory; (2) a type of commission house which often advances funds to the consignor, identified chiefly with the raw cotton and naval stores trades. Committee on Definitions, *Marketing Definitions* (Chicago: American Marketing Association, 1960), p. 13.

Keep in mind that the ideal has been described in all these descriptions. There is wide variance in capabilities of manufacturers' agents as in all other types of middlemen. Indeed, one may easily find among agent middlemen as a class a fairly large number of incompetent agents who are attracted by the lure of potentially large earnings and who enter the field without the knowledge and abilities that make them valuable representatives of their principals' products.

A particular type of manufacturer's agent, not classified separately in the wholesale census, but always considered as a distinct group in the trade, is the *food broker.* These agent middlemen, as described by their title, deal almost exclusively in grocery store and food products. Many of the most familiar products on the shelves of grocery stores are sold nationwide through food brokers. Generally, food broker establishments are small, usually consisting only of the broker and, at most, one or two assistants, although small numbers of them have fairly large staffs.

Quite commonly, food brokers handle from 6 to 12 or 14 noncompeting items for that many clients. They cover clearly defined territories that are of sufficiently small sizes to enable them to provide intensive coverage. They (we are assuming, of course, efficient operators) know their territories intimately and by spreading their costs over several items are able to cover them thoroughly. Their main job is to sell the principals' products by the best means available, such as store display, samplings in stores, assisting retailers with promotions that help to move the goods off the retailers' shelves, and intensive coverage of wholesale and chain-store buying offices. Food brokers are not expected to store, deliver, or otherwise handle goods, but often they maintain a small stock of each of their items from which they may make emergency deliveries if a retailer runs short before a regular order arrives.

Selling Agents. Selling agents, like manufacturers' agents, primarily sell goods for a client on a commission basis. Frequently confused with manufacturers' agents, selling agents do differ, chiefly in their scope of authority. Whereas the manufacturers' agent is limited geographically and policywise, selling agents arrange to assume full responsibility for selling the entire output of one or more products, but not necessarily the full line of their principals' plants; and they usually receive authority commensurate with that responsibility. Typically selling agents handle the output of two or more manufacturers, using their best judgment, based on wide experience, to choose the most desirable markets and selling methods. In some lines it frequently is found that selling agents perform such services as credit and collections, product design, and even production scheduling for the principals.

The extent and type of services rendered by selling agents and other middlemen are reflected in their cost of doing business. Table 15-3 reveals that selling agents as a group receive commissions of only 4.2 percent on sales. One must remember that the figures given for all agents and brokers is for commissions earned and not just expenses, as are the figures reported for merchant middlemen (see the footnote to Table 15-3). Further, the figures are averages—with a possible range existing between 2 and 9 percent. This is true of most of the operating expense figures stated for agent middlemen.

Selling agents are well suited to handle the output of a factory operated by skilled product specialists who have not become experienced in marketing techniques. Plant managers frequently are more efficient if they direct their skills exclusively to production, leaving marketing problems to a sales specialist.

As a result, selling agents often are found in industries that are characterized by many relatively small producing units which turn out products suitable for sale through many kinds of outlets and to a large number of users. Cotton textile mills in the middle and deep South are often served by selling agents. The manufacture of quality cotton fabrics requires tremendously specialized training and attention to detail and may well be conducted by relatively small mills. Customers of fabric mills are often also small-scale operators who are demanding in quality and design requirements. Hence, production specialists in that field generally find it profitable to attend to manufacturing and to have a selling agent seek out and satisfy the buyers.

Auction Companies. Auction companies are most commonly found in the marketing of leaf tobacco, livestock, fruit, and vegetables. These establishments usually provide places where the merchandise may be inspected prior to the auction sale, and then they either sell from that floor or provide an adjacent room where buyers and auctioneers meet.

Almost all cigarette tobacco is sold from auction barns by auction companies or single auctioneers who travel with the harvest. In large terminal markets, such as Chicago and New York, a majority of produce is sold through auction companies; and in many rural areas livestock auctions account for an important portion of total livestock marketing.

Fruit and produce auctions in terminal markets illustrate the essential features of this kind of marketing. Typically the goods are moved from rail cars or trucks throughout the night and early morning onto the floor, where "lots" of fruit and vegetables are on display. Around 5 or 6 A.M. a catalog is available for buyers. Buyers inspect the goods until sale time, usually about 7 A.M. At sale time the buyers move to their places in the auction room, which is simply a large hall with seats for buyers and a platform for the auctioneer and the shippers' representatives. Individual sales proceed rapidly, but it still takes a buyer most of the morning to obtain a full line of produce.

Auction companies are among the oldest types of wholesaling establishments and are found in all parts of the Western World, as well as in lesser numbers throughout the Middle East where they first may have developed. Auction companies furnish the selling staff and, in some though not all instances, the physical facilities wherein the sale can take place.

An auction is an excellent place to observe free interplay of price-making forces at work. Quality of goods on display, expert judgment on the part of buyers competing for the goods, and amounts of stocks on hand all play a role in establishing the price.

Auctions are rather cumbersome marketing agencies in that the buyers must physically inspect the goods and be on hand during the entire selling period. It is much less expensive to pick up a telephone and order a given quantity of a specific grade of an item. Nevertheless, auctions remain fairly important in sales volume since many goods do not readily lend themselves to simple classification.

Auction companies usually are paid a commission on the goods sold, although in a few markets a flat fee is charged. Table 15-3 indicates that auction companies have operating expenses of 2.9 percent of sales. Thus, it can be readily observed that they do not have great investments in facilities and services. Compare that operating expense ratio with a typical department store gross margin of 38 to 40 percent of sales.

Purchasing Agents.   Purchasing agents, resident buyers, and syndicate buyers who are in business for themselves and who purchase for clients on a commission basis are included in the category of purchasing agents. Actually these agent middlemen differ from buying brokers only in name and in the fact that they confine their operations to the dry goods, apparel, and general merchandise fields, while the group known as buying brokers is commonly found in industrial goods fields.

One classification of this group, resident buyers, is clearly distinctive in manner of operation and in the clients served. Resident buyers are found in the apparel and dry goods manufacturing and trading centers, where they maintain offices to serve retail store buyers. Resident buyers, or resident buying offices, become specialists in certain lines. Larger offices have quite large staffs organized somewhat along typical department store lines, with each person concentrating in the merchandise his or her retail counterparts will buy. When retail buyers go to market, they get product and price information bulletins from their resident buyers. Through such cooperation and service, resident buyers learn the needs of their clients; and when it is not practical for the store buyer to make a market trip, often the resident buyer is able to buy needed fill-in merchandise particularly suited to any given store client.

Farm Products Assemblers

Assemblers of farm products exist because there is frequent need to gather quantities of products from several producers to provide efficient performance of marketing functions, such as having optimum shipping lots. They are "establishments primarily engaged in purchasing from farmers and assembling and marketing farm products in local producing markets and in cities of producing regions."[7]

CHOOSING A CHANNEL

Choice of proper outlets and channels of distribution for a product is one of the most important decisions to be made by the producer of a good. There is no formula by which the choice may be made. Since quality of performance by various firms within a given category of middlemen varies widely, and because one can

---

[7]U.S. Department of Commerce, Bureau of the Census, *Census of Business: 1972.*

never know for certain whether the product will move better through another channel, it is difficult to determine which is the best type of outlet to use. The brief description of middlemen given here does indicate the kind of service that may be expected from each of the more important wholesale institutions and does show that in large measure one gets what one pays for. This is evidenced by the fact that a broker provides less service and advice than a selling agent. Hence, the broker's fee, on the average, is less than selling agent fees. Nevertheless, it must be stressed that differences in abilities of people and firms within wholesaler categories are great. Producers should exercise great care in selecting the institution through which to sell. They should learn how similar goods go to market, the reputation and abilities of various kinds of middlemen, and the type and quality of services available.

Remember that a wholesaler cannot do anything for producers or retailers that they could not do for themselves. The value of middlemen lies in their ability to do better and more economically the jobs required for effective distribution.

QUESTIONS AND ANALYTICAL PROBLEMS

1. If you made a sales call on a manufacturer of a low-priced, widely used consumer good in the United States, Europe, the Far East, or any other place, the manufacturer would almost certainly remark, "We use general wholesalers because_____. However, we don't like to use them entirely because_____." Fill in the blanks with what you think the manufacturer would say.

2. List the advantages of wholesalers as given in your text. For each of the stated advantages, explain why wholesalers can perform the economic activity more efficiently than retailers or manufacturers.

3. (a) What inherent disadvantages do wholesalers have? (b) What disadvantages, not inherent, often appear when a manufacturer chooses to use wholesalers rather than his own sales force?

4. Using cost as the only basis, how can you justify the existence of wholesalers in the grocery field?

5. List the criticisms that manufacturers often level against wholesalers.

Opposite each, state the wholesaler's answer to the criticism. Evaluate both the criticisms and the answers.

6. How have wholesalers, as a class of institution, met the problem of increasing operating costs over the past two or three decades?

7. Why is there an apparent trend toward specialized wholesaling?

8. What can a manufacturer's sales force do better than a wholesaler?

9. Check the wholesale section of the most recent *Census of Distribution* and prepare a list of the chief lines handled and the sales volume of each. What conclusion do you draw from the table you prepared?

10. In a large western city the oldest general line wholesaler has been selling parts of the business during the past few years. First, the firm sold its grocery business. Next, the drug department was sold, and recently the company sold its hardware department. A speaker at a business lunch referred to those sales and to examples of purchases direct from the factory in his own

business. His conclusion was that wholesale institutions were doomed since better transportation and communication facilities had rendered them no longer necessary. Do you agree? What can you learn from the wholesale portion of the *Census of Distribution* about the increasing or decreasing importance of wholesalers? Is the trend for various types of wholesalers the same as the trend for all wholesale business?

11. Why are service wholesalers more important in the distribution of consumer goods than they are in industrial goods?

12. Why have rack jobbers been a development of recent years? Why were they not prominent wholesalers ever since 1900, for example?

13. Draw a chart on which you show the distinguishing characteristics of each type of agent middleman.

List the various agent middlemen on the left side. Make headings across the top that describe characteristics. For example, *length of contract, extent of authority,* etc., could be headings.

14. A cannery that is one of the three or four largest volume processors of various fruits and vegetables in the United States is reviewing its sales methods. The company packs under its own label as well as under chain store brands. There is reason to believe that the present company sales force is too expensive. What middlemen should the company consider? Which one would you choose? Analyze the alternatives and give detailed reasons for your choice.

15. Explain the statement that there is nothing wholesalers do that manufacturers or retailers could not do for themselves.

Case 15.1 • THE SEA FRESH COMPANY

The Sea Fresh Company is a medium-size northwestern fish packer and canner that deals mainly in shellfish, Alaskan halibut, and salmon. The company currently maintains a sales force of 20 representatives who call on wholesalers and chain stores in 15 principal markets.

Because of increasing expenses, company executives are considering a change in the present distribution policy. As an alternative, Sea Fresh is considering the use of food brokers in each of the areas now covered by a sales representative, based on the belief that better area coverage as well as decreased costs will result. In large cities more than one broker can be used.

Brokers normally receive commissions of 3 to 5 percent of sales. The wholesalers to whom the brokers sell receive a margin of 12 percent, and retailers take a markup of 25 percent. The total marketing expense ratio of Sea Fresh Company currently stands at 20 percent of net sales, of which $350,000 is spent on national magazine advertising. Last year's sales were just over $4,000,000.

What losses in effective marketing will be incurred if the contemplated change is adopted? Will there be any gains? Estimate the savings in cost that may result from the adoption of the change.

Case 15–2 • REAL LINE LUGGAGE, INC.

Steven Schneider, general sales manager of Real Line Luggage, Inc., and the firm's president, Val Johnson, have been discussing the firm's distribution strategy. Schneider's position is that the current distribution strategy is adequate and, in fact, has many advantages for the firm. Johnson, however, disagrees.

Essentially Real Line Luggage, Inc., sells direct to various types of small and medium-size retailers. Sales representatives call on some retailers; other retailers place orders either by phone or mail. The number and quality of retailers is closely controlled by Schneider, who believes that Real Line Luggage should be sold only through dealers. Moreover, he believes that the competitive position of each dealer should be protected by limiting the number of dealers in an area and by encouraging all dealers to maintain the suggested retail price. Schneider thinks that selective distribution, quality dealers, and, as much as possible, uniform retail prices lead to lower volume but higher profits, better distribution control, and a better product and company image.

Johnson, however, thinks that the time for change has arrived. He has stated that using wholesalers instead of going direct to retailers will solve many problems. The advantages, as he sees them, include better territorial coverage, since the sales force will be able to contact directly all wholesalers rather than the hit-and-miss approach now being used to contact retailers. Also, physical distribution costs will be reduced. Large shipments can be sent to wholesalers at truckload rates rather than the more expensive less-than-truckload rates currently in use. Finally, wider distribution and therefore greater volume will result through the use of wholesalers.

Whose view do you support and why? Will the firm's production capacity have any effect on your decision?

6

Special Aspects of Marketing

16

international marketing

Ninety-two percent of all American firms sell only in this country. Ridiculous! For most, the cost of constantly changing product lines, with all the attendant start-up and marketing expenses, is greater than learning to export existing products. Exporting adds years to many a product line. Take the case of a Texas manufacturer of car and truck air conditioners. The domestic market was leveling off as more cars and trucks were sold with air conditioning as original equipment. The Texas firm "diversified" by exporting products to Japanese car manufacturers--with great success.

--"Seven Surprising Facts About Exporting,"
published by the United States
Department of Commerce

International trade exists for the same basic reason that trade between persons or firms within one country exists: human satisfactions are enhanced by such exchange.

Simply put, trade results because of *comparative advantage.* Differences in climate, natural resources, levels of technology, and craft or management skills provide one group of people (call them A) the facility to produce some goods easier, of better quality, or less expensively than others can produce them. Group A then trades goods with another group which has comparative advantage in producing something that A needs. People in Iowa or Ohio could grow bananas and papayas in greenhouses; but it is more efficient for them to grow other crops or to manufacture something else and sell it, and then to spend the revenue on tropical fruit produced where it grows better than corn, for example.[1]

---

[1]For a thorough and readable explanation of the theory of comparative advantage and new trade theories see Franklin R. Root, *International Trade and Investment,* 4h ed. (Cincinnati: South-Western Publishing Co., 1978), Chapters 2–4.

THE DECISION TO ENTER INTERNATIONAL MARKETS

As in any important business decision, prime motivation for entry into international markets will depend on how each individual firm views its challenges and opportunities. Among the principal reasons for the decision to "go international" are (1) opportunity for increased profits and (2) protection of present operations.

Opportunity for Increased Profits

The firm may identify a need for its present products in another country and decide that it is easier to increase volume by meeting that need than to penetrate further into the domestic market.

For example, a manufacturer of specialized mining equipment in the Rocky Mountain states found opportunities in other countries such that domestic market sales now account for less than half the total earnings of the company.

United States pharmaceutical producers found that relatively little expense was required to sell certain products in other countries; European automobile manufacturers found markets in other countries for the same reason. After expending large sums for product development these firms welcome the extra business.

Sometimes a firm takes a long view and enters a market that appears to be developing in the belief that when the country provides large and profitable opportunities it will be those firms with early entry that benefit. Hence, we saw five automobile manufacturers establish assembly plants in Peru. Any one of the firms could easily meet the total demand, but each wanted a foothold on what appeared to be a profitable market several years in the future.

Protection of Present Operations

Advertisements and news stories about Chase Manhattan Bank, Bank of America, J. Walter Thomson, Marsteller (advertising), Booz, Allen & Hamilton (accounting and counseling), as well as other service businesses, publicize their ability to serve clients in international trade. Many of these firms had to follow important clients to other countries or lose them to competitors in those countries.

An examination of the data on international trade reveals that marketing and processing raw materials account for approximately 50 percent of the total each year. Hence, companies requiring those materials have long been in international markets.

The Marketing Planning Guide (Illus. 2-2) and Integrated Analysis for Strategy Development (Illus. 2-1) in Chapter 2 can serve to evaluate markets and develop marketing plans and strategies for operations in any country or for trade between countries. It must be stressed, however, that more emphasis must be placed on studying and evaluating the external environments than is usually true for domestic marketing.

The range of variations such as size, age, and other demographic characteristics between individuals within a country, may be greater than the variation between "averages" of two countries.

If you prick us, do we not bleed? if you tickle us, do we not laugh? if you poison us, do we not die? and if you wrong us, shall we not revenge?
[William Shakespeare, *Merchant of Venice*, Act II, Scene 9.]

However, differences in all or some of the external environments—economic, cultural, physical, technological, political/legal, and competitive—are usually more striking and extreme than between regions within a country. Success or failure will depend on the assessment of whether the disparate influences impinge on acceptance or rejection of your product.

To heighten awareness of the effects of those differences and to stimulate interest in recognizing opportunities in international trade are the purposes of this chapter.

A MACRO VIEW OF TRADE

Leaders in volume of world trade are the industrialized nations.

Although the ranking of countries may vary from year to year, the countries in the list in Table 16-1 were the top ten a decade before, with the exception of Belgium-Luxembourg, which has been replaced by Saudi Arabia in the export column (oil, of course). Almost two thirds of world trade is done by these ten countries, which means that the 140-plus remaining countries shared in only one third of the total.

Table 16-1   **The Ten Leading Exporting and Importing Countries (1975)**

Percentages of Total Exports and Imports

	Exports		Imports
United States	13.5	United States	12.8
Germany (Federal Republic)	11.4	Germany (Federal Republic)	9.2
Japan	7.1	Japan	7.2
France	6.6	France	6.7
United Kingdom	5.6	United Kingdom	6.6
Netherlands	4.5	Italy	4.8
Italy	4.4	Soviet Union	4.6
Soviet Union	4.2	Netherlands	4.3
Canada	4.0	Canada	4.3
Saudi Arabia	3.5	Belgium-Luxembourg	3.8
TOTAL	64.8	TOTAL	64.3
World	100.0	World	100.0

Source: Derived from United Nations, *Statistical Annual Yearbook,* 1977.

Not only do the industrialized nations of the West dominate total world trade, but most of their trade is with each other. Over 70 percent of the exports of industrialized—i.e., economically developed—countries went to other industrial countries.[2]

CONTRIBUTION OF INTERNATIONAL TRADE TO GROSS NATIONAL PRODUCT

Even though the United States is the largest volume exporter and importer, international trade does not assume the same interest and importance as a contributor to that nation's total business as is true in many other countries.

At the end of 1978 merchandise exports from the United States, valued at approximately $142 billion, contributed 6.7 percent of the nation's Gross National Product (GNP), which was an increase from 4.9 percent in 1972. Many countries have much higher portions of GNP derived from international trade. In the Netherlands, Belgium, the Federal Republic of Germany, Switzerland, and Norway, export contributions to GNP of each country exceeded 30 percent.[3]

Those data do not reflect the importance of foreign trade for numerous individual companies. Singer, IBM, Coca-Cola, Gillette, Hoover, NCR, and other larger and smaller companies derive over half their earnings from international business.[4]

UNITED STATES FOREIGN TRADE

Broad categories of merchandise traded by United States firms, shown in Table 16-2, indicate the comparative advantages in agriculture and technical goods, and also illustrate that industrialized countries buy many goods in the same

Table 16-2   Percentage Distribution of United States Merchandise Exports and Imports (1978)

	Exports	Imports
Food, Beverages	14.5	9.2
Crude Materials and Fuels	14.9	30.2
Manufactured Goods	67.0	58.3
Other	3.5	2.3

Source: 96th Congress, First Session, *Economic Indicators*, January, 1979.

---

[2]See current United Nations, *Monthly Bulletin of Statistics.*
[3]Derived from United Nations Statistical Office, "Individual Country Data," *Yearbook of National Accounts Statistics*, 1977.
[4]United Nations, *Multinational Corporations in World Development* (New York City: United Nations, 1975), and "Big Players in the Global Game," *Business Week*, January 12, 1974, p. 53.

categories as those they sell. Manufactured goods are the major items sold and bought by United States firms. Notice also the large percentages of total trade from foods and crude materials. The United States sells many minerals and much lumber. You are aware, of course, that the United States imports much oil.

The principal trading partners of the United States are shown in Table 16-3, along with the portion of total United States exports and imports.

Table 16-3   Percentage Distribution of United States Trade by Area / Country (1977)

	Exports	Imports
Canada	21.0	21.7
Western Europe	28.2	18.9
20 Latin American Countries	13.5	11.0
Japan	8.8	12.8
Principal OPEC Countries	7.5	8.5
Others	21.0	27.1

Source: U. S. Department of Commerce, Bureau of the Census, *Highlights of U. S. Export and Import Trade, 1977.*

INITIAL INTEREST IN FOREIGN MARKETS

An owner of a relatively small plant that produces woven woolen goods received an invitation to an export development seminar sponsored by the Department of Commerce and the Small Business Administration. Before that he had not thought about export possibilities.[5]

Micro-Gen Equipment Corporation makes a somewhat unique and highly effective insecticide and pesticide spray device. The company received inquiries about the product from abroad before anyone in the company had even considered anything beyond a domestic market.[6]

A major corporation, as part of long-range planning, makes continuous assessments of markets all around the world.[7]

However the interest is sparked, the firm must answer this question: Is the return worth the effort, and what is the risk?

---

[5]Personal interview with one of the owners.
[6]Personal interview with the president of the company.
[7]Wilson, George, and Solomon, "Strategic Planning for Markets," *op. cit.,* describes General Electric's long-range planning.

The extent of risk will depend in a large measure on the method of entry into foreign markets.

ALTERNATIVE METHODS OF ENTERING FOREIGN MARKETS

Methods or strategies employed in entering a foreign market, ranked in order of least risk and investment to greatest involvement, are (1) exporting, (2) licensing, (3) joint ventures, and (4) fully owned manufacturing and distribution facilities. A fifth means is by management contract. Usually such contracts come about involuntarily because the government of the host country either expropriates a company and offers a management contract or the host country refuses to permit ownership of particular industries and will contract out the management.

These are not necessarily sequential steps, even though exporting is apparently most common as an initial entry. It is also the recommended entry strategy for small businesses.

Exporting

Quite often the motivation to enter foreign markets is to provide an outlet for the firm's excess manufacturing capacity with existing facilities. Hence, profits rise faster than total sales because fixed costs are being covered by the domestic sales.

Exposure to risks of a foreign environment, which includes possible misunderstanding or misinterpretation of the external environments, is minimized when the firm exports its already-existing products. It may make minor modifications, such as changing the electrical current components and using colors more acceptable in the foreign market, but fundamentally it is doing what it knows best. Consequently, the only risk is its investment in finding middlemen, producing some extra promotional materials, providing samples, and the cost of visiting the market.

Some companies with large commitments to foreign markets use exporting as a permanent means of selling abroad, for all or part of their product lives. Friedrich Manufacturing Corporation, a major supplier of refrigeration and air conditioning equipment, for instance, continues to sell its supermarket display cases through export agents because the volume outside the United States is not large, and the cost of using its own sales force would leave no profit. For other products the company maintains sales offices either alone or in joint venture.

Methods of accomplishing export sales may be divided into three general categories: (a) sales through a firm's domestic marketing organization, (b) indirect exporting, and (c) direct exporting.[8]

---

[8]See *Export Marketing for Smaller Firms,* 3d ed., available from the Small Business Administration.

Sales Through a Firm's Domestic Marketing Organization. These sales usually are made through individuals or firms located in the exporting country and known as buyers for export. A buyer for export usually is treated as a domestic customer and may be served by the domestic sales force.

Buyers for export can be independent or under contract. Independent buyers for export commonly watch for merchandise that can be purchased at a bargain, perhaps distress merchandise that can be sold abroad. They do not represent a manufacturer on a continuous basis. Buyers under contract act for clients abroad much as do resident buying offices that purchase for retail store clients in the domestic market. Many foreign department stores retain buyers for export in New York City, and United States department stores retain buyers in Western Europe.

Indirect Exporting. Indirect exporting involves delegating foreign sales responsibility to an export representative located in the United States. The representative works with the manufacturer to see that the firm's products and related material are appropriate for foreign markets, and then most of the sales effort is carried on by the representative's own export sales force and/or network of foreign distributors.

A large portion of companies engaged in indirect exporting use either a combination export manager (CEM) or a manufacturer's export agent (MEA). A CEM typically handles exports for several clients. They work closely with their clients, operate under the client's name in business transactions, and in essence function as low-cost, independent export departments. A domestic parallel is the selling agent. MEAs operate in foreign markets very much as manufacturers' agents do in the domestic market. (Review selling agents and manufacturers' agents in Chapter 15.) Their main benefit to their clients is the understanding they have of the foreign markets in which they operate.

Piggybacking, or having their product sold by manufacturers of related products, has proved to be profitable for a fairly large number of United States producers. This arrangement works well when a firm, not experienced in foreign markets, has a product that complements those of a firm with a well-established distribution system abroad. As examples, electronic components, ancillary or auxiliary equipment for communications systems, as well as supplies and equipment needed to service the products of the established manufacturer, have been marketed successfully by this means.

Direct Exporting. Direct exporting means that a firm retains control of its export marketing effort and deals directly with its own representatives or customers in foreign countries. This is done through marketing intermediaries, agents, or merchant wholesalers located in the foreign market, or by establishing sales branches in the market. Some companies employ traveling export sales representatives. Small firms frequently appoint foreign firms as representatives. These alternatives are not mutually exclusive; it is possible to use two or more methods simultaneously.

Direct exporting requires a much greater commitment than the indirect methods. The burden of evaluating market opportunities and the problems of management fall on the firm. It is beyond the scope of this chapter to present the attendant means, methods, and execution of such an operation. The brief introduction to analyzing markets in the discussion of the market/product profits in a later section will illustrate the magnitude of the task. Reference to sources of information presented near the end of the chapter will provide guidance.

Licensing

Licensing provides another means of entering a foreign market without large capital or executive investments. Patents, designs, manufacturing processes, and trademarks are licensed to a firm in the desired foreign market. Frequently the arrangement is for a one-time disclosure fee (patents and processes are provided), plus a royalty on all units produced. To insure quality the licensor will likely train and supervise production employees initially and then either maintain a production specialist in the licensee's plant or have randomly selected units sent to the home plant for testing and inspection.

Licensing may be the least profitable alternative for market entry. Scarce capital, import restrictions, or government prohibition of or sensitivity to foreign ownership may, however, make this the only feasible means to sell in a particular market.

Problems can arise when the licensee develops sufficient capability to enter the local market with its own brand or to become a serious competitor in other markets.

License agreements vary according to the host countries' laws and policies. A common royalty practice is for royalties to be paid for five years; a few agreements allow ten years. In some countries the agreement can be renewed once, but in other places no renewal is allowed.[9]

Franchising is a form of licensing and has been widely used by consumer goods companies in recent years. Holiday Inn, McDonalds, and Kentucky Fried Chicken, as examples, have made rapid growth through franchising and licensing their names, management techniques, and supplies.

Joint Venture.

A joint venture is an enterprise in which two or more companies share ownership, control over operations, and intellectual property rights (patents, trademarks, and technical processes).

Joint venture is the only means of entry when there are legal requirements for local participation. The Andean countries, Mexico, and others require that existing foreign-owned companies dispose of at least 51 percent equity to local investors,

---

[9]For a good list and explanation of precautions and care to be used in selecting a licensee or a joint venture partner, see Small Business Administration, *Export Marketing for Smaller Firms, op. cit.,* p. 129.

and no new companies may be formed where foreign ownership exceeds 49 percent.[10] In some countries existing domestic firms can elicit influence to prevent wholly owned foreign ventures. General Motors, as an example, had to modify its 100-percent-or-nothing policy and enter a joint venture with ISUZU in Japan.[11]

Total control is desired by firms which have sufficient capital and management personnel because that control facilitates implementation of company policy. The examples, however, show that it is not always possible.

For a small company it may be wise to enter a joint venture despite the possibility of conflict because of different management styles and philosophies, as well as disagreement over appropriate expenditures for marketing plans and strategies. A local firm will have access to channels of distribution and have an established reputation as a quality producer (assuming that care is exercised in selecting a reputable venture partner). Access to manufacturing facilities, understanding of the local culture, including acceptable business practices, and, in general, knowledge of acceptable and unacceptable behavior—both legal and societal—will be contributions the local partner can make.

Manufacturing and Distribution in the Foreign Market

An entry strategy of a company-owned subsidiary to manufacture and distribute in a foreign market is undertaken when a perceived large demand justifies the investment and risk.

The company now must understand the external environments thoroughly. Knowledge of the host country customers and language becomes essential.

This may be the only practical avenue to a foreign market, such as much of Europe, where the member nations of the European Economic Community (EEC) adopted a common tariff and essentially eliminated tariffs between member nations. It then became attractive for firms of nonmember countries to get behind that tariff wall by building or buying manufacturing plants in one of the EEC countries and thereby gain access to markets in the others.

The commitment and investment required by this entry strategy will be examined in the discussion of market opportunity analysis, planning and execution of marketing strategies, and transnational management sections that follow.

BEYOND THE DOMESTIC MARKET

As in domestic marketing, it is essential to identify target markets for international trade. First, it is useful to have an understanding of the general characteristics of world areas.

---

[10]See "Columbia in the Andean Group," *Colombia Today,* Vol. 8, No. 2, 1973, p. 8.
[11]"New Strategies for a World Auto Market," *Business Week,* December 24, 1973, p. 39.

General Classifications of Areas

Most nation-states are not willing to let *only* market forces determine their transnational trade policies; hence, one categorization of areas is by degree of political influence. Thus, there are the *market economy* countries where business is done largely by private firms as in North America, Western Europe, and Japan. Then there are the *managed economies* with state enterprises dominating trade—the Soviet Union, Eastern Europe, and the People's Republic of China. Those classes are further delineated by degree of economic and industrial development and the existence and maturity of the necessary infrastructure of transportation, communication, energy sources, and education. Lesser developed economies lack some part or nearly all the infrastructure development.

For market analysis today a classification suggested by Dr. James H. Gardner, former president of Armac and its predecessor company, Armour Chemical, is useful.

> *Resource rich—industrialized nations/areas*
>   Examples: United States, part of Europe, the Soviet Union, East
>   Germany
>
> *Resource rich—developing nations/areas*
>   Examples: OPEC countries, China
>
> *Resource poor—industrialized*
>   Examples: Japan, Switzerland
>
> *Intermediate—some resources, fair political stability*
>   Examples: Mexico, Brazil
>
> *The unfortunate vast majority*—either poor in resources or having abysmal
> political situations

Trade View Classification of Nations

Identification of a country's level of development or of where it fits in the resource rich/resource poor schema can provide preliminary information on the general types of goods required.[12]

At a low level of industrial development income is derived largely from agricultural goods and other basic raw materials. Demand is for specialized, expensive equipment to extract basic raw materials and for building transport facilities.

The development of primary manufacturing creates a demand for machinery to process materials previously shipped in raw form. Ores are pelletized, sugar is partially refined, processing of some foodstuffs is undertaken. Such items as fertilizers, basic chemicals, such as alum and bleaching power for a sugar refinery, and cloth bags are frequently imported in this stage.

When a stage of manufacture of nondurable and semidurable consumer goods is reached there are small, local manufacturers of such goods as shoes, batteries, plastic items, and home building materials. Total factories and supplies required

---

[12]Philip Cateora and John M. Hess, *International Marketing* (3d.; Homewood, Ill.: Richard D. Irwin, Inc., 1975), p. 363.

to support them may be imported. The supplies provide a submarket for repair facilities and tools, special lubricants, and special fasteners, for instance.

A fairly well-industrialized country, in the next stage, manufactures durable consumer goods and some capital goods. Refrigerators and, perhaps, automobiles and machinery are produced for domestic and export markets. A demand for heavy capital equipment and specialized machinery to support local manufacturing is evident.

> In Italy, for example . . . as a result of an increase in auto ownership . . . there is a sizable increase in the need for diagnostic and testing apparatus. There are presently about 2,000 shops that have this equipment, but there is need for approximately 23,000 repair shops with such modern equipment as wheel alignment indicators and motor analysis.[13]

When a country reaches the next stage, complete industrialization, it will have leadership in a large variety of goods, with specialization in certain lines. That means that the country will not produce everything it needs and will trade with other industrialized economies—the theory of comparative advantage at work.

Multi-Nation Markets[14]

Recognition must be made of the various forces of multi-nation economic groups. Opportunity to develop a market for your product may be either constrained or assisted if the attractive market lies in one of the economic cooperation areas. The arrangements for regional economic integration are regional cooperation for development (RCD), free trade areas, customs unions, and common markets.

RCD. A regional cooperation for development arrangement is an agreement among several countries to participate with one or more business firms to develop basic industries. Each country contracts to provide joint-venture financing and to purchase a share of the output produced.

Free Trade Area. The purpose of a free trade area is to build a larger market by reducing or eliminating the barriers to trade, including those between member countries. Rivalries and political tensions, as well as geographical barriers, keep some of them from full realization of the benefits, as is true of the Latin American Free Trade Association (LAFTA). However, free trade areas still exist and provide increased communication and cooperation. The European Free Trade Association performed well for over ten years until some of the strongest members joined the European Economic Community.

---

[13]*Ibid.*, p. 364.
[14]Derived from Ruel Kahler and Roland L. Kramer, *International Marketing* (4h ed.; Cincinnati: South-Western Publishing Co., 1977), Chapter 8; also Cateora and Hess, *op. cit*, Chapter 9. For a list of the major multi-nation economic groups see Vern Terpstra, *International Marketing* (2d ed.; Hinsdale, Ill.: The Dryden Press, 1978), p. 42.

Customs Union. A customs union agreement usually eliminates tariffs, or at least greatly reduces them, between members and also establishes common external tariffs on imports from nonmembers. Benelux countries (Belgium, the Netherlands, and Luxembourg) have had a customs union since 1921.

Common Market. To the dimunition of trade barriers between members and agreement on a common external tariff a common market adds agreements for free flow of capital and labor within the common market. The European Economic Community (ECC) stressed full economic integration, including common investment funds for industrial development, similar wage and welfare payments, antitrust legislation and common agricultural policies. Other common markets exist in Central America, the Andean countries, the Caribbean, and Africa. COMECON, whose members are the USSR, East Germany, Poland, and other Eastern European countries, features a common market.

WHICH MARKET? WHICH PRODUCT?

That brief, general review is a first step in selecting a market. The company cannot use a shotgun approach; it cannot supply the world. It must pay attention to volume. It takes as much effort to serve a 500-unit market as a 5,000-unit market. Further, most companies do not have sufficient research facilities and other resources to make it possible to understand all the political, legal, cultural, and economic constraints around the world.

Careful selection of target market segments is necessary. A market/product profile analysis is useful in determining which areas the company's resources fit or can be made to fit most profitably. A first step is to take the elements from the integrated impact analysis schema (Illus. 2-1, Chapter 2) and display them as is shown in Illus. 16-1, the Market/Product Profile. Next gather *pertinent* information about each of the external environments (left-hand column). Careful analysis

MARKET: X PRODUCT: Y	PRODUCT	PRICING	PROMOTION	DISTRIBUTION
ECONOMIC				
CULTURAL				
PHYSICAL- GEOGRAPHIC				
TECHNOLOGICAL				
POLITICAL- LEGAL				
COMPETITIVE				

Illus. 16-1   **Market/Product Profile**

of the information will let you know what modifications from domestic strategy are necessary. For example, economic and cultural information will very likely affect all four of the strategy elements: product, pricing, promotion, and distribution.

Thorough, careful preparation of country profiles pays off even though it is a demanding and tedious process. The company that exports only its excess and uses agents to handle its product will, of course, have to do a less thorough analysis than a firm that assumes more control of marketing in foreign markets. Information on the external environments helps identify products that meet needs and which will be accepted. The company's capabilities are known. The task then becomes to match company objectives and resources with the needs/opportunities in the target market.[15]

Company Foreign Market Objectives

How a company uses the information gained from an analysis of the market/product profile depends on its objectives in entering foreign markets.

At one end of a spectrum is a manufacturer whose interest is to derive most of its revenue from domestic markets; any sales abroad will be only excess production over domestic demand. Further along is a company that derives as much business from foreign markets as it can develop with its existing products or with slight modification of those products. On the other end is a company whose objective is to serve as many customers as possible wherever they may be.

Alternative Product Strategies

Product alternatives and management alternatives will be a reflection of the objectives sought.

Alternative product decisions to meet the company objective can be to (1) sell the same product at home and abroad, (2) individualize the existing products to suit needs and wants of each new area, or (3) develop new products. Those alternatives with the inclusion of promotion can be developed into basic strategies for foreign markets:[16]

1. Same product with same promotion wherever product is sold, as Pepsi-Cola and Coca-Cola do.
2. Same product but promote a different use for the product. For example, a small tractor used for gardening in the United States is sold as agricultural equipment abroad.
3. Alter the product to meet a local need but promote the same use as in the United States. Detergents that work in cold water are an example. (Detergents for cold water later become a product promoted in the United States, also).

---

[15]See Richard P. Carr, Jr., "Identifying Trade Areas for Consumer Goods in Foreign Markets," *Journal of Marketing,* October, 1978, p. 78 for a method of selecting a trade area for general product classes.

[16]Simon Mojaro, *International Marketing, a Strategic Approach to World Markets* (London: George Allen & Unwin Ltd., 1977), p. 53, and Cateora and Hess, *op. cit.,* p. 34.

4. Develop a new product for foreign markets. For example, Quaker Oats makes Inca Parina, a soft drink which is a dietary supplement based on a cereal grain for use in Andean countries. Both General Motors and Ford Motor Company designed rugged, basic trucks which are simple to manufacture, with a production line that is highly labor intensive, to be made and sold in lesser developed countries.

Avoiding Self-Reference Criteria

In an analysis of markets and evaluation leading to business decisions we operate without conscious reference to cultural norms and conditions around us at the home base. When firms go abroad, however, careful analysis is required to avoid an unintentional violation of the host country's cultural norms.

A self-reference criterion (SRC)—the unconscious reference to one's own cultural values—is the root of most business problems encountered by people operating outside their own country, according to James Lee.[17] We tend to agree. Therefore, as the market/product profile is developed it is a good idea to list the traits, economics, values, and needs or habits that are fundamental to the success of the product at home. Recognize that those are home market factors. From the market/product profile develop a similar list for the proposed new market from the information gathered, being aware of SRC. Data will not provide all the answers, of course; judgment will be required for decisions. This exercise should, however, help to diminish the influence of SRC.

EXAMPLES OF EXTERNAL ENVIRONMENT INFLUENCES

It is beyond the scope of this chapter to present a complete analysis for a specific product in a proposed market. The following examples are presented to illustrate how factors in the external environments may influence the decision of whether to enter a market and, if that is a go decision, which product strategy to use.

Economic Influences

A licensee manufacturer of office equipment in Peru estimates his market potential to be about equivalent to that of Toledo, Ohio, even though Peru has a population 20 times larger than that of Toledo.[18] Food expenditures, as a percentage of total family expenditures are about 20 to 25 percent in the United States, approximately 30 percent in the United Kingdom, and 70 to 80 percent in many less-developed countries.

The obvious point of these examples is the need to know how much income there is and how it is distributed in a country. Also, in countries where the average

---

[17]James A. Lee, "Cultural Analysis in Overseas Operations," *Harvard Business Review*, March–April, 1966, p. 106. He suggests a four-step process to minimize the effect of one's value systems on one's analysis of conditions in another society.

[18]Interview with the owner.

family income is abysmally low there may well be a market for luxury items. A two tier market is common. The few wealthy families buy high priced goods. The majority will provide a market for inexpensive transistor radios, textiles, pots and pans, and simple tools.

Cultural Influences

Errors arising from the difficulty of assessing and adapting to cultural differences can involve product design, advertising or other promotional methods, and marketing methods.

Variations in the use of household appliances and expenditures for other family purchases in Western Europe are explicable only, or in large measure, when cultural influences are considered. Use of automatic washing machines in the United Kingdom is about one third that in Italy; vacuum cleaners in Italy are one third the use in the Netherlands; food mixer sales per family in the United Kingdom are just half what they are in the Netherlands; and expenditures per family for holidays abroad are one fourth as high in Italy as in Germany.[19]

Language has an obvious potential for misunderstanding; many expressions in one language are pure nonsense when translated directly into another language. To convey the meaning of "He murders the King's English" in French, one should say "He speaks French like a Spanish cow."[20] Getting an *interpretation* rather than a straight *translation* would have avoided the oft-repeated General Motors blunder when "Body by Fisher" came out in Flemish as "Corpse by Fisher."[21] Sometimes a company is fortunate. Fresca is sold in both North America and South America. In Spanish, *fresca* means fresh—both in the sense of refreshing and of being new, as in a fresh idea.

Campbell Soup had success with condensed soups in the United States but failed in the British Isles where only ready-to-eat soup was acceptable.[22] A low-calorie promotional theme was inappropriate for snack items in Peru because poor people, who comprise a significant part of the market for the products, have a low-calorie intake.

A food processor erred in advertising canned fish in Quebec magazines and newspapers. The advertisement, which ran repeatedly, showed a woman in shorts playing golf with her husband. The copy message was that she could spend the day on the links and still serve a delicious dinner that evening if she used the canned

---

[19]See *Consumer Europe* (London: Euromonitor Publications, 1976), Chapter 3, for data and discussions of other variations in expenditures for household appliances, vacations, and other consumer purchases. Also see Robert T. Greene and Eric Langeard, "A Cross-National Comparison of Consumer Habits and Innovator Characteristics," *Journal of Marketing,* July, 1975, p. 34, for differences between consumer buyer behavior in France and the United States.

[20]See Maurice Brisebois, "Industrial Advertising and Marketing in Quebec," *The Marketer,* Spring-Summer, 1966, p. 10, for this and other references to French-Canadian cultural influences on buyer behavior.

[21] & [22]See David Ricks, Marilyn Y. C. Fu, and Jeffrey S. Arpan, *International Business Blunders* (Columbus, Ohio: Grid, Inc., 1974), p. 11, for this and other blunders.

fish. A cultural anthropologist advised the processor to change the promotion campaign because

> . . . every element in it violated some theme of French Canadian culture; a wife would not likely play golf with her husband, she would not wear shorts, and would not serve that particular kind of fish as a main course.[23]

Physical/Geographical Influences

Friedrich Manufacturing Company, the commercial refrigeration and air-conditioning equipment producer mentioned earlier, has found a number of geographic-related problems that affect international trade. Such problems include, for instance, fungus developing in such equipment in certain high humidity areas in Africa. In Saudi Arabia, sand and ocean air cause maintenance problems. In addition, certain potential markets are great distances from good central service facilities. Hence, modifications in the domestic product are required, including simplifications.

The Andes Mountains and the Amazon basin jungles affect distribution patterns and methods in the western part of South America. There is no integrated transportation system; nor is there good, rapid communication between the coastal cities and the high mountain towns. Types of vehicles required, placement and types of service facilities for mechanical products, and promotional methods must be modified to solve these problems.

Political-Legal Influences

Some countries have restrictions on entry into business, especially in retailing. In particular, France, Denmark, and the Netherlands have had such restrictions; but these countries are relaxing many of their stringent codes. France, among others, has had restrictions on chain store development. No unit of a chain could be located in cities under a specific population. Regulation of business hours is still quite common there and in England.

Labor laws on distribution policies must be observed. A bakery and snack items producer in Peru could neither revise nor reduce the number of driver-salesman routes, since labor laws place rigid limitations on firing people and on changing work conditions.

Tax laws, import regulations, both tariff and nontariff requirements, and currency exchange provisions vary greatly. Current and accurate information can be obtained from the U. S. Department of Commerce. Small businesses probably will want to rely on freight forwarders or other intermediaries to help them comply.

Almost every day newspapers report political changes in particular countries that not only affect the products that business may market but also determine the extent of marketing activities permitted to business. Political decisions

---

[23]Charles Winick, "Anthropology's Contribution to Marketing," *Journal of Marketing.* July, 1961, p. 55.

that affect currency exchange influence the activities of special marketing intermediaries. Barter brokers, who arrange trades of goods among countries where it is difficult or impossible to effect exchange of currencies, often play a dominant role in trade with eastern European and some developing countries.[24]

Summary Exercise

Use the analysis in Chapter 2 and the Market/Product Profile to illustrate an evaluation of the market for, say, automatic washing machines. Is a large supply of hot water available? If not, will cold water detergents and your company's machine perform well? Is electrical power available? Can your product adapt economically to the power supply? (The United States, Canada, and Saudi Arabia have 60 hertz [60 cycle]. The rest of the world uses 50 hertz.) What are the rating and standard requirements for electrical appliances? What is the per capita income? Do any but a few families have sufficient income to purchase an automatic washer? Do those who can afford a washing machine have servants who do the laundry? Are distribution and service facilities available? Do any regulations prohibit importation of fully assembled units, thus requiring that assembly take place in the country?

This list of questions is not exhaustive but does illustrate the necessary analysis.

SOURCES OF INFORMATION AND ASSISTANCE FOR EXPORT MARKETS

In this section the emphasis is on information sources that are of most value to small businesses interested in entering the export market. Firms that have reached the level of global or multinational business usually have developed their own sources.

The principal difficulties encountered by a small firm desiring to enter the export market are (1) obtaining market information that will enable it to assess the level of demand for its product, (2) selecting the best channel for distribution of its product, and (3) determining cultural differences that affect business and social practices that will in turn affect its relationships with the country and its customers.

The nearest Field Office of the United States Department of Commerce can provide materials and assistance that will be of significant help to the business manager who is seeking market information.

Trade Lists

Each trade list gives the names and addresses of firms that make, buy, or sell specific commodities or services in one country. It also contains a summary of the

---

[24]Falko Schuster, "Bartering Processes in Industrial Buying and Selling," *Industrial Marketing Management*, April, 1978, p. 119.

market potential for the commodity in question, government regulations affecting trade, basic information about each firm listed, and some general information on the country concerned.

Bureau of International Commerce (BIC) Trade Contact Surveys

The Field Office will help prepare the request for a trade contact survey that is tailored to specific requirements of a firm. The survey is made by the staff of the commercial attaché of the embassy in the country in which the company is interested. It is designed to help find several qualified firms in that country that are interested in selling the entrant's product.

Exposure of the Product in a Country

The manager of a firm may also request the Field Office for aid in getting the company's product introduced into a country by any of the following methods.

Trade Missions.   Trade missions may be organized by the government or by industry; in any case, the functions of these missions are similar. Four to six business people from the United States visit a country to introduce business proposals from the United States to that country. They meet with local business people who wish to examine each proposal and who, if interested, are put in touch with the United States firm concerned. Trade missions also carry back to the United States business proposals made by foreign companies. These proposals and trade mission reports are published in *International Commerce,* a publication available at the Field Office or by subscription.

Trade Fairs and Trade Centers.   With the aid of the Field Office, a product can be put on display in one or more of the 400 international trade fairs held each year at the six permanent trade centers in London, Frankfurt, Milan, Tokyo, Stockholm, and Bangkok, or at the Sample Display Centers located in Beirut, Manila, Nairobi, and Bangkok. There are also small versions of the trade centers, such as the Business Information Centers, which are distribution centers of business proposals by firms that do not wish to display their products. Such centers are established at international trade fairs where officers from the United States Department of Commerce are available to discuss the proposals with interested local business people and to help make commercial arrangements between interested companies.

Chamber of Commerce

The United States Council of the International Chamber of Commerce can provide guides to understanding and complying with trade requirements. Such publications as "Uniform Customs and Practice for Documentary Credits," I.C.C. Publication No. 290, which interpret international trade rules, are available.

American chambers of commerce and international chambers, such as German-American and Anglo-American groups, are established in over 40 countries to facilitate trade and understanding between the trade partners. Members can direct business executives to people in their trade, give advice on local customs, and generally facilitate entry into the market.

Assistance in Understanding the Country

Department of Commerce offices in the United States and commercial offices at United States embassies and consulates are primarily service offices whose mission is to help in the initial stages of entry into a market. That service has been valuable to many firms, especially those that are small or new entrants in foreign trade. According to one experienced commercial officer, a company that has experience and its own office in a country will usually be better prepared to solve specific problems than will the commercial office of an embassy or the U.S. Department of Commerce.

Interviews with managers of foreign operations and commercial officers in embassies of Europe, South America, and the Far East produced the following suggestions to business executives for gaining understanding of a country and its business practices:

1. Obtain from a Field Office, local library, or marketing departments of firms already doing business in the country a reading list that will acquaint you with the particular country.
2. Make a personal visit to evaluate the market. The embassy will usually be able to arrange interviews with people you should know, such as managers of other United States companies doing business with your potential customers.
3. Do sufficient homework before visiting the country. Allow enough time for the trip, considering holidays, working hours, and customs of negotiations. A most common fault is to plan an itinerary that does not allow for delays due to closed offices on holidays, long negotiations, and the like. An understanding of the language aids in interpreting polite acceptance or polite rejection and in making an overall evaluation of your acceptance. Hence, you should start at home to arrange interviews with persons who can help you make such interpretations and evaluations.
4. Be careful of decisions based on one or two visits with United States citizens in the country. Some will have "gone native" and not understand your dilemma and others with only short exposure will be full of misinformation. Local executives of United States firms already doing business in a sector allied to yours will probably be good sources of information.
5. Do not be too ready to assess all differences in trade practices as inferior to your own. It is trite but essential to be flexible and understanding. Enough sensitivity and perception should be developed to allow you to make an objective appraisal of the capabilities of the representative who will carry your business in that country.

Conditions Favorable to International Trade

International trade probably will continue to increase in volume. Two conditions will influence this trend: (1) the lowering of the distance barrier due to improved transportation and communication facilities and (2) the development of a political climate conducive to favorable relations between trading nations and an accompanying willingness to facilitate the exchange of different national currencies.

There can be no doubt that improvements in communication and transportation will continue. Air travel is decreasing the distance between world points. By means of modern communications, every community today is sensitive to what is taking place in other communities of the world. An increasing proportion of space on the front pages of newspapers is devoted to the foreign scene. Developments in communication and transportation and increased travel make people aware of foreign products. While trade between nations is somewhat more complex because of political barriers that do not exist in domestic trade, it is to be hoped that the well-being of people that is possible through increased trade will override political barriers.

QUESTIONS AND ANALYTICAL PROBLEMS

1. Define the theory of comparative advantage.
2. The prime motivation for seeking foreign markets is the same as it is for seeking domestic markets. Comment on this statement.
3. Who are the major trading partners of the United States? What general classes of goods do they sell to United States firms and buy from United States firms?
4. What effect will initial interest in export trade have on the distribution system selected?
5. What are the principal methods by which a firm may enter foreign markets? What are the advantages and disadvantages of each?
6. Define and explain how each of the following can be accomplished:
   (a) selling through the domestic marketing organization
   (b) indirect exporting
   (c) direct exporting
   (d) piggybacking
7. Why would a manufacturer in the United States decide to enter into a licensing arrangement in a foreign market?
8. What are some of the major risks in a joint venture?
9. Why do some companies establish manufacturing facilities and company-controlled distribution organizations in a foreign market?
10. List and define, in order of international cooperation, the various forms of multi-nation economic groups.
11. How can the market/product profile, as displayed in Illus. 16-1, help a manager avoid self-reference criteria?
12. Find examples of external environmental factors that influence
    (a) product design
    (b) distribution methods
    (c) promotional themes and programs
13. Find at least five examples of marketing blunders that occurred because of lack of information or understanding of environmental influences.
14. The owner of a small business is pondering the possibility and profitability of exporting part of the company's output. Outline the steps she should take to help determine whether it is a wise action to take. Include principal sources of information in your answer.
15. What is a trade mission?
16. What benefits are expected from participation in trade fairs?

Case 16–1 • L&N INDUSTRIES

Bob Beckstead, the acting president of Young Knives, of Gary, Indiana, has been contemplating the future of his career. The former president of Young Knives, Stewart Houston, recently was forced to resign by the board of directors because of certain legal problems the company is facing. Bob Beckstead, marketing vice-president and long-time Young employee, has been asked to temporarily run the firm. Since taking over, however, he has been besieged by lawyers, brokers, and others who want to purchase Young Knives. Bob is now attempting to decide the course of action he should take.

Young Knives is primarily a knife wholesaler. The firm purchases knives from various suppliers all over the world. The knives are built especially for the company and always carry the Young brand name and trademark. Young markets an entire line of knives for domestic and outdoor recreational use. The firm had sales in 1979 of about $18 million and has consistently been a good performer. In general, the Young line of knives appeals to discriminating buyers. This is because Young's quality and prices are somewhat higher than major competitors.

Young Knives was started in the early 1900s. The business has always been owned by the Young family, and the former president's father-in-law, Clyde Young, is now chairman of the board. The company has always been led by one of the family members until the recent hiring of Bob Beckstead. Clyde Young now wants to leave the business. He has recommended to the family that the firm be sold. Additionally, he has instructed Bob Beckstead to find a buyer.

Bob has received many offers. However, many of the offers are inadequate or potentially damaging to him and other company personnel. Being fired at the age of 55 is not something Bob wants to happen. He is aware that frequently the first act of the new management of an acquired firm is to fire all the remaining top executives.

The latest offer Bob has received is from L&N Industries in England. L&N has been one of Young's chief suppliers and a long-standing relationship has developed between the two companies. L&N's general manager has never been able to get along with Young's former president, Stewart Houston, but Bob Beckstead has always had a good relationship with the L&N executive.

According to the formal L&N offer, the entire stock of Young Knives is to be purchased at $5 above the current market price. Additionally, no changes in top management or current operating practices are contemplated. The offer sounds ideal, but Bob is uneasy. He can't understand why a foreign supplier wants to buy a company in the United States. He is also perplexed because the market for knives in the United States has grown very slowly.

What are some of the reasons that the British firm of L&N Industries would want to purchase Young Knives?

Case 16–2 • GLEEM COAT POLISH

Troy Christensen, the owner and chief executive officer of Christensen, Inc., manufacturers and marketers of Gleem Coat Polish, is facing a major decision: how to market Gleem Coat polish outside the United States.

Christensen, Inc., was started by Troy three months after her graduation from college. She borrowed $20,000 from her cousin, obtained the distributorship rights to a newly developed car polish, and went to work. She floundered for awhile, but soon established adequate distribution for the product. She paid back the loan and over a three-year period increased sales by 500 percent. Three years after starting the company, she added a new product to the line, an interior fabric protector. Both products sold well, and one complemented the other.

Troy is considering the international market for a number of reasons. First, competition is tough in the United States market and becoming tougher. Second, sales volume achieved by the company is much lower than is plant capacity. Finally, like all good business people, Troy recognizes that the international market offers tremendous opportunities. Troy also realizes that a high-risk factor is present when entering the foreign market. She believes that unfamiliarity with the country and its culture is the primary reason for the increased risk.

Troy has a number of questions about marketing outside the United States. First, she wonders where she should begin expansion. Second, she is unsure about the type of middleman structure to utilize. In the United States she sells through wholesalers and large chain retailers. Finally, she lacks knowledge of the government rules and regulations governing the exporting and importing of products.

In what country or countries do you recommend that Troy initiate the program and why? How can Troy investigate the middleman structure of a potential target country? Finally, how can Troy learn about government rules affecting her international marketing plans?

17

marketing of services

Marketing students and some professionals frequently associate the practice of marketing with physical products and the companies and corporations that market these products. For example, who among us has not admired the efficiency of General Motors in marketing automobiles or the excellence of Proctor & Gamble in developing and marketing products for household and personal use (i.e., Crest toothpaste, Tide detergent, etc.)? However, the marketing of goods is only one aspect of marketing. The marketing of service is a second broad concern of the field of marketing.

Before analyzing services and service marketing, consider the following contemporary examples. H & R Block and other income tax preparation services now complete over half of all personal income tax forms in the United States. Marketing techniques are used by these firms to gain both customers and employees. A second example of the growing importance of service marketing is found in the banking industry. Current bank marketing practices are far different from what they were ten or even five years ago. Banks advertise extensively, are constantly developing new products (i.e., automatic tellers, new forms of checking accounts, check guarantee cards, etc.), and even occasionally compete on the basis of price, as evidenced by such items as no-service-charge checking accounts. One bank has even used sales promotion coupons to increase business. Customers displaying a coupon when requesting a bank service received a discount.[1]

SERVICES: AN OVERVIEW

To understand service marketing one must be familiar with the distinction between a pure service and a product-related service.[2] Although both are important, this chapter will focus primarily on pure services.

Products can be defined as "a complex bundle of satisfactions which are related to the manner in which the product is perceived by the prospective buyer." Therefore, a product can include both functional attributes and psychological attributes. Additionally, some products are augmented with various services. Consider Illus 17-1. The end points of the line in Illus. 17–1 represent a pure good and

PURE
PRODUCT

PURE
SERVICE

Source: Adapted from John M. Rathmell, "What Is Meant by Services?" *Journal Of Marketing*, October, 1966, p. 32.

Illus. 17-1   **Goods-Services Continuum**

a pure service. The horizontal oval indicates where the majority of marketed products fall with respect to being either a pure good or a pure service. Specifically, most products are tangible in nature, but are sold with certain services implicitly or explicitly related to the sale. For example, computer sales representatives frequently emphasize the programming, software, and maintenance-related services of the firms they represent more than the actual computers and hardware. An example of a product-related service for a consumer product is the free alteration policy of many retail stores when clothing items are purchased.

Pure services, as noted in the far right of Illus. 17-1, are the primary concern of this chapter. The reason for this emphasis is not because product-related services are not important, but because the marketing of pure services is different in some respects from the marketing of tangible products.

Definition of Services

Pure services are activities, benefits, or satisfactions that are offered for sale where there is no exchange of tangible goods involving a transfer of title. Observe

---

[1]B. L. Steel, "Using Coupons to Sell Bank Services," *Banking* (September, 1973), p. 82.

[2]John M. Rathmell, "What Is Meant by Services?" *Journal of Marketing,* Vol. 30, No. 4 (October, 1966), p. 32.

the three important aspects of this definition. First, a marketing exchange occurs; that is, each party is giving up something of value to gain something of value. Second, the something of value acquired by the purchaser is an activity, benefit, or satisfaction. Finally, an exchange of title for a tangible good does not take place. Therefore, this definition does not exclude services that are frequently offered in conjunction with a tangible good such as air transportation or hotel accomodations. Examples of services included in this definition are amusements, hotels, electric services, hairstyling shops, repair and maintenance firms, financial institutions, and professional service providers such as doctors and attorneys.

Classification of Services

Services can be classified in many ways. Common classification criteria include type of seller, type of buyer, buying motives, buying practices, characteristics or attributes, and degree of government regulation. A synthesis of these methods follows.[3]

Some services are totally or primarily for ultimate consumers; other services are targeted toward businesses, nonprofit institutions, or governments. Examples of the former include life insurance, household maintenance services, and personal care services such as those provided by beauticians and barbers. Examples of services provided primarily to the industrial, nonprofit, or government market include consulting firms, advertising agencies, and accounting firms.

A second classification of services is based on whether the services are human or machine centered. Human-centered services are those in which the benefit to the user of the service comes primarily from direct contact with the service provider. Masseurs, lawyers, and doctors fall in this category. Machine-centered services include household utilities and all types of transportation and communication services.

Services can also be classified in terms of whether they are privately or publicly owned, and whether they are profit making or nonprofit making. Three categories of services are predominant here: private profit making, private nonprofit making, and public enterprise. Examples of the three types are, respectively, an accounting firm, a private college, and the Tennessee Valley Authority.

Finally, services can be classified with respect to the degree they are governmentally regulated and with respect to functions performed. Some service providers, such as utility companies, are highly regulated, while other service providers rely primarily on self-regulation. A common list of functions which classify services includes communication; consulting and business facilitating; educational, financial, health, and household operations; housing; insurance; legal, personal, recreational, and transportation services.[4]

---

[3]This classification of services was taken from John M. Rathmell, *Marketing in the Service Sector* (Cambridge, Mass.: Winthrop Publishers, Inc., 1974), p. 10.
[4]*Ibid.*, p. 17.

Services in the United States Economy

The service industry is an important and integral part of the United States economy. As shown in Table 17-1, the service segment of the economy is growing

Table 17-1   Services as a Part of the Gross National Product

(Billions of Dollars, Current Dollars)

	1930	% of Total	1960	% of Total	1965	% of Total	1970	% of Total	1976	% of Total
Gross National Product	164.5	100	506	100	688	100	982	100	1,692	100
Durable Goods	20.5	12.5	43	8.4	63	9.1	85	8.6	157	9.2
Nondurable Goods	63.0	38.2	151	29.8	189	27.4	265	26.9	440	26.0
Services	59.3	36.0	131	25.8	179	26.0	269	27.3	483	28.5

Sources: U.S. Department of Commerce, Bureau of the Census, *Statistical Abstract of the United States: 1973* (94h ed.; Washington: U.S. Government Printing Office, 1973), p. 320, #517, and U.S. Department of Commerce, Bureau of the Census, *Statistical Abstract of the United States: 1977* (98h ed.; Washington: U. S. Government Printing Office, 1978), p. 429, #690.

at a faster rate than the product sector. The reaction of many business people to this phenomenon was best summed up by one executive when he exclaimed, "Seventy percent of (GNP) growth is supposed to be in services and 30 percent is supposed to be in products; and I want to be in on that 70 percent."[5]

There are many ways to illustrate the increasing role that services play in the United States economy. This expanding role of services has been called a service revolution.[6] Evidence indicates that the service revolution has been spawned as a consequence of an increasingly affluent society: as people grow more affluent they have a greater desire or need for various services.[7] The usual explanation for this is that, as people become more affluent, they substitute pleasant activities for less pleasant activities. However, the less pleasant activities (cleaning the house or car or computing income tax) must still be accomplished. Therefore, people use some

[5]K. W. Bennett, "Service Industries," *Iron Age* (June 12, 1969), p. 78.

[6]William J. Regan, "The Service Revolution," *Journal of Marketing,* Vol. 27, No. 3 (July, 1963), p. 57.

[7]William J. Regan, "Economic Growth and Services," *The Journal of Business,* Vol. 36, No. 2 (April, 1963), p. 57.

Table 17-2   **Employment in Goods and Service Industries**

(In Thousands)

	1950		1970		1976	
	Number	Percentage	Number	Percentage	Number	Percentage
Construction, Manufacturing, and Mining	18,189	41.8	26,066	34.7	25,976	30.9
Services, Trade, Government, Finance, Insurance, Real Estate, and Transportation	25,337	58.2	48,994	65.3	58,092	69.1

Sources: Derived from the U.S. Department of Commerce, Bureau of the Census, *Statistical Abstract of the United States: 1960* (81st ed.; Washington: U.S. Government Printing Office, 1960), pp. 209–211, #271, and the U.S. Department of Commerce, Bureau of the Census, *Statistical Abstract of the United States: 1977* (98h ed.; Washington: U.S. Government Printing Office, 1977), p. 399, #651.

of their growing affluence to pay others to perform the less pleasant but nevertheless necessary tasks.

Perhaps one of the best indicators of the increasing importance of the service industry is that of service expenditures as a percentage of GNP. As illustrated in Table 17-1, service expenditures were very high in the late 1920s and early 1930s. As the full impact of the Depression was felt, consumers began to cut back on service expenditures. However, starting in the mid-1950s service expenditures as a percentage of both GNP and personal consumption expenditures have continued to grow.

A second way to evaluate the increasing role that services and service marketing play in the United States economy is in terms of the percentage of the work force engaged in providing services. As shown in Table 17-2, a steady increase in the proportion of employees in the service industry has occurred. This increase is indicative of how the United States economy is changing.

The Future of Services

The most widely held view of service marketing in the future is that services will continue to take an increasing share of the consumer's dollar. This forecast is based not only on extensions of past trends but also on the basis of cultural changes. As more and more material goods requirements are satisfied, people may turn more to services to gain satisfaction and self-fulfillment. Also, as two- and three-working-member households become more common, the limited time of household members may dictate that more services be purchased.

Service requirements by businesses and other institutions will also likely grow. As the business environment becomes more competitive and complex, the need for service-providing specialists will also increase. Additionally, many firms caught in today's inflationary period may attempt to save cash by contracting the performance of certain services that were once performed within the firm. Perhaps some day product development, product testing, or even planning, may be performed by outside experts who, in the short run, cost less than maintaining the capability within the firm.

Although the picture for service marketers in the future looks fairly bright, some concerns also exist. For example, severe inflation and, as a result, falling real incomes could cause many consumers to rethink their purchases of consumer services. Because many consumer services can be performed in the household if necessary (for example, car and house repairs, hair cuts, income tax preparation, etc.), consumers may cut back on their consumer service purchases if economic conditions drastically deteriorate. Services can be performed by household members, or at least postponed, but food purchases must be made on a regular basis. As a result, the potential exists that consumer services may not continue to grow as predicted.

INTANGIBILITY—THE KEY DIFFERENCE

The key difference between products and services is the intangible nature of services. Intangible, in this context, means two things.

> The crucial point about services is that they are doubly intangible: they are impalpable—they cannot be touched by the consumer; and they are difficult for the consumer to grasp mentally—what does the consumer purchase when buying life insurance?[8]

Because of these two factors, services are unique in some ways. These unique factors are discussed in the following pages.[9]

Consumed When Produced

Many consumer and business services are consumed as they are produced. For example, consider the doctor giving a physical examination, or the hairstylist cutting a person's hair. Although the utility of the service may last for some time (i.e., the feeling of well-being resulting from a new and flattering hairstyle), the service is actually consumed as it is produced. This one factor can cause many difficulties, including the participation of the consumer in the service, the inseparability of the service personnel and service

---

[8]John E. G. Bateson *et al., Testing a Conceptual Framework for Consumer Service Marketing* (Cambridge, Mass.: Marketing Science Institute, 1978), p. 11.

[9]*Ibid.,* p. 11.

environment from the client, and the interrelated nature of production and marketing.

Participation of the Consumer

Many services are human centered and can only be performed by people. An attorney, at least initially, must counsel the client; a doctor must examine the patient; and a portrait photographer needs a subject to create a portrait. In all cases the receiver of the service must be present for the service to be consumed. If the client is not present, the service is not produced.

A dentist's services cannot generally be produced and stored until consumers need the service. The patient must participate for the service to be performed. If the consumer refuses to participate, or more likely cancels an appointment, the service is not performed and the dentist's capabilities are underused.

Service Personnel and Environment

The simultaneous nature of production and consumption implies that consumption occurs in the service factory (i.e., the dentist's office). Therefore, long channels of distribution and middlemen are not possible in the service industry. Two options are available: service providers must either go where the market is, or they must bring customers to their location. This can result in a high fixed-cost operation because of the necessity of many sites to provide service, instead of one large plant which takes advantage of economies of scale.

The existance of many small sites of service production generally implies three things. First, capital requirements are not large and, therefore, entry into the service industry may not be difficult. Second, because entry is not difficult, and because of the difficulty of differentiating one service from another, the service industry is frequently very competitive. Finally, because of many small service-production sites, quality control or standardization in the service industry is very difficult. The quality of service can vary greatly among service producers.

Production and Marketing—Interrelated

The production and marketing of services are frequently interrelated. Service providers are frequently small, and many consider themselves professionals rather than business people marketing products. This explains the aversion of some doctors, attorneys, and other professionals to advertising. This fact also emphasizes the importance of word-of-mouth advertising in the success of some service providers. An attorney, dentist, or physician may easily and unknowingly develop a good or bad reputation through the word-of-mouth process.

THE MARKETING OF SERVICES

All products, including services, are marketed. However, because services are intangible, and because of the simultaneous nature of production and consumption, service marketing is somewhat different from physical product marketing. These differences are pointed out in the illustrations that follow.

Pricing of Services

Many factors determine how services are priced. Services differ so dramatically with respect to size and degree of government regulation that generalities are difficult to draw. Nevertheless, some generalizations are possible.

Some service providers such as physicians and dentists are frequently required to be members of a professional society. To a degree, these societies set standards of professional conduct and may even suggest fees for various services. Additionally, the providers of these services are in a unique position regarding pricing. Within limits, these professionals could charge exorbitant fees. A large majority of doctors and dentists practice what is called ethical fee setting. They recognize their responsibility and, in fact, their obligation to society; therefore, their fees are set in a range that gives most patients access to the medical services they require.

Because the standardization of services is difficult, considerable variation in service pricing exists. Consider the example of two women's hairstylists. One stylist may charge higher prices than another stylist for the same service simply because of factors such as reputation, experience, quality of work, or even professional background (European trained, for example) of the individual providing the service.

To a great extent, much of the service industry is composed of small suppliers of services. Moreover, a large number of small businesses providing a service is one characteristic of perfect competition. A second characteristic of the service industry is that of heterogeneity of the product. As mentioned previously, services are less frequently standardized than physical products. In spite of this, some similarity in service prices does exist. Competition is one reason. Competitive factors tend to keep prices fairly similar. A laundromat with washer prices set at 25 cents a load will attract more customers than one set at 50 cents. However, as the importance of the service to the individual increases and as nonstandardized services are called for, price variations will become evident. Prominent attorneys retained by clients involved in criminal trials are frequently able to ask for and receive fees that are much larger than the norm.

Regardless of the type of service, methods of setting prices are eventually the same as for product pricing. Prices can be set on the basis of cost, on the basis of demand, or on the basis of competition. Frequently a combination of two or three of the methods is used. Typically prices are set to cover costs, to provide a profit, and to be competitive with other service providers in the marketplace.

Finally, in the area of service pricing, government regulations and public opinion are perhaps of greater importance than in product marketing. Formal government regulation of pricing occurs in government-sponsored, but privately owned, public utilities. The local power company, the regional division of American Telephone and Telegraph, and the mass transit system all provide necessary and vital services. Various economic reasons exist for granting public utilities monopoly rights. However, because the monopolies are allowed to exist, prices are regulated.

Promotion of Services

The promotion of services, like the promotion of products, is an important factor in determining whether the service offering will be successful. Unlike products, however, service promotion presents some unique problems. These problems, in part, revolve around the intangibility of the service.

As already mentioned, intangibility of services means that a service lacks physical form or substance. When General Motors advertises an automobile, or when Proctor & Gamble advertises a detergent, the actual physical product can be illustrated, displayed, and pictured in various settings. In promoting a service the actual product cannot be so easily visualized. For example, what does life insurance protection look like?

Because of the intangible nature of many services, the benefit of the service is frequently emphasized in the promotional program. For example, New York Life Insurance Company emphasizes the primary benefit of financial security in its advertising program. This benefit is presented and emphasized in many effective and creative ways. The E. F. Hutton Company, a securities firm, emphasizes the quality of the investment advice it provides with its advertised motto "When E. F. Hutton speaks, people listen."

A second factor relating to the intangible nature of services is the importance of the reputation of the service provider. Potential purchasers cannot inspect the actual product or can do so only with some difficulty. Consequently, the reputation of the service provider is critical to success. The reputation that accompanies a service provider is, to some degree, related directly to the quality of the service provided. The service provider, however, can influence his or her reputation by effectively using promotion.

Traditionally certain types of service providers were ethically or legally prevented from engaging in formal promotional activities other than through the use of an office sign, business card, and through selling their services through the process of community involvement. However, taboos preventing doctors, dentists, lawyers, and other professionals from advertising themselves and their services are now changing. Lawyers can now use various promotional methods, but only in restricted ways. Additionally, some states have passed laws which will allow physicians to advertise their services.

Generally all promotional tools can be used in the promotion of services. Traditionally personal selling has taken on a critical role because of the personal nature of many services. Additionally, some services are in a sense unsought products.[10] People usually do not set out on their own initiative to purchase life insurance, for example. Thus, a service of this type relies heavily on the personal sales function.

Recently, the demand for many services has exceeded the capacity to deliver these services. Utilities providing basic household energy requirements and doctors and dentists providing basic medical care are examples. Also, some evidence

---

[10]E. Jerome McCarthy, *Basic Marketing: A Managerial Approach* (6h ed.; Homewood, Ill.: Richard D. Irwin, Inc., 1978), p. 287.

exists that people are not satisfied with the services they are receiving.[11] In these situations the promotion function (perhaps in conjunction with the price function) frequently is used to reduce, redirect, or conserve services.

Distribution and Delivery of Services

Traditionally the channel of distribution for services has been very short and direct. The reason for this is that for many services production and delivery are performed simultaneously. As an example, consider the services of a barber or a hairstylist. The direct nature of delivery for many services is one reason why large-scale concentration in the service industries has not occurred until now. The direct nature of many services has inhibited the use of intermediaries or middlemen. However, there are exceptions to this.

Airlines are in the transportation business, and users of the service must eventually come into direct contact with the service provider. However, airlines have employed independent middlemen—travel agents—to arrange reservations and write tickets.

Frequently creative thinking and implementation can offer service marketers many new ways to distribute their services. A bank that uses 24-hour automatic tellers is a good example. An example in the nonprofit area is the use of mobile units by public libraries to make their services available to all members of society in an efficient and economical manner.[12]

Franchising has been used extensively in many areas of service marketing. The hotel/motel field is a good example. Ramada Inns provide away-from-home lodging for business and pleasure travelers. Each Ramada Inn is independently owned and operated, but in accordance with a franchise agreement.

Service Development and Management

Service development and management are as important for the service marketer as product development and management are for the product manufacturer marketer. Product or service development refers to modifying the current product or service offering by elimination, modification, or innovation. Product or service management refers to the day-to-day activities necessary to insure that the products or services achieve the objectives outlined for them by management.

The service offering is changed and adjusted for several reasons. One primary reason is a fundamental change in the marketing environment. For example, as inflation rates have crept steadily upward over the last 10 to 15 years, traditional savings accounts with low interest rates have lost appeal to savers and investors. Consequently, banks have offered time certificates of deposits with higher interest rates.

Change in the competitive environment is a second important reason for modifying service offerings. A good example is no-charge checking accounts of-

---

[11]James E. Bell, Jr., and David Appel, "The Service Gap—Marketing Crisis in the Seventies," *Southern Journal of Business*, Vol. 5, No. 3 (July 1970), p. 1.

[12]Theodore Levitt, "Production-Line Approach to Services," *Harvard Business Review*, Vol. 50, No. 5 (September–October, 1972), p. 41.

fered by banks. At times a bank may want to increase its deposits. Offering low or free checking is one way to accomplish this. However, when one bank offers free checking, other banks in the area may also have to offer the same service or lose customers.

Like the product marketer, the service marketer must read the environment, formulate new service ideas, test-market these service ideas, and arrange for widespread distribution and promotion of the service.

Perhaps a classic example of implementing the marketing concept by offering a service is H&R Block, Inc. The management of H&R Block recognized that income tax preparation is an ordeal for most people. Consequently, H&R Block began offering income tax preparation services. These types of services, now offered by many firms, have been very successful in helping people solve the problem of preparing their tax forms.

Service marketers, like product marketers, must be continually aware of competitive or environmental threats to their business. Additionally, service marketers must continually scan the environment for new opportunities. As in product marketing, those individuals and organizations that can satisfy the need in the best manner, and in the quickest way, will have an excellent chance of earning good profits. To clarify this point, consider investors who recognized ten years ago the trend toward small homes and the increased demand for rental apartments. For many households storage of goods then became a problem. The solution to the problem was the mini-warehouse, a common phenomenon today in small, medium, and large towns.

SERVICE MARKETING: SELECTED EXAMPLES

Several examples of industries primarily involved in providing services illustrate both the differences and similarities in service product marketing and physical goods product marketing.

Financial Services

One of the major services that are bought and sold at the marketplace is financial service. This service includes making money and credit available, protecting it, and in some instances selecting investment opportunities that provide a major occupation and income to many. The money flow managed by financial institutions contributes a significant facility to the functioning and growth of the economy and provides satisfactions to many that would otherwise be impossible. There are many types of financial institutions, but most of them are included in these general classifications: banks, insurance companies, and investment houses. The relationship to marketing of each of these types of financial institutions is discussed here.

Banks.　Only in recent years have banks departed from traditional patterns and entered the competitive race. Since the base from which a commercial bank operates is its deposits, a bank aggressively seeks the patronage of depositors. Such aggressive seeking of deposits is economically desirable because banks can render improved services with various degrees of excellence and achieve different levels of efficiency. They can dignify or abuse their customers, the depositors. It is, therefore, important that banks be stimulated to higher levels of performance by competition, just as are other marketing institutions.

Competition in banking services has some of the characteristics of product competition. A bank uses depositors' funds as a base for making money available to other parties; thus, the main marketing efforts of banks move in two directions. First, a bank attempts to sell people on the practice of depositing money with its institutions. In most instances the bank pays a price determined by the interest rate for this money set by the Federal Reserve Board. Second, the bank lends money to others for which it collects interest. Both the interest that is paid the depositor and the rate that is charged on loans are prices that are determined by marketplace forces. The management of a bank, though, still has a certain amount of leverage in charging higher or lower interest rates, depending on its specific strategy. The interest that the bank pays the depositor, as compared with the rate charged the borrower, is somewhat similar to the wholesale price paid by the retailer and the retail price charged the ultimate consumer, although one should be cautious in pushing this comparison too far. In the last ten years, most states have passed legislation limiting interest rates.

A commercial banker does more than buy the money from depositors at one price and sell the same money to borrowers at a higher price. The commercial banker can multiply the volume of loans to exceed the base provided by the deposits, as limited by the amount of deposits required. Furthermore, skill in dealing with money is quite different from skill in retailing.

The fact that banks must compete on a price basis, both in terms of loans and deposits, is particularly significant to marketing students. Customers for loans are secured by innovations in the interest-rate price and in contract provisions designed to make it convenient for the individual to repay the loan. Innovations in the interest-rate price and in the frequency with which the interest is computed to obtain a multiplying effect are means by which depositors are secured. To achieve a degree of stability in deposits, banks employ the merchandising inducement of paying a higher rate of interest on a certificate of deposit than is paid for the ordinary time deposit.

Banks also engage in nonprice competition by selecting convenient locations and providing night depositories, drive-in service, an adequate number of tellers to avoid lines and waiting, cheerful service, a friendly atmosphere, and cash dispensing machines, which give 24-hour banking to the consumer. While these areas, both in the price and nonprice fields, are subject to different policies, means of performance, and innovations, they are all designed to win the support of bank customers, be they depositors or borrowers.

Bank Credit Cards.   Large banking firms offer credit cards that are honored in a majority of businesses in all parts of the nation. Holders of the card can use it for all kinds of purchases or payments and pay all their bills with one check to the bank issuing the card. The cost of the card to the bank is paid by charging a certain percentage of sales to the firms where the credit purchases are made.

Bank Marketing Opportunities.   The Meadow Brook National Bank (now known as the National Bank of North America) in New York, is an example of what a bank can do if it uses the marketing tools available to it. This bank had assets of less than $50 million and two offices in 1959; by early 1965 it had 66 offices and $850 million in assets. The bank hired six young and aggressive sales representatives from industrial companies. These people surveyed the respective areas to which they were assigned to discover the best prospects for expanding business. They then studied the business opportunities of individual businesses before calling on them. With a clear knowledge of each firm's opportunities, they called on these businesses and sold them on the idea of using bank loans and services to improve their business. The rapid growth of the bank attests to the success of this marketing program. Today the bank has 141 offices and approximately $4.5 billion in assets.

Insurance Companies.   Only a short time ago all an insurance sales agent had to know was the provisions of three main kinds of policies: term insurance, twenty-pay life, and the twenty-year endowment policies. Today even small companies have almost as many kinds of policies as General Motors has automobile models. The productive insurance underwriter now studies the entire financial condition of the prospect and sets up an insurance program tailored to the specific needs of the individual. It is common for insurance programs to be designed to begin repayment when the children start to college, to provide retirement at a specified income, and to build up an emergency fund as preparation for unexpected crises. Today even small insurance companies employ actuarial experts to assist them in fashioning policies that will differentiate their offerings from their competitors' policies.

Insurance companies have adapted to the needs of our economy. Inflation has been accepted as a permanent characteristic of the economy. Insurance or annuities with fixed dollar values are less likely to appreciate in value than common stocks. To adapt to this change, insurance companies have merged with mutual funds and sell both insurance and mutual funds with insurance and appreciating income provisions in one package. Others have adopted a means of disbursing gains of portfolio appreciation in their dividend program. Still others have tied the cash value of the customer's claims to stock price levels and advertise and sell variable annuities. Thus, it appears that the success of insurance companies is tied closely to marketing skills. The effectiveness of the selling and advertising program of insurance companies is strategic and an absolute necessity. The constant adaptation and improvement of the kinds of policies and contracts closely resemble an industrial firm's program of product research and development. The other source of income for insurance companies is from investments. Excellence in this area also requires expertise in the area of analyzing markets.

Just as insurance companies have made effective use of the innovation concept, they have also pioneered in the field of demand creation. Not nearly as many people would be aware of the circumstances that might result from accident or death were it not for the effective advertising and selling of insurance companies. They also dramatize effectively the positive effects that result from a well-managed insurance and annuity plan. Whichever motive or selling appeal is used, demand for the product is created in true marketing fashion.

Investment Companies. The growing affluence of the population has created opportunities for an increasing proliferation of different kinds of firms that sell investment securities. Now even small cities with 50,000 people have access to direct wire services to Wall Street and have several investment agencies competing for business from which they realize a commission on the sales they make. In large centers security firms tend to specialize in certain kinds of stocks and bonds, for large populations and income make specialization possible, as is the case in the marketing of goods.

Another financial service organization that has grown significantly is the mutual investment fund. This organization is composed of security specialists who invest the money of the company's clients in securities as defined by the company's policy. Many of these companies offer their clients a choice of investment programs or a combination of plans. Some programs emphasize safety with a low but certain income such as can be obtained by the purchase of bonds. Other programs are designed for the individual who prefers slightly less security and more income. Still a third possibility is one that places less emphasis on income and more on growth and appreciation of capital values. The organizers of mutual funds profit by charging loading fees to cover the cost of their selling campaign and their expertise in the selection of securities. Thus, their income is for the service rendered and not from the income of the securities. Their success depends upon their ability to combine securities into contracts that are attractive to customers and to sell them. Like the product sellers, they are concerned with effective marketing of their services at minimum costs.

Transportation Services

Transportation of people is a service of both private and public concern, and, unfortunately, the services available at present are very unsatisfactory. Metropolitan highways are jammed to the point of frustration, a difficulty which is being compounded by population and automobile sales increases. Although subsidized, commuter agencies in many metropolitan areas are losing money and are providing substandard service. It is evident that at many points the demand for people transportation is outrunning the supply. Neither the genius of free enterprise nor the assistance of government has provided the answer, as has been typically done in other fields. Nevertheless, there are some hopeful signs on the horizon. San Francisco's Bay Area Rapid Transit System (BART) moves a greater volume of traffic at higher speeds than any known system has heretofore accomplished.

From the foregoing it can be concluded that nonproduct enterprises such as transportation services and financial services are strongly committed to marketing programs. They utilize market studies to determine their competitive weaknesses and to discover opportunities for greater and better service. They conduct sales and advertising programs with growing insight. Finally, they are acquiring a growing awareness of their customers' needs and characteristics and are involving themselves in both research and promotion to satisfy those needs.

PERSONAL SERVICES

In personal and miscellaneous services, there is an almost infinite diversity of levels of marketing skills. A knowledge of the marketing concept and the need for market orientation could be useful to these services, but awareness of such needs is nil. The repair technician, the barber, and the beautician would prosper by being more intelligently articulate about their services and reasonably aggressive in selling and explaining them. Such an approach could be almost as important as the quality of their work.

The legal and medical services have ethical codes that prevent aggressive advertising and selling. Since these services are highly professionalized, it is assumed that a person or organization should be judged by performance and not by selling skill. Obviously demand creation has no place in either profession. Other areas that absorb the service dollar, such as education and government, are major fields of study in their own right. Marketing knowledge is helpful to them, though hardly in the same sense that it is to the business segment.

RECREATIONAL SERVICES

The marketing of recreational services is somewhat different from that of financial services or utilities. Recreational services are more heterogeneous in nature. It is difficult to compare the activities of the New York Mets or the Los Angeles Rams with those of the Bank of America. Nevertheless, these athletic teams must either make a profit or be financed by some form of philanthropy. Moreover, the owners of athletic organizations share the same entrepreneurial drives as do other marketing organizations. For example, the Baltimore Orioles moved from St. Louis, where they shared baseball fans with the Cardinals, to Baltimore because of a promise of greater financial return.

QUESTIONS AND ANALYTICAL PROBLEMS

1. Define pure service products and distinguish them from physical good products.
2. List five examples of consumer services and five examples of business services.
3. Many services tend to be human centered. What does this mean?
4. What arguments, pro and con, can you make about the statement, In the future, services will continue to take an increasing share of the consumer's dollar?
5. Discuss the two meanings of the word *intangible,* when *intangible* is used to describe services.
6. Why do doctors practice ethical fee setting?
7. Does the intangible nature of services make promoting services more difficult?
8. Compare the duties and functions of the marketing department of a service firm with those of a product firm. What similarities and differences occur?
9. What would you emphasize in a marketing program for a financial institution, such as a bank?
10. Choose any personal service and explain how you would promote it.

Case 17-1 • THE MERCHANTS AND FARMERS BANK

The president and the vice-president of the Merchants and Farmers Bank are not in agreement on a proposal to improve and modernize the drive-in depository and teller service of the bank. The vice-president favors an investment of $100,000 to purchase real estate and build a small unit apart from but connected with the bank building. The president of the bank is not convinced that such an investment is merited.

The Merchants and Farmers Bank, with total resources of $10,000,000, is located on a prominent corner of a city with a population of 45,000 and a trading area of 110,000 people. This location is three blocks west of the intersection of the two main commercial arteries which are considered the center of the business district. There are three other banks in the city. One was organized only five years ago and is located in the center of the city. It has total resources of $1,500,000. The second bank—one of the oldest in the city and part of the regional chain—is located one block north of the intersection at the center of the city. This bank has total resources of $12,000,000. The third bank is located across the street and south of the regional chain, away from the main intersection. This bank recently merged with a progressive bank in a small city only six miles away and is engaged in a vigorous promotion program. It has total resources of $6,000,000.

The Merchants and Farmers Bank presently has drive-in arrangements at a window of the main bank building. The entrance to the window is the same as the entrance to the bank's parking lot. There is room for only two lines of traffic. Often a single car pulls into the driveway at such an angle that it blocks the entrance to the parking lot. Such incidents frustrate traffic to the extent that during busy periods the automobiles often line up until the street itself is blocked. The vice-president proposes to purchase additional real estate and build a small building opposite the present window. The new building will have depository windows on both sides. Thus, during the busy periods of the day, the bank can use the present facilities along with the new ones and serve three lines of traffic. The additional purchase of real estate will provide adequate space for both entering and exiting the depository service and the parking lot.

In spite of the fact that two of the competing banks already have more adequate depository service than the Merchants and Farmers Bank, the president is not convinced that three windows are necessary. He believes that, if a boy is employed to direct traffic during busy periods so that the parking lot lane is not blocked, the depository patrons will not mind waiting. In support of his position the president contends that (1) drive-in banking will not increase, (2) patronage of a bank is not determined so much by convenience as by the integrity, financial skill, and respect which the public has for an institution, (3) an increasing amount of banking will be done by mail, and (4) electronic data processing equipment will make it possible to clear balances by automatic communication, thereby making visits to the bank less necessary.

Whose views do you support? Why?

Case 17-2 • PALMER HOUSEHOLD CLEANING SERVICE

William O. Palmer retired from the United States Army in 1974, after 20 years of service. While in the army, Sergeant Palmer frequently used a house-cleaning service, which was available at most army posts. When an army family moved from an on-post government house, the house was inspected for cleanliness before the officer or enlisted person was released from his responsibility for the house. Many families did not want to go through the effort of cleaning the house and waiting for the inspection. Consequently, the project was turned over to a house-cleaning service. The service then cleaned the house and arranged for the inspection. The fees for the service increased through the years, but in 1974 were as follows:

> Two bedroom $100
> Three bedroom   135
> Four bedroom   160

Bill Palmer believed that a similar type of service could be marketed in civilian life when people move or simply want a thorough annual house cleaning. With approximately 20 percent of the United States population moving every year, Bill was optimistic about his chances for success.

In 1974 the former sergeant—now civilian Palmer—and his family returned to their favorite city, Indianapolis, Indiana. He settled his family, and set up his house-cleaning business. In 1975 he lost about $3,000; however, in 1976 he broke even, and in 1977, 1978 and 1979 he made a profit of $4,000 a year.

As Bill looked over his financial performance for the past four years, he realized that his expenses had increased as rapidly as his revenues. Because of this, he believed that his chances of increasing his profit in the house-cleaning business were not good.

Bill Palmer was not a man to give up. He had some new ideas about how to make his service business more profitable. These ideas revolved around offering several new services.

Snow Shoveling

Midwest winters are hard, and appear to be getting more severe. Many people are tired of spending two hours digging out every morning. A snow-shoveling service may find many eager customers.

Lawn Care

A lawn-and-garden-care service may also have appeal. Many people garden and mow their lawns simply because they cannot find anyone trustworthy to perform the service. The lawn-care service could also balance out the labor requirements of the winter snow-shoveling service.

House and Pet Sitting

For many families, vacations and travel present problems in taking care of the house and the family pet. A service to provide a watchful eye over the house and pet may also find a ready market.

Sick and Convalescent Care

Finally, Palmer is considering the possibility of establishing a service to the sick and convalescent. This service will not entail nursing care, but such things as food preparation, house cleaning, shopping, and when necessary child care. Again, Palmer thinks a good market for this type of service may exist.

Advise Bill Palmer as to whether he should expand his service offerings, and which, if any, of the new services he should select.

18

✗ social issues ✗ in marketing

Within the broad context of the interface between business and society, marketing has its fair share of important social issues. As the element of business practice that has the closest contact with members of society (in their role as consumers) marketing tactics are scrutinized and subject to vigorous criticism at times.[1] The purpose of this chapter is to identify several important social issues in marketing. The discussions are not intended to provide definitive answers. Rather, the issues are raised to establish a forum for inquiry and thoughtful consideration of the marketing process.

Social issues in marketing range from very broad social and economic considerations to very specific elements of the marketing function. Issues of both types are addressed in this chapter through a discussion of the following concepts: marketing and a free enterprise economy, consumer information and education, the cost of marketing, consumerism, the creation of need via marketing, product safety, advertising, marketing to the poor, and future social challenges.

---

[1]See for example Vance Packard, *The Wastemakers* (New York City: David McKay Co., Inc., 1960) and David Caplovitz, *The Poor Pay More* (New York City: The Free Press, 1967).

MARKETING AND A FREE ENTERPRISE ECONOMY

At the outset of a discussion of social issues relating to marketing it is important to recall that marketing was not the brainstorm of the gray-flannel Madison Avenue crowd. To reinforce the discussion of marketing in Chapter 1, the marketing process emerges in industrialized societies from a need for efficient and effective movement of goods to and through a marketplace. The fundamental basis for the existence of the marketing function is an economic one. Products that are centrally located and produced in large quantities cost less and are more easily obtained. In a society based on the free-enterprise principles of economics, a process such as marketing is implicitly required.

In our society, however, it must be recognized that the economy of the United States functions only partially on the principles of free markets. The complex nature of an industrial state has brought about regulations and government intervention. The result is that a *mixed economy* has evolved. There are restrictions and guidelines imposed on the fundamental exchange process. Marketing has progressed and evolved simultaneously. It now functions as part of a somewhat free, partly socialistic, and heavily regulated economy.

Marketing continues to exert a useful and important influence on the economy. This function, however, is vastly different from its original form. Rather, marketing has evolved to a broadly based and pervasive process that must face many difficult tasks in meeting consumer and government demands.

CONSUMER INFORMATION AND EDUCATION

With the evolving nature of the role of marketing in society have come great demands for consumer education and information. The issues involved in this area are to determine how much information is useful to consumers and how that information should be provided. It is important to make a clear distinction between the areas of consumer information and education because their functions are different and the tactics for satisfying demands in each area are, therefore, also different.

Consumer information is the provision of facts and descriptions of goods and services through advertising, labeling, warranties, consumer reports, and other information vehicles. The marketing process is held directly responsible for the availability and content of many of these sources. The difficult issue to address in this area is the type of information to provide consumers. In the early 1970s it was intuitively believed that providing consumers with unit-pricing information in grocery stores would lead to more informed consumer choice. After great expense in institutionalizing the program nationwide, various estimates indicate that only 10 percent of consumers use the information. Both government and marketing proponents of the unit-pricing strategy have learned the expensive lesson that consumers employ a multitude of information cues in the choice process and price is only one source of knowledge.

A criticism of marketing that is offered frequently is that marketer-controlled sources of information frequently carry very little if any actual product information. As pointed out in the Consumer Decision Making Process (Chapter 3), however, in some instances consumers are buying more than a physical, tangible material good. When a buyer is seeking satisfaction of a motivating need, the functional attributes of a product are secondary in both the choice process and information search. What becomes relevant to the consumer at this point is information relating to the need satisfaction characteristics of the product. This information often arrives in the form of an emotional appeal. It is true that this type of message carries little product information. That is because the consumer is *not seeking* product information. The relevant information for the buyer in this situation is the need satisfaction appeal the message is transmitting.

If the consumer is to retain a controlling position in the product decision process, then the firm is required to provide the desired information. There are times when the relevant information does not include facts about functional product features. It is, however, the appropriate information in the eyes of the consumer.

If the argument is forwarded that consumers *should not* use nonfunctional product information in the choice process, the issue is one of *consumer education;* that is, training consumers to recognize and use objective information about product features, use, and warranties. The consumer education issue is one that is receiving more attention through organizations such as the Consumer Advisory Council. For consumer education to become a moving force in the marketplace, formal steps need to be taken to facilitate the process.

The implementation and success of consumer education will depend on two significant changes in the consumer behavior process. First, rather than having people learn of the consumption process through *doing,* formal programs can be implemented in the educational system. Courses in grade schools and high schools can teach students how to identify significant product differences based on performance, use, and warranties. The second necessary change in the process may not be easy to implement or even rationalize. Based on the premise that consumers should not use information related to nonfunctional product attributes, the second requirement for effective consumer education is to point out to consumers that they suppress the human tendencies for psychological and sociological need satisfaction through product acquisition. It seems unreasonable to expect that consumers can cease to be human beings during the product choice process. Such a proposal obviously is unworkable.

The reasonable approach to informed consumer choice that coordinates and integrates both consumer information and consumer education is that relevant information about products be made readily available to consumers and that formal consumer education programs alert consumers to the appropriate use of the information. In this fashion control of the choice process is retained by the individual buyer and he or she is free to engage in decision making as an individual.

THE COST OF MARKETING

Many issues surrounding the criticisms of the marketing process relate to the charge that marketing costs too much. The costs of the marketing process are high. If the total cost of product development, pricing and price determination, distribution, and promotion are charged as marketing expenses, then the cost of marketing is, in fact, about 50 percent of the final price paid for a product by consumers. Certainly this would seem to be a heavy financial burden for the consumer to bear. There are, however, several conditions related to the cost of marketing that should be considered when judging whether marketing costs too much.

It is fundamentally difficult to accurately assess what the value of the marketing efforts are versus the costs of the process. It would be difficult for the consumer to state how much it is worth in dollars and cents to have a variety of products from which to choose. Further, what does it mean to consumers in monetary terms to have products conveniently located, for a store to have convenient shopping hours, or for products to come in different forms and package sizes? Each of the marketing tactics alluded to have become firmly established in business operations. Consumers have demonstrated a desire to have and a willingness to finance convenience, variety, and service. Whether having these market utilities costs too much or too little is almost impossible to determine. Perhaps the strongest argument for the viability of a marketing practice is that it survives and proliferates. The test of market survival indicates consumer sanctions of various marketing efforts.

A second issue related to the general consideration of marketing costs is the efficiencies created by the function that result in actual costs savings. The stimulation of demand which can provide benefits from economies of scale must be deducted from the marketing costs. Exactly what are these savings? This, again, is difficult to determine. Efficiencies also accrue to the consumer as products are readily available and in the proper form for use and gaining greatest satisfaction.

The costs of marketing must also be considered within the context of the benefits to society that the process generates. First, it can be claimed that a high and rising standard of living is a valid social objective. As such, marketing can be instrumental in facilitating the attainment of this goal. By providing the distribution of goods and information concerning product availability, marketing directly contributes to the standard of living enjoyed by a society. Second, the competitive environment in an economy stimulates product improvements and technological advances. Again, the marketing process contributes to the drive for market success of a product. In the search for product differentiation (a marketing advantage) firms invest heavily in research and development.

Further, marketing costs have increased in recent years because of demands placed on the system by consumers. Some of these demands—longer store hours and a wide assortment of products—have been discussed. Consumer demand for more services, however, is an area where significant cost increases have occurred in the marketing process. Consumer demands for credit, delivery, repair, installation, and liberal return policies are expensive services to provide. Certainly if a business operated on a cash-only basis, refused to make refunds, and had no service staff, the cost of doing business would be reduced appreciably. Consider, however, the attractiveness to the consumer of this type of service. Consumers have clearly demonstrated their desire for these related services, and the retailer who snubs these desires will find consumer patronage very low.

Finally, a discussion of the costs of marketing must address the question of whether the system responds quickly enough to consumer desires. On this point, the efficiency of the process is questionable. There are reasons for this type of inefficiency. For the firms that are truly consumer-oriented, the desires expressed by consumers must be verified and then built into product features. This process can be a lengthy and costly one. The price of an error in this assessment is even more costly; so firms proceed cautiously and, yes, slowly. Also, there are those firms that simply have not adopted the marketing concept as a business philosophy and, in fact, do not respond at all to consumer desires. This type of firm has a high probability of failure in the marketplace, however, and therefore will suffer the consequences of a lack of responsiveness to consumer desires.

The issue of marketing costs is a complex one. Due to the several elements of the issue raised here and the lack of techniques for accurately measuring marketing productivity, the best that can be hoped for is that there is an appreciation for positive and negative aspects of marketing costs. Marketing will always cost the consumer something. It is necessary, however, that the marketing process add value in the marketplace above and beyond the costs it generates.

CONSUMERISM

It is difficult to separate consumerism from the other social issues in marketing. Certainly the consumer movement is related to product safety, consumer information, the cost of marketing, and the other issues addressed in this chapter. There are, however, issues central to consumerism that can be isolated and discussed as a separate consideration. These are (1) the actions affecting marketing that have been stimulated by the consumer movement and (2) the activities of corporations designed to explicitly deal with consumer demands.

The consumer movement can be traced back to the early 1900s and has emerged on a regular basis as the economy of the United States has advanced. The 1960s consumer movement marked an era when consumers gained their greatest inroads. The uprisings of consumer discontent at that time culminated in President Kennedy's issuance of a statement of consumer rights. These rights are as follows:

1. The consumer has the right to safety.
2. The consumer has the right to be informed.
3. The consumer has the right to choose.
4. The consumer has the right to be heard.[2]

The impetus created by the movement itself and the broad public awareness created by President Kennedy's call for consumer rights resulted in several actions that have had a great impact on society: the passage of more legislation intended to aid the consumer, the creation of consumer protection agencies at both the federal and state level, and the implementation of class action suits. Each of these responses function to provide consumers with increased powers in the marketplace and additional influence on firms in cases of dissatisfaction. The area that some believe will have the greatest impact, however, is consumer education. As was

---

[2]These consumer rights are outlined in E.B. Weiss, "Marketers Fiddle While Consumers Burn," *Harvard Business Review* (July-August, 1968), p. 45.

pointed out, this area of consumer activity is capable of providing buyers with the ultimate marketplace power; to simply eliminate (through lack of patronage) the firm or product that does not provide satisfaction.

The other side of the consumer movement is the corporate response to increased consumer activities. Firms have attempted to comply with the increased demands by initiating several strategies directed specifically to enhance corporate-consumer relations. These include holding executive-consumer panel discussions, increasing corporate product servicing practices, and establishing separate departments to handle consumer affairs.[3] This is not to say that *all* firms have recognized the consumer movement and tried to respond. Rather, these are merely indications that consumerism has greatly increased the awareness of the need to comply with consumer desires.

A final general consideration in the area of consumerism is the philosophical conflict between consumerism and the marketing concept. The consumer movement is said to be an indictment that the marketing concept is either not working or not really being implemented by firms. For, if firms were truly endeavoring to first identify consumers' needs and then developing products specifically to satisfy those needs, there would be no need for a consumer movement.

On the surface, it would appear that consumerism and the marketing concept could not exist side by side. Actually there are several reasons why they can and do exist at the same time. First, because of the diversity of human interests and desires, it would be virtually impossible to design and market a product geared to every individual's exact desires and specifications. A firm attempts to design and market a product that meets a range of needs. As such, in many ways it does not exactly fulfill the needs of one individual perfectly, but rather meets the needs of a mass market. Second, the firm must try to develop products and services that satisfy market demands within a reasonable cost parameter. Certainly each of us would value and find satisfying the craftsmanship, durability, and service that are inherent in a Rolls Royce automobile. Few of us, however, are willing or able to pay $60,000 for these product features. To make products accessible to the masses, they are sometimes less than the absolute best they can be.[4]

The variety of human needs and the need to make products available to the masses make consumerism and the marketing concept strange bedfellows. The appropriate view of this area is that consumers and corporations must continue to develop a more effective dialogue so that consumer satisfaction continues to be enhanced.

MARKETING CREATES NEEDS

A common cry of critics is that marketing creates needs and makes people buy things they don't need or want. In thinking about this claim, there are several areas of inquiry a thoughtful analysis should consider.

---

[3]For a comprehensive treatment of the corporate response to consumerism see Leonard L. Berry, "Marketing Challenge in the Age of the People," *MSU Business Topics* (Winter, 1972), p. 7.

[4]For a broader discussion of this concept that includes its relationship to corporate profits see Y. Hugh Furuhashi and E. Jerome McCarthy, *Social Issues in Marketing in the American Economy* (Columbus, Ohio: Grid, Inc., 1971), p. 102.

A good starting point is to reexamine the basic human motivators that provide the catalyst for the consumer decision-making process (Chapter 3, page 47). It will be recalled that several conditions can motivate the product search. These search motivators can be classified as two general types: practical (stock-out conditions) or psychological/sociological (the need for esteem, status, affiliation, etc). With regard to the need to replace a depleted or worn-out item, the criticism of marketing is somewhat less intense. Consumers engage in the routine restocking of items and may be drawing upon firmly established and frequently employed decision criteria. It is the second type of search motivator that is cited as the dastardly practice of marketing. Close examination of these motivators for product search, however, clearly indicates that these are basic human needs far beyond the control of marketing or any other artificial stimulus. Humans will find these needs emerge at different periods of their individual life experiences. The search for satisfaction of these needs many times leads people to the marketplace as an alternative for satisfaction. Firms, in turn, will devise (or portray products) capable of satisfying these needs.

Needs are fundamental to human beings and cannot be created by marketing tactics. The legitimate social issue regarding human needs and the marketing process is not that marketing creates needs, but rather that marketing can appeal to these needs in devious and questionable ways. The adolescent consumer provides a good example of questionable appeals to the buyer. At this delicate stage of human development, the typical young adult's need state is dominated by the overwhelming urge to gain acceptance, love, and an assurance of belonging. Products can easily be portrayed as useful in gaining the desired acceptance. The essence of these messages then can simply be: If you don't use this product you won't be as popular as you could be. Certainly the firm using this type of appeal would receive high marks for providing the young decision maker with relevant information. The need to be popular is the most relevant factor in the adolescent's life. However, is it appropriate to prey on this need or to appeal to it with such brute force that conflict is created in the mind of the decision maker? Herein lies the essence of marketing and its relationship to needs.

On a higher conceptual plane marketing and need satisfaction must be considered as they affect human achievement. Our consumer-oriented society has come to value many products that provide prestige and status simply because of their rarity or excessive cost. Thus, it becomes possible to simply *purchase* prestige or status in the marketplace. In a less industrialized society that lacked a proliferation of products and the mass communication to publicize their existence, the achievement of status and prestige had to be earned rather than purchased. Our affluent industrialized society acts as a deterrent to behavior that generates esteem and prestige. Rather, it becomes the norm to simply *buy* need satisfaction. Therefore, society suffers, since many valuable human efforts tend to be lost through the ease of achieving recognition by the possession of material goods.

A final point of consideration regarding the ability of marketing to create needs relates to the rate of success of new products. It was pointed out in Chapter 8 that about eight out of ten new products fail. If marketing had the powerful effect that some critics attribute to it, certainly this condition could not exist. Products could be eased into the marketplace with little difficulty and would enjoy instant success. The consumer is simply too intelligent to buy just anything. Since, as has been pointed out, consumers possess cognitive faculties that provide an evaluation of a product's pertinence and usefulness, products fail because they do not fulfill the needs and demands of consumers. Thus, marketing cannot, again, *create* needs.

PRODUCT SAFETY

The right to safety was identified earlier as one of the goals of the consumer movement. Perhaps the most significant governmental response to date relates to the issue of safety hazards of products and their use.

In 1969 the National Commission on Product Safety issued a report indicating that 600 household products in 400 product categories posed serious safety hazards to users. In the top 20 were several frequently purchased or widely used items such as cleaning agents, bicycles, liquid fuels, power lawn mowers, and space heaters. The estimates of annual injury from household product use are staggering. Each year 20 million Americans will be injured seriously enough to require some form of treatment.[5]

In response to the Commission's investigation and report, Congress created the Consumer Product Safety Commission in 1972. Because of the perceived seriousness of the product hazard problem, the newly created Commission was granted far-reaching powers. It can investigate products for safety hazards either by individual brand or through examination of entire product categories. It also has the power to ban products or issue product design standards to meet safety requirements. Finally, the Commission can plan educational messages for radio and television broadcast to encourage the safe use of products.

This last power of the Commission focuses on an issue of product safety that represents the most difficult aspect of the problem. Product failure or hazard is only one element in the danger products pose for consumers. The product, the user, and the way in which the product is used are all part of the safety problem. Each of these variables of product application is capable of being solely responsible for an accident. The Consumer Product Safety Commission itself identified stairs as the second most hazardous product category. The stairs themselves represent a recognizable use risk to consumers. The incidence of accident, however, is only partly due to the inherent hazard posed by stairs. Consumer use of the product is a significant contributing factor. Legislation and other forms of government intervention can solve only part of the product safety problem. The informed use of products by consumers is a significant element in reduced hazard risk.

The most philosophically complex and involved aspect of the product safety issue is one that has been referred to as "normative authoritarianism."[6] The approach represents a Big Brother approach to consumer problems. The position is taken that consumers are incapable of determining what is good or appropriate.

[5]*Final Report of the National Commission on Product Safety* (Washington, D.C.: U.S. Government Printing Office, June, 1970), p. 9.

[6]This concept appears in James F. Engle, David T. Kollat, and Roger D. Blackwell, *Consumer Behavior,* (2d ed. Hinsdale, Ill.: Dryden Press, 1973), p. 619.

Adopting such a position initiates paternalistic legislation to aid the consumer in overcoming the deficiency. To date several such types of legislation have been enacted. Equipping automobiles with seat belts and mandatory helmet laws for motorcyclists are examples. Another related legislative effort relates to cooling-off laws affecting door-to-door sales, whereby consumers have a period of a few days to rescind their decisions, which may have been made on the spur of the moment.

The seriousness of the issue underlying normative authoritariaism needs to be recognized. Who are the groups or individuals who will specify what is *right* for consumers. When a democratic society foregoes its right of freedom of choice, the relinquishment of this basic privilege must be carefully considered. This is not to say that business or any other major institution in a society can conduct its affairs free from public scrutiny. Rather, the idea of relegating consumption decision powers to another party is a concept that requires judicious thought by every consumer.

ADVERTISING

Many of the social issues related to advertising have been addressed within the context of earlier discussions in this chapter. The costs of marketing implicitly consider the costs of the advertising effort. Consumer information and education factors require the use of advertising as one of the vehicles for effecting change. A discussion of creating needs through marketing efforts is inextricably linked to the messages transmitted through advertising. There are issues, however, that are crucial to advertising itself. This discussion will focus on these issues. Specifically, the issues of deception in advertising and the developmental social effect advertising may have will be discussed.

Deception in advertising was originally singled out as an unacceptable business practice by the Federal Trade Commission Act (1914). In its original form the FTC Act was designed to reduce the adverse effect of deception on effective competition. Consumer protection from deception was not achieved until 1938 when the Wheeler-Lea Amendment was added as legislation. Most recently the FTC has been empowered with the ability to require a firm found guilty of misleading or deceptive advertising to run corrective advertisements which revise and correct previous allegations.

It is impossible to offer a defense for deception in advertising. The practice is simply unacceptable as a market mechanism. The difficulty regarding this issue, however, is to determine what is deceptive. The manufacturer who claims the firm's laundry product can remove grease stains is subject to legislation and punishment if the product cannot perform the task. The manufacturer who claims to have the best laundry product in the world, however, is free from legislative mandate. This is *puffery* and is considered completely legal.

Deception in advertising is so complex that it hardly even qualifies as a "grey area." The FTC has dealt with the problem by restricting its activities and investigations to product claims that relate to functional product attributes that can be investigated in quantifiable, measurable terms. Therefore, the grease-cleaning power of a detergent or the cold-prevention capabilities of a mouthwash are functions which the Commission can investigate and pursue. A question arises, however, when nonfunctional (emotional) product claims are considered in the context of deception. If a toothpaste promises sex appeal, is the firm engaging in deception? Thus far no good solution exists to the problem of emotional appeals and their relationship to deceptive advertising. Some marketers believe that consumers are the best judge of deception and can retaliate in the marketplace by withholding patronage.

One of the most difficult aspects of rectifying deceptive practices in advertising is the inefficiency of the policing process. First, as a federal agency, the Federal Trade Commission has jurisdiction only over interstate violations. The local advertiser who actively engages in deception on an intrastate basis may find it easy to continue the practices. Few states have powerful policing or prosecution mechanisms established to deal with the offender.

In light of these problems of effective monitoring and prosecution, several cooperative efforts from independent organizations and advertising industry sources have tried to aid in the process. Local Better Business Bureaus try to gather and organize consumer complaints and through adverse publicity and legal actions try to deter firms from deception. The advertising media certainly have a vested interest in maintaining accuracy in the advertising claims they carry. Magazines and newspapers can refuse to print advertisements judged to be in poor taste or deceptive in their claims. TV and radio stations that belong to the National Association of Broadcasters (NAB) follow the NAB's guidelines for advertising contained in its Code of Good Practice.

Other cooperative efforts to reduce deceptive practices come from several organizations. The advertising industry itself, through the American Association of Advertising Agencies, issues guidelines to member agencies regarding fair practice. Another advertising industry organization, the National Advertising Review Board, screens advertisements to determine if they meet the standards of good taste and truthfulness. Several product industries also have made efforts at self-regulation of advertising that are intended to bolster the efforts of regulation in the area and provide the consumer with accurate product information. These related efforts point to encouraging prospects for the nature of advertising in the future.

The second social issue central to the advertising function of marketing relates to the societal effect the proliferation of mass media exposure to advertising may be having. The extreme view in the controversy states that advertising is shaping cultural norms. Perhaps a more reasonable line of thought poses doubt about the effect the ongoing exposure to persuasive product information is having. The issue is of particular concern with respect to advertising directed at children. Critics have questioned the uses of sophisticated techniques to grab children's attention and the use of fantasy situations to make products appealing. The most recent controversy in children's advertising will produce the "Kid Rule" from the FTC. This rule is expected to provide guidelines for advertising aimed at children—especially advertisements for presweetened products, which currently constitute the dominant form of children's advertising.

Other aspects of the social effect of advertising relate to the use of sex and the portrayal of stereotypes in advertisements. Sex in advertising has long been an area of criticism. The use of sex in advertisements is seen to contribute to a decline in morals. It is claimed that mass media accentuation of sex endorses promiscuity. Stereotyping of women and ethnic groups is another charge leveled at advertising. The critics note that women are portrayed as housewives, mothers, or sex objects; ethnic groups, they say, have been relegated to stereotypical roles in advertising at times. Firms and advertising agencies are sensitized to the emotionalism surrounding these issues and have attempted to show both women and ethnic group members in a wide range of activities and situations.

Advertising has emerged as an important social issue in marketing for two reasons. First, there are some serious considerations regarding the use of advertising and its techniques which have been raised in the foregoing discussions. Second, advertising is in a position of prominence because of its visibility. It surrounds us not only as consumers but also as citizens conducting our daily affairs. When confronted with impertinent or poorly conceived advertisements, we are annoyed and complain. The serious issues of advertising must retain a prominent position in the marketer's thought. As a major element in the marketing process, effective and acceptable practice of the process is a requirement.

MARKETING TO THE POOR

One of the casualties of a mass-consumption society is the poor. Low-income consumers struggle to maintain a reasonable living while engulfed in the allurement of a myriad of goods and services. The poor are isolated in urban ghettos and various rural pockets of poverty. Their members are dominated by ethnic groups and the elderly. Aside from welfare legislation and minority hiring practices, few efforts have been directed at the consumption problems of low-income consumers. There are and have been, however, both conscious and inadvertent abuses of the poor stemming from the marketing process.

No other area of marketing has suffered more from unethical practices than consumer credit in low-income areas. Preying on the low-income consumers' lack of education and their desire for an improved standard of living, poverty area credit merchants have, in the past, been found to use illegal and fraudulent enticements to lure the low-income consumer. Bait-and-switch tactics, easy credit terms, and shoddy merchandise are examples of the abuses. Further, it was found, in at least one ghetto area, that retailers were charging low-income consumers interest rates from 50 percent to 82 percent of the purchase price for a new television.[7] Credit practices in other nonghetto parts of the city under study were within the legal limit for the state. Credit abuses of the poor appear to occur in more than isolated cases, as other authors have observed the same phenomenon.[8]

Another issue regarding low-income consumers and the marketing process relates directly to the basis upon which unethical merchants were capable of exploiting the poor through credit enticement. Simply because the poor are iso-

---

[7]Frederick D. Sturdivant and Walter T. Wilhelm, "Poverty, Minorities, and Consumer Exploitation," *Social Science Quarterly,* Vol. 49, No. 3 (December, 1968), p. 649.

[8]Homer Kripke, "Gesture and Reality in Consumer Credit Reform," *New York Law Review,* Vol. 44, No. 2, (March, 1969), p. 1.

lated sociologically does not mean that psychologically they do not have the same needs and desires as their affluent counterparts. The human urgings for belonging, prestige, esteem, and dignity are irrepressible, as the discussion motivators in Chapter 3 point out. Low-income consumers are not immune to these desires and are aware of several marketplace alternatives that directly address these needs. Unfortunately, many of these products are designed and marketed for affluent consumers. The result is that, because of financial incapacity, the low-income consumer cannot afford to acquire these goods and anxiety results. The impoverished consumer is then put in a position of trying to cope with the reality that these sources of satisfaction are beyond his or her means. The stress is especially difficult for low-income parents as they try to cope with demands of their children——demands that have been stimulated by commercials.

Marketers, attempting to provide want-satisfying products in the marketplace, have accidentally been the source of stress for the poor. This is not a devious plot on the part of marketers to expose the poor to products they can't afford and which actually don't satisfy their current needs. Rather, the products are appealing to low-income consumers because the consumers aspire to rise above their current state. Further, the imperfections of mass media result in messages communicated to the poor that were designed and placed in media directed at a totally different segment.

The creation of anxiety and stress in low-income consumers generated by inaccessible products and services is a difficult issue. To suggest that the consumers *shouldn't* feel the desire for these products seems unreasonable. This merely fosters a normative authoritarianism of a different type. Marketers cannot be held solely responsible, since product design and demand stimulation were not planned for this segment of society in the first place. Perhaps one way the marketing process can contribute to a solution in this area is through a better understanding of low-income consumers and their basic needs. Marketing research and the striving to understand consumer behavior typically concentrates on the mass market. The mass markets in America constitute the most economically feasible and viable segments for product marketing. The poor in this country are referred to as the "other America" from a sociological perspective. They are isolated and ignored with the hope the problem will disappear. In a very real sense, the same thing has happened with regard to the ability of marketing to serve this segment of society. Since they do not constitute a mass market and since their financial condition provides little spending flexibility, marketers have not concentrated on servicing low-income consumers.

Recently, however, some research has been conducted which attempts specifically to identify ways in which low-income consumers can be served efficiently and effectively.[9] Through marketing research that can identify the unique needs and desires of this special segment of consumers it may be possible to improve their

[9]See Richard J. Semenik and Robert Hansen, "Low Income Versus Non-Low Income Consumer Preference Data as Input to Socially Responsive and Economically Profitable Decision Making," Kenneth L. Bernhardt (ed.), *Marketing: 1776–1976 and Beyond* (Chicago: American Marketing Association, 1976) p. 205. Also see Arieh Goldman, "Do Low-Income Consumers Have a More Restricted Shopping Scope?" *Journal of Marketing,* Vol. 40, No. 1 (January, 1976), p. 46.

overall consumption capabilities and satisfaction in the marketplace. The low-income consumer remains, however, one of the most difficult social issues in marketing.

FUTURE SOCIAL CHALLENGES

The social challenges facing marketing in the future are abundant. But, as with most challenges, there are tremendous opportunities. Marketing and its functions are capable of making a significant contribution to the development and progress of society. Also, marketing can be instrumental in helping society deal with several difficult problems it is likely to face in the near future.

Most closely aligned with marketing's normal responsibilities is the continuous necessity of technological innovations. In the last century more products have been introduced than in the accumulated history of the world. Many of these products were landmark innovations which improved the quality of life. The challenge remains to keep pace with technological development and effectively deliver beneficial products to consumers. Marketing can help insure that a worthwhile innovation survives and serves the people rather than permitting it to become a marketplace casualty.

Solid waste disposal problems and a general public concern for the environment will continue to pressure marketing organizations into devising products that are ecologically sound. Product packages that are recyclable and product materials that are biodegradable are examples. Also, marketing techniques can be used to help alter consumer behavior so that wasteful consumption can be reduced. The returnable-bottle example is a good one, although marketing practitioners continue to wage the war against consumers' desires for convenience.

As this country faces the threat of severe energy shortages, marketing can take part in two major aspects of solving the problem. First, marketing tactics can be used to stimulate behaviors designed at conserving energy. Promotional techniques can be used to make consumers aware of steps that can be taken to save energy, such as driving at reduced speeds, insulating their homes, and reducing the consumption of heating fuels. Also, attempts to stimulate the use of mass transit and car pooling can be facilitated by marketing tactics.[10] Using the concepts of consumer choice critera discussed in Chapter 3, efforts can be made to try to change consumers' attitudes about using their personal vehicles. Second, when plentiful and affordable energy alternatives are made feasible, marketing can aid in the introduction of these energy sources to society. The introduction of new products has long been the responsibility of the marketer, and these techniques can

---

[10]Research on this topic has been in progress for sometime now. For examples see U.S. Department of Transportation, *The Transit Marketing Project: Summary of Consumer Research, Baltimore MTA and Nashville MTA* (Washington, D.C.: Office of Transit Management, Urban Mass Transportation Administration, June, 1976) and Alice M. Tybout, John R. Hansen, and Frank S. Koppelman, "Consumer-Oriented Transportation Planning: An Integrated Methodology for Modeling Consumer Perceptions, Preference, and Behavior", *Advances in Consumer Research,* Vol. 5 (Association for Consumer Research, 1978), p. 426.

be used to alleviate the problems that will come from switching to new forms of energy.

The social problem of overpopulation is a serious one. There are several steps society can take to ease the pressures created by population increases. Technological, sociological, and individual changes need to occur as increased demands are placed on a country's natural resources. From the standpoint of technological advancement and implementation, the potential contributions of marketing have already been cited. The other tasks a society faces in dealing with population growth largely have to do with education of the citizenry. The experience of marketing experts with mass communication may prove to make an important contribution in this area.

Marketing applications in various nonprofit organizations have made significant strides in recent years. These nontraditional, noncommercial applications of marketing techniques have matured to the point that general texts on nonprofit marketing have appeared.[11] The use of marketing in the arts has advanced rapidly. Arts organizations plan to achieve improved financial stability by turning to marketing as a vehicle for generating additional revenue through increased patronage. In the health care field, interest in marketing has been fostered by pressures to hold down the cost of medical care. Through marketing techniques, more efficient and effective methods for health care delivery and the use of medical facilities are being investigated. Also, attempts are underway to change behavioral patterns as a way to improve health conditions in society. Public service campaigns for increasing physical exercise and avoiding household hazards are examples.

Colleges and universities across the nation are turning to marketing as they begin to compete for students. As the composition of the age groups changes in this country, schools are attempting to continue to make use of existing facilities. Attracting additional students and introducing various adult or community education programs are strategies that rely on the marketing process.

The inroads being made by marketing in nonprofit organizations represent an important achievement for the discipline. First, this is an area where marketing can help contribute significantly to the quality of life. Second, the typical nonprofit organization manager or director has a misperception of the marketing process. The crass and manipulative image of marketing is soon disspelled, however, once the benefits to the organization and the heightened satisfaction of the consumer are realized.

In looking to the future and the social role of marketing in a changing environment, important changes internal to corporations must also be considered. First, corporations must continue to look for ways to improve the efficiency and effectiveness of the marketing effort. Increased efficiency will help keep the cost of products to consumers as low as possible, thereby providing a countervailing force to inflation. Improved effectiveness, achieved through research that accurately as-

---

[11]For an excellent summary of applications and literature in this area see Christopher H. Lovelock and Charles B. Weinberg, "Public and Nonprofit Marketing Comes of Age," in Christopher H. Lovelock and Charles B. Weinberg (eds.) *Readings in Public and Nonprofit Marketing* (Palo Alto, Calif.: The Scientific Press, 1978) p. 3.

sesses consumer desires, will increase satisfaction in the marketplace and help enhance the quality of life. Second, corporations themselves can work harder in the future to reduce abuses in the marketplace. By devising programs to facilitate dialogue between consumers and corporate personnel, problems in the system can be more quickly identified and solved. Also, the establishment of better working relationships among corporations and the various entities (governmental and societal) that are trying to deal with consumer problems can also help improve the system. Finally, firms can step up their efforts to improve product quality, service, and safety through research and development.

QUESTIONS AND ANALYTICAL PROBLEMS

1. What is the difference between consumer information and education? How are the two dependent on each other?

2. Is it your opinion that marketing costs too much? Can you offer ideas that will reduce the costs of marketing?

3. Which marketplace activities stimulate consumerism? What dangers are there to the firm in reacting to consumerists' demands?

4. Why can't marketing create needs? What is the relationship between marketing efforts and human need states?

5. Cite the main issues surrounding product safety. Why is this area so difficult to deal with from the marketer's perspective?

6. Advertising has long been a target for criticism. Why is advertising attacked so frequently and what efforts have been made to enhance this marketing effort?

7. What is *normative authoritarianism?* How does it pose a threat to a democratic society?

8. Why are low income consumers called casualties of a mass-consumption society? How can the marketing process more effectively serve this segment?

9. What are some nontraditional applications of marketing? Can you cite some areas where marketing may be applied in the future?

10. How can corporations more effectively meet the social challenges of the future? What changes in business operations will facilitate the effort?

Case 18-1 • THE REALCOLD ICE COMPANY

Hamad Kamal is seeking a solution to a problem of conflict between business ethics and custom. Kamal is the general manager of the Realcold Ice Company, which employs approximately 50 driver/sales representatives in the area of a large city in a developing country. Since there are few electric refrigerators in some sections of the city, there is a large market for ice. In June, July, and August, the demand for ice is more than double that of the regular season. With the incomes of the low and middle class increasing, Realcold

Company finds it does not have the capacity to meet the summer demand. In the face of this scarcity, the sales representatives are instructed to favor their steady, oldest, and largest customers. Rather than follow instructions, however, the driver/representatives deliver the ice to the highest bidder and pocket the difference between what they collect and the regular price. Spot checks on this operation indicate that the practice enables a significant number of the drivers to triple their monthly income. The pay scale of the driver/representatives is on the basis of a fixed minimum plus a commission. Compared with other workers in the same class, it is considered adequate.

Mr. Kamal was educated and worked in England and the United States. As of result of this experience, he is convinced that productivity and efficiency in business are closely related to the honesty and integrity of the workers. He also recognizes that extra tipping or "baksheesh," as it is termed in the Middle and Far East, is a long-established custom which is not considered dishonest by a large portion of the population.

What steps should Hamad Kamal take, and how should he proceed to make them effective? Is there a relationship between productivity and efficiency and business integrity?

Case 18-2 • SIMOMILK

Simomilk, a mother's milk substitute for newborn infants, is manufactured by Milk Products Industries, of Racine, Wisconsin. Joyce Kelley, the director of marketing for Milk Products Industries, is on the horns of a dilemma. Mrs. Kelley is wrestling with a recommendation that she must make to the firm's board of directors. The subject of the recommendation is whether Simomilk should be marketed in developing Third World countries.

The dilemma that concerns Mrs. Kelley is of a moral and ethical nature on one hand and a business nature on the other. Specifically, mother's milk substitutes have been successfully marketed by other companies in various developing nations. From a business perspective, the ventures are extremely successful and, in fact, very profitable. But, some unfortunate consequences have also resulted.

The culture and technology in the developing countries are frequently not well suited to mother's milk substitutes. The product usually requires mixing with water. Unfortunately water supplies in many countries are not purified to the degree necessary for infants. The result is that many children contract dysentery and stomach and intestinal diseases.

A second health-related problem found among children raised on mother's milk substitutes is malnutrition. Income levels in developing countries are commonly very low. Mother's milk substitute products can be a rather difficult economic burden for a family. To lessen the burden, many mothers mix more water with the product than the directions call for. Infant malnutrition often results from the practice. Unfortunately, by the time the malnutrition is detected, there is little that can be done. The infants' families cannot afford additional milk substitute, and the mother's natural milk is no longer available.

Mrs. Kelley realizes that technically the infants' families make the decisions to use a mother's milk substitute product. But she also realizes that the culture, economic level, and education of the people prevent them from making informed decisions. She is truly confounded by the choices.

What recommendations do you think Mrs. Kelley should make to the board? Why?

appendix 1

career opportunities in marketing

In the words of a sage, "The two most important decisions you will ever make are who you will marry and the career you will follow." With the first decision we wish you good luck. To the latter decision we address this appendix.

The field of marketing is broad and diverse. Because of this diversity it is frequently difficult to explain to marketing students exactly what marketers do. The purpose of this appendix is to help define those activities and to discuss careers and career planning.

KNOW YOURSELF

Perhaps one of the most difficult aspects of choosing a career is to truly know your likes and dislikes, your strengths and weaknesses. This is not easy knowledge to acquire, and frequently people wrestle with these problems for years. Finding the answers is especially difficult for those in the traditional college-age group of 18 to 22.

Certainly not everyone of you faces the problem of knowing what you want to be. No doubt, some of you have known children of ten who knew their lifework and had already set their course. You may be that fortunate type of person. If so, persevere to reach your objectives and to attain your goals!

However, many of you—perhaps most of you—fall into another category. You find many activities interesting and enjoyable. And you are dually frustrated by your inability to choose one area in which to concentrate and your lack of specific knowledge of any one career or job. If you find yourself in this majority, there are steps you can take and places you can go to get help.

The college placement center or counseling service at your university or college can be of great help. These offices usually are equipped to administer vocational tests to help you identify your interests and, to a degree, your talents. Additionally, these centers probably can furnish literature describing various types of jobs.

Work at Different Jobs

Perhaps a more useful way to identify your likes and dislikes is through a variety of work-related experiences. Many opportunities are possible. Summer jobs and part-time work during the academic year can provide many useful and worthwhile experiences. Many business schools maintain cooperative or intern programs with various businesses or organizations. In some programs you will work right with a business and earn college credit for doing so. In other programs you may actually take a semester or quarter off to experience on-the-job training.

If you are having difficulty identifying your interests, try various jobs. You may find exactly what you are seeking and, at a minimum, you will begin to identify occupations and jobs that are not suited for you. A broad range of experiences can be a great teacher.

Talk to People

Another thing you can do is to talk to people who are working in areas that you find interesting. One good way to meet and talk with these kinds of people is through professional and business associations. These organizations provide many opportunities to meet with members of the business community and to learn what these people do and what problems and challenges they face on a day-to-day basis.

In the marketing area there are at least two professional organizations that give you the opportunity to broaden your education and range of experiences. Many colleges or universities have student chapters of the American Marketing Association. Other schools have the Pi Sigma Epsilon professional business fraternity. Although formally referred to as a fraternity, Pi Sigma Epsilon is composed of approximately 17,000 men and women active in marketing, sales management, and selling. Both organizations deal with the many aspects of marketing and frequently feature interchanges with practitioners in the field. The Pi Sigma Epsilon fraternity, which is associated with the many local chapters of Sales and Marketing Executives, also features marketing and sales projects as part of the fraternity program.

Knowing yourself and your career goals is not easy; but there are things you can do to better identify your interests, talents, and strengths. However, simply knowing yourself is not enough. You must plan for your career.

CAREER PLANNING

Perhaps you remember the following dialogue from Lewis Carroll's *Alice's Adventures in Wonderland:*

> "Cheshire-Puss," said Alice, "would you tell me, please, which way I ought to go from here?" "That depends a good deal on where you want to get to," said the Cat. "I don't much care where . . ." said Alice. "Then it doesn't matter which way you go," said the Cat. ". . . so long as I get somewhere," Alice added as an explanation. "Oh, you're sure to do that," said the Cat, "if you only walk long enough."

As Alice soon learned, "If you don't know where you're going, you'll probably end up somewhere else."[1] Career planning can help you be where you would like to be in 5, 10, or even 20 years.

One of the great challenges of career planning was addressed at the beginning of this appendix: identify your likes and dislikes, your strengths and weaknesses. And this may take time. But, while you are learning to "know thyself," there are some traps you should avoid and some roads you should follow to help you decide what you want to do and to enable you to reach your goal. To see how this is possible, let us inspect two different ways of viewing life.

Don't Look for Endings

Many of us go through life always looking forward to either endings or beginnings. For example, how many of you have thought that life will be so much better when this semester or quarter is over? Other events we tend to look forward to, but not past, are graduation, a job, and perhaps marriage. However, when these events occur, life still goes on. The occurrence of these events does not automatically make us happy or satisfied in our job or family situation.

A second way to look at life is shown in Illus. A1-1. Life is, in one sense, a road we are moving along. As we proceed along the road, various side paths branch off from the main road we are traveling. These paths represent opportunities and alternatives that we may, if we are prepared, have the chance to take. However, whether an opportunity is open to us depends on us and how well we have prepared ourselves.

If you complete your college education and successfully graduate, you may immediately encounter two side paths branching off from your main road. One contains a Graduate School sign, the other an Attractive Job Offer sign. To a degree, whether you are able to grasp either of these opportunities will depend on the things you do from this point until the opportunities present themselves. You cannot relive the past; you had better make the best of the present. Good grades, work experience, useful relationships (with your professors, employers, etc.) and personal development (good manners, attractive appearance, ability to

---

[1]The Lewis Carroll quote, the quote noted by the footnote, and many of the ideas for the career planning section were taken from David Campbell, *If You Don't Know Where You're Going, You'll Probably End Up Somewhere Else* (Niles, Ill.: Argus Communications, 1974).

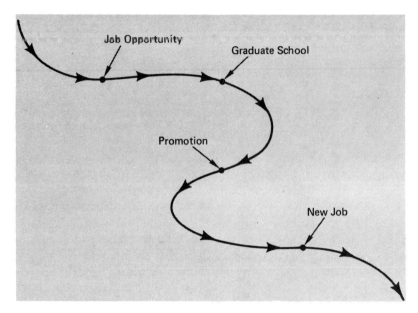

Illus. A1-1   **A Pathway of Opportunities**

express yourself) can positively influence the advantages that are open to you when your road crosses an opportunity path.

To summarize, one principle of career planning is to be prepared for opportunities. To do this, you must strive to grow and improve in those areas of life that are central to your development. This principle applies even on the job. As an employee, if you don't try to learn anything beyond your immediate task, the chances are that you will not be eligible for promotion when the opportunity comes. Even if your career goals are not completely formulated, you can still do something. Not knowing what you want to do is no excuse for not doing anything.

Use Time Effectively

A second principle of career planning is using time effectively. Regardless of the career you now want, or the one you eventually adopt, learning to use time wisely will always be of value. Although this is neither the time nor the place for a time management lesson, you might try the 168-hour exercise as a first step in effective time utilization.

There are 168 hours in the week, 7 days times 24 hours. From this 168-hour week, subtract the time that is committed for personal maintenance or other responsibilities, such as school, study, work, etc. One busy student discovered 15 hours of free time after carefully analyzing the time he had available. This schedule is shown in Illus. A1-2.

Two observations can be made from the 168-hour exercise. First, there is only so much time in any one week; if you learn to make the best use of it, your chances for a successful career will be greatly improved. Second, you may be surprised at the amount of free time you are supposed to have but can't seem to find. To

Category	Hours
Sleeping	49
Study	30
Work	20
Class	15
Eating	14
Dressing	7
Traveling	7
Exercise	5
Recreation	4
Club Meeting	2
Subtotal	153
Free Time	15
Total	168

Illus. A1-2   A Weekly 168-Hour Time Schedule

remedy this, begin to observe how you use time and where you waste it. Remember that effective use of time is a habit like caring for your teeth. The sooner you adopt the habit, the better off you will be.

Many people resist effective time utilization because they say that schedules, lists, and deadlines limit their freedom. In reality, however, using your time effectively means you will have more time to do the things you want.[2]

Set Goals

A third principle of career planning is properly setting goals. As we mentioned, if you don't know where you are going, you will probably end up somewhere else.

One key to goal setting is to set goals for different lengths of time. One career expert has recommended that we all have long-range goals, medium-range goals, short-range goals, mini-goals, and micro-goals.[3] Long-range goals concern the basic questions about life-style, type of family situation you desire, and perhaps the overall economic status you want to achieve. Medium-range goals concern the next five years, while short-range goals are concerned with the period of about one month to one year from now. Mini-goals cover one day to one month, and micro-goals cover the next 15 minutes to an hour. Ideally these goals should be consistent with one another. In others words, the accomplishment of a micro-goal should indirectly contribute to your long-range goals.

The process of setting goals is not easy, but once accomplished, the goals will be of great value to you. These goals will help you decide which activities you elect

---

[2]An excellent book on time management is Alan Lakein, *How to Get Control of Your Time and Your Life* (New York City: The New American Library, Inc., 1973).

[3]Campbell, *op. cit.*, p. 36.

to engage in and how you spend your time. Planning and goal setting take time, but the time spent is well worthwhile.

One aspect of determining your career goals is to attempt to match your strengths as a person with the characteristics of the job best suited for you. The following section attempts to enumerate job characteristics in the marketing field.

THE MARKETING FIELD

The field of marketing is very broad; therefore, people of various talents and orientations can frequently find the type of job best suited to their individual needs. However, before describing various types of jobs in the marketing area, it may be helpful to review a few job characteristics that are common to a great majority of marketing jobs.

Marketing Is People Oriented

Perhaps the most common characteristic of all marketing jobs is the constant interaction with and orientation toward people. The marketing function exists to satisfy the needs and wants of customers—the needs and wants of people. Thus, marketers are frequently interacting with current associates and meeting new ones. Because of the people-oriented nature of marketing, marketers at all levels usually find themselves dealing continually with people. A sales representative who calls on customers is an obvious example. But even top-level marketing managers spend much of their time dealing with other employees as well as with customers, competitors, suppliers, and others.

Marketers Must Be Creative

A second characteristic of many marketing jobs is that of creativity. Marketers must continually utilize their creative abilities to solve their marketing and business problems. Sales people must unceasingly devise creative ways to find and sell new customers, to retain present customers, and to use time efficiently. Product managers use their creativity in designing and implementing effective marketing strategies, while copywriters create fresh flows of copy for effective promotions. In addition, creativity and the ability to spark ideas into reality underlie the entire new product development process. Perhaps in no area of business is there more opportunity to utilize and develop creative talents than in marketing.

One other characteristic common to many but not all marketing jobs is the necessity of working with numbers. The talent required is not necessarily the ability to understand statistics and quantitative methods; the requirement is more one of being able to draw implications and formulate strategy from marketing data. Marketers are constantly concerned with market share, profit margins, prices, markups, inventory levels, sales volume and quotas, and marketing research information. These data are summarized in numbers, and it is up to the marketing personnel to derive meaning from the numbers. Again, marketers in general don't have to understand advanced statistical methods, but they must be able to look at averages and percentages and correctly interpret their meaning for managerial purposes.

Jobs Available in Marketing

Given these characteristics, what kinds of jobs are available in the marketing area? There are many kinds of jobs available. One specialist describes the types of jobs available this way: "Marketing offers something for the artist as well as the statistician and for all shades in between."[4] However, if you are going to work for the first time, your opportunities will be somewhat limited. These limitations are the same as those faced by other first-time employees. For example, your friends who are graduating in finance will not start out as company controllers. They will spend some time learning the business before they are transferred to jobs of more responsibility.

One entry job for first-time employees is that of selling. Many selling jobs are in the industrial market; that is, calling on wholesalers, retailers, and manufacturers. Sales are made to or through purchasing agents, buyers, or perhaps to the owner or manager. This type of selling, as with most types, requires skill and training. Moreover, sales positions in the industrial market usually pay exceptionally well.

In addition to good pay, many managers consider selling experience a prerequisite for other marketing level jobs. Typically even people recruited specifically for product manager jobs will have spent some time in selling. Sales people interact directly in the marketplace. They are close to the consumer and, because of this, they must know the business. If a selling job is open to you, investigate it. You may be surprised at the responsibilities the job involves, the pay it offers, and the potential for advancement it presents. Always remember: there is no marketing without a sale.

Another excellent opportunity lies in the retailing area. Jobs are available in almost all areas of the country, and many large retailers, such as Sears, have management training programs for college graduates. Training may include some classroom work, but the majority of time will be spent in an apprenticeship program in on-the-job training. Time will be spent learning product lines and merchandising, as well as store operations and management.

Some jobs are available in specialty marketing areas such as advertising agencies and marketing research firms. These jobs present the opportunity to become a specialist in one part of the marketing field. However, the number of jobs in these areas is limited; therefore, landing a job of this type will probably require far more than simply signing up for interviews at the placement center.

Perhaps one of the most interesting and demanding jobs in the marketing field is that of product or brand manager. A product or brand manager is given some or all responsibility for a given product or brand, or series of products. The product or brand manager must develop a marketing plan, coordinate it with the advertising and sales personnel, and monitor the product through time. Because of the varied nature of the product manager job, many executives consider the job good

---

[4]Robert H. Williams, "The How, What and Why of Marketing: A Brochure of Answers" (Unpublished working paper, College of Business, University of Utah, no date), p. 12.

From a Bottling Works Executive

The major responsibilities in marketing include sales forecasting, media planning, budget management, financial planning, promotional development and planning, marketing research analysis, sales analysis, and distribution systems analysis. Additionally, a large portion of our time is spent in developing creative approaches to the marketing of soft drinks.

From a Marketing Account Supervisor

Sales—calling on direct wholesale grocery accounts—calling on headquarters accounts of major store chains in the Salt Lake area—acting as a consultant when asked for this service.

From a Manager of a Small Plastic Fabricating Firm

Coordination of our wholesale program. This includes such items as advertising, trade shows, catalogs, and pricing.

From a Market Analyst

Determine the nature of markets our products compete in, market share analysis, potential for new products, image analysis, concept testing, making recommendations for action to management.

From a District Sales Manager

Advertising—determine how much and in what form (TV, radio, outdoor). Promotion—plan cents-off campaigns, packaging, pricing, timing. Merchandising—plan in-store position space displays, point of purchase material.

Illus. A1-3   **What Do Marketers Do?**

training for higher level positions. The jobs are also challenging because of the many communications necessary between the product manager and the sales manager, advertising agency, etc.

One of the consequences of the consumer movement has been the increasing attention that firms pay to customers and their complaints. Customer relations departments have often been positioned under the marketing vice-president. Increasingly, career and job opportunities lie in this area.

Many of the jobs described so far illustrate the customer or demand side of marketing. However, many people are employed in getting the product to the customer. Transportation specialists, warehouse managers, inventory control experts, and packaging personnel are all required to market effectively. The marketing concept emphasizes customer satisfaction, not just making a sale. People are required to help satisfy customer demand.

The foregoing are only examples of the many and diverse kinds of jobs available in marketing. For more detailed job descriptions you may wish to consult *Job Descriptions in Marketing Management,* by JoAnn Sperling (Chicago: American Marketing Association, 1969), and *Careers in Marketing,* by Neil Holbert (Chi-

From a Steel Supplier Executive

> Marketing affects financial planning, purchasing, and, in fact, all operations. Summing up, the marketing plan must first be made before any plans for return on investment, dividends, capital purchases, etc., can be made.

From a Secretary and Treasurer of a Leading Financial Institution

> Marketing does play an important part in my business, even though we do not market merchandise. Marketing money is our job, and many principles used in merchandise marketing are used in selling money.

From a Bottling Works Executive

> Marketing is the most important part of our business—our firm is marketing oriented.
>
> Accounting, finance, and management are considered integral functions within the total marketing area.

From a Medical Products Sales Representative

> In the hospital products area of the medical products industry a company's future is rated directly proportionate to the quality of their marketing staff and their right arm, the sales force. Usually with any medical product there is a mountain of both pro and con clinical data. The marketing staff must make a very complicated decision as to which product to offer the market, in what form, and at what price. The luxury of being certain of a demand for medical products gives the marketing staff the pleasure of concentrating on the more pleasant functions of marketing.

From a Sporting Goods Executive

> Our company is primarily a marketing firm, distributing sports equipment throughout all the United States and Canada and in a minor degree in the Far East and Europe. We distribute to 17,000 dealers in the United States and some 1,500 in Canada. Only about 15 percent of our annual volume of approximately $55 million is manufactured by our own company. The remainder of our merchandise is manufactured for us under contract by other suppliers. About 75 percent of our operating costs and personnel are involved in some phase of the marketing function directly or in supporting functions. So marketing is a very important and fundamental part of our business operation.

Illus. A1-4   How Important Is Marketing in Your Firm?

cago: American Management Association, 1976). However, many of you may still be somewhat unclear about exactly what marketers do. To enlighten you further, a survey was conducted of past marketing graduates of a major university. Two questions of concern to you were asked of the subjects: What do marketers do? and How important is marketing in your firm? Illus. A1-3 should give you an indication of how marketers view their job responsibilities.

Illus. A1-4 examines how much importance various business executives attach to the marketing function in their jobs or industries.

Whatever your career choice, the authors hope that this appendix on career opportunities has been of value to you. Additionally, whether you work in accounting, production, marketing, or any other field, we hope that you take with you from this course a fundamental understanding of the importance of marketing to a firm. Best of luck in your careers!

appendix 2

a guide for case analysis

When you completed the second chapter in the text, you probably read the cases describing various business situations that followed the Questions and Analytical Problems. These cases are provided as learning aids to assist you in becoming more knowledgeable about marketing. The cases are designed to complement the reading in the text and to provide topics for discussion among you, your classmates, and your instructor.

Many first-time marketing students are unfamiliar with the process of analyzing and discussing cases. Because of this initial unfamiliarity and because many of you will use cases extensively in other classes, this appendix is provided to assist in increasing your skill in case analysis. The ability to conduct an in-depth analysis of a case is a skill that can be learned; but, like all skills, the basics must be mastered to eventually achieve a high degree of proficiency. The material that follows includes the basics—as well as advice and recommendations—on how to focus your own abilities on the case you are analyzing.[1]

---

[1]The material for this appendix is drawn extensively from Alfred G. Edge and Denis R. Coleman, *The Guide to Case Analysis and Reporting* (Honolulu: System Logistics, Inc., 1978).

WHY STUDY CASES?

The answer to the question, Why study cases?, is best answered by first defining what a case is. Many definitions exist, but perhaps the most famous is this: a case is "typically a record of a business issue which actually has been faced by business executives, together with surrounding facts, opinions, and prejudices upon which the executives had to depend."[2] In other words, cases are real or contrived situations about businesses or other organizations. A case is composed of many items, including information about people involved in the organization, statements summarizing financial information and other quantitative material, the history of the firm and its past performance and strategy, and, frequently, data about competitors and the industry. Interwoven throughout the material presented in the case is one or more problems that the organization is currently facing. The problem may or may not be obvious to the casual reader; but hidden in the case somewhere is a problem to be identified, clarified, and solved.

One underlying concept of case analysis is identifying the problem the case presents. Consequently, this is one of two reasons why case study is an integral part of a business student's education. Problem identification as practiced in the analysis of cases is similiar in many respects to on-the-job problem identification. The decision maker is typically dealing with complex problems in the face of limited amounts of information and time. Thus, the experience of analyzing and discussing cases brings an element of realism to the educational experience that is frequently missing in lecture or other teaching methods.

Cases as learning devices offer other advantages in addition to problem identification and realism. One of the greatest advantages of cases is the intellectual exercise that is required of the students who analyze the case—hard thinking. Sitting through a lecture and reading can (but not necessarily should) be done on a fairly low level of intellectual involvement. The instructor speaks and the student absorbs. The student reads diligently, but remembers little. However, with cases, the level of involvement is much deeper; and, therefore, the educational experience is richer and more meaningful.

Cases also provide the student the unique experience of applying theory and classroom learning to real life situations. The distinction between knowing *about* something and truly *knowing* something is relevant to this point. Many people can get an *A* in a marketing course, yet when it comes time to sell their car they haven't the slightest idea where to start. These people know about marketing, but not how to market. The case method of instruction helps students bridge the gap between knowing and doing, between theory and practice.

The purpose of using the case method is no different from the purpose of using lectures. "Cases impart action abilities to students by giving them practice in decision making; lectures impart action abilities to students by giving them facts, principles, and theories which will guide them in decision-making situations. Both

---

[2]Charles I. Gragg, "Because Wisdom Can't Be Told," *Harvard Alumni Bulletin,* October 10, 1940.

are used to the same end: to cause the student to *act* correctly in decision-making situations."[3]

CASE ANALYSIS

Perhaps the principal benefit of the case method of instruction is the practice in structured thinking that the case method provides. Case analysis, if done correctly, forces one to process information, to structure one's thinking, and to creatively develop solutions to problems. Once case analysis is mastered, the skill will be useful in analyzing business problems on the job.

Proficiency in case analysis, like all skills, can be learned. Each of us may have an inherent tendency toward case analysis. However, through study and practice this tendency can be improved. Presented and discussed here is a series of steps to follow when performing case analysis. These steps are summarized in Illus. A2-1.

Comprehend the Case Situation

The first step in case analysis is to grasp the facts and situations described in the case. Quickly reading the case to develop perspective and an overall idea of what is going on in the case is a good first step. If you are not working under great time pressure, you may want to allow a day or two between a first reading and further analysis. This will allow you to unconsciously analyze the case and deepen your understanding of the situation.

The second reading of the case should be undertaken slowly and carefully. Making notes and underlining are useful at this stage to help you remember and locate key points and bits of information. The purpose of the second reading of the case is to allow you to grasp and understand the facts as presented in the case.

Diagnose Problem Areas

The second step in the process of analyzing a case is to diagnose potential problem areas. The process followed here is similar to a doctor analyzing a sick patient. The doctor conducts a physical examination, looks at test results, and analyzes symptoms. As you analyze cases, you must identify various areas in the firm which may be potential problems (i.e., advertising, sales promotion, pricing, etc.).

Once the problem areas are identified, evidence about each problem area should be drawn from the case. Underlinings and previously made notes will be valuable here. The purpose of collecting evidence about potential problem areas is to determine whether the potential problem area is really a problem.

---

[3]Edge and Coleman, *op. cit.,* p. 4.

Step 1: Comprehend Case Situation

    1. Speed read the case
    2. Read the case carefully, taking notes and underlining.

Step 2: Diagnose Problem Area

    1. Identify problem areas.
    2. List facts by problem area.
    3. Use evidence to diagnose each problem area.

Step 3: State Problem

    1. State major problem.
    2. State minor problems.

Step 4: Generate Alternatives

    1. List solutions to major problem.
    2. List solutions to minor problems.

Step 5: Evaluate Alternatives and Select

    1. Construct a T account for each alternative.
    2. List pros on one side and cons on the other side.
    3. Carefully weigh pros and cons, and select the best alternative.

Step 6: Defend Your Selection

    1. List questions about the workability of the solution.
    2. Develop a defense for each question.

Source: Adapted from Alfred G. Edge and Denis P. Coleman, *The Guide To Case Analysis and Reporting* (Honolulu: System Logistics, Inc., 1978), p. 28.

Illus. A2-1   **Steps in Case Analysis**

State the Problem

The output of the effort you put into Step 2 is the ability to clearly and specifically state the problem. "The problem statement itself is about one to five sentences in length and explains the basic disequilibrium or opportunity that underlies the situation."[4] The formal statement of the problem serves at least two advantages. First, it forces you to crystallize your thinking on what the problem really is. Until you can write a concise and clear statement about the problem, you do not understand the case situations well enough and you should return to Step 2.

---

[4]Edge and Coleman, *op. cit.,* p. 38.

The second advantage of formally stating the problem is that it can now be communicated fairly easily to your instructor or other students. Once the problem is communicated, it can be analyzed and discussed to determine whether improvements can be made.

As you begin to think about and formulate the problem statement, consider the significance of the problem you have selected. One way to judge the significance of the problem is to determine whether managerial action could lead to a substantial improvement in the firm's situation.

Finally, consider the time aspects of the problem you have selected. Is it a short- or long-run problem? Both the short and long run are important, and both are interrelated. Frequently failure to solve immediate problems may make the long run unimportant. The firm may simply go out of existence before the long run arrives. Additionally, if management chooses to ignore the long-run problems, short-run difficulties may be inevitable. Thus your problem statement should consider both the short and long run.

In addition to the major problem in the case, there may be one or more minor problems. You may also want to identify and confront the minor problems. Your decision regarding the minor problems will doubtlessly be affected by the time you have available for working with the case.

Generate Alternatives

After the problem has been stated and identified, you must formulate various alternatives to solve the problem. Although not exactly like brainstorming, generating many alternatives to solve the problem can be helpful. As you approach the task of generating alternatives, you may initially identify one or two alternatives that seem obvious and natural. However, further thought and analysis may lead to a great many potential answers to the problem.

As you devise alternatives, let your past work or classroom experience, your common sense, and your creative ability guide you. If you have sufficient time and interest, researching the industry and trade journals covering the industry may be useful. Regardless of the source of your ideas, do not attempt to evaluate the alternatives until you have generated a sufficient number.

Evaluate Alternatives and Select One

In this stage of the case analysis you must analyze the advantages and disadvantages of each of the alternatives developed in the previous stage. One good way to do this is to use a T account framework shown in Illus. A2-2.

A T account for each alternative is constructed. Next, the advantages and disadvantages of each alternative are identified. As you develop the advantages and disadvantages of the alternatives, consider at a minimum the following aspects: implementation, differential advantage, timing and likelihood of occurrence.

Implementation refers to putting the alternative into action. Some alternatives will be more easily implemented than others. Additionally, some alternatives will require more resources and time than others. Also related to implementation is the amount of change required from the people in the firm. Generally the

ALTERNATIVE 1

Advantages	Disadvantages
1. _____	1. _____
2. _____	2. _____
3. _____	3. _____
4. _____	4. _____
5. _____	5. _____

Illus. A2-2   T Account Framework for Case Analysis

greater the behavioral changes required, the more difficult implementation will be.

Differential advantage refers to the unique strength or critical capability that the firm possesses. An alternative that capitalizes on the firm's critical capability or takes advantages of a competitor's weakness will be superior. Also, any alternative that recommends direct confrontation with a competitor holding a differential advantage over the solution-seeking firm should generally not be chosen.

Timing in the context of alternative evaluation and selection can mean at least two things. First, it takes time to implement an alternative. If the time frame for implementation is too long or if the environment is changing too rapidly, an alternative may be obsolete before it is implemented.

Second, you must distinguish between what may have caused the problem originally and the action necessary to solve the current problem. As you evaluate and select alternatives, take a policy approach; that is, consider the problem, the desired end state, and the tools available to move toward the end state. It may be interesting to know why and how the problem developed, but this information may be of little value in actually solving the problem.

Finally, you must attempt to predict the outcome of each of the alternatives. As you attempt to make these decisions, consider the economic and social environment and the organizational climate. Admittedly you are operating in the area of speculation and intuition, but the situation is not much different from that of business people in actual practice.

Now that you have thoroughly analyzed each alternative, you must select one. Your selection should be based on all your previous comparisons and analysis. When the selection is made, you are ready for the last step in case analysis.

Defend Your Selection

It is likely that the evaluation of the alternatives that you completed previously helped you realize that more than one of the alternatives may have solved the problem. One of the unique attributes of cases in the business world is that there is not necessarily just one optimal solution. Many potentially good and workable solutions may exist. Because of this, many questions about the alternative you selected will be raised. You should be prepared to answer these questions.

The best way to defend the alternative you have selected is by anticipating the questions that will be asked. Once the questions have been anticipated, you can work out responses for the questions that are raised. In this way you will be able to defend your selection and will not be surprised when a fellow classmate or the instructor challenges your conclusion.

In the process of defending your alternatives, you should not close yourself off entirely from your critics. It is entirely possible that you missed or misinterpreted some information that may have changed your mind about the case and the problem solution you chose. Remember that cases are learning experiences that can be valuable to all participants in the case discussion.

CASE DISCUSSION

Discussing cases in class is perhaps the most important aspect of the case method. As a student you will want to take an active part in the discussions. Your participation will signal the instructor that you are prepared and interested in the topic. Your participation will require preparation and thus insure that you will benefit from the case method of instruction. The following suggestions, summarized in Illus. A2-3 and briefly discussed here, will assist you in becoming a good case discussion participant.

One of the best ways to become involved in a case is to attempt to experience the situation. Place yourself in the position of the individuals in the case. Try to perceive the situation as they do and assimilate the difficulties they are facing. If you do this, you may find yourself enjoying the case method of instruction because it involves you personally. For a short time you may actually lose yourself in the case quandary.

To correctly participate in the case discussion you must do at least three things. You must attend class regularly; you must master the facts of every case before the case discussion; and you must analyze the cases before the class period. The case

---

1. Experience the situation.
2. Attend class regularly.
3. Master the facts.
4. Analyze the cases before class.
5. Respect fellow classmates.
6. Respect the instructor.
7. Accept responsibility for carrying class discussion.

Source: Adapted from Alfred G. Edge and Denis R. Coleman, *The Guide to Case Analysis and Reporting* (Honolulu: System Logistics, Inc., 1978). p. 20.

Illus. A2-3   **Suggestions for Case Discussion**

method develops perspective and the potential for action in a student. Failure to attend class regularly prevents the potential and perspective from evolving. Additionally, you may find yourself in an embarassing position when common knowledge to the class is a new discovery to you.

Mastering the facts of a case is different from case analysis. Frequently the instructor will introduce a case discussion saying, "Describe the situation found in the case." No analysis is desired or expected at this stage, just a brief restatement and summary of the facts. If you want to get the instructor's attention, one good way is to volunteer to answer the lead-off question.

Also, the case method of instruction will be of little value to you if you have not analyzed the case prior to the class discussion. Frequently, those students who dislike the case method most are those who put the least effort into case analysis.

Finally, your participation in case discussion will be more valuable and enjoyable if you develop a respect for your fellow students and the instructor. The instructor has a job to do and, to a degree, must manage the class discussion. Recognize that he or she must walk a fine line between dominating the discussion and allowing the discussion to develop its own momentum. Also, the instructor must encourage comments and participation. Therefore, directing students who have become sidetracked requires tact and understanding.

Try also to display respect and understanding for the efforts of your fellow classmates. Case discussions do not have to deteriorate into a we-are-right-and-you-are-wrong impasse. If you will accept responsibility for carrying your share of the class discussion and if you will use common sense and courtesy, you will find the classroom very conducive to learning.

WRITING AND PRESENTING CASE REPORTS

Many sources are available to provide guidance to the student who must submit a written case or present one orally.[5] You should consult one of these sources if given such an assignment. Also, your instructor will usually provide guidance in these matters. The instructions provided by your teacher should be adhered to closely. Frequently the instructor's grading practices and his or her instructions will be closely related. Failure to follow the instructions can result in a grade that does not reflect the effort you have put into the case.

Finally, it is important to remember that the quality of a written or orally presented case can be no better than the quality of the analysis of the case. Therefore, attention given to a thoughtful and thorough analysis will be very beneficial whether the case is to be discussed, presented, or written.

The authors of this text wish you well with your case study. We hope that you will find the suggestions in this appendix useful and that you will enjoy your experiences with the case method.

---

[5]For example see Alfred G. Edge and Denis R. Coleman, *The Guide to Case Analysis and Reporting* (Honolulu: System Logistics, Inc., 1978); Malcolm P. McNair (ed.), *The Case Method at the Harvard Business School* (New York City: McGraw-Hill, Inc., 1954); Robert Ronstadt, *The Art of Case Analysis: A Student Guide* (Needham, Mass.: Lord Publishing Co., 1977).

index